WRATH OF THE DRAGON

WRATH OF THE DRAGON

THE **REAL** FIGHTS OF BRUCE LEE

JOHN LITTLE

This book is also available as a Global Certified Accessible™ (GCA) ebook. ECW Press's ebooks are screen reader friendly and are built to meet the needs of those who are unable to read standard print due to blindness, low vision, dyslexia, or a physical disability.

Get the ebook free!*
*proof of purchase required

Purchase the print edition and receive the ebook free. For details, go to ecwpress.com/ebook.

Published by ECW Press
665 Gerrard Street East
Toronto, Ontario, Canada M4M 1Y2
416-694-3348 / info@ecwpress.com

Cover design: Ben Little
Cover photo of Bruce Lee: Courtesy of Steve Kerridge

LIBRARY AND ARCHIVES CANADA CATALOGUING IN PUBLICATION

Title: Wrath of the dragon : the real fights of Bruce Lee / John Little.

Names: Little, John R., 1960- author.

Description: Includes index.

Identifiers: Canadiana (print) 20230237401 | Canadiana (ebook) 20230237444

ISBN 978-1-77041-742-7 (softcover)
ISBN 978-1-77852-218-5 (ePub)
ISBN 978-1-77852-219-2 (PDF)
ISBN 978-1-77852-220-8 (Kindle)

Subjects: LCSH: Lee, Bruce, 1940-1973. | LCSH: Martial artists—United States—Biography. | LCSH: Actors—United States—Biography. | LCSH: Jeet Kune Do. | LCGFT: Biographies.

Classification: LCC GV1113.L44 L58 2023 | DDC 796.8092—dc23

This book is funded in part by the Government of Canada. *Ce livre est financé en partie par le gouvernement du Canada.* We also acknowledge the support of the Government of Ontario through the Ontario Book Publishing Tax Credit, and through Ontario Creates.

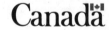

PRINTED AND BOUND IN CANADA

PRINTING: FRIESENS   5 4 3 2

MIX
Paper from responsible sources
FSC
www.fsc.org   FSC® C016245

"Come not between the dragon and his wrath."

— Shakespeare (*King Lear*)

To the fans.
You were right all along.

CONTENTS

PROLOGUE

"I don't call the fighting in my films *violence*. I call it *action*. An action film borders somewhere between reality and fantasy. If I were to be completely realistic, you would call me a bloody violent man. I would simply destroy my opponent by tearing him apart or ripping his guts out. I wouldn't do it so artistically."

— Bruce Lee (*Hong Kong Standard*, February 10, 1973)

Nineteen seventy-three was an interesting year in America. The war in Vietnam ended, the Watergate scandal led all the way to the presidency, the first cell phone was invented by Motorola, and something called Kung Fu had crept into the nation's consciousness.

The martial arts phenomenon was ignited by the *Kung Fu* television series, which premiered in October 1972. A mere seven months later it was the highest-rated show in the country, with a viewership of twenty-eight million households.[1] The success of the series caught everyone completely by surprise — particularly the executives at Warner Bros., the studio that produced the show. Sensing a trend, in early 1973 the movie division of Warner Bros. purchased the North American distribution rights to a horrendously dubbed, low-budget Kung Fu film produced by Hong Kong's Shaw Brothers Studios. It starred the Indonesian-born actor Lo Lieh and went by the provocative title of *Five Fingers of Death*; when Warner Bros. released it into theaters in March 1973, it quickly went to number one at the box office.[2] The genre now proven to be a bona fide money maker, a glut of "Chop-Socky" flicks quickly followed, and soon, in the theaters at least, the lyric from Carl Douglas's song "Everybody was Kung Fu fighting" appeared to be true.

But not everybody who was Kung Fu fighting would become a global superstar. That honor was reserved for only one person: an American-born Kung Fu wunderkind by the name of Bruce Lee. When Lee's movies hit the theaters, audiences were left spellbound and an international martial arts craze was born.

A ONE-MAN INDUSTRY

Bruce Lee's sudden death in July 1973 at the age of thirty-two, just prior to the release of his final film, *Enter the Dragon*, resulted in a worldwide fascination with the man that soon developed into an industry unto itself. Bookstores carried multiple titles devoted to him. Alex Ben Block's *The Legend of Bruce Lee*, Linda Lee's *Bruce Lee: The Man Only I Knew*, and Felix Dennis and Don Atyeo's *Bruce Lee: King of Kung Fu* were biographies that were read and reread multiple times by a rapidly growing fan base, pored over as thoroughly as others might study scripture. Magazines such as *Fighting Stars*, *Black Belt*, *Deadly Hands of Kung Fu*, *Official Karate* and *Inside Kung Fu* — and many others that came into and passed from existence during the 1970s — were purchased, often multiple copies of the same issue at a time, as they were certain to feature articles on Lee almost every month.

And when books and magazines weren't coming out in sufficient quantity to feed the voracious appetite of Lee's fans to learn more about the late martial arts superstar, some would travel to their respective cities' Chinatown districts to visit the bookstores there. Most of these stores had magazines (and later poster magazines) that had been imported from Hong Kong, featuring photos and stories that the publications in the West didn't have access to. These, likewise, were consumed in a ravenous desire to learn more and more about Bruce Lee. Walls of bedrooms soon were bedecked with posters of the man, representing international shrines to his burgeoning legacy. Indeed, Lee was the first image his fans saw upon opening their eyes in the morning and the last image they saw before they closed them at night.

From the books, magazines and posters proceeded the martial arts schools, which began to mushroom on street corners and in strip malls. And outside of formal classes, on schoolyards and in basements, an army of Bruce Lee wannabes filled the air around them with kicks and punches, aping the movements their hero had displayed in his movies (which seemed to reappear in theaters several times a year during the mid-1970s).

I know this because I was one of these people. When the wait in between theatrical re-releases of his films was over, I'd sneak an 8mm (and later a Super 8mm sound) camera into the movie theaters and, scrunched down in my seat to avoid detection, I'd film the master in action. Weeks later, after Kodak had developed my film, I'd spend innumerable hours studying the biomechanics of Bruce Lee's kicks and punches, often frame-by-frame, until I better understood how he used his body to execute such a dazzling repertoire of martial arts techniques. When a Karate school opened down the street from my house, I begged my parents for the money to enroll me, which they graciously did. The dojo had a black-and-white poster near the change room depicting Lee in a martial stance from *Enter the Dragon*, which served to further inspire us as we received instruction in the art.

To me, and tens of thousands like me, Bruce Lee was the greatest fighter of all time — bar none. But then came the backlash. And it started within the very dojos that displayed his posters. The instructors, perhaps not wishing to share the respect and adulation of their students with a dead practitioner of a different martial art than the one they represented, pointed out that Lee had never fought in martial arts competitions; indeed, there was no record of him having fought anybody at all. Such opinions carried weight. They were, after all, uttered by black belts, who had put years into the very arts that we were now training in. Soon, Lee's legend of martial art supremacy began to erode; it seemed more were against him than for him. Eventually, all his fans were left with was the image of a movie actor who engaged in choreographed scuffles on the screen, a man who was all form and no substance.

Some seriously damaging blows to Lee's image came when Karate tournament champions Bob Wall and Chuck Norris (both of whom had supporting roles in Lee's 1972 film *The Way of the Dragon*) began to run him down in the American press. Wall said "Bruce was very, very insecure. He had no confidence . . . At 136 pounds he sure wasn't going to take and beat any Joe Lewis or Chuck Norris."[3] For his part, Norris told American talk show host David Brenner in 1986, "The thing is, I was a fighter, I fought for years. Bruce . . . never competed, he never fought professionally."[4] That Wall and Norris had only ever competed in non-contact "point Karate" tournaments was a fact that neither man brought to the attention of their respective interviewers. It didn't matter. And when another national Karate champion, the aforementioned Joe Lewis (who was a world champion in both point Karate and full-contact Karate), threw his hat into the ring, describing Lee as "a little Chinese actor, not a fighter,"[5] the damage was done. In the martial arts world, Bruce Lee wasn't a "real fighter."

CINEMATIC TOUGH GUYS

It must be said that Wall's and Norris's proposition wasn't an unbelievable one. After all, movie actors seldom turn out to be as tough in real life as they appear in the movies. A case in point would be Sylvester Stallone, a man who reignited interest in the sport of boxing during the mid-1970s when he wrote and starred in the movie *Rocky*. His performance was so believable that most fans believed Stallone could really box. Even he believed it, right up until he made *Rocky II*. That was when he decided he had what it took to step into the ring to spar with Roberto Duran, the Panamanian fighter who is generally considered to be the greatest lightweight boxer of all time. Duran left the "Italian Stallion" swinging at nothing but air, while peppering the actor with punches that left him helpless. "At first I thought, this will be pretty interesting because, you know, I was a few pounds heavier, a little taller," Stallone recalled of the experience. "And then I realized the difference between amateur and consummate pro. The way he could move his head just an inch . . . it's impossible to hit him. This man would demolish me in the ring. Put it this way: if there was a fight, the fight would be eleven seconds including the count."[6] Some years later, Stallone evidently forgot the lesson that Duran had taught him and made the mistake of thinking that he was up to swapping real punches in his fight scene with professional kickboxer Dolph Lundgren in the movie *Rocky IV*.

Lundgren obliged — and Stallone ended up in the intensive care unit of a Los Angeles hospital.[7]

THE BLOOM COMES OFF THE ROSE

As the years passed, more martial artists found their voice and echoed Wall, Norris and Lewis's criticism of Bruce Lee. While these same people had welcomed the influx of new students that Lee's image had brought into their martial arts schools (read: businesses), they now believed that they no longer had need of him. Their martial arts expertise was more than sufficient to run a successful studio, and Bruce Lee was simply a distraction from the business at hand. Lee's fans were cowed into silence. Who were they to argue with America's most decorated martial arts champions? When pressed, Lee's fans had to admit that they didn't have any evidence that their hero had fought for real. Sure, there were stories circulating that Lee had won a few fights in his youth, but who hadn't? Such minor league skirmishes were grossly insufficient evidence to warrant a belief that he was "the greatest fighter" of any era, let alone of "all time." Although their numbers were diminishing, there were still those who remained steadfast in their belief that their eyes had not deceived them, that what they'd witnessed Lee do in his movies in terms of skill, speed, power, and agility wouldn't simply evaporate in a real-life encounter. Indeed, the very thought seemed nonsensical to them.

Nevertheless, by the late 1970s the global fanaticism for Bruce Lee had waned. His films were no longer making the rounds in movie theaters with any degree of regularity, and he was not being talked about with the same reverence that he once was within the various martial arts schools that were then thriving in major cities all over Europe and North America. Moreover, while Lee had taught dozens of people his approach to martial art over the years, locating an instructor of his art was like finding a needle in a haystack. Indeed, there were only two people in the entire world who were actively teaching Bruce Lee's art at the time — Dan Inosanto in Los Angeles and Taky Kimura in Seattle. By contrast, there were more than 1,200 Tae Kwon Do instructors in the United States alone.[8] The martial arts had become big business; every martial arts school was competing with other schools for revenue, and, being outnumbered by several thousand instructors to two, Bruce Lee's art was gradually getting lost in the din of the marketplace. Some of Lee's students, most notably Seattle's Jesse Glover and California's Dan Inosanto, wrote books in which they testified to their late teacher's considerable fighting prowess, but because these books were available only through mail order, their audience was largely Bruce Lee fans who didn't need much convincing on the matter. And apart from these fans, the word didn't spread very far.

During the many years of my love/hate relationship with martial arts, I have witnessed a lot of street fights, as well as amateur and professional fights, and I've been a judge for the Ultimate Fighting Championship (UFC). I've even been involved in a few altercations myself, which quickly convinced me that as a fighter, I made a pretty good writer. I've come to learn over the years that a good fighter not only has to be skillful in the techniques of hurting people, but when fighting another person who is similarly skilled, they must possess certain elements of dexterity, coordination, balance, timing, speed, power, mobility, an ability to fight through anxiety and often pain, courage, perception, reflex reaction and self-confidence. Most of us possess some of these attributes; real fighters own a good number of them. World-class fighters possess all of them. Did Bruce Lee have these attributes — or were the long-standing assessments of Wall, Norris and Lewis correct? I wanted to find out.

SEEKING ANSWERS

By the early 1990s I found myself living in California and working for bodybuilding mogul Joe Weider. Joe employed me to write articles for the various magazines he published, such as *Muscle & Fitness*, *Shape*, *Men's Fitness* and *Flex*. It was there that an opportunity to interview Bruce Lee's students and friends presented itself. I suggested to my editor-in-chief that I wanted to write an article for *Muscle & Fitness* about Bruce Lee's training and bodybuilding methods. After all, while his fighting ability might have been called into question, it was undeniable that he had a very impressive physique. My editor-in-chief thought it was a good idea, and I was given a green light to proceed. It was an article that I truly looked forward to writing, as it gave me the opportunity to seek out and communicate with people who not only knew how Lee trained, but also if he could really fight. I went at my research like a man possessed and interviewed everyone and anyone who knew, worked or studied with Bruce Lee: those who were with him in Hong Kong in the 1950s; his friends and private students in Seattle in 1959; those who studied his real-life fighting art privately and directly from him, or at his modest-sized schools in Seattle, Oakland and Los Angeles, throughout the 1960s; and those who knew and worked alongside him when he made his movies in Hong Kong from 1971 to 1973. From this preliminary sampling sprang additional research, some of it culled from trips to Hong Kong, others from forays into San Francisco, Oakland, Los Angeles and Seattle. In analyzing all this testimony, a far different picture of Bruce Lee's real-world fighting ability slowly came into focus. One that stood in sharp contrast to the one his naysayers had painted over the decades.

What follows, then, is the "street record" of Bruce Lee, related by those who were there and witnessed it firsthand.

A NOTE ON THE TEXT

The term "Kung Fu" doesn't necessarily have a martial arts connection. It's a generic term that's used to describe the skill and excellence obtained after years of dedicated study. Therefore, it can be applied to any skill cultivated through hard work and constant practice. Here, both "Kung Fu" (Wade-Giles spelling) and "Gung Fu" (Pinyin spelling) are used to indicate the Chinese martial arts generally, but "Kung Fu" is also employed as a part of terms for specific styles of martial art, such as Wing Chun Kung Fu and Northern Shaolin Kung Fu. When Bruce Lee employed the term, he used the Pinyin spelling, but the two versions should be taken as interchangeable.

CHAPTER ONE

THE CONCRETE JUNGLE

"It should be remembered that violence and aggression is part of everyday life now. . . . You can't just pretend that it does not exist."

— Bruce Lee (*New Nation* [Singapore], August 15, 1972)

I n 2009 I found myself standing in the principal's office of St. Francis Xavier's College in Hong Kong. I hadn't been summoned there for misbehavior; rather, I was told to wait in the office while the vice principal, Joseph Lu, searched for something in a back room.

St. Francis Xavier's is a Catholic secondary school for boys — one of no less than eighty-five Catholic secondary schools in Hong Kong. The school was constructed in 1955, when it relocated from Shanghai, China, once the communist takeover on the mainland threatened the existence of Christian educational institutions. Here, students are taught their lessons primarily in English, but Chinese and other languages are also spoken. It's a big school, featuring a large central building that stands five stories high, bookended by two smaller buildings of four stories each. These structures are set atop some 35,251 square feet of prime real estate in Kowloon, Hong Kong's most populous area. The school has added buildings and carried out renovations since 1955, but for the most part, it hasn't changed all that much.

Mr. Lu returned from the back room holding a manila folder in his hand. He opened it up and flipped through a few pages. Finally, his focus rested on one particular piece within the folder. "There it is," he said, as he turned the folder around to show me the object of his attention. I looked to see a photograph that had been stapled onto the lower left corner of an 8 × 10 inch sheet of faded white cardboard. It was a student record from fifty-three years ago. Various categories were typed on the card, along with statements written in blue ballpoint pen. The date of the student's admission was indicated: "10 Sept., 1956." That put the age of the boy in the photo two months shy of his sixteenth birthday. The image revealed the face of an apparently happy, handsome, clean-cut young man. I noted that the date entered as his birth year was wrong: "27 Nov., 1941." I knew that the boy was actually born in 1940, which in Chinese culture would be the Year of the Dragon. If he had been born a year later, in 1941, it would have been in the Year of the Snake. Not a chance. Even if I hadn't previously seen his birth certificate from a hospital in San Francisco, this kid was a dragon. Perhaps the most famous dragon of all time.

There was additional writing on the paper indicating the boy's name, address and phone number. It also contained the assessment "Poor student," an appraisal that was evidently made by the principal of La Salle College, the high school he had transferred in from.

I was surprised that St. Francis Xavier's still had his record in their files; after all, it was from over half a century ago. Tens of thousands of students had come and gone since the time of this student's arrival. Despite the boy's lowly academic assessment, the staff at St. Francis Xavier's College spoke of him with pride. Not one but two vice-principals, along with the current day administrator, then entered the principal's office and stood alongside me, craning their necks to have a look at the lad's student card. They were quick to bring up the fact that the boy once won an inter-school boxing championship on behalf of the school just two years after he had enrolled here. It was a major point of pride for them, which surprised me, since it had little to do with anything of an academic nature, which, of course, is the very purpose of the school. In truth, three St. Francis Xavier's students competed in the inter-school boxing tournament in 1958, but the boy in the photo was the only student who brought home a gold medal from the competition. It might well have been a moment in time long since forgotten, just like the names of the other student boxers from St. Francis Xavier's that competed alongside him that day, but for the significance of the name of the boy in the photograph: Bruce Lee.

Bruce's transfer to St. Francis Xavier's occurred shortly after his expulsion from La Salle College, another Catholic secondary school in the same district — and his removal had been immediate. Psychologists might find a case study in the teenage Bruce Lee, what with all the fights and hyper-macho mischief that he engaged in during this period. They might even conclude that what drove him to such behavior would continue to serve as a psychological spur to continue fighting well into the final years and months of his life. It seemed that Bruce was always trying to prove his masculinity to the world and, if one looks even further back into his history, one might conclude that he was always, perhaps, trying to prove it to himself.

In 1983, author Albert Goldman, best known for his scathing biographies of Elvis Presley (*Elvis*, 1981) and John Lennon (*The Lives of John Lennon*, 1988), made Bruce Lee the subject of a two-part article that appeared in *Penthouse* magazine. As per Goldman's modus operandi, the picture he painted of Bruce was decidedly negative.[1] One statement from the article was particularly ignorant: "The Eastern Bruce Lee — to phrase it bluntly — put balls on 400 million Chinamen."[2] The assertion drew a sharp rebuke from Bruce Lee's friend and student, Dan Inosanto, who rightly condemned its content.[3] Goldman's statement was patently false, of course, as the Chinese male population totaled 458,760,000 in the year that Bruce Lee's last film was released, a rather clear indication that Chinese males had no need of Bruce's help in the cojones department.[4] However, his taking aim at that particular region of Bruce's anatomy was not without significance, particularly in light of the fact that Bruce was born with an undescended testicle (a condition known as cryptorchidism).[5]

It was a condition that would majorly impact certain periods of his life. For example, it was the reason he was declared "unfit" by the Washington state draft board for induction into the army during the Vietnam War[6] — a decision that might well have saved his life, and, at the very least, saved him from the severe psychological trauma that so many of the soldiers who returned home from the war had to endure. However, this condition, working in conjunction with other issues of a psychological/environmental nature, would serve as a strong impetus for Bruce to seek to define his own sense of masculinity over the years. In other words, and contrary to Goldman's claim, Bruce

Lee would be far too busy putting balls on himself to worry about attaching them to the remainder of the male Chinese population.

BIRTH OF THE DRAGON

Bruce Lee was born in San Francisco Chinese Hospital on November 27, 1940, which is to say that he was (and always considered himself to be) American.[7] This would prove to be another fact of his birth that would majorly impact him throughout his life, both negatively and positively. His mother, Ho Oi Yee (referred to as "Grace" in English), was alone in San Francisco when he was born. Her husband, Lee Hoi-chuen, a renowned actor in the Cantonese Opera (an equivalent of American vaudeville), was over 2,900 miles away while his wife was giving birth, plying his trade on stage in New York's Chinatown district. She named the boy Lee Jun Fan, which roughly translated from the Chinese means "Return to San Francisco."[8] However, Bruce's parents later would come to believe that the Chinese characters in "Lee Jun Fan" were a little too similar to the ones that appeared in Lee Hoi-chuen's father's name, and this would have been disrespectful, at least from the Chinese perspective.[9] And so the baby's name was changed to Lee Yuen Kam, meaning "protector of San Francisco."[10] "We were alone [in San Francisco]," his mother recalled, "and he was my protector."[11] Neither "Lee Jun Fan" nor his anglicized name "Bruce" (both of which were included on his United States Department of Justice Immigration and Naturalization Service records) would see use until many years later, when the boy was enrolled in an English secondary school in Hong Kong.

When the newly expanded Lee family returned to their apartment in Kowloon in early 1941, the baby boy's name changed yet again — along with the family's attitude toward him. The Lees had suffered the death of their first child, a three-month old boy they had named Lee Teung.[12] The Lees had not taken this to be merely a tragedy that occurred during the risky task of bringing a new life into the world, but rather a sign that evil spirits were at work. Demons, they believed, were responsible. And these demons evidently were on the hunt for little boys whose souls they sought to snatch up and take away with them to the netherworld. In an effort to thwart these evil spirits' intentions, the Lee family adopted a baby girl,

Fung (called Phoebe in English), in 1938. A mere forty days later, Grace Lee gave birth to a biological daughter, Yuen (called Agnes in English). It wasn't long after Agnes was born that Grace found herself pregnant again.

As both of their daughters were healthy, the Lees concluded that it was only baby boys' souls that were in demand by the evil spirits; baby girls' souls evidently not so much. And so, when Grace and Hoi-chuen's union produced a son in October of 1939, they were ecstatic — but terrified at the same time. The baby, Sum (English name: Peter), had to be protected; the evil spirits were certain to return and snatch their baby boy away from them. To confuse the spirits as to the gender of the child, Grace pierced Peter's ear and dressed him in girl's clothes.[13] She would continue to dress him in female clothing until she was certain that he was strong and healthy enough to openly acknowledge his biological gender. The tactic seemed to succeed. Peter grew into a hale and hearty thirteen-month-old by the time baby Bruce was brought into their crowded apartment in 1941.

CONFUSING THE SPIRITS

From the Lees' perspective, the gender masking had proven a successful demon-deterrent for Peter, so there was no reason to think it wouldn't do so for Bruce. While within their apartment, the Lees referred to their new child as "Sai Fong" ("Little Phoenix"), which was a feminine name. And as with Peter before him, they pierced Bruce's ear, and every night when he went to bed, they put a skirt on him.

When the boy grew old enough to attend public school, they continued in this vein, sending him to a girls' public school.[14] However, while Peter only had to endure this subterfuge for, perhaps, two years, such would not be the case with Bruce, who would have to withstand a very confusing gender identity until he was nine years old. Being treated as a girl by his family, combined with his cryptorchidism, made him different from the other young boys he palled along with, and slowly instilled in the youth a burning desire to clearly establish — to everybody — that he was *male*.

With each passing year Bruce grew more determined to assert the masculinity that his parents had so long sought to suppress. His ninth birthday was evidently a rite of passage in this respect, as his parents had decided — finally — that it was okay to drop the feminine pretense. A friend of his, William Cheung, later recalled: "Bruce came over and talked to me and he said he was really happy to get over his ninth birthday, because all these years he had to wear a skirt to go to bed to confuse the evil spirits. And, also, he went to a primary school, a girls' school, and so on the way home I was feeling really sorry for [him]."[15]

THE YOUNG MOVIE STAR

Bruce Lee's childhood was unorthodox, to put it mildly. Prior to the enduring attempt to confuse the evil spirits about his sex, he'd been brought onto a movie set and thrust before a camera while still in San Francisco less than one month after he was born.[16] His role? That of a baby girl. The film was entitled *Golden Gate Girl*[17] and was directed by the famous (and first female) Chinese movie director, Esther Eng.[18] The film was released in San Francisco in 1941, but would not be shown in Hong Kong until 1946,[19] at which time Bruce found himself before the cameras once again.

Despite being only six years of age,[20] he appeared as a supporting actor in the movie *The Birth of Mankind*. Two years later, he was in front of the cameras again, this time in the film *Wealth is Like a Dream*.[21] Sometime after his ninth birthday, he was cast as the lead actor in a feature film entitled *Kid Cheung* (also known as *The Kid* and *My Son, A-Chang*). This proved to be a significant film for the boy, as it not only became quite a hit in Hong Kong, but also marked the first time he would be billed as "Lee Siu Loong" ("Lee Little Dragon"), the name by which he would be known throughout the Cantonese-speaking world forever after. His nom de l'écran was created by Yuen Bo Wan, a famous comic strip writer in Hong Kong, whose comics had provided the inspiration for the film.[22]

The character that Bruce portrayed in this film was fascinating: a young, streetwise tough guy who fought frequently, stole occasionally and carried a knife. It closely mirrored a phase of the young boy's real life that would endure throughout his teenage years in Kowloon. For the moment, he was the most famous nine-year-old in the (then) Crown Colony of Hong Kong, which instantly established him as being both popular and a target while attending public school.

THE LURE OF TAI CHI

Bruce's love affair with the martial arts began when he was around ten. His father was a devotee of Tai Chi Chuan and had studied it under the tutelage of Liang Tzu-peng (1900–1974).[23] Young Bruce often watched Hoi-chuen performing its slow, circular movements, and listened intently as his father read aloud to him passages from fighting novels and magazines that praised the ancient Tai Chi masters. He drank this up, particularly the stories of the Tai Chi practitioners' almost superhuman powers that were able to repel people without touching them. Also inspiring were the tales of weaker people beating stronger people, older people defeating younger people, and Tai Chi defeating all of the more aggressive styles of Chinese self-defense.

Bruce's young mind was also struck by the yin-yang philosophy that underpins the art, and how all things arise out of the Tai Chi — or "Grand Terminus," the eternal energy of the universe — and exist in an interdependent relationship with everything else. On the surface (and even more deeply) it made perfect sense; what we think of as opposites cannot exist without their counterparts. Without night, what is day? Without up, what is down? Without female, what is male? Moreover, the black dot in the white portion of the yin-yang symbol and the white dot in its black portion symbolize this mutual interdependence: in the purest strain of one, there exists a tiny bit of its opposite. Thus, within every saint is a touch of the devil, and vice versa. The symbol further represents that if any single attribute is carried to its ultimate extreme, it will morph into its opposite.

This is the basic Chinese understanding of the Tao (道), or "way of nature," which was said to be set down in 400 B.C. by a mysterious figure by the name of Lao-Tzu. In Chapter Two of the *Tao Te Ching*, Lao-Tzu states:

> When the people of the Earth all know beauty as beauty,
> There arises (the recognition of) ugliness.
> When the people of the Earth all know the good as good,
> There arises (the recognition of) evil.
> Therefore:
> Being and non-being interdepend in growth;
> Difficult and easy interdepend in completion;

Long and short interdepend in contrast;
High and low interdepend in position;
Tones and voice interdepend in harmony;
Front and behind interdepend in company.[24]

That a fighting art could be based on such a mind-blowing philosophy captivated Bruce. Yin-yang philosophy would forever after be his martial arts touchstone. Delighted in his son's interest in the art, Hoi-chuen taught him the 108 movements of the Tai Chi form, which Bruce gradually came to perfect.[25] He could recite from memory the name of each movement within the form, all the while believing in the power of "chi," the internal energy that the masters of Tai Chi Chuan were said to possess and could infuse into their techniques at will. Bruce would soon have the opportunity to put his daily practice of the art to the test.

BRUCE LEE'S FIRST FIGHT

One day while walking to school, Bruce happened to step on the foot of a student from a different school. An argument ensued, and suddenly the boys were surrounded by students from both schools who were now urging them to settle the dispute with their fists. Being pressured by the crowd, the two retired to a nearby playing field to have it out. The other student, much bigger and heavier, looked on as Bruce stretched out his arms and began going through the movements of the Tai Chi form, calling out the names of each posture to the crowd.

This certainly looked and sounded impressive, not only to those who had gathered around the pair, but also to his opponent, who was now beginning to have second thoughts about what he had just gotten himself into. Growing impatient for the fight to commence, the classmates of the larger student pushed him towards Bruce to get things started. The lad smashed into Bruce, terminating his performance of the Tai Chi form and knocking him down. The spell of Bruce's martial wizardry now broken, the student promptly sat on Bruce's chest, pinning him to the ground. The larger boy rained down punches on a defenseless Bruce in a more primitive version of what MMA aficionados would refer to as "ground and pound." Bruce's classmates ran away in horror, and Bruce endured an embarrassing beating until his opponent lost interest in the enterprise, got up and continued on to school. Bruised and battered, Bruce slunk home to nurse his wounds (particularly the one to his pride) and seriously reevaluated his pre-fight belief that Tai Chi Chuan was an invincible fighting art.[26]

THE EIGHT TIGERS OF JUNCTION STREET

The year that Bruce turned twelve he entered Hong Kong's prestigious Catholic secondary school, La Salle College. Unfortunately for his teachers, he was a kid with a chip on his shoulder and was constantly looking for opportunities to assert himself and prove his masculinity. "He was angry," recalled Robert Wang, a former classmate of Bruce's at La Salle. "He had a reputation as a troublemaker, and was involved in so many fights that he was summoned to see the principal frequently."[27] He drew other boys to him in crowded Kowloon that were of a similar disposition. Some of these kids had formed their own street gang: the Eight Tigers of Junction Street. The more pedestrian names of certain of the gang members were John, Robby and Au Chun. The more intriguing names were Kings, Big Mouth, Lunny, One-Eye and Speedy.[28] Sensing a kindred spirit in Bruce, they invited him to join their gang. Bruce accepted without hesitation. However, apart from the natural rebelliousness of youth, the teenagers had other reasons to band together.

Hong Kong in the 1950s was a British colony where seismic change was taking place. Once the communists had assumed control of China, refugees (particularly from its southern region) began immigrating to Hong Kong in droves. And it wasn't just business owners fleeing the mainland; the communists, led by their chairman, Mao Tse-tung, were actively purging the republic of triads, the organized crime groups.

It didn't take long for the displaced triads to start their nefarious enterprises afresh in the colony. "The streets of Hong Kong were like a jungle then," recalled William Cheung. "The triads wanted to recruit young people to do their dirty work, as those under eighteen didn't get sent to jail, they were sent to reform school."[29] This meant that when the teenagers were sent away, new recruits from the streets were brought in, leaving the triad leaders unscathed and free to continue on with their criminal operations. In an effort to protect their turf from the growing menace of the triads, smaller street gangs began popping up all over Kowloon and Hong Kong Island. Ultimately, however, the street gangs found the lure of money and power to be irresistibly seductive, and would gradually become subsumed by the better-organized triad societies.

Cheung, whose father worked on the Hong Kong police force, remembered that "the triads liked to recruit celebrities, their families and children, because celebrities commanded a lot of respect and could draw a lot of other people into their gang." As a result of Hoi-chuen's connections within the Hong Kong entertainment industry, by the time Bruce had turned thirteen, he had appeared in no less than eight major films (nine if you count his appearance in the film *Golden Gate Girl*).[30] In other words, he was just the kind of guy the triads were looking to move in on.[31] However, the triads' initial efforts were easily rebuffed; Bruce's gang, for the moment at least, provided him with sufficient protection against the organized crime influence.

Being a teenage movie star living in an overcrowded city, where literally millions of people knew his face, brought additional problems that were quite separate from merely avoiding the clutches of organized crime. Bruce also had to cope with constant challenges to fight to prove that he wasn't just a pretty boy actor, and that he was actually as tough as the streetwise characters that he portrayed in certain of his films. To the shock of many of his fellow students, Bruce seemed to welcome such opportunities for violence. "The challenges came from newcomers who were eager to gain instant fame and recognition by prevailing over him," Robert Wang recollected. "Bruce met these challenges head-on, and with pleasure each time. He was fearless. It was as if he went into every fight either to kill or be killed."[32]

On one occasion, Bruce was approached while at school by a student looking to extort money from him. The two students headed for the bathroom. Bruce led the way, and his would-be extortionist followed close behind. When they arrived, Bruce turned and pushed his adversary into the bathroom wall. He pulled out a switchblade knife and held it against the boy's stomach.

His adversary's tough-guy persona suddenly evaporated.

"All right, now take off your clothes," Bruce demanded. "*All* of them!"

The student did as he was commanded. Bruce gathered up the teenager's clothing and exited. He tossed the student's clothes into a nearby bush and headed home.

The naked student, too embarrassed to leave the restroom, entered a stall, closed and locked the door, and stayed there for hours. He eventually fell asleep. When the sun went down and the boy hadn't returned home, his parents became frantic. They telephoned the school, but no one on duty had seen the lad. The parents then contacted his teacher, but she reported that she hadn't seen the boy since earlier that afternoon. The parents' next call was to the police. Officers were dispatched to the scene to search the school and its neighboring grounds. Eventually they found the boy, shivering and terrified, all alone in the school bathroom.[33]

On another occasion, when Bruce spotted a belt that a Caucasian student from a different high school was wearing, he approached the teenager and again pulled out his switchblade, demanding that the young man give it to him. The youth understandably complied.[34] Bruce would later recall that during this period of his life he was "a punk and went looking for fights. We used chains and pens with knives hidden inside."[35] And in a city of 2.2 million people,[36] many of whom were displaced and desperate, fights weren't hard to find.

He got into trouble again when he fought with another tough kid in the area named David Lee. The two had locked horns on prior occasions, but this time both boys pulled out switchblades. A few jabs and misses occurred before Bruce's knife found the other boy's arm, drawing blood. The pair were then either separated or agreed to stop, realizing that, if the matter escalated any further, it would only end tragically. When word of the encounter reached the principal of La Salle, he couldn't discipline Bruce as the fight had occurred off school property. However, the young man's actions were now being watched closely; one more misstep and he would be expelled.[37]

ENTER YIP MAN

What the young Bruce Lee possessed in fearlessness, he lacked in fighting technique. "I wondered what would happen if I didn't have my gang behind me if I got into a fight," he told a reporter in 1967. "I decided to learn how to protect myself and I began to study Gung Fu."[38] For a short time he studied Hung Kuen (also known as Hung Gar), a southern style of Kung Fu.[39] But he would soon switch allegiances once he witnessed his friend, William Cheung, easily dispatch an opponent using Kung Fu techniques that he had never seen before. Intrigued by the explosiveness of the techniques, he badgered Cheung for details until he revealed the name of his instructor: Yip Man.

Yip Man (now more popularly rendered "Ip Man") was a venerable, chain-smoking man of sixty at the time and already something of a legend within the martial arts circles of Hong Kong. He had grown up in Foshan, China, where he'd received instruction from Chun Wah-shun in the art of Wing Chun Kung Fu, a close-range fighting system that taught its adherents to strike throughout the centerline of a person's body with rapid-fire punches, while using leg kicks to attack the lower extremities. In 1909, Yip traveled to Hong Kong to attend St. Stephen's College, a secondary school that wealthy foreigners sent their children to. While in Hong Kong he was said to have received additional instruction in Wing Chun by a man named Leung Bik (generally believed to be the son of Leung Jan, the man who had taught Yip Man's teacher Chan Wah-shun). All of Yip Man's training in Wing Chun occurred at the beginning of the twentieth century.

Like most Chinese martial arts, any history of the art beyond this point is largely apocryphal, and fades off into the twin mists of myth and legend.[40] Perhaps more impressive to Bruce Lee was a rumor that had been floating around Hong Kong in the early 1950s that Yip Man, when challenged at his Kung Fu school, had killed a man with one punch.[41] The story is undoubtedly apocryphal as well, as there exists no record of Yip Man ever being charged with manslaughter from when he returned to Hong Kong in 1949 until his death there in 1972. But a teenage Bruce Lee certainly was of the opinion that such an event *could* have happened, and that kind of lethal technique was something that he wanted to learn.

At Bruce's prompting, Cheung brought him to Yip Man's Wing Chun school to meet the master. Wong Shun Leung, the school's top fighter, remembered laying eyes on Bruce Lee for the first time:

> I practiced my Kung Fu in Master Yip's institute. I also helped to instruct the students. At that time, [William] Cheung brought in an Elvis-like youngster. He leaned his body to one side with his hand on the wall. The other hand was in the back pocket of his trousers. His body was supported by one of his legs only. He swayed his body continuously. His manner was very frivolous, as though he thought that he was smart. I really did not like his appearance. After he went away, I told Cheung that I did not welcome this young man.[42]

Apart from Wong, there was another obstacle that Bruce needed to overcome before he could start his training at Yip Man's school: his parents. Like many Chinese families, the Lees considered Kung Fu to be a direct gateway to the triads, and they wanted no part of that for their son.[43] Lee Hoi-chuen had observed the triad presence expanding within the entertainment industry, and he was determined that the taint of organized crime would never touch his family. However, Bruce knew which parent to work on, and over the course of the next several months he keyed in on his mother, Grace, until she ultimately capitulated and gave him the money to begin his Wing Chun lessons. Grace then soft-soaped her husband into accepting her decision.[44] Once again, Wong Shun Leung was present when Bruce returned to Yip Man's school: "A few months later, [Bruce] came for the second time. This time, he dressed properly and was more polite. Master Yip liked him very much, so he took him to be his disciple. He immediately came over and greeted me. This was so sudden that I just could not understand. We became fellow students and friends."[45]

Yip Man was actually eager to accept Bruce Lee as a student. Not only had he seen several of Bruce's films[46] (celebrity students then, like now, are always good for business), but Bruce's enrollment also meant that an additional eight Hong Kong dollars a month would soon be coming Yip's way in the form of Bruce's membership fees.[47] While there is a belief in the West that the Chinese art of Kung Fu, in its purest form, has always been free from the taint of money, the reality is that ever since Kung Fu lessons were taught to the public, money had been changing hands.[48] While living in Foshan, Yip Man had been required to pay twenty taels of silver to be accepted as a student of Chan Wah-shun, and then another eight taels of silver a month for his Wing Chun lessons.[49]

Bruce began his lessons as soon as his mother's cash was in Yip Man's pocket.[50] During the first two lessons, he proved himself to be a model student — but that all changed in the third session. According to Yip Man's son, Yip Chun:

> As a rule, my father did not like to teach new students immediately. So, after the procedure of accepting them, the first lesson was taught by [senior Wing Chun student] Yip Bo-ching. . . . On the third day after the first lesson Bruce finally caused some trouble. Early in the day, Bruce came to find Yip Bo-ching to practice sticking hands [called *chi sao* in Cantonese, a Wing Chun tactile/sensitivity drill]. They put their full attention at it. But suddenly, without letting other people know, Bruce sent out a kick. Yip was a bit older. Moreover, he was not [expecting] it. So, he was hurt. Fortunately, Bruce was willing to apologize on that day and William Cheung explained for Bruce Lee. Otherwise, Bruce would be discharged [from the school].[51]

That misstep behind him, Bruce took to his Wing Chun training as though his life depended on it; not a day went by when he wasn't practicing. As a result of such diligent training, he improved rapidly — so rapidly, in fact, that he was soon surpassing many of Yip Man's most senior students, many of whom had been studying Wing Chun for several years. While such rapid improvement was impressive, Bruce's dedication to Wing Chun didn't make him any less bellicose.

During a gym class at La Salle College, the school's physical education teacher decided to take his students outside and have them run three laps of the school's soccer field. When students slacked off or didn't run as quickly as he wished, he whacked them on the back of their legs with a ruler. The sting of the ruler on a bare leg seldom failed to produce the desired effect. That is until he whacked Bruce in the hamstrings. Instead of picking up his stride, Bruce wheeled around and glared at the teacher — and then pulled out his switchblade. The gym teacher's eyes widened in terror and he took off running as fast as he could in the opposite direction with Bruce in hot pursuit. He ran into the principal's office before Bruce caught up with him. This was the last straw: Bruce Lee was immediately expelled from La Salle College.[52]

Hoi-chuen and Grace were shocked and embarrassed by their son's behavior. They quickly pulled whatever strings they could to have him transferred to another secondary school to complete his education. Due to the influence of a family member who happened to be a benefactor to St. Francis Xavier's College, the school agreed to his enrollment there. However, along with admission to the new school came a warning that *this was it* — there would be no more second chances. Bruce was told in no uncertain terms that he needed to dedicate himself, body and soul, to his academic studies at the new institution. Although it was the proper sentiment, it could only be fulfilled by half. While the boy's body would indeed attend classes at St. Francis Xavier's, his soul had already been pledged to another school: Yip Man's.

"When I first learned martial art, I, too, have challenged many established instructors. And, of course, some others challenged me also."

— Bruce Lee (Radio Hong Kong, 1971)

Yip Man was impressed with Bruce's dedication. He would later tell his son, Yip Chun, about the numerous times he had looked out from his window to observe Bruce throwing kicks and vertical fist punches while walking towards his school, or performing Wing Chun hand techniques such as circling hand (*huen sao*), pulling hand (*lop sau*) and darting hand (*biu sau*). Other students from the Wing Chun school saw Bruce walking through the streets carrying a pair of dumbbells and throwing punches while holding them.[1] Even at home, Bruce pounded stools on either side of him with his fists to strengthen his arms and toughen his hands.[2] Yip Man appreciated that Bruce was never a pushy student; he never grew impatient drilling on fundamental techniques over and over and never demanded more of his teacher and senior instructors than they were willing to give.[3] "He would stay on one technique for weeks and months until he mastered it," recalled William Cheung. "So, just with that quality, it made Yip Man like him."[4]

When Bruce wasn't training at Yip Man's school, he was training with William Cheung. The two young men were inseparable during 1956 and 1957. "In the 1950s we were training 1,000 punches, 500 kicks every day," Cheung recalled. "Most of our training sessions were over four hours nonstop. And one of the main things that we trained was that we repeated each technique until we mastered it. So, we never tried to skip something. And so, our basic foundation was so good that it made us superior to all the other martial artists."[5] Similarly impressed with Bruce's dedication to Wing Chun was Wong Shun Leung, who by this point had been studying the art for five years under Yip Man's guidance:

> Apart from having good potential, he also paid attention to the use of equipment in training himself. Under my advice, he had made two steel bars to strengthen the power of his wrists. When he had time, he would train with his bars. This helped a lot in increasing his punching power. The things he practiced every day included punching, sidekicks, and training on the wooden dummy. When he had finished with all this, he would sit down and meditate on what he had done. He trained himself in this way for a long time.[6]

Frank Clausnitzer, a student at St. Francis Xavier's College, was one of a number of students who would gather around the Little Dragon at recess to watch him practicing his Wing Chun moves. Occasionally, Bruce would teach them some of the techniques from the art. Frank's older brother Rolf recalled once getting yanked off his feet and having his arms completely locked up when Frank performed the Wing Chun pulling hand technique on him that he'd learned from Bruce earlier that day.[7] And then, two weeks later, Rolf recalled meeting a seventeen-year-old Bruce Lee for the first time:

> Frank brought home this wizard and introduced him as Bruce Lee Jun Fan. It was the one and only time I met Bruce face to face, but I recall he was clean-cut, well groomed, about my height, but considerably lighter. He began by demonstrating what I reckon was part of the Sil Lum Tao form. This had the same effect on me as it has had on countless people since who know nothing about Wing Chun — not very exciting and somewhat puzzling!

Then came the mind-blowing experience which was to confirm my interest in Wing Chun that my brother had aroused a few weeks earlier with his own little demo. Bruce invited me to "spar" with him, assuring me that I wouldn't get hurt. . . . He asked me to bring my arms in contact with his, turned his head through 180 degrees so that he couldn't see me, and he gave me the go-ahead to box, to go for his face and chest. I tried for what seemed like a minute to score, but he deflected and trapped every jab, hook, cross and uppercut I threw, and his fist kept ending up under my nose. I realize now that what he was doing to me was "blindfolded" *chi sau* [sticking hands] of a very high order.[8]

Bruce was very tribal at this point in his life, in the sense that if any of his family, gang members or fellow Wing Chun students suffered an impertinence, he didn't think twice about heading out to track down and fight the person who had caused it. When his younger brother Robert accidentally touched a soccer ball during a match on a nearby field, one of the players punched him in the stomach. Robert ran home and told Bruce, who immediately hit the streets and the local soccer fields looking for the culprit. He never found him, but Robert recalled that Bruce let out a string of Cantonese curse words that made him proud.[9] "Bruce was very protective of me and the rest of our family," Robert recalled.[10]

When a member of the Eight Tigers of Junction Street was jumped and beaten up by two members from a rival gang, Bruce again went out to hunt down the ones who did it. When he spotted the two gang members, he approached them as if to talk, but as soon as he got close enough, he suddenly lashed out and punched both of them, knocking them down.[11] There is no record of the street gang ever bothering any member of the Tigers of Junction Street again.

WING CHUN TOUGH GUY

By 1957 Bruce had cultivated a serious disdain for practitioners of Chinese Kung Fu who didn't train as hard as he, Wong Shun Leung and William Cheung did. He particularly grew to detest the teachers of these arts who seldom trained at all, possessed no fighting experience, and attracted students to their schools solely as a result of the legends and reputations of their respective arts. If he saw such teachers performing in the parks of Hong Kong, he often felt obliged to confront them.

On one such occasion he saw a crowd gathered around a teacher who was demonstrating the Tai Chi form. The master announced that when he sank his chi into his lower *dantian* (one of the energy centers located in the lower part of the body, as taught in certain of the "internal" styles of Kung Fu) he could withstand a punch from anybody and asked for a volunteer to help him demonstrate. Bruce stepped forward. When the instructor set his stance and sank his chi, Bruce promptly cracked him in the ribs. The teacher collapsed to the ground, where he writhed and moaned. Bruce stood over the man and glared at him. "Next time, don't show off." Bruce then turned and made his way through the crowd of startled onlookers.[12]

As Bruce was now a loyal member of the Wing Chun clan, his attitude toward rival schools of Kung Fu was what one might expect from a teenager who wanted desperately to raise his stock in the eyes of his fellow practitioners. However, it was also an attitude that lacked deference and respect, two qualities that young men were expected to show older men within Chinese culture. When one of his Wing Chun classmates (whom we only know by the surname of Ng) came to class one afternoon complaining that a master from a different Kung Fu clan had challenged him to a fight, Bruce automatically responded that he would take him on.[13]

Wong Shun Leung heard what was said — and what Bruce planned to do about it. However, Wong happened to know the master from the other school, a certain Sifu Li, and believed that Ng was suffering from a misunderstanding. Wong knew Master Li to be an honorable and humble man; certainly not the kind of person to instigate fights between Kung Fu schools. However, before he could offer an opinion, Bruce approached him. "We're having the match on Saturday. I'm fighting him."

"What match? Has the other side agreed to this? And to a specific date and place?"

Bruce shook his head. "But I know where Li teaches on Saturday mornings." He gestured toward several Wing Chun students standing nearby. "*We* will meet him there. You know that man who issued the challenge?"

"What man? Who made this proposal?"

"It's Li. He made the proposal."

Wong wasn't convinced. "I can't believe Li challenged Ng. He's a good man. I've met him — he's not the kind to cause any trouble."

But Bruce wasn't to be dissuaded. While Wong was skeptical, he also didn't want to discourage him if, in fact, Master Li had issued such a challenge. It was, after all, a Wing Chun student's duty to defend his school.

"Don't force Li," Wong counseled. "It's only okay by me if he *agrees* to fight. I don't want to destroy your plan, so I'll come, but I'll look on from a distance."

Bruce smiled. "If *I'm* there, he will fight," he said. "Just wait and see."

While Wong reluctantly agreed with Bruce's plan, he also resolved to head down to Master Li's compound on the morning of the match, just in case the problem might be avoided. By 8:00 a.m. Saturday, Bruce Lee and eight of his Wing Chun brothers were on the march to Li's training area, which turned out to be a deserted house next to a railway track. Wong Shun Leung followed the group from a distance. As the Wing Chun brigade drew closer they spotted Master Li and twelve of his students training in the front yard of the house. Wong looked on as Bruce broke away from his group, made his way into the yard and stood before Li and his students. Placing his hands on his hips, he announced, "Hey! Who is the one that wants to fight? Let me satisfy your desire. Quick! I don't have much time!"

Wong noted a look of puzzlement on Master Li's face.

"We will not fight," Li said. The teacher turned and walked away. His students followed.

"You cowards!" Bruce yelled, hoping to rile up the Kung Fu master. "Yeah, go home! Why do you even practice Kung Fu? You are not a man! You *challenged us* to fight — and I'm not a patient man. I won't wait!"

Sensing that his words weren't having the desired effect, Bruce chased after Master Li. He caught up to the man, positioned himself in front of him to block his way, and stared at him. He made a gesture that was meant to insult the teacher.

Master Li made no response.

Bruce now began to mock the man; he broke into a dance, he pretended to shake in fear. "Oh! I beg you," he exclaimed sarcastically, "have mercy on me!" When that didn't work, he offered a new challenge to the master. "I'll *let* you beat me. I won't fight back, okay? You don't have to be afraid. I like you. Come on, let's start!"

Master Li was clearly embarrassed by the young man's actions. Spotting Wong Shun Leung looking on from afar, the old teacher walked over to him. The two men shook hands. "Mr. Wong, have we done anything wrong?" Li asked. "Since we are friends, you can tell me frankly. I respect you and I don't want to have any misunderstanding."

Now Wong was the one who was embarrassed. Master Li — clearly — had not challenged anybody.

Bruce piped up again. "Leung! *Please* ask him to fight with me. If you do, I'll invite you out to dinner tonight!"

Wong Shun Leung looked at him with daggers in his eyes. He marched over to Bruce and took hold of him firmly by the arm. "Bruce, *cool down!*" he said in a harsh whisper. "Listen to me: You should not force people to fight. Your behavior is not very good. If other people learn of it, they will think that we are rough and rude. If Master Yip finds out about this, he won't be happy. It is useless to provoke Li."

Bruce shrugged his shoulders.

Wong returned to Master Li and placed his hand reassuringly on the old man's shoulder. "These youngsters are still green, and some of them just want to see how people fight. That is why they make so much nonsense. Forgive them for my sake. I don't want to hurt our relationship. If there is anything wrong, come and tell me."

"Yes, that's right," Li replied. "We are all members of the Chinese martial arts family. I know that you, Mr. Wong, are a good man. I hope we'll have more interactions in the future." And with that, Master Li turned to leave.

Bruce rolled his eyes at what was now playing out. Rather than putting the instructor in his place, Wong Shun Leung had instead calmed the waters. The fight was off. Bruce walked over to one of his fellow Wing Chun students and pulled the young man's arms up into a fighting stance. Then he pretended that he was Master Li; he walked as though he was drunk, and when a light strike from the student hit his chest, Bruce dramatically fell to the ground and flailed his limbs as though convulsing.

As insulting and juvenile as Bruce's behavior was, Wong actually found himself stifling a chuckle at the performance. "Lee's acting was good," he later recalled with a laugh. By now Master Li and his students had left the premises, which allowed Wong to relax a little bit.

Still, the incident did nothing to endear Bruce Lee to the long-established Hong Kong martial arts community. When word reached Yip Man about the encounter, he somewhat facetiously nicknamed Bruce Lee "Upstart,"[14] but never reprimanded him. Not that Bruce cared. His sole interest in formally studying Kung Fu was to improve his fighting skills, and he was pissed that an opportunity to test himself in action against the master of another clan had slipped through his fingers.

A STUDENT WITHOUT A SCHOOL

Bruce Lee's brazen behavior, combined with his rapidly evolving skill set, had slowly but steadily eroded the goodwill of many of the senior students at Yip Man's school. Not only had his out-of-class antics increased the chances of their being challenged by members of a rival school, but during sparring sessions within Yip Man's studio, Bruce was mopping the floor with students who had been studying under the master for many years.[15] The possibility that Bruce might soon eclipse them in Yip's eyes, not to mention the celebrity status that he enjoyed as a movie star in Hong Kong, fostered a deep-seated resentment among certain of the senior students. They wanted Bruce Lee off the scene, and the sooner the better. The problem was that none of them had the means to best him in a fight, and, by most reports, Yip Man was fond of the Little Dragon.[16]

But a little digging on the senior students' part revealed an opening that could be exploited. Bruce's mother, Grace, it was discovered, wasn't a full-blooded Chinese person. Indeed, her mother was a Caucasian woman from England.[17] While the students weren't sure of her precise ethnicity, they were certain it was European. Some thought German.[18] It didn't matter; the fact that she wasn't pure Chinese was sufficient. Ever since the communist victory in 1949, a damper had been placed on the open teaching of martial arts throughout China. Those who did teach did so beneath the government radar and in small groups whose loyalty could be trusted.

Teaching foreigners or non-Chinese was something that could get a martial arts instructor in trouble within his community. It simply wasn't done.[19] Knowing this, a band of Wing Chun students approached Yip Man and laid out their evidence that Bruce Lee was — at best — only three-quarters Chinese, and that he had to go for the good of the reputations of both Yip Man and the school.[20] "Reluctantly," William Cheung later recalled, "Yip Man told Bruce Lee to go."[21] Bruce would never forgive his Wing Chun brothers for having him kicked out of Yip Man's school.[22]

The decision to banish Bruce from his school had been a problematic one for Yip Man. Not only had he liked Bruce, but he had long been good friends with Lee's father, Lee Hoi-chuen.[23] To kick his friend's son out of his school, and to do so because Lee's grandmother on his mother's side had been Occidental, was an insult to Hoi-chuen's family. To mitigate this problem, Yip came up with a way to keep Bruce in the art and still satisfy the demand from certain of his students to have him expelled from the school. It was a solution that would save face for both parties.

TRAINING WITH THE "KING OF TALKING HANDS"

Wong Shun Leung's reputation within the Wing Chun clan was such that he didn't need to say anything to command the respect of Hong Kong's Kung Fu community. A veteran of over 100 challenge matches (*beimo* in Cantonese) by some accounts, Wong had handily defeated some of Hong Kong's best Kung Fu practitioners. While many Kung Fu masters talked about how good their fighting skills were, Wong always let his hands (and feet) do the talking for him. Consequently, he had been dubbed the "King of Talking Hands." While Yip Man may have been the headmaster of the Wing Chun school, Wong Shun Leung was the man the master tapped on the shoulder whenever a rival martial artist needed sorting out.

Yip approached Wong and asked him to train Bruce privately at the apartment of Wong's father, where Wong was living at the time.[24] This new arrangement could be interpreted by Bruce as not so much getting turfed out of the main school, but rather getting special attention from the clan's best fighter. It might even be taken to represent a promotion of sorts. Bruce accepted the proposal with some alacrity; he wanted to learn how to become a better fighter, and who knew more about fighting than Wong Shun Leung? Wong was already training some of the more advanced students at his apartment, so one more wouldn't pose a problem. "Bruce Lee learned all three sets [forms] of Wing Chun," Wong recalled.[25] "At the time I taught Bruce, I did not know the whole Wooden Dummy form. [I knew] about the first sixty moves of the Wooden Dummy form. He worked very hard at learning."[26]

Surprisingly, the first sixty moves of the Wooden Dummy form were all that Yip Man knew as well.[27] The Wing Chun system has six forms, or series of practice movements, three of which are performed with empty hands; a fourth, the Wooden Dummy, is performed as a training aid, and the final two forms are performed with weapons (a long pole in one, and two butterfly knives in the other). Many years after his death, there would be criticism leveled at Bruce by certain parties in the Wing Chun community that he "never learned the complete system," which, while true, is a little too dismissive of his capabilities in the art. He certainly was fluent in its first two forms and the majority of its dummy set, and sufficiently proficient in its trapping, kicking and striking to excel far beyond most Wing Chun practitioners in fighting. And becoming a better fighter was his only reason for practicing the art.

While training with the other students who came to Wong's apartment was fine, Bruce recognized that he would progress faster if his lessons with Wong were private. He first approached Wong directly, stating that he should only teach him. Wong refused such a preposterous request on principle.[28] Since that tack didn't work, Bruce quickly devised another. After his high school classes ended, he caught a bus to Wong's home before the other Wing Chun students arrived. The Wong family's apartment was on the third floor of a building in Mong Kok, in the midwestern region of Kowloon. Bruce raced up the stairs to the first landing and waited for his fellow students to show up. Upon their arrival he intercepted them, his head hung low in dejection. "Wong isn't home today," he said, regret tinging his words.[29] Bruce then walked with the disappointed group back to the bus stop and saw them onto the bus. Once the bus pulled away, he rushed back to Wong's apartment and, feigning surprise that the other students hadn't shown up for class, he would receive one-on-one instruction from Wong Shun Leung.

This happened on several occasions, until Wong discovered the ruse and scolded his cheeky student. Bruce never repeated the trick again. Despite the scolding, Wong would later smile at the recollection. "You could tell that he was an intelligent kid."[30] Training directly under the King of Talking Hands resulted in Bruce Lee's fighting skills taking a quantum leap. Wong stressed practicality in fighting, and had no use for ornate techniques with no real-world application. Wong's approach was wholeheartedly embraced by his eager student. Long after he settled in America, Bruce would write a letter to Wong: "Even though fighting theories are important, practicality is even more important. Both are necessary. I thank you and Master [Yip Man] for teaching me the Wing Chun approach in Hong Kong. Actually, thanks to you I was guided more toward the path of practicality."[31]

It was well that Wong stressed practicality, for the Little Dragon was still fighting in the streets. On one occasion, sometime after he had started training with Wong Shun Leung, Bruce was walking south through the slums of Sham Shui Po on his way to St. Francis Xavier's. As he made his way toward the school, a man suddenly appeared and charged at him brandishing an ax. According to Sid Fattedad, a friend of Bruce who happened to be with him that day, the man had been giving Bruce a rough time for several days in succession and, when he saw him again on this particular morning, he lost his mind and charged at him. According to Fattedad, Bruce was neither surprised nor scared by the attack. Instead, he deftly side-stepped the man's ax swing and simultaneously fired a kick directly into the man's groin. As the man doubled over from the strike, Bruce drove his elbow into the back of the man's neck. "The guy dropped his ax as he fell to the ground," Fattedad recalled, "and Bruce picked it up and put it to his neck saying, *mo yuk!* ('don't move!') The fight was over, and [I had] the feeling that Bruce would have used the ax on this fellow if he did not do as he was told."[32]

Within the Ving Tsun Athletic Academy today sits a bust of Yip Man. Affixed to it is a brass plaque that contains nine rules of conduct known as the "Ving Tsun Jo Fen" (roughly: "The Wing Chun Ancestral rules"), which are said to have been created by Yip Man during the 1950s. The sixth rule states: "Learn to develop spiritual tranquility. Abstain from arguments and fights." It seems a worthy rule to follow. However, at seventeen years of age, "spiritual tranquility" was not on Bruce's radar. Despite the danger involved, the truth is that Bruce enjoyed fighting — and he had no intention of abstaining from it.

CHAPTER THREE

FIGHTING FOR ST. FRANCIS

"Water is the softest substance in the world, yet it can penetrate the hardest rock or anything — granite — you name it. Water also is insubstantial. By that I mean, you cannot grasp hold of it. You cannot punch it and hurt it. So, every Gung Fu man is trying to do that: to be soft like water, and flexible, and adapt himself to the opponent."

— Bruce Lee (screen test, 1965)

One day, Brother Edward Muss heard swearing and banging emanating from the ground floor bathroom at St. Francis Xavier's College. Muss was a large, powerful man who also had a background in Western boxing.[1] Most of the students did their best to stay clear of him. With determined strides Muss made his way to the bathroom and threw open the door. He was shocked to discover Bruce Lee and another student in a wild brawl. He separated the two youths and rebuked them. He dismissed Bruce's adversary, but then turned to Bruce and gave him a choice — he could be suspended from school, or he could join the school's boxing team.[2]

In truth, Muss had had his eye on Bruce ever since the pair exchanged cross words several months previously. Bruce had evidently challenged Muss to step into the ring with him. It was a brazen move by such a young man, particularly one with no boxing experience. However, to the surprise of everybody in the school gym who witnessed the match, Bruce not only held his own with the bigger and more seasoned man, but tagged him with punches and evaded everything the teacher threw his way.[3] Muss had been trying to figure out a way to get the boy on his school boxing team ever since. That way had suddenly materialized.

An inter-school boxing tournament was coming up and with Bruce Lee now on board, the St. Francis Xavier's boxing team's chances of winning a gold medal had improved considerably. Not only was Bruce reputed to be a fearless and talented fighter, but he was possessed of an almost preternatural athleticism. One of the teachers, Brother Gregory Seubert, had once looked out the window from his office on the third floor of the school to witness Bruce perform more than fifty consecutive chin-ups.[4] Later, when the teachers were talking among themselves, Brother Gregory mentioned what he saw and this immediately piqued the interest of Brother Edward. Now Muss had to fight the urge to pinch his pudgy flanks knowing he had Bruce Lee on the St. Francis Xavier's boxing team.

THE TRAINING BEGINS

In the weeks leading up to the tournament, Brother Edward taught Bruce the fundamentals of the "sweet science" and was impressed at how naturally the young man took to it. "When he came to our school I knew at once he was a boxer — he was already that good," Brother Edward would later recall.[5] While Bruce may have been a natural at boxing, Muss would have raised an eyebrow when he saw the name of the young man Bruce would be facing in the tournament: Gary Elms.

Elms had won his division of the inter-school boxing championships for the past two years in succession. He was a tough, seventeen-year-old student from King George V School, which catered mostly to the children of British soldiers stationed in Hong Kong. Elms knew how to fight and clearly was a formidable opponent. A boxing ring was Elms's office, a place where he was not only comfortable but dominant. As might be expected, once the names of the fighters were made known among the student bodies of the schools that would be competing, the "Elms Versus Lee" bout was the chief point of discussion.

Few who attended the schools entered in the competition — St. Francis Xavier's, St. George, La Salle or King George V — gave Bruce, who was as green as the St. Francis Xavier's logo, any chance against Elms whatsoever. To better his chances, Bruce sought out Wong

Shun Leung for guidance on how he might incorporate some of the hand techniques from Wing Chun into his forthcoming bout. Wong sparred with him as a Western boxer would, while Bruce defended and attacked using the principles and techniques of Wing Chun Kung Fu.[6] After a few weeks of diligent training, Wong was confident that if Bruce didn't win, he would certainly give Elms all he could handle.

THE COMPETITION BEGINS

The boxing card featured no less than nineteen bouts. Twelve of the boxers were Caucasian and seven were Chinese. The host school, St. George's, entered twenty-three boxers in the competition, King George V brought seven and La Salle had five. Try as he might, Brother Edward had only been able to rustle up three boxers to represent St. Francis Xavier's. The tournament was a relatively new inter-school competition. Indeed, it was billed as just the "Third Annual Inter-School Individual Boxing Championships."[7]

When the doors to St. George's finally swung open on the evening of March 29, 1958, the auditorium quickly filled to capacity. Friends and family of the thirty-eight contestants were in attendance, in addition to students and members of the public.[8] Given that the British were then calling the shots in Hong Kong politically and socially, any event in which it was legal to punch a *gwai lo* (foreign devil) in the mouth was looked upon by the native Chinese as an event that was well worth seeing. Among those in the audience that evening were Wong Shun Leung, who was there primarily to observe how his student would employ what they'd worked on; Frank Clausnitzer, who, as a student of St. Francis Xavier's, was there to lend his vocal support to the boxers from his school; and Frank's brother Rolf, who was rooting for the boxers from King George V.

The format for the tournament was straightforward:

- Each bout would consist of three one-minute rounds.
- Each fighter would have one bout only.
- Judges would decide the winner of each match.
- The referee had the authority to stop the bout in the event of a knockout, or if a fighter was seriously hurt and in no condition to continue.[9]

In no time at all, St. George's school pulled ahead with a 3–0 record. Their boxers had easily outpointed those from King George V, and one match actually featured two boxers from St. George's competing against each other. The first boxer representing St. Francis Xavier's, a teenager named Hawkins, wouldn't see action until the sixth bout of the tournament, when he was outpointed by a fighter named Austin from St. George's. This brought the leaderboard to five wins for St. George's and one for King George V. By the time the seventeenth fight of the night had concluded, St. George's was miles ahead of the other schools with twelve wins, followed in second place by La Salle with four. King George V had a tenuous hold on third place with one win, while St. Francis Xavier's was sitting dead last with no wins at all.

The seventeenth bout of the evening caused considerable excitement, as it was the only fight of the night that didn't go the distance. A local newspaper would name St. George's Peter Burton as "the most promising boxer of the evening when he won his bout inside the prescribed three one-minute rounds." Burton, who had been boxing for three years, pummeled his opponent from King George V so relentlessly that the referee was forced to stop the fight on a technical knockout (TKO). Burton had either been brought in specifically for the tournament on account of his boxing skill, or had recently started attending St. George's school, as the newspaper indicated that he had not been present at the tournament the year before and that this was his "first fight in Hong Kong."[10]

GARY ELMS VERSUS BRUCE LEE

Despite sitting through seventeen matches, the energy from the crowd was palpable when Bruce Lee and Gary Elms stepped into the ring.

Both opponents knew the other's reputation — as did all of the students in attendance. Elms was the defending champion of his weight division, while Bruce was known for his street fighting prowess, along with having appeared in some seventeen Cantonese-language films by this point. The fact that he had been studying Wing Chun Kung Fu for the past two years was also known to certain of those in attendance. This was going to be a fight to remember: each fighter weighed about 120 pounds, both were legitimately tough guys, and the winner would claim the bragging rights for the school that he represented. Would it be the representative of the predominantly British King George V School, or the Chinese Catholic school of St. Francis Xavier's? Both institutions had their supporters. None of this was lost on Brother Edward and the rest of the St. Francis Xavier's contingent — Bruce Lee was their school's only hope of winning a gold medal in the competition.

The Chinese fans in attendance were rooting for Bruce to triumph over his foreign opponent. Five Chinese fighters had already competed prior to the Lee Versus Elms bout, using what the press would describe "as their own style of boxing," which is open to interpretation. Presumably this phrase referred to Chinese fighters using elements of Kung Fu in the boxing ring, or it may simply have been a euphemism for them flailing away at their opponents without any indication of Western boxing technique. In any case, all five Chinese boxers won their matches, a source of considerable pride for the pro-Chinese crowd, who now looked on excitedly as Bruce prepared to start the match. The fact that Bruce intended to use the striking techniques and principles from Wing Chun would make for, in Rolf Clausnitzer's words, "the weirdest, most bizarre boxing match I had ever, ever seen in my life. I don't think I'll see another one like that again."[11]

When the bell sounded to start round one, Elms immediately assumed the orthodox stance of Western boxing; his jab probed in and out, high and low, like the tongue of a snake, searching for an opening. Bruce raised his arms in the traditional ready position (*bai jong*) of Wing Chun. He stood square to his opponent, right arm extended, palm up; his left palm, fingertips pointing upwards, was placed next to his right elbow. He extended his right leg perhaps twelve inches and pivoted his foot slightly to the left.[12] Many of those in attendance jeered when they saw this posture in the ring. To the minds of the boxing purists, whatever Bruce intended doing in this bout clearly wasn't Western boxing.

Bruce, oblivious to the catcalling from the crowd, simply waited as Elms shuffled towards him, still pawing the air with his left jab. Using his left leg as a pivot, Bruce turned his body to ensure that wherever Elms was, he always faced him head on. Elms now fired off several jabs in quick succession, which, by subtle turns of his arms and body, Bruce deflected without difficulty. Suddenly Bruce exploded forward with a series of Wing Chun chain punches (so called because, like links in a chain, each punch seemed attached to the previous one, following one another in rapid succession). As per the Wing Chun method of the time, each of Bruce's punches concluded with his wrist tilting sharply upward, generating a little extra torque with each strike. To the surprise of many, all of Bruce's punches penetrated Elms's defense, each making solid contact with the Britisher's face and chest. Bruce's final punch of the series landed flush on Elms's jaw, dropping the two-time champion flat on his back. The crowd exploded in applause, believing they just might be witnessing an upset in the making.

Elms, however, could take a punch. He pulled himself to his feet and indicated to the referee that he was fine to continue. Wiping off Elms's gloves on his shirt, the referee signaled for the bout to resume. Elms, embarrassed at having been knocked down, began to throw more powerful punches. Once again, Bruce used his Wing Chun training to deflect each and every blow. Finally, the bell rang to signal the end of the first round, and each fighter returned to his corner for the one-minute rest interval.

The crowd applauded — or rather, most of it did. The students in attendance from King George V were strangely silent. They hadn't expected this; their fighter was the defending champion. An Elms victory had been all but assured. To have witnessed him knocked flat on his back was not only a novelty, it meant that he had lost the first round and put the gold medal for this bout clearly in jeopardy. Elms knew this as well, and going into the second round he was determined not to take his opponent as lightly as he had in the first.

When the bell rang to begin round two, Bruce once again assumed the ready position of Wing Chun. But this time Elms came out swinging — hard. A palms-up block from Bruce with his extended right arm (*tan sao*) deflected the first blow away from his face, while a low left arm block (*bong sau*) deflected Elms's attempted body shot off to the side. Elms now pressed his attack harder — with the same result. The frustration on his face was evident to all; no attack he launched could find its intended target. And then Bruce Lee did it again: he fired off a rapid series of chain punches that drove his opponent across the ring, and capped it off with a vertical fist punch that hit Elms square on the jaw, once again depositing him on the canvas.

The crowd broke into rapturous applause and cheers as Bruce resumed his Wing Chun stance, waiting for his opponent to get back to his feet. Elms stood up and the referee checked him over to make sure he was okay to continue. Once more, Elms nodded. The referee stepped back and the fight resumed. Elms now approached Bruce cautiously, his previous all-out assault clearly not having brought him the result he'd anticipated. After some ineffectual jabs from the King George V fighter, the bell rang to end the second round.

There now was considerable concern in Elms's corner; his coaches were talking over each other in an attempt to solve the Wing Chun techniques that had prevented their fighter from landing a single punch during the previous two rounds. Everybody in attendance knew that Elms was so far behind in the scoring that he now needed a knockout to win. Back in Bruce's corner the jubilation was barely suppressed; Bruce merely had to survive the next round to win the match. Brother Edward was beaming.

When the bell sounded to start the third and final round, Bruce once again assumed the ready position of Wing Chun, while Elms employed lateral movement in an attempt to find an opening to land a haymaker. But every time Elms moved in one direction, Bruce pivoted slightly to keep himself square to him. The tip of his upturned glove at the end of his extended right arm was always directed at Elms's nose. Recognizing that his opponent's unorthodox defense wasn't providing any openings, Elms now launched a desperate attack, swinging wild hooking punches, left and right, as fast as he could. Some fell short of their target; others were parried by Bruce's arms. Elms made one last desperate rush to swarm his opponent. Bruce deflected each of his blows, and then exploded forward with yet another series of chain punches to his opponent's chest and head that concluded, yet again, with Elms flat on his back. By the time the fallen fighter had regained his feet, the bell sounded to end the bout and the referee raised Bruce's arm to make it official: Bruce Lee had won the match.

The crowd cheered when Bruce was presented with his championship gold medal and cheered again as he made his exit from the ring. Friends and fellow students mobbed him and asked to look at his medal — the only one that any of the fighters from St. Francis Xavier's had won that evening. Elms had lost his crown and left the ring bewildered, still unable to figure out what had gone wrong. His friends from King George V gathered round to console him, but it had little effect.

The final match of the evening brought a small measure of redemption for the King George V fighters when their boxer, Metrevelli, outpointed his opponent, Chen from St. Francis Xavier's. The final medal count saw host St. George's school standing atop the heap with a record of twelve wins and eleven losses, La Salle College finished in second place with a record of 4–1, King George V was third at 2–5, and St. Francis Xavier's finished last at 1–2.

One of the fighters from La Salle, Robert Wang, who had won his bout against a fighter named Clowson from St. George's, was among the group that approached the heavily sweating Bruce Lee immediately upon the latter's exit from the ring.

"Congratulations, Big Brother!" Wang exclaimed.

Bruce shrugged in dissatisfaction. "Give me one more round and I will knock the hell out of the limey," Bruce said. "Three rounds are too short; it's no fun. They should do it like the professionals — fifteen rounds — *then* it's exciting!"

Wang was intrigued by Bruce's use of Kung Fu in the ring. "But you don't box like we are taught. What kind of boxing is that? It's not the kind that Brother Eugene teaches us."

"To hell with Brother Eugene. I punch Wing Chun style. It's a lot more effective than boxing. I will teach you Wing Chun one day. You will learn to be a better fighter from me than from Brother Eugene."[13]

Despite the win, and what it meant for his school, Bruce wasn't pleased with his performance. When Frank Clausnitzer approached him to offer his congratulations, the fighter shook his head in a show of frustration.

"What's up?" Frank asked.

"I couldn't knock the bastard out."

Bruce said he was annoyed that all of the fighters had to wear sixteen-ounce gloves, which seemed to him so large as to resemble pillows. The padding in the gloves had spread the power of his punches over too broad a surface, reducing their impact. Bruce also felt frustrated that he had not quite mastered the quick upturn of the wrist technique at the end of his punches, which, to his way of thinking, had also diminished the force of his strikes. "I'm going to train until I can get *that* punch working," he said. "That's the way I want to fight next time."[14]

He also mentioned that he wanted to box the St. George's fighter Peter Burton, who had won his bout by TKO just prior to Bruce's match. However, given that Burton was several weight classes above Bruce, there was no way that either his or Burton's school would ever sanction such a contest. Later that evening Bruce Lee scribbled the following entry into his diary:

> March 29, 1958: Win the interschool competition (champion) against 3 years champ Garie Elm.
> Place: St. Georgie School.[15]

Despite his critical evaluation of his performance in the tournament, Bruce Lee's classmates, along with the teachers and staff at St. Francis Xavier's College, treated him like a conquering hero. "Bruce was the king gorilla of the whole school," his brother Robert recalled.[16]

CHAPTER FOUR

BATTLE ON THE ROOFTOP

"Efficiency in sparring or fighting is not a matter of correct, classical, traditional form. Efficiency is anything that scores."

— Bruce Lee (*Black Belt* magazine, 1968)

Bruce Lee didn't bask long in the glow of the positive attention. He understood that having success in a sporting event was one thing, but having success in the street against qualified practitioners from rival Kung Fu styles was something else entirely — and it was those kinds of victories he longed for.

The boxing match proved that Bruce's fighting skills had risen to a significant level over his past two years of training. However, as someone who was by this point in his life totally consumed with martial arts, he coveted a combat reputation like the one his Wing Chun senior Wong Shun Leung enjoyed. Everywhere Wong went, he was given a wide berth; his long list of beimo victories over the best Kung Fu fighters in Hong Kong had earned him that respect. By contrast, Bruce had won a solitary boxing match. Even his victories in the streets counted for nothing. Wong hadn't made his bones by fighting nondescript denizens of the shadier parts of Hong Kong. If Bruce wanted a solid reputation in the martial arts world of Wong Shun Leung, he needed to earn it in battle against the best martial artists that the region had to offer.

Whenever his Wing Chun brothers fought against students from rival martial art schools, Bruce often tagged along to watch. Sometimes the Wing Chun fighters won, sometimes they lost. Wong Shun Leung taught his students the reality of fighting, which was that few if any people will emerge from a fight unscathed — and that they had better make their peace with that fact if they were thinking of following him into beimo. That counsel diminished the enthusiasm of many students. Wong counseled that victory in a fight is guaranteed to no one, irrespective of the style of Kung Fu one was practicing. Indeed, a lot of what turns the tide of a fight resided in the tenacity and will of the individual practitioner.[1] These were lessons that would remain with Bruce Lee for the remainder of his life.

Not long after defeating Gary Elms, Bruce attempted to broaden his reputation by engaging in two separate challenge matches. According to Wong Shun Leung, the first of these took place when he wasn't around to witness it. He heard that Bruce won but that his opponent hadn't been all that skillful.[2]

That was about to change.

Bruce agreed to participate in a beimo on May 2, 1958, against Robert Chung, who was an assistant instructor under master Lung Chi Chuen in the Northern Shaolin style of Kung Fu. He also convinced a newcomer to Wing Chun by the name of Chen to compete in a beimo that same day against another Northern Shaolin student. Chen had trained in the Northern Shaolin style, and so, Bruce reasoned, the young man should know what to expect from any opponent who used it. Once the Northern Shaolin practitioners agreed to the matches, Bruce approached Wong Shun Leung to serve as his coach for the beimo. Wong agreed.[3]

On Friday, May 2, Wong, Bruce and Chen made their way to a large multi-story apartment complex on Union Road in Kowloon City. The beimo would take place on the rooftop to avoid any chance of police intervention. Fighting in Hong Kong was against the law, and both parties wanted to keep the contest on the down low.[4] As the trio made their way toward the apartment building, Wong noticed a small crowd in front of the complex. One of them called out, "That's Wong Shun Leung! We'll have something to see today!" The three-some ignored the accolades and kept walking. "The atmosphere was very tense," Wong recalled, "as if a great thunderstorm was going to break out." If these people already knew about the beimo, perhaps the police did too.

"Why are there so many people here?" he asked Bruce. "Did *you* tell them to come here?"

Bruce shook his head. "Maybe they heard about it from the other side."

Bruce headed for the entrance, but Wong stopped him. Lowering his voice, he said, "keep walking." Bruce nodded, understanding that Wong didn't want the group that had gathered outside to know where the beimo would be taking place. Wong, Lee and Chen walked past the apartments, turned a corner and continued along the block a short distance, before doubling back and entering one of the apartment buildings through a stairwell. The three climbed the stairs to an upper-level unit where a friend of Bruce's lived, and remained there for about ten minutes. At this point, one of them took a quick scan of the hallway, and, determining that the coast was clear, the trio made their way to the top of the building.

They were surprised to see people already on the roof — by Wong's estimation, some twenty to thirty people were present. Some sat on the parapet, others leaned against the sides of the water tanks, and still more simply stood around and stared.

JUDGE AND COACH

The Northern Shaolin group arrived. After conversing among themselves, several of its members walked over to Bruce for a brief dialogue. Bruce then approached Wong Shun Leung. The two exchanged words and Bruce brought Wong across to where the Northern Shaolin students had gathered. All of the Northern Shaolin students knew of Wong and respected him not only as a superb fighter, but also as a man of integrity and inherent fairness.

Speaking on behalf of the Wing Chun clan, Wong called for everybody's attention.

"Both parties are here today to *gong sao* [talk with their hands; to test their Kung Fu against each other] without ill intentions," he announced. "It is important that this be so for the young students who are training in martial art. However, in order to ensure that the outcomes of these matches are fair, I suggest that we first set the rules and then elect a judge who is acceptable to both parties." Someone from the Northern Shaolin side called out, "As for the choice of the judge, we trust Master Wong totally, since he is well known in the martial arts circles and has more experience than us. We think it would be best if Master Wong is the judge."

Wong was flattered but troubled. "At the time I was Bruce Lee's coach. To do that and be the referee for the fight, it was quite hard to balance roles." While Wong had been in matches of all stripes — ranging from light sparring to fights behind closed doors in which only the victor walked out, and the loser was taken to the nearest hospital — he wanted to make sure that the matches this day were of the former, tamer variety.

After finally accepting the role of judge, Wong laid out the rules:

- Each match would consist of two rounds of two minutes each, with a one-minute break provided between rounds.
- If either fighter was knocked down or fell, the other fighter must stop his attack.
- If one of the fighters stepped out of the designated fighting area, a chalked circle drawn around a 324-square-foot radius, he would lose a point. If a fighter stepped out of the fighting area three times consecutively, he would be disqualified and his opponent declared the winner.
- If one of the fighters became incapacitated and unable to defend himself, the judge had the right to stop the contest to ensure the injured fighter's safety.

Wong asked if anybody present objected to these rules.

All parties agreed. All that remained to be decided was who would fight first.

After some discussion, Bruce broke away from his group and approached Wong. "Leung," he said, "Chen will have the first match."

Wong raised an eyebrow. He'd already had second thoughts about Chen's readiness for the bout. He had seen martial arts students in the past who'd been quite dedicated — until they were humiliated in a challenge match. After that, they quit martial arts altogether and had to deal as best they could with the disgrace of having lost. Some didn't deal well with it at all.

Wong called Chen over. "You're still green when it comes to fighting. Are you sure you want to do this?"

Chen said that while it was true he was a newcomer to Wing Chun, he was not a newcomer to martial arts. He had, after all, trained in the Northern Shaolin style and he knew the opponent he would be fighting. He understood what he was getting himself into.

Wong had his doubts. "I'm not sure that it's a good idea for two people from the same style to fight publicly."

Chen said he was fine with it and repeated that he was good to go. And with that, Wong motioned for the fighter from the Northern Shaolin school to step into the chalked circle.

The fighter was a twenty-year-old man named Choy, who stood about five feet six inches. Chen was three years younger and stood about five feet nine. Wong turned to the crowd and announced, "Since Chen is earnest in his desire to compete, I have no other choice than to allow him to do so." He then turned to the fighters and explained that this should be a friendly contest; rather than considering themselves to be representing different clans, they should recognize that both Wing Chun and Northern Shaolin were *gwok sut* (Chinese national arts) and therefore fell under the same umbrella. He emphasized that their match was "just a demonstration and learning experience."

Choy turned to Chen. "Who is your master?"

"I'm not good enough to represent my master. You shouldn't presume to represent your master. Since that's the case, let's not talk about masters. This is not a life or death fight but sparring. So, let's spar with control and have some fun."

It was good counsel. And it held right up until the timekeeper announced the start of the match.

As soon as the bout commenced, the two combatants launched themselves at one another. They threw backfists, right crosses and hooks, some directed at the body, some to the head. This was not a friendly contest but a real fight. While many punches missed their intended targets, many more found their mark, leaving instant bruises and swellings on both fighters' faces. They flailed away until the time-keeper announced that the first two-minute round was over. There would not be a second round.

The fighters were exhausted. Chen, being taller and having the longer reach of the two fighters, had landed the most strikes, but Choy had been the aggressor during the round. In Wong's estimation, the bout was a draw. Both sides grumbled, but as the match was intended to be a friendly competition, a draw was acceptable. Then came the main event.

BRUCE LEE VERSUS ROBERT CHUNG

Robert Chung walked into the chalked circle first. Chung was eighteen years old and stood five feet ten inches tall and weighed about 130 pounds. "Bruce Lee's opponent was pretty big," Wong recalled. "He was a well-known assistant instructor of Northern Shaolin at the time."

Next to step into the circle was Bruce Lee, who, at seventeen, was a year younger than his opponent and stood just a little under five feet eight inches tall, and weighed 125 pounds.

The two young men walked to the center of the circle to receive their instructions from Wong. "As neither of you have had a problem with each other in the past, this gong sao is not about which style of Kung Fu is best, but rather is being held so that both of you obtain some beimo experience," Wong explained. "Winning or losing isn't important, so don't worry about that. You both understand that injuries are a possibility, so if one of you should get injured, don't get angry about it. Even if you have had a problem with one another in the past, perhaps after today's contest you might become friends. If either of you think otherwise, then I won't allow the gong sao to go on." Chung nodded. He had looked at Wong the whole time he'd been speaking. Bruce, for his part, looked bored. Arms folded across his chest, he gazed skyward as Wong spoke, nodding occasionally to indicate that he understood what was expected of him.

Wong recalled, "I told Bruce's opponent that since I was Bruce's coach and the referee that I would not coach Bruce during the fight, but that I would still offer him some advice in between rounds." The Northern Shaolin fighter was fine with this, as he too had people in his corner that would advise him of any weaknesses they detected in Bruce's technique and of any changes in strategy he should employ. Wong produced a coin and said he would flip it. If it landed heads,

Bruce would have to wait for his opponent to initiate the attack before he could go on the offensive; if it landed tails, Bruce would be the one to attack first. Wong tossed the coin into the air and all parties looked on as it came down and bounced off the ground. The coin landed heads. Chung would launch the first offensive.

Both fighters stepped back into the stances of their respective arts. Lee, as he had done in the boxing match, immediately assumed the ready position of Wing Chun. Chung assumed a stance from Northern Shaolin: legs wide with knees bent, his left arm extended with his fingers clenched like a claw. His right hand was balled into a fist, which he held next to his hip. The timekeeper pulled out his watch and counted down the seconds until the start of the match: "Three, Two, One — *Fight!*"

Chung cautiously circled Bruce. With every step he took, Bruce's lead arm followed him. Chung then made his move: he hit his opponent's extended hand to create an opening for a right punch. The punch was partially deflected by Bruce's lead arm, but enough of it made it through to land a glancing blow off his jaw. Bruce immediately returned fire with a punch of his own that landed squarely on Chung's chest. Both fighters stepped back.

Bruce reassumed his stance and waited for Chung to attack. The wait wasn't long. Chung came at him quickly with a series of long, looping overhand strikes, one hand following the other in rapid succession. Bruce did what he could to deflect the blows, but the power of the assault drove him backwards until he had inadvertently stepped out of the chalked circle. A point was awarded to Chung.

A look of disgust washed over Bruce's face as both fighters returned to the center of the circle and reset their stances. Once again, Chung barreled in, launching a series of strikes that rained down on Bruce from overhead. Unlike the boxing punches he had faced in the ring against Elms, Bruce found the overhead blows much harder to defend against, as the Wing Chun blocking positions seldom went higher than nose height. As Chung struck at him, Bruce attempted some counterstrikes of his own, but he was backing up to dodge the blows that Chung fired at him and most of his punches missed their targets. Chung stepped in, putting him within Bruce's striking range. Both fighters threw — and connected with — punches fast and furious.

Bruce took a sharp blow to his eye, which immediately started to swell. Another punch from Chung caught him flush in the mouth. In desperation, Bruce grabbed Chung with his left hand and Chung grabbed Bruce with his right hand. Both fighters now threw jackhammer punches at each other from short range, almost all of which connected. They pummeled each other in this manner for several seconds until the timekeeper yelled out that the first round was over.

Wong Shun Leung separated the two fighters and immediately escorted Bruce off to one side of the chalked circle, where his Wing Chun brothers had gathered. Wong later said that "because the opponent was bigger than him, Bruce had received a few punches to his face; his nose was bleeding slightly." So was his mouth, and the left ridgeline of his brow was noticeably bruised and swollen.

Across from Bruce on the opposite side of the chalked circle, the Northern Shaolin students were checking out the punishment that Chung had received. To their relief, Chung's wounds were minor; his chest displayed several red welts where Bruce's vertical fist punches had landed, and a small amount of blood was seen trickling down from a cut on his lip. It was evident from a comparison of the fighters' wounds that Chung had landed the more damaging strikes — and more of them — in the first round.

While Wong had tried to stay neutral, he hated to see any of his Wing Chun students lose ground to a competitor from a rival school. It angered him because any potential loss to another Kung Fu style served to whittle away at the status he'd achieved for Wing Chun through his many beimo matches over the years, which had established the art's reputation as the premier fighting system in Hong Kong.

"Is my eye swollen?" Bruce asked.

"Yes, it's bruised. Your nose is bleeding, too, but it's okay."

From Wong's observation, Bruce had only been "posing and showing off" during the first round. It didn't seem that his fighter was taking the match seriously.

"Where was your *offense*?" Wong asked. "That *whole round* you just stood there waiting for him to attack!"

Bruce looked at Wong somewhat surprised. "I didn't attack him because I lost the coin toss — you said that he was to attack first! That's why I waited for him to attack before hitting back!"

Wong couldn't believe what he had just heard. He stomped his foot on the ground in exasperation. "That only applied to the *first exchange* of the fight," he said between clenched teeth, "not the whole round!" Wong shook his head. He was fighting to control his own temper.

"You're a greenhorn. An absolute greenhorn!"

Bruce's face flushed. "My performance today is bad," he said. "If I get hurt too badly, my father will notice it. I think we better call it a draw and end the match."

Wong couldn't believe that either. What kind of attitude was this? What example would it set for Wing Chun's reputation in the eyes of the other martial arts styles in Hong Kong — and for the younger and newer students in the art?

"Lee, if you do not continue in the second round it means that you *surrendered*. How can that be regarded as a *draw*? Moreover, you're capable of fighting on." Wong looked over at Chung and saw him breathing heavily.

"Your opponent is wheezing now," Wong said. "If you fight on, you will win."

Bruce's eyes widened. "I will win? Leung, are you sure?"

"Why would I lie to you?" Wong insisted that Bruce finish the final round. If he chose not to, then it would be on Bruce — not Wong — to announce to everybody that he was quitting the match.

Bruce nodded. His eye was throbbing. He knew that if it hadn't turned black already, it would soon. If he took another punch to his face, he would end up looking like a raccoon.

"If my face gets any more screwed up, when I go back home my dad will really punish me badly."

Wong knew that Bruce feared his father's wrath. Hoi-chuen had made it clear to Bruce on several prior occasions that he disapproved of his fighting and wanted him to focus instead on making something of himself in school — not on the streets. Moreover, his son was in the movie business, and having a bruise-free face and a mouth full of teeth was a requirement in that industry. Wong's upbringing wouldn't allow him to say anything that would contradict the wishes of Bruce's father, but, to his mind, a bigger issue was at stake.

"How are you going to answer our master, and your fellow Kung Fu brothers, if you quit? Are you more afraid of your father yelling at you than you are of being laughed at for the rest of your life? No matter what, you have to fight on!"

The look on Bruce's face suddenly became more serious. He hadn't considered that — being laughed at was intolerable to him.

"Look," Wong explained, "in the next round, don't think about defense or how to deflect his punches, or how to make yourself look good. Just think about hitting the guy and *you* be the aggressive one this time! Don't worry about whether or not your fighting technique is perfect; you are now in a *fight* — not a demonstration. Punch only at his face. Don't worry if you get hit or not. Get in close to him — and attack!"

Bruce stared straight ahead and wiped the blood from his mouth.

By now the one-minute rest period was up. The timekeeper signaled that it was time for the second and final round to begin.

Chung's group was feeling confident. Their fighter had dominated the action in the first round and they expected him to do likewise in the second. Chung walked to the center of the circle and once again lowered himself into the wide stance of Northern Shaolin.

Bruce stood up and made his way into the circle. He looked surprisingly relaxed. Once again, he assumed the bai jong of Wing Chun. He placed most of his weight on his rear leg. He was now a compressed spring waiting to be released.

Chung advanced. Bruce remained stationary.

Bruce suddenly made as if to strike and Chung jumped back. But Bruce didn't move. He simply remained in his stance — and smiled. He repeated this feint three more times, and each time Chung reacted to it by jumping backwards to avoid a blow that didn't come. He found Bruce's calmness and smile unsettling. As Chung bit on each feint, it was Bruce who was now dictating the action of the fight. He once again moved his arm as if to strike, and this time Chung, anticipating another feint, decided to blast through the ruse with a punch of his own. It was just the opening Bruce had been waiting for. No longer tethered to the belief that he had to wait for his opponent to strike first, he now sprung forward and punched Chung square in the face. As Chung's head snapped back from the blow, Bruce charged in using the same vertical chain-punching he had employed to such good effect in his boxing match against Gary Elms.

The suddenness of Bruce's attack, combined with the tactical switch from defense to offense, caught Chung completely by surprise. So much so that every punch Bruce threw landed with a resounding thud on Chung's face. The first four strikes had a concussive effect, and Chung staggered two or three steps back and stumbled to his right. Bruce quickly darted to his left so that he remained square to Chung and fired off another salvo of chain punches, one of which snapped Chung's front tooth, which went spiraling skyward. Chung's back now hit against one of the parapets, and a punch from Bruce's right fist caught him square on his left eyebrow, splitting the skin and causing his head to bounce off the wall behind him. He was out before he hit the ground.

Chung lay motionless at the foot of the wall, his face a bloody mask of crimson. At this point Bruce Lee's killer instinct took over. In what would have been a clear violation of the fourth rule that Wong had established, he now moved in for the kill.

Mortified, the members of the Northern Shaolin clan called out for Wong to stop the contest. Before Bruce could deliver a coup de grâce, Wong threw his arms around him and yanked him away from the fallen fighter.

After settling Bruce down, Wong returned to examine Robert Chung's injuries. He worked on him feverishly until finally Chung's eyes fluttered open. A wave of relief washed over the Northern Shaolin troupe.

Chung took stock of his injuries. "Why didn't you tell him to stop," he yelled.

"Because you had not stepped out of the ring at that point and still had the ability to fight back." Wong spoke loud enough for everyone to hear him. "So, I had no right to call for a stop."

Wong's words did little to pacify Chung. According to Wong, "Bruce Lee's opponent told me that since I was the judge, I shouldn't have forced Bruce Lee to continue fighting after the first round."

Chung was right, of course. However, despite how Wong Shun Leung had framed the match as a learning exercise, it was obvious that nothing of the kind had happened. It had been, unmistakably, a fight between two people who were representing something far larger than themselves. To the fighters' (and Wong's) eyes it had been a match between two schools of Kung Fu — Northern Shaolin and Wing Chun. Besides, as Wong had cautioned both fighters prior to the bout, injuries were a distinct possibility in such a contest.

While the Northern Shaolin students gathered around Chung to inspect his injuries, Bruce Lee's Wing Chun brothers congratulated him on the victory for their style. Wong, despite the criticism from the opposing side, now looked upon Bruce with a fair degree of pride.

While Bruce was pleased with his performance in the second round of the fight, he was nevertheless angry at himself for having been struck so frequently in the first round, even though he'd believed that it was his job to defend rather than to attack. Jesse Glover, who would later become Bruce's first student in the United States, recalled what Bruce told him about the fight a year or so after it occurred: "Bruce said that his blocking was less than it should have been and he was dazed by a partial strike to the head. . . . After the fight, Bruce started immediately to train against overhand strikes. Bruce said that this [fight] set a pattern for him that he was to follow all his life. The pattern that he spoke of was the practice of correcting his weaknesses after each fight."[5]

But such reassessment came later. For the moment, Bruce Lee — and his rapidly blackening eye — had to go home and face the wrath of his father.

CHAPTER FIVE

CROSSING THE TRIADS

"Well, let's face it, in Hong Kong today, can you have a fight? I mean a no-holds barred fight? Is it a legal thing? It isn't, is it?"

— Bruce Lee (Radio Hong Kong, 1971)

The Lee family were now living in a large apartment on the second floor of a building on Nathan Road in the Tsim Sha Tsui district of Kowloon. It was a congested household back in the 1950s, consisting of Grace, Hoi-chuen, their five children Phoebe, Agnes, Peter, Bruce and Robert, Wu Ngan (an orphan boy whom the Lee parents had more or less adopted), servants, and Hoi-chuen's mother. Adding to the menagerie were nine dogs, seven cats, birds, an aquarium full of fish, a pet chicken[1] and a monkey.[2] Entry into the crowded apartment required passage through two doors that were locked to prevent vagrants from entering the flat, and also to delay any possible police raids on the apartment, as Bruce's father was an opium smoker and opium was contraband in Hong Kong.[3]

So, after his rooftop battle with Robert Chung, Bruce had to wait for one of the family servants to unlock the doors and let him in. Bruce's younger brother Robert happened to be in the hallway when his older brother entered. Their father was in a room just off the entranceway — and Bruce wanted no part of his father that evening. Robert looked on as Bruce, covering his right eye with his hand, made a beeline to the servants' quarters. This seemed odd, and so the young boy followed Bruce into the room. "Hey, what happened?"

Bruce took his hand away from his face and revealed that he had a black eye.

"Fighting, right?" This was not the first time Bruce had come home in such a state.

"Yeah, but that guy got it from me. I got a couple of his teeth knocked out, you know. I got a black eye, but I sure did a lot better than he did!"[4]

Robert left the room in search of his sister, Phoebe. Upon learning of Bruce's injury, Phoebe went into the kitchen to retrieve a hard-boiled egg from the refrigerator, which she brought to the servants' quarters and handed to Bruce, who pressed it against his bruised eye. The cold egg would help to reduce the swelling. While Grace Lee was made aware of what had happened, the family were able to keep the matter hidden from Bruce's father, for a few days at any rate.[5]

While Lee Hoi-chuen may have been temporarily kept in the dark, word about the fight traveled quickly through other parts of Hong Kong. When Yip Man learned of the encounter, he took Wong aside and told him he did the right thing in insisting that Bruce fight on.[6] According to Wong: "I really think that fight and that victory were very important to Bruce Lee [and his development], because, had Bruce Lee lost that fight, he would most likely have lost his interest in the martial arts."[7]

By this point, Bruce's time in Hong Kong was rapidly drawing to a close. He was eighteen years old now, and his parents had always intended for their son to return to San Francisco to claim his American citizenship. However, the trip across the ocean to the land of his birth might have been delayed for a few more years had it not been for an incident in a Hong Kong café.

DUELING ACTORS

In early 1959, Bruce had recently completed a new movie entitled *The Orphan*, and the advance buzz was centered on his performance, which by all accounts was electrifying.[8] In a case of art imitating life, Bruce's role in the film was that of a troubled, angry teenager living in Hong Kong who was running with a street gang. In one scene, Bruce's character pulls out a switchblade and threatens his teacher with it. Word quickly spread that this movie was going to be a huge hit, and that Bruce Lee was poised to become the new superstar of Hong Kong cinema.

Such advance publicity and praise was thrilling for the Hong Kong film industry, and for Bruce particularly, but there were others operating within and on the periphery of the film world that were not pleased.

Despite trying for many years, the local triads had been unable to bring Bruce under their control. And now that he was poised to become the biggest film star in Hong Kong, he represented money and influence that had slipped through their hands. And there were local actors who were both irritated and confused by Bruce's success. After all, they had paid the extortion fees and kickbacks to the triads with the belief that the gangsters would see to it that their careers advanced, only to see someone who did neither of these things skyrocket past them in popularity and status within the industry.

One actor in particular made his displeasure with Bruce's impending success known to all who came within his circle. Known throughout Hong Kong as "Handsome Fo," the actor Leung Zai Fo was a popular movie star in the region, and an actor who was very much under the control of the triads.

One afternoon, Bruce was enjoying a light lunch with Wu Ngan (the young man adopted by the Lee family) at a teahouse in Kowloon when in walked Handsome Fo and some of his friends. Bruce was probably well aware of Fo's resentment toward him, but if so, he didn't care; many young wannabe actors in the movie business had been jealous of his success for many years now. Leung was just another name on a rather long list.

Fo and his entourage sat down at a table not far away from Bruce and Wu. Fo had a newspaper with him and opened it up to read. He soon happened upon an article that referred to Bruce as "the Eastern James Dean."[9] Such high praise disgusted Fo, and he and his friends began to loudly critique the newspaper article's sentiment, making sure their disparaging comments were loud enough for Bruce to hear them. "If this kid knows how to act, then Handsome Fo here is so much better that he should win the Haw Nan Academy Award!" The award was the Hong Kong equivalent of an Oscar.

Bruce and Wu ignored the insults and continued to talk. Their refusal to respond angered Handsome Fo's friends. "Hey, kid! Do you have any triad connections?" one asked. "If not, if you still want to continue acting, then come over here and kneel down and offer a cup of tea to Handsome Fo. After Fo accepts your offer, your future will be bright forever!"

Teahouse patrons got up and left at the mention of triads. But the overture only served to piss Bruce off. He turned in his seat to face Handsome Fo and his group. "None of you guys would know whether Fo's acting is good or not. All you know is how to kiss his ass — and that won't bring him any academy award!"

Handsome Fo looked at Bruce. "Listen up: you were just lucky that Lee Hoi-chuen brought you into this industry. If he had died two years back, you wouldn't be sitting here in this teahouse like a bigshot, eating your pineapple bun!"

Bruce gestured toward the front door of the café. "If you're looking for trouble, step outside. I'll take you on!"

Fo and his friends stood up and headed for the door. Bruce and Wu followed. Almost immediately the fight was on. Bruce quickly began to pummel Fo quite severely, which caused a crowd to gather round to watch the spectacle of two popular actors fighting each other. And why wouldn't they? It was the 1950s Hong Kong equivalent of Brad Pitt engaged in a punch-up with Leonardo DiCaprio. The owner of the teahouse called the police, who arrived on the scene within a matter of minutes, and all involved in the altercation were hauled off to jail.

When Bruce's family arrived at the police station to post bail for their son, the superintendent informed them that not only was fighting in the streets illegal, but if Bruce was caught doing it again the police would have him formally charged. He also pointed out that whoever Bruce fought was eligible to bring a lawsuit against him for damages. And, if Handsome Fo had suffered a broken nose or some other injury that prevented him from making a movie, both he and the production company that employed him could legally come after Bruce for damages, which could end up being a considerable amount of money.

A few days later, Bruce's mother learned that Handsome Fo was not only a member of a local triad, but that his triad group were now looking for Bruce, and were quite prepared to kill him if he should venture into their territory in the future. Fearing for her son's life, Grace conferred with her husband and the parents decided that, all things considered, their son's immigration to the United States should be bumped up to the soonest date possible.[10]

And so, on April 29, 1959, Bruce Lee, in the company of his family, went to Victoria Harbor. His father pressed a newly minted U.S. $100 bill in his hand and bid him farewell. Tearful goodbyes were exchanged among the Lee family members, who now stood back and looked on as Bruce boarded the SS *President Wilson*. Within hours, Bruce Lee found himself alone among strangers on a ship that was cutting its way through the rolling waves of the South China Sea. He was headed toward America, and a future that nobody could have predicted.

CHAPTER SIX

COMING TO AMERICA

"Gung Fu originated in China. It is the ancestor of Karate and Jiu-jitsu. It's more of a complete system and it's more fluid. By that I mean, it's more flowing; there is continuity in movement, instead of one-movement-two-movement and then stop."

— Bruce Lee (screen test, 1965)

Twenty-three-year-old Jesse Glover, a powerful African American from Seattle's inner city, had been searching for a more effective form of self-defense for some time. Prior to a stint in the Air Force, he'd grown up in the mean streets of East Los Angeles, where he embraced the Chicano gang culture. A pachuco tattoo between his index finger and thumb bore testimony to his past.[1] But quite apart from Jesse's proven willingness to use violence, he was a sensitive and highly intelligent man, in addition to being a natural and talented athlete. He had boxed a bit while in the Air Force,[2] and was well on his way to becoming a second-degree black belt in Judo. Indeed, while still a brown belt in the art, he won the Pacific Northwest Judo Championships a staggering fourteen times in a row.[3] "He'd go out there and flatten black belts," recalled Jesse's best friend and long-time roommate, Ed Hart. "Finally, Judo clubs in the northwest got together and demanded that the Seattle Judo Club make him a black belt because he was beating everybody."[4] But neither boxing nor Judo satisfied Jesse's desire to learn a more efficient way to fight and survive in the city streets.

BRUCE LEE'S FIRST STUDENT

Upon Bruce's arrival in the United States, he spent some time in San Francisco before heading north to Seattle to complete high school, and then to attend university. During his first few years in Seattle, he lived in a very small room above a restaurant owned by a woman named Ruby Chow, who was an old friend of Bruce's father. Bruce hadn't been in Seattle long when word got out that he could fight — and that his style of fighting was the Chinese art of Wing Chun Kung Fu.

One day on his way to Edison Technical School, which prepared adult students to enter the workforce, Jesse spotted the young man whose reputation for fighting was rapidly spreading throughout the neighborhood. "I went up to him and asked if his name was Bruce Lee," Jesse recalled. "He said it was. I asked him if he did Gung Fu. He said he did. And I asked him if he would teach me. He asked me if I had a place where there was no one around. I said 'yes.' And that evening he started to instruct me."[5]

Bruce's willingness to teach came with a stipulation, however. He would only teach Jesse if he agreed not to tell anybody — and this was important. Yip Chun would recall his father, Yip Man, telling him of a conversation that he had with Bruce prior to the latter's leaving Hong Kong for America in 1959: "My father reminded him that Chinese Kung Fu is one of the sophisticated arts of China, that we need Kung Fu techniques to defend ourselves and to keep good health, and that the techniques of Chinese Kung Fu should not be taught freely to foreigners (it was typically Chinese traditional thinking of the old Kung Fu masters). Bruce Lee promised to bear this in mind before he left for the USA."[6]

While Bruce did bear this mind, he also recognized that he could not progress in his Kung Fu without having someone to practice with. And certain training techniques within Wing Chun, such as *chi sao* (sticking hands) practice, could only be performed with a training partner who knew the movements and purpose of the exercise. The problem was there were no Chinese Wing Chun practitioners in Seattle who were available to train several hours a day.[7] Jesse was willing to learn, but if Bruce instructed him at Ruby Chow's, Ruby had a direct pipeline back to his father — and to Yip Man.

From his father's perspective, the family had sent Bruce to America for an education, to go on to university and make something of himself — not to while away his time teaching Kung Fu to Americans. However, if Bruce taught Jesse away from Ruby Chow's, and Jesse didn't tell anybody, there was no chance of the news getting out. It seemed like a no-brainer. Bruce agreed to take Jesse as a student, and to teach him privately at the apartment Jesse shared with Ed Hart and another man, Howard Hall. And with that, Jesse Glover became Bruce Lee's first student.

TEACHING KUNG FU

Jesse couldn't contain his enthusiasm for what Bruce was teaching him and told his roommates. It wasn't long before they pressured Jesse to approach Bruce on their behalf to see if they too could learn Wing Chun Kung Fu. Surprisingly, Bruce was receptive to the idea. To him, more people meant more practice, and more practice meant more improvement. Soon word of Bruce Lee's Kung Fu spread to friends of the roommates.

However, not all of Jesse's acquaintances shared his enthusiasm for Bruce and Kung Fu. Jesse hung out with a tough crowd; all of his friends were experienced fighters who fought almost weekly in the Seattle streets. Certain of them were doubtful that what Bruce was teaching had any use whatsoever.

Take James DeMile, a U.S. Air Force boxing champion:[8]

> I met [Bruce Lee] by going up and sort of challenging him. . . . I was about 225 pounds and in really good shape. Bruce was 135. Bruce asked me to take a swing at him. So I did — and he just ate me alive! He trapped my hands and just immobilized me. So, it was an interesting time because I was just sort of coming out of my punk days, being tough and fighting a lot, and I realized that I was growing older and I had to kind of figure out what I wanted to do with my life. But still the basis of who I was, was built around my ability to fight. And then here is this kid who beat the hell out of me in about five seconds. So, I could either take this as

total deflation and take away my ego, or I could use it as a learning experience. . . . Well, obviously, I joined Bruce's training group.[9]

With the addition of DeMile, a small, tight-knit group formed around Bruce, and all of these first-generation students had a solid fighting arts background:

- Jesse Glover was a boxer and regional Judo champion
- Ed Hart had been a professional boxer, a bouncer and Judo black belt
- James DeMile was the U.S. Air Force heavyweight boxing champion
- Skip Ellsworth was a Judo practitioner
- LeRoy Porter was a green belt in Judo
- Pat Hooks was a black belt in Judo
- Leroy Garcia was a boxer, wrestler and street fighter

"All of us were street fighters," DeMile recalled. "And Bruce could beat us all. And I don't mean it would be a struggle . . . we didn't have a chance."[10]

The group went everywhere together, and with no other friends in a new country, Bruce welcomed the companionship. Despite being rough around the edges, these young men from the streets of Seattle knew their way around; they taught the teenager how life was in America, took him to movies, taught him the latest slang and went to restaurants with him. They even took him to British Columbia, Canada, so that Bruce could shop in Vancouver's Chinatown for books on Kung Fu that had recently arrived from China, Taiwan or Hong Kong. And they helped Bruce with his homework assignments to free up more of his time so that he could teach them more Kung Fu.

. Bruce was intrigued by the fact that most Americans were physically bigger and stronger than he was, and set about researching what areas of the human body remained vulnerable to attack irrespective of one's physical size. Strikes to the eyes, throat and groin were obvious examples, and he worked tirelessly on perfecting such strikes. To work on his finger jab to the eyes, he hung a domino mask from the ceiling in his room and every night practiced jabbing his fingers through its small eyeholes, doing multiple sets of thirty to forty thrusts each in an attempt to lay down the neuromuscular pathways necessary to scratch the cornea of a person's eyes as a reflexive strike. He became so precise at this that he was able to thrust his fingers through the eyeholes without the mask moving.[11]

THE STREET FIGHTING RESUMES

Given their ages, testosterone levels and passion for all things fighting, the reputation of the group began to spread. Soon the workers at Ruby Chow's were hearing rumors that their new boarder was getting into fights. Greg Luke, a long-time friend of the Chow family, recalled that "Lee was up at Dick's Drive-In, and people tried to cut in. He didn't appreciate that, so he took out, like, five guys with an umbrella."[12] Another friend of the Chows, Betty Lau, also heard the rumors: "The boys on the dragon team were talking about going to watch some Japanese kid who'd challenged Bruce. [They said] he broke the guy's arm and leg."[13] Annie Galarosa, a resident of Seattle's Central District, recollected: "My older brothers at Garfield [High School] were always complaining about this Chinese kid who was getting notorious around the neighborhood. He was known for being able to beat up more than one guy. Apparently, they were jealous of Bruce Lee."[14]

When word of her boarder's street fighting reached Ruby Chow's ears, she wanted him gone. She had worked too hard and too long to build up her business in Seattle. She had parlayed that success into becoming a well-respected representative of her community. She'd been the first Asian American elected to the King County council; she and her husband, Ping Chow, had raised five children in their house/restaurant on Jefferson Street; and her business not only attracted patrons from the local population, but was also frequented by high-level entertainers such as Louis Armstrong and Bob Hope whenever they were in the city.[15] She was not going to see her well-respected name and reputation sullied by some fight-intoxicated teenager from Hong Kong, no matter how good a friend his father was.

She made a transpacific telephone call to Lee Hoi-chuen in Hong Kong to bring him up to speed on what his fourth child was getting up to. Bruce's father was both embarrassed and furious. Ruby's youngest son, Mark Chow (now a King County District Court judge), recalled that Bruce's father was "demanding his return to Hong Kong."[16] Once again, Grace Lee interceded and pleaded with her husband to let Bruce stay in Seattle a little while longer. Bruce was only months away from graduating from Edison Technical School (now Seattle Technical College), which meant he was already on the cusp of being eligible to enroll at the University of Washington. She didn't want to prevent that from happening by having him return to Hong Kong, where it was feared he would only continue on in his previous ways. Somehow, Hoi-chuen decided to give his son another chance, and Bruce was allowed to remain in Seattle.[17]

AMERICAN REBEL

Bruce Lee had no intention of leaving America anyway. He was by this time nineteen years old, he had friends and he was having fun. America had opened his eyes to a whole new world: it was bigger and bolder than other countries with its modern buildings and flashy cars, and its population was less crowded than what he had grown up with in Hong Kong. America had cleaner air, the latest music, different martial arts, Hollywood movies and people of all varieties and persuasions. There weren't the same venerated traditions that were ritualized in Hong Kong, traditions that were expected to be observed simply by virtue of being traditions. Youth — not the ways of the ancients — was worshipped. Americans looked upon the younger generation as the future; *they* were the important ones, as they embodied the qualities of life, progress, enthusiasm, health, fitness and growth. The old simply went into politics or nursing homes, where their babbling was heard but not taken too seriously. In America everything was happening *now*, and people were opening themselves up to the notion that the present, not the past, was where one's focus ought to be.

America was also the land of rebels. It had been established by rebels and was a country that bent its knee to no one, particularly the British, who had stamped their royal and dusty imprint all over Hong Kong. Rebelliousness was not an attitude that was punished but rather celebrated in America: its movie stars were rebels like James Dean and

Marlon Brando, and the Beat Generation and counterculture were in full swing, permeating the country's music and its literature. Writers like Jack Kerouac, Allen Ginsberg, Alan Watts, Timothy Leary and Aldous Huxley were introducing new and dangerous ideas into the culture.

Everything about America was agitation — and exciting. It was as if the country had been designed for nineteen-year-olds. How weary, stale, flat and unprofitable Hong Kong seemed by comparison. Moreover, Bruce's new friends were fun to hang around with; there were always get-togethers, parties — and fights. They even taught Bruce how to shoot guns of various calibers,[18] something that was absolutely forbidden in Hong Kong. America was the center of the universe and Bruce Lee wasn't going anywhere.

HELPING SOMEONE TO THE FLOOR

Bruce continued to train hard and to give freely of his martial arts knowledge to his friends. But, even more than before, he insisted on secrecy — particularly when it came to his fighting. And it was a pledge that his Seattle friends, for the most part, kept. Skip Ellsworth, for example, even twenty years after Bruce's death, wouldn't speak to anybody about Bruce's fights in Seattle who hadn't first been vetted by Jesse Glover. And even then, he only touched on the details:

> When Bruce and I went into an all-Black pool hall near 23rd and Madison, there was an incident involving some Black guys. When Bruce and I drove a truck to Montana to pick up some freight, and we stopped at a "cowboy–honky-tonk–tavern–restaurant" for dinner, there was an incident involving some cowboys that were hanging out under a mercury light in the parking lot. When Bruce and I were leaving the Kokusai Movie Theater one night in the International District in Seattle there was an incident involving three Black dudes. The list goes on . . . Bruce had altercations all the time. Nothing serious, because with Bruce an altercation went like this: a guy would try to hit him and he would miss. And Bruce would hit the guy and

the fight was over. On average, an altercation lasted a second and a half. Maybe three seconds, depending on if there was a discussion first. But invariably it would be a matter of someone swinging and missing and then Bruce hitting the guy and down he goes. And Bruce had this thing where it was extremely important to help a guy to the floor, so to speak, so that the guy wouldn't hurt himself. The guy would immediately become unconscious, so Bruce would have to grab him and "help him to the floor" is the way he put it.[19]

THE EMERGENCE OF SPEED, SKILL AND POWER

Bruce was fixated on improving his skill set. He typically spent two to four hours a day training with his friends, but then several additional hours training on his own. He desperately wanted to become faster and more powerful.[20] To this end, he began training with weights, performing countless numbers of push-ups, as well as additional exercises to enhance his tactile sensitivity.

He had previously studied the footwork of fencing by watching his older brother Peter in action. Peter had been the British Commonwealth fencing champion, and his footwork, particularly in closing the gap between his opponent and himself, had made an indelible impression on Bruce. Wishing to incorporate this closing move from fencing into his street fighting, Bruce purchased books on fencing, studied its tactics and worked tirelessly on applying the lunge step from fencing to his Kung Fu training. Eventually he got to the point where he could move in to touch someone so quickly that the person couldn't stop him.

"Bruce could have a person stand with their hand four inches from the side of their face," Jesse recalled, "and he'd close from a distance of seven feet and touch the side of their face before they could block his hand. I saw him demonstrate this skill several times and no one was ever able to react to his hand before it had returned to its starting position. His punch was so fast that your eyes couldn't pick up the movement. The only way that you could tell that he had punched in front of your face was by the wind that the punch created."[21]

In all his years in boxing and Judo, Jesse had never seen anybody who could punch so fast. Curious as to the actual speed of Bruce's punch, Jesse had a friend, Gary Barnhard, an electronics student at Edison Tech, devise a means of testing it. Barnhard created an electric timer. He wired one end into a light switch and the other into a cutoff switch attached to the back of a small pad. The timer started the instant the light was turned off. It stopped when somebody hit the pad. Jesse would kill the light, and Bruce would hit the target. Jesse and Gary told Bruce to strike the pad from varying distances and, after each hit, they recorded the data from the timer. From five feet away, Bruce's time was eight one-hundredths of a second (0.08 seconds). From three feet away, his reaction time was a mere five one-hundredths of a second (0.05 seconds).[22]

Not only Bruce's speed but his athleticism impressed everyone who witnessed it. Trisha Mar, a niece of Ruby Chow's, recalled that she and her teenage cousins ate at Ruby Chow's restaurant every Saturday. Almost as a ritual, when they left the establishment each of them would jump into the air to touch the fringe of a tassel that dangled from a hand-painted lantern hanging from the ceiling near the exit. It was eight feet off the ground and most of them could barely touch it with their hands. But Mar recalled that one Saturday Bruce was watching them as they performed their exit ritual and, when they were finished, he did a small dance toward the lantern and then leapt up and kicked the tassel with his foot. The Mars were dumbfounded.[23]

Evidently Bruce was able to perform this maneuver rather routinely. Anthony Laigo Cordova remembered, "There was a high school house party in the Central District one night. Everybody was having a good time. Bruce Lee is there and he's very calm, cool, super-polite, and mingling on the side. As he's leaving he shocks the room. Out of nowhere, he just jumps up in the air and kicks the ceiling! Then he just walks out the door."[24]

Bruce continued his lengthy practice sessions,[25] punching a wall pad, thrusting his hands into garbage cans filled with gravel,[26] engaging in sticking hands (*chi sao*) practice with his students and, once it arrived from Hong Kong, making prolific use of the wooden dummy. The dummy was mounted beneath the fire escape stairway at the back of Ruby Chow's restaurant. The fire escape offered some protection from the elements, allowing Bruce to practice on the dummy even if it was raining outside (which, in Seattle, was more often than not). "When he practiced he was another person," recalled Trisha Mar. "His intensity and the noises were almost animalistic. He was so fast and so incredibly strong."[27] Mar's recollection was seconded by Jesse, who remembered that "Bruce's attacks on the dummy were very noisy, and he was only allowed to practice with it during certain hours of the day."[28]

COOKING UP TROUBLE

The noise Bruce made practicing on the wooden dummy had grated on the nerves of one of the cooks at Ruby Chow's restaurant ever since Bruce first set it up. The two men almost got into a fight about it at the restaurant on one occasion, when the cook picked up a meat cleaver and threatened Bruce. When Bruce dared him to take a swing at him with it, the cook ended up putting it down and backing away.[29] But the peace between them didn't last, and one day when the racket from Bruce's training was particularly loud, the cook stormed outside where Bruce was practicing with his friend Skip Ellsworth and told him to knock it off. Bruce offered a few choice Cantonese words in reply. The man went into the kitchen and returned brandishing a knife. He now had Bruce Lee's full attention. The man moved towards Bruce uttering threats. Ellsworth was looking for something to use as a weapon when Bruce made his move. Whether it was a kick or a punch happened too fast for Ellsworth to tell. All he knew was that the cook was lying on the ground, out cold. "The guy made some threats, had a knife, and it got to the point where it was threatening to Bruce," he recalled. "So, Bruce just hit him and rendered him unconscious and 'helped him to the floor' and that was it."[30]

Despite his young age, Bruce Lee's martial arts skills were undeniable. His friends were convinced that he was exceptional, a genius of unarmed combat. They pressured him to open a school and promised that they would help him do it. The idea appealed to Bruce. It would give him more time to train and develop to an even higher level. Toward this end, Bruce and his students began giving demonstrations throughout Seattle whenever they could in order to get the word out about the budding young master and his art. The first of these demonstrations was performed at Edison Technical School. And it was there that trouble appeared in the form of a black belt Karate and Judo expert named Yoichi Nakachi.

CHAPTER SEVEN

ELEVEN SECONDS
OF MAYHEM

"The object of Gung Fu is a maximum of anguish with a minimum of movement."

— Bruce Lee (*Seattle Times*, 1967)

Yoichi Nakachi grew up in the small fishing village of Kushimoto, which is at the southernmost point of Japan's main island, Honshu. At the age of twelve, he began training in the Shinpu-Ren style of Karate under the mentorship of instructor Yon Pon Gun.[1] Little is known of Yon Pon Gun, other than that he was a practitioner of the Korean Hwa-Rang style of Tae Kwon Do. When his business ventures brought him to Kushimoto, he began to train a select group of students in the art. He mixed his Tae Kwon Do training with some Okinawan Te Karate, and the fusion of these two arts he christened Shinpu-Ren.[2]

During the mid-1940s, when Nakachi was studying under Gun, the practice of *Budo* (Japanese martial arts) was banned in Japan on the order of the American military, then under the direction of General Douglas MacArthur. Despite the ban, Gun continued to train his students in secret, usually in the mountains, open fields and beaches. When the ban on the Japanese martial arts was lifted in 1948, Gun continued teaching for two more years before leaving Japan for Korea in 1950. Upon his departure, he left the instruction of Shinpu-Ren to Nakachi, who by then had earned his second-degree black belt in the art.[3]

Nakachi, as the senior student (*sempai*), taught Kushimoto students in Shinpu-Ren's various kicking drills and *katas* (forms), along with some weapons training and lots of sparring (*kumite*).[4] In 1959, at the age of twenty-six, Nakachi left Kushimoto, boarding a ship that was bound for America. Once on U.S. soil, he made his way to Seattle, where he enrolled as a student at the University of Washington. He attended on a scholarship in philosophy, which had been provided by the Tenrikyo religion back in Japan. Not long afterward, Nakachi resumed his teaching of both Karate and Judo, in which he was also a black belt, in Seattle's University District.[5] According to Jesse Glover, the Karate man was known throughout the city for being a legitimate badass. "He was not a slouch. I'd known him from Judo where he was a black belt, too. He used to get in fights around town and go against guys with knives."[6] When Nakachi happened upon a flyer announcing that there was going to be a martial arts demonstration that included Judo at Edison Technical School, Nakachi and some of his students decided to attend.

AN OFFENSIVE DEMONSTRATION

The original plan for the demonstration had been to feature Kung Fu exclusively. But after discussing it with his students, Bruce concluded that Kung Fu was too obscure to the American public to attract much of a crowd and added a Judo component to the presentation.[7] Joining Bruce on stage that day were Skip Ellsworth, Ed Hart (who was the master of ceremonies), Pat Hooks and Jesse Glover. Skip and Jesse, both long-time Judokas, were the obvious choices to handle the demonstration of that art, while Bruce and the remainder of the group would command the stage for the Kung Fu portion of the presentation. After the Judo demonstration concluded, Bruce and the others took to the stage.[8]

Bruce performed a dramatic, visually pleasing form from the Praying Mantis style, and the others demonstrated forms from other styles of Chinese Kung Fu that they had been taught by Bruce.

After the Kung Fu presentation, Bruce took the microphone from Ed and spoke to the audience about the history of Chinese Kung Fu. He commented on the many different iterations of the fighting arts practiced throughout China, and how there were "hard" styles that required the output of a great amount of energy for kicking and striking, such as Hung Gar and Choy Li Fut, as well as "soft" styles such as Tai Chi that used an opponent's energy against him, requiring comparatively little energy. From the Chinese perspective, he said, the soft styles were considered to be of a higher level than the hard styles, as they were more in accord with Tao and "going with the flow," rather than using unnecessary muscular force and strain to subdue an opponent. In effect, a soft style practitioner allowed his opponent to defeat himself, as the harder an adversary directed his energy towards a practitioner of a soft style, the harder that energy was directed back at him, resulting in one's opponent bringing about his own defeat. As a discussion of Chinese philosophy and its application to unarmed combat, it was a beautiful message. But to certain martial artists from different disciplines who were in attendance, Bruce's comments were interpreted as a dig at the hard arts, which, by definition, included the Japanese art of Karate. And that was exactly how Yoichi Nakachi interpreted Bruce's statements.

CHALLENGE ISSUED

The next public demonstration Bruce and his students performed took place on October 28, 1960, at the Yesler Terrace Gymnasium. Both Judo and Kung Fu were featured, but with the added attraction of Bruce exhibiting his prowess on the wooden dummy. The show went off without a hitch until the wooden dummy demonstration. The dummy was attached to a wooden stand and had six of Bruce's students supporting it from behind, but when he began to hammer away at its trunk and arms, his students were, in Jesse's words, "flying all over the stage. Our combined weight and strength weren't enough to effectively brace the dummy against the power of Bruce's punches."[9]

Yoichi Nakachi, once again in attendance, was still fuming from the comments Bruce made at his previous demonstration. At the end of the performance he dispatched one of his students to deliver a challenge to Bruce on his behalf. From Nakachi's perspective, it was a matter of national pride: he wanted to prove that Japanese Karate was a superior martial system — despite what the old guard in China thought. The challenge caught Bruce completely off guard. He spoke to his students about Nakachi's challenge and asked if any of them thought he should fight the Karate practitioner. To a person, none of his students believed it was necessary. Indeed, they told Bruce that it would be beneath his dignity to accept such a challenge.[10] Satisfied that his friends didn't think he had anything to prove, Bruce and the group left the venue. That his challenge was ignored struck Nakachi as a further affront; clearly the alleged Kung Fu wunderkind was all bark and no bite.

Nakachi thought about it over the weekend, and when Monday morning arrived, he was still hot under the collar. He remained convinced there was only one way to resolve the matter, and that was for him and Bruce to fight it out. And so, early Monday morning Nakachi arrived at Edison Technical School, pushed open the doors and headed straight for the student lounge. The lounge was in the basement of the school, but as all students went there before classes started, he believed that's where he'd find Bruce that morning. Entering the lounge, he quickly scanned the room. He soon caught sight of Bruce talking with some students at the other side of the room. Nakachi stood by the doors waiting for Bruce to notice him. When eventually their eyes met, he gestured for Bruce to come and fight him.[11] Bruce wasn't interested.

Not to be thwarted, Nakachi waited in the hallway and, when Bruce appeared, he stepped out in front of him and dared him to fight. Bruce, however, simply smiled, walked around him, and continued on his way to class. His intentions frustrated yet again, Nakachi left the school as angry as he had been when he arrived there that morning. Later that evening, Joe Cowles, a thirty-two-year-old marine, encountered Nakachi at the downtown YMCA on the way to a Judo class. "Nakachi bragged to me how he had challenged Bruce to fight him, and Bruce had turned him down," Cowles recalled. "And this bragging took place before I even knew Bruce. Nor did I know the Karate man. So, I didn't know what he was bragging to me for."[12]

It didn't take long for the news to spread. Chinese Kung Fu practitioners passed word along to Bruce that his passiveness in the face of Nakachi's taunting was an insult to Chinese Kung Fu — and that if Bruce wouldn't fight him, one of them would. Bruce waved them off, stating that no one was going to goad him into a fight.[13] His word on the matter was final. But less than twenty-four hours later, he changed his mind.[14]

CHALLENGE ACCEPTED

On Tuesday morning, Bruce was back at the student lounge of Edison Tech when, once again, Nakachi appeared. "Bruce said the man walked right up to him and stared right in his face," Cowles recalled. "Then he reached out, shoved Bruce aside, and walked past him. Bruce said to us, 'As long as he talked, I just let him talk. But when he put his hands on me, then I accepted his challenge.'"[15]

Later that afternoon, Bruce pulled Jesse aside as he was leaving his final class of the day. "I'm going to fight the son of a bitch! And I want you to be my second." Jesse nodded and the pair headed off in search of the Karate expert.[16]

As Nakachi had last been seen in the basement of the school, that was where Bruce and Jesse headed. En route, Bruce told Jesse that he wanted to fight Nakachi on the top floor of the building. The news stopped his friend in his tracks. "I don't think that fighting in the school is a good idea, Bruce," he said. "You could get expelled."

Bruce hadn't considered that possibility. If he was expelled, Ruby Chow would find out — and she would inform his father right away and Bruce would have to face yet another family conflict. Now Bruce was angry and frustrated.

"Where then?" he asked.

For some reason, the first location that popped into Jesse's mind was the downtown YMCA. In truth, it wasn't a bad venue; it wasn't unusual for people to practice Karate there, and if people saw a fight going on they might simply interpret what they were seeing as a sparring match, which wouldn't raise any red flags. Bruce agreed but told Jesse that he was too mad at the moment to allow himself to get within six feet of Nakachi. Were that to happen, he was likely to start the fight as soon as he saw him. He told Jesse to set things up, and if the YMCA wasn't an acceptable venue for Nakachi, then screw it, they would have it out on the top floor of Edison Tech then and there. Jesse nodded and then continued down into the basement to look for Nakachi, while Bruce went up to the top floor to wait for Jesse's report.

It didn't take long for Jesse to locate Nakachi. He told him of Bruce's proposition and Nakachi indicated that the YMCA was okay; he was not only familiar with the institution, but also taught Karate classes there during the week.[17] As far as Nakachi was concerned, the venue gave him home field advantage. Both parties agreed to bring along some friends to serve as seconds and witnesses to the match. Jesse suggested that everyone should meet in front of the school in one hour and they would all head to the "Y" together. He then hiked up the staircase and told Bruce the news.

In short order, Ed Hart and Howard Hall (who by now had become another student of Bruce's) were collected and the group then walked to the bus stop in front of Edison Tech. The quartet hadn't been there long when Nakachi and his crew arrived. One of them was an exchange student named Masafusa Kimura. Kimura had previously taken Kung Fu lessons from Bruce along with Jesse and the others; for him to now be siding with Nakachi didn't sit well with Bruce's group. According to Ed, "We believed that he [Kimura] had been the one advocating for the fight by telling Nakachi one thing and telling Bruce another, until a confrontation was unavoidable."[18]

Such suspicions were academic at this point, however. The fight was going to happen and the tension between Bruce and Nakachi was palpable. "There was electricity in the air at the bus stop when the Karate man and his group walked up," Jesse recalled. "And for a moment I thought the fight was going to happen right there. Bruce kept looking away from Nakachi in an effort to control his anger, but the Karate man kept moving into Bruce's line of vision in an attempt to break down his confidence. I was a happy man when the bus arrived because the tension in Bruce was increasing and I felt that he could explode at any moment."

The bus pulled away from the school, and Nakachi turned to Bruce and began listing off the rules of the match.

Bruce waved him off. "Forget the rules because I'm going all-out!"

When they arrived at the YMCA, Nakachi's crew went directly to a dressing room where the martial artist kept his Karate uniform in one of the lockers. Nakachi's two friends looked on as he put on his white Karate top and Karate pants, and then fastened his black belt around his waist. In the meantime, Bruce and his crew walked along a corridor and into an empty racquetball court. Once inside, Bruce kicked off his shoes and removed his shirt. A tank top and jeans would be his fighting attire. After a few deep knee bends, he turned and faced the door of the racquetball court and waited for Nakachi's arrival.

Nakachi and his supporters left the dressing room and walked towards the court with a confidence that bordered on arrogance. Upon entering, one of Nakachi's friends approached Jesse and asked if he would serve as the referee for the match. Jesse agreed. Next, Ed Hart was asked to be the timekeeper for the bout. Acting in his capacity of referee, Jesse then put forth what he thought should be the rules of the encounter:

- There would be three two-minute rounds, with the winner being the person who won two of the three.
- A round would be scored a win if a man was knocked down or knocked out.
- If, for any reason, one of the two fighters proved unable to continue, his opponent would be awarded the match.

Both parties accepted the rules. Nakachi then began a series of preparatory Karate moves, which he did for the dual purpose of warming up and intimidating his opponent. When he had finished, he stood and faced Bruce.

"Are you sure you want this fight?" Bruce asked.

"Ya, ya, ya."

Bruce turned to the witnesses in the room to make sure they would hear what Nakachi's answer to his next question would be. "And *you* are the one who pushed to have this fight, right?"

Nakachi repeated his previous reply.

Bruce smiled. "All right, then."

THE FIGHT BEGINS

Bruce assumed the ready position stance of the Wing Chun style, and Nakachi settled into a wide front stance — his left leg forward and his right fist clenched and at his hip, ready to strike. He extended his left arm toward Bruce with the palm open.

Ed Hart looked down at his wristwatch and waited for the second hand to hit twelve. Seeing that the fighters were facing each other and in position, he held up his left arm and said, "Ready . . . *Begin!*"

Nakachi fired a front kick toward Bruce's chest, which Bruce deflected with his right arm. Before Nakachi could reset, Bruce struck him flush in the face with a left-hand vertical fist and then reeled off a series of rapid-fire chain punches. Each punch landed in Nakachi's face and drove him across the length of the racquetball court until his back slammed hard into the far wall. Nakachi had attempted to punch back during the initial onslaught, but all of his strikes had been easily deflected. With his opponent now momentarily trapped, Bruce unleashed several more punches to Nakachi's face.

The Karate man, in a move of desperation, now attempted to grab hold of Bruce's arms. But at that very moment Bruce pivoted and delivered a double fist punch, one fist striking Nakachi's face, the other his chest. Because he threw the double punch while twisting, both strikes landed with considerable power. He sent Nakachi, by Jesse's account, "flying six feet through the air." When he landed, Nakachi came down on both knees — and was instantly met with a full-force front kick to his face. Blood exploded from the man's nose, and the force of Bruce's kick flipped Nakachi over onto his back. According to Jesse:

> I hollered "Stop!" because that was one of the rules; if you hit the floor, that was it. But then the guy just went out. He looked like he was dead. I was afraid. I thought, "Damn, I hope this guy's not dead." That guy was out of it; I mean, he was unconscious. When I walked over and looked at him, his face looked like somebody thought he was a baseball and had taken a bat to him.

Ed and Jesse looked at each other in muted shock. "Shit," Ed said under his breath.

Since Nakachi's friends were frozen in disbelief, Ed and Jesse approached the fallen fighter, each taking hold of an arm. The pair then dragged him across the floor to the nearest wall and propped him up against it.

As Nakachi regained consciousness, his eyes blinked, and, recognizing Ed Hart as being the timekeeper, he struggled to articulate a question. "How long [did] it take him to defeat me?"

"I felt so sorry for this poor guy," Ed recalled. "The total time of the match was only eleven seconds, so I doubled it, and told him, 'ah, twenty-two seconds.' And the guy said, 'Oooohhh!' and collapsed back against the wall. That he should lose so quickly was disgraceful to him. Shit, if I had told him the match was only eleven seconds."[19]

DAMAGE CONTROL

Bruce Lee quickly took stock; he did not want this getting out — to anybody. He told everyone present that as far as he was concerned, he wasn't going to mention what had taken place and wanted everyone else to vouch that they wouldn't speak a word of it either.[20] All in attendance pledged to keep silent about it. This lasted about a day, until someone from outside of Bruce's group broke ranks and told somebody else. Soon everybody knew about the fight at the downtown YMCA,[21] and of Bruce's preternatural performance in it.

When Howard Hall, a tough Newark, New Jersey, native who was rooming with Ed and Jesse at the time, returned to their apartment later that night he immediately pulled Ed aside. "Damn it, Hart," he exclaimed, "*that* guy's dangerous!"[22] Indeed. It was later discovered that Nakachi had suffered a cracked skull during the fight, the fracture extending from his orbital bone down to his cheekbone.[23]

When Bruce returned to his room at Ruby Chow's, he recorded the following entry in his diary:

> Against karate black belt today (Shodan [first-degree black belt])[24] and 2nd degree black belt in judo
> Place: downtown YMCA
> Date: 1st Nov. 1960
> Result: won knock him down in 13 second; [he] couldn't fight anymore.[25]

Bruce evidently had not spoken with Ed Hart at this point to learn the exact duration of the match. According to Jesse, how quickly Bruce had dispatched the Karate man was impressive. "Nakachi was pretty fast and his technique was pretty good. He was just fighting the wrong guy."[26]

CHAPTER EIGHT

FAMILY, GUNS, AND BUSINESS

"At long range, you use a kick to the shins in the same way a boxer uses his left jab."

— Bruce Lee (*Seattle Post-Intelligencer*, 1966)

Bruce hadn't been home in four long years, and, in March 1963,[1] after the spring semester concluded, he boarded a plane for Hong Kong for a reunion with his family. Some big changes had occurred since he'd last seen his parents: he had graduated from Edison Technical School, moved out of Ruby Chow's, opened his own Kung Fu school and been admitted as a student to the University of Washington. His parents were over the moon. Their boy — finally — had straightened himself out and was now on a path to making something of his life. They were absolutely overjoyed by his homecoming; indeed, the atmosphere was so positive that Bruce decided to remain in Hong Kong for the duration of the summer. There were other reasons for his return, too, of course, such as reconnecting with old friends and picking up some additional martial arts pointers from Yip Man.

TRAINING WITH YIP MAN

Three months after Bruce arrived, Doug Palmer, a friend and student of Bruce's from Seattle, arrived in Hong Kong at Bruce's invitation. Palmer had just completed his freshman year at university, where he majored in Chinese studies, but he had never been to Asia before. He was understandably keen to see the sights and experience firsthand the culture he had read so much about.[2] He hadn't been in Hong

73

Kong long when Bruce offered to introduce him to Yip Man. "I had to pretend that I didn't know any Gung Fu," Palmer recalled, "because Bruce wasn't supposed to be teaching non-Chinese at that point."[3]

The two men arrived at Yip's apartment, which Palmer recalled was small and sparsely furnished. There was a spare room, however, and in short order the master and student retired there to train. According to Palmer: "It was fascinating; they did mostly the sticking hands. I don't really know if Bruce was holding himself back because it was his teacher, or whether his teacher really was dominant. I mean, Bruce dominated everybody else, and he clearly *wasn't* dominating Yip Man in the sticking hands. It was more like two equals, from my limited perspective, watching."[4]

According to Jesse, Bruce told him he had not been holding back in his sticking hands sessions with Yip Man: "The first time he returned from Hong Kong, Bruce told me that there were still three people who he couldn't get by — his teacher [Yip Man], his teacher's assistant and [Wong Shun Leung]."[5]

By contrast, when Bruce first moved to Seattle in 1959 he told Jesse there were five members of the Wing Chun School that he couldn't get by.[6] That list had now been trimmed by forty percent. Bruce knew his skills were improving and that he was heading in the right direction.

TROUBLE ON THE STAR FERRY

While Bruce Lee's Kung Fu skills were evolving, his ability to avoid fights hadn't improved. He frequently went out on dates in the evenings, and Doug Palmer usually stayed behind with Bruce's younger brother Robert and his friends. One evening, Bruce set out via the Star Ferry service to see a girl who lived on Hong Kong Island. The Star Ferry is a long-time staple in Hong Kong, shuttling people back and forth between Hong Kong Island and the Kowloon peninsula since 1888. Bruce, who was always fashion-conscious, dressed to the nines. When the date ended, Bruce took the girl home and then boarded the ferry to return to Kowloon. Just as the ferry was preparing to pull out from Wan Chai Pier, two men looking for trouble stepped on board. Spotting the nattily attired Bruce, the pair sauntered over and plunked themselves down on the passenger bench directly behind him. Soon they began to mock Bruce's voguish clothes. Bruce recognized that the two troublemakers were trying to goad him into a fight and simply ignored them. This, of course, had never come easy for the hot-tempered martial artist, who would later say that "it takes a hell of a lot [more] for me *not* to do anything than to do something."[7] Nevertheless, he kept his mouth shut and endured the verbal abuse for the duration of the ferry ride.

Upon the arrival of the ferry at the Tsim Sha Tsui pier, Bruce disembarked and began his walk along Nathan Road towards the family apartment. The two troublemakers also stepped out and began following him.[8] Soon the men caught up to Bruce and resumed their taunting. When Bruce picked up his pace, they picked up theirs.

"Hey, where you going so fast?"

"Do you have to hurry home to Mommy?"

By this point, Bruce had had enough. He whirled around and kicked the man nearest to him in the shin as hard as he could. The fact that Bruce was wearing hard-heeled dress shoes made the impact particularly painful. The man cried out and instantly fell to the ground, clutching his lower leg.

Bruce now advanced toward his second antagonist, but the man quickly retreated and held up his hands; he wanted no part of what his friend had just received. Bruce proceeded to cuss them out in Cantonese, and then headed home. When Bruce entered the apartment, Palmer and one of Bruce's cousins noticed that he was chuckling to himself. When the cousin asked what was so amusing, Bruce related the incident, blow-by-blow, to the pair. The cousin laughed and said, "Gee, you've really mellowed a *lot*, Bruce. In the old days, you would have beaten both of those guys up as soon as you got off the ferry!"

CHANGING TIMES

Upon his return to Seattle at the end of the summer, Bruce resumed teaching Kung Fu to whoever was interested, irrespective of their ethnicity. According to Jesse:

> Bruce's mother was half German or English, so Bruce himself was part white. . . . the first [student] group was, like, there was Leroy Garcia, [who] is Mexican

and Norwegian; Jim DeMile, he's Filipino and Irish; Taky Kimura, he's Japanese; Tak Miyabe, he was a Japanese exchange student; John Jackson, he was Black; I'm Black; Ed Hart, he's Irish; Howard Hall, he's English; Pat Hooks, I think he was Caucasian and maybe part Ute Indian. Yeah, that [not teaching non-Chinese] wasn't Bruce's agenda at all. He didn't care about that kind of shit.[9]

While Bruce's refusal to discriminate based on the color of someone's skin or nationality impressed Jesse, he wasn't impressed that Bruce's Kung Fu school, now called the Jun Fan Gung Fu Institute ("Bruce Lee's Kung Fu Institute"), had become more formalized in its instruction. To Jesse, his friend and Kung Fu instructor had always just been "Bruce," but in the school the students were instructed to address him as Sifu (the Cantonese word for teacher). This had seemed an unnecessary formality. When he and the first wave of students began learning Kung Fu from Bruce, the lessons had always been free-form and informal; they could ask Bruce any question that they wanted answered about fighting with no pretenses involved. Then, their Kung Fu school was anywhere in Seattle — street corners, outside Edison Tech, in Jesse's apartment, in public parks. Now the lessons were only being taught in one place within the city — and spontaneous questions and answers had been replaced with a rigid curriculum.

And some of the techniques that were being taught, Jesse believed, were not nearly as effective as what Bruce had shared with him when the lessons were more extemporaneous. "The first night of my training I began to learn the first Wing Chun form and sticking hands," he recalled. "In his formal school, in Seattle at any rate, few of the students practiced sticking hands."[10] Jesse's was a sentiment shared by another of Bruce's early students, James DeMile: "He left out pieces of the puzzle that made everything work. He de-emphasized the center-line, closed bai jong and spring energy."[11]

The content of the new Kung Fu lessons seemed, to James and Jesse at least, to be watered down. While they continued to encourage Bruce in his quest to bring more students to his school, they just weren't interested in having to pay for something that was less practical than what they had received before. In truth, what money the two men possessed was limited, and neither could absorb the expense required for formal lessons, particularly when in the past they had received such instruction simply in exchange for their friendship and helping Bruce in any demonstrations he was putting on. All that had changed.

In fairness to Bruce, teaching a group required a much different approach than did simply sharing techniques informally among friends. Besides, he needed money just as much as they did. And he also wanted to share certain aspects of the art of Kung Fu that went beyond its fighting techniques. To this end, he taught the new students Chinese terminology, the history of the Chinese fighting arts and Chinese philosophy. He referred to his art as "Chinese Gung Fu: The Philosophical Art of Self-Defense." Indeed, this would be the title of the one and only book he published on Kung Fu during his lifetime. And, as certain of the original students fell away, newer ones stepped forth, such as Taky Kimura, a man whom Bruce selected to assist him in teaching classes at his formal school, or to run the classes if Bruce couldn't be present.

Kimura took readily to the philosophy Bruce taught. In the 1940s he and his family had been uprooted from their home and business in Seattle and taken away by train to Tule Lake in California, where they were put into a prisoner-of-war camp (euphemistically referred to as an "internment camp") for the "crime" of having Japanese ancestry. The Kimuras, and thousands like them, were held in these camps until the Second World War had concluded. Upon their release, the Kimuras discovered that their former home of Seattle had changed. The family was now looked upon with suspicion and was refused service in restaurants. Kimura was a beaten man — until he met Bruce Lee. Bruce, a fellow Asian, never took a backward step for anybody, and he told Kimura — repeatedly — that, despite the tragedy he had gone through, he was just as good as anybody else. The lesson stuck. Soon Kimura regained his dignity. He would become Bruce Lee's best friend and most devoted student.

FRIENDS BECOME RIVALS

Believing that he had absorbed most (if not all) of the good stuff that Bruce had to teach, Jesse eventually approached Bruce to see if he had any objections to him and James DeMile opening a Kung Fu school of their own. "He said he had no objection to that," Jesse recalled, "as long as we didn't call what we did Wing Chun or Jun Fan."[12] The two clubs operated independently of each other for a time, with Bruce pulling in more students as a result of both his phenomenal skill and his art's broader range of interests — self-defense, philosophy, physical fitness, meditation and history — whereas James and Jesse only offered a better way to kick the shit out of someone. Nevertheless, the three men remained friends and would often meet up after Bruce finished teaching a class to go out for dinner.

It was with that intention in mind that James and Jesse dropped by Bruce's Kung Fu school one evening.[13] As the pair headed down the stairway to Bruce's Kung Fu studio on the lower level of the building, they encountered some of the newer students leaving the school. One of the students, recognizing James as one of Bruce's earliest students, asked him why he wasn't attending the classes anymore. And that's when James made a grievous mistake — he told him. According to James, "I said that we did not feel the training was as practical as when we trained, since certain fighting concepts were changed or missing. I felt that Bruce was leaving out a few concepts and applied principles that I thought were very important." When the students returned for their next class at the school later that week, they confronted Bruce and asked him why he wasn't teaching them the important concepts and principles that he had shared with James and the previous generation of students.

Bruce was stunned by the allegation and became furious. The next time that James and Jesse dropped into his studio after class, he was in no mood for chitchat. Bruce already had on his coat and held a pair of leather gloves in his hands. When he saw them, he confronted James. "Why did you say that to my students?"

James turned ashen. A foreboding silence now filled the room, broken only by the sound of Bruce slapping his leather gloves into the open palm of his other hand. He stared hard into James's eyes. "Are you challenging me?"

James saw that Bruce was ready to attack. "I knew I was on very dangerous ground," he recollected. "To fight Bruce when he was calm was insanity, but to do it when he was mad was to invite sudden death."

"I was out of line, Bruce," he said. "I'm sorry."

"You have no right to make any comments to my class!"

James was terrified. He didn't know what else he could say to pacify his former teacher. "He just stared at me, as if lost on what to do next," he recalled. "I felt he wanted to provoke a fight." The silence was deafening. Again, James apologized, and then he turned and left the school. He later recalled: "That moment could have changed both of our lives. I always carried a gun. It was a habit while in the service and after being discharged. It was only later, I remembered, I had my hand on the gun in my coat pocket. Jesse and I talked about it later, and I had to admit that if Bruce had attacked, I probably would have shot him. I do not know if it reflects badly on me, but that was who I was at that time."

This marked the end of James DeMile's association with Bruce Lee.

AN ALLY IN OAKLAND

While Bruce may have lost a friend in DeMile, he was about to gain a new ally in the Bay Area in the form of James Yimm Lee. James held a reputation as both a formidable fighter and an exceptional athlete. He had been involved in gymnastics and wrestling while in high school, and, as a member of the Oakland YMCA, he set a weight-lifting record in the 132-pound division for all of Northern California. He had also boxed as an amateur and held a brown belt in Judo,[14] having trained in the art while working as a welder in Hawaii during the Second World War. His real passion, however, was Kung Fu, which he practiced for a time under the watchful eye of the highly respected Sil Lum (Shaolin) master Wong Tim Yuen. Wong had studied Kung Fu in China prior to his coming to America, and later became an enforcer for the San Francisco Hop Sing Tong, a Chinese secret society that dabbled in organized crime.[15] He was not a man one wanted to fool around with.

While Wong was a traditionalist, James was something of a visionary. He had started his own book publishing company and was among the first to publish books on Kung Fu in America. The two men had collaborated on a book that James published entitled *Chinese Karate Kung-Fu: Original 'Sil Lum' System for Health & Self Defense*, which was released on January 1, 1961. However, the two men had a falling out. Why James Lee left Wong's school is by no means clear; some claim it was over a dispute in book royalties,[16] whereas James would state publicly that it was because Wong had not been teaching him anything of practical use.[17] In any case, when James heard through the grapevine about a martial arts phenom named Bruce Lee who was kicking the stuffing out of black belts in Seattle, he was intrigued. Whatever the style was that Bruce was employing, it was obviously effective. He made a phone call to Bruce, and not long after headed north to Seattle for a face-to-face meeting. James found out that the young man was everything the stories he heard had led him to believe. "I wish I could have studied under Bruce Lee when I was twenty-one," he would later recollect. "Unfortunately, I'm more than 20 years older than Bruce, Still, it's better to learn a realistic approach to the martial arts late than never at all."[18] It was to be the start of a lifelong friendship between the two men.

James told Bruce about some of the unique martial arts training equipment he had welded together in his shop — equipment that was practical, cutting edge and nowhere else to be found. Bruce couldn't wait to come to Oakland to try it out. James was completely won over by Bruce's approach to fighting, which, combined with his own beliefs and unique training equipment, caused the two to believe that they were on the verge of a martial arts revolution that would bring Kung Fu into the twentieth century. Soon Bruce was shuttling between Seattle and Oakland.

THE PUBLISHED AUTHOR

To make some additional money,[19] James suggested that Bruce write a book that James could publish through his company, Oriental Book Sales, in Oakland. Inspired by the prospect of becoming a published author, Bruce returned to Seattle and set to work writing the book. Its title was *Chinese Gung Fu: The Philosophical Art of Self-Defense*. It turned out to be a small but interesting publication that featured a general overview of Kung Fu, along with some sample training exercises and combat techniques, in addition to an essay on how the philosophy of yin-yang applied to the Chinese fighting arts. He drew illustrations for the book and supplemented the text with photographs of him demonstrating Kung Fu techniques against certain of his Seattle students.

One of these students was Jesse Glover, who thought the whole enterprise was a waste of time:

> There wasn't that much to it. . . . Some of the techniques would work, but some . . . they're not at all what Bruce would have done. It was, like, "okay, we've got to have something to show the people who are going to buy this book, so let's try a little of this, a little of that." . . . [The photographer was] a guy from Hong Kong who was going to Edison Tech and he was studying watch repair or something. He also knew something about photography, so he came and took the pictures. It cost Bruce $600, I think that's what he told me. . . . But it wasn't a very good book and I never bought a copy of it. I mean, I have had people give me copies since then, but I didn't think it was worth five dollars then, and it's not worth it now.[20]

In an attempt to bolster the credentials of its author, the book also contained a few falsehoods: "Bruce Lee, one of the highest authorities in the Chinese Art of Gung Fu in the United States today, came from China three years ago."[21] While Bruce was certainly knowledgeable about the various styles of Kung Fu, he had only been practicing it for about seven years at this point. Other Kung Fu teachers in the United States, such as Lau Bun and T.Y. Wong (James Lee's former master), had been teaching the art for several decades and doubtless would not have considered such a young and comparatively inexperienced practitioner of Kung Fu as being one of the discipline's "highest authorities."[22] As to his having arrived in the United States from China, this was another bit of misleading window-dressing; Bruce came from the British colony of Hong Kong. He had never been to China in his life.

And then there was this passage: "At thirteen, he met Master Yip Man, leader of the [Wing Chun] School of Gung Fu, and since then he has devoted himself to that system. After years of daily training and engagements in competitive matches, he was awarded the rank of instructor — the youngest to achieve it in that School."[23] This was patently false. Bruce was never awarded the rank of instructor in Wing Chun Kung Fu (and never would be). Yip Man was the only official instructor of the art and there were several of Yip's senior students who were more advanced than Bruce in both practice and knowledge of Wing Chun by this time. Nevertheless, apart from such minor self-serving passages, and Glover's criticism of the publication, the book went on to sell reasonably well, bringing in US$5,000.[24]

James urged Bruce to leave Seattle and open a Kung Fu school in Oakland. California was a hotbed of martial arts activity, and James was convinced that Bruce could take the state (or at least Oakland) by storm. And he wouldn't have to give up his Seattle school, as Bruce's assistant instructor Taky Kimura could continue to run it, which meant that Bruce would be earning two incomes. The prospect appealed to him as a second school was seen as the next step in his master plan; he had written to family friend Pearl Tso two years previously that his goal was "to establish a first Gung Fu Institute that will later spread out all over the U.S."[25] He had already opened one institute in Seattle, so a second one in Oakland seemed a logical progression. Suddenly the University of Washington was viewed as an impediment, rather than an asset, to his future. Who needed a Bachelor of Arts degree to teach Kung Fu? And so, when the university's spring quarter concluded, Bruce dropped out and headed south to Oakland.

MARRIAGE AND MOTIVATION

By July 1964, two things had changed. Bruce Lee was living in Oakland with James Lee — they even had a storefront in Oakland picked out for the location of the second Jun Fan Gung Fu Institute — and Linda Emery, a university schoolmate from Seattle whom Bruce had been dating for the past ten months, was pregnant. This had *not* been part of Bruce's master plan. Linda recalled that "the idea of commitment scared him to death. He wanted to be financially secure before undertaking the responsibilities of a wife and family."[26] Taky Kimura recollected Bruce contacting him at the time and asking the older man,

"What do you think about Linda?" Kimura thought for a moment that his friend and teacher was thinking of leaving her (Taky may not have known about the pregnancy), and replied, "Bruce, she supports you one hundred percent and does everything you could possibly ask. You will *never* find another girl like her." Bruce paused and thought it over. "You're right," he replied.[27]

As a result of Linda's pregnancy, the couple had to get married right away. They set a wedding date for August 17, 1964. If anything, the prospect of soon becoming a father served to light a fire under Bruce; the Oakland school now became his top priority. He had to do everything he could to ensure it would be a success — his family's future depended on it. The master plan expanded: Linda would continue on at the University of Washington until the end of the semester, at which point she would join Bruce in Oakland. To save money, they would move in with James Lee, his wife and two children. But until then, Bruce had to get the word out about his Oakland school and make some money.

A NEW SALES PITCH

But the product Bruce was pitching in Oakland was far different from the one he sold in Seattle. In Washington, he was selling an ancient and (to Americans) exotic art that had been refined and handed down over thousands of years.[28] It was the distilled essence of the Tao, or "way," of unarmed combat — but it also represented a unique and total approach to human well-being. The practice of this special art cultivated health, strength and peace of mind. In Bruce's words, it was an art of "gentleness and unity of mind and body."[29] Overall, Chinese Kung Fu had something for everyone, so the potential market for such a product was as large as it could possibly be. If, as Bruce believed, "Ideas are what America is looking for,"[30] then Kung Fu was a pretty good idea to get behind.

But this wasn't what he was selling in Oakland. It was now about speed, power and putting the hurt on someone as quickly as possible. It remained to be seen if scaling down the benefits until what was left was simply a more efficient way to punch someone in the face was the "idea" America was looking for — and that enough people would be willing to pay money for. In Seattle, Kung Fu was an umbrella term that encompassed all types of Chinese martial arts; indeed, Bruce had compiled a list of twenty-three different styles of Kung Fu, and indicated that there were many others.[31]

While his teaching of non-Chinese students was frowned upon, the fact that he was effusive in his praise for China's martial arts culture served to underscore the validity of what the Chinese Kung Fu masters in America had been practicing and teaching their students for quite some time. At that point, Bruce Lee and the Chinese Kung Fu community in America were reading off the same song sheet. But ever since he had hooked up with James, a different Bruce Lee had emerged, one that was no longer saying "China first" no matter what the Kung Fu style, but rather that the Chinese martial culture was stuck in the past and it was high time it got its clock fixed.

A FEUD DEVELOPS

The turning point in Bruce's thinking seemed to be James Lee's break with Wong Tim Yuen. From that point, James never missed an opportunity to ridicule Wong or his style of Sil Lum Kung Fu. Wong, in turn, responded in kind, even publishing a new book on his art that mocked James's brick-breaking skills by featuring a picture of Wong's eight-year-old son breaking a brick in the same fashion. This move to belittle James's reputation in print seemed a petty thing to do, well beneath the dignity of a man in his sixties. But then, few decisions about Kung Fu instruction in the U.S. were based solely on what was good for the art. These were business moves, pure and simple. James had defected along with his monthly fees, taking several of Wong's students (and their monthly fees) along with him. Wong's book simply indicated that his former student's product was inferior to his own.

Wong's opening gambit in his war with James did not come without a response. When James published Bruce's book, he made sure to include a selection of photographs of Bruce demonstrating how his Kung Fu techniques easily overcame those of Wong's Sil Lum. To emphasize the point, James, who assumed the role of Bruce's adversary in the photographs, made sure to wear the uniform of the Sil Lum school. Above the photos ran the statement: "The techniques of a superior system of Gung Fu [are] based on simplicity. It is only the half-cultivated systems that are full of unnecessary wasted motions. . . . Here are some examples of a slower system against the more effective Gung Fu techniques."[32] The section had clearly been added as an afterthought. The photos for this section of the book were taken in James's garage in Oakland, while all of the other photos were taken in the parking lot of Ruby Chow's restaurant in Seattle. The section was included for no other reason than to fire a return shot over the bow of Wong Tim Yuen.

Having such statements and photos appear in his book drew Bruce into the feud between Wong and James. Moreover, such animus seemed highly out of place in a book extolling the virtues of Chinese Kung Fu generally, as it forced the book's narrative to change course. It went from being a general introduction to the wonderful art of Chinese Kung Fu to a statement on certain types of Chinese Kung Fu being more wonderful than others. The yin-yang principles of moderation and opposites complementing and being interdependent on each other (pages 80–83 of the book) had, with the turn of a page (quite literally, as the critique appears on page 84), now gone out the window.

"Gung Fu," Bruce wrote in his introduction, "is for health promotion, cultivation of mind, and self-protection. Its philosophy is based on the integral parts of the philosophies of Taoism, Ch'an (Zen) and the *I'Ching* (*Book of Changes*)."[33] If true, then Bruce's compass had drawn him seriously off course; he had forgotten the words of Chien-chih Seng-ts'an, the third Chinese Patriarch of Ch'an, who wrote in his principal text *On Trust in the Heart*:

> The Perfect Way is only difficult for those who pick
> and choose;
>> Do not like, do not dislike; all will then be clear.
>> Make a hairbreadth difference, and Heaven and
> Earth are set apart;
>> If you want the truth to stand clear before you,
> never be for or against.
>> The struggle between "for" and "against" is the mind's
> worst disease.[34]

The ending of Bruce's book made it quite clear that one style of Kung Fu was "superior" to all the others. And such a distinction, one might say, was considerably greater than a "hairbreadth difference." Bruce was advocating "for" his method, and "against" the method of Wong Tim Yuen. The martial arts community in San Francisco now became invested in the James Lee–Wong Tim Yuen feud, and Bruce Lee, as the chosen representative for James's side of the dispute, was center stage in the fracas. Even Bruce's friends and supporters in the martial arts community were a little taken aback by his new attitude. "When he ridiculed people, he wasn't very tactful," recalled Kenpo Karate master Ed Parker. "He didn't pull his punches at all. You don't make friends by telling people their way of doing things is full of shit. In Chinatown, I'd hear how unhappy they were about Bruce. They'd call him a wise punk."[35] Nevertheless, Bruce's former pitch about the glory of Chinese Kung Fu was out; that all other Kung Fu styles but his own were "full of shit" was the product he was selling in Oakland.

CHAPTER NINE

TURF WAR IN CHINATOWN

"Let us put it this way: ninety-nine percent of the whole business of Oriental self-defense is baloney. It's fancy jazz. It looks good, but it doesn't work."

— Bruce Lee (*St. Paul Dispatch*, 1968)

O n a fall evening in 1964, Bruce Lee walked through the front doors of the Sun Sing Theater in San Francisco's Chinatown. By his side was the famous Hong Kong movie star Diana Chang. That night, the Sun Sing was screening Chang's latest hit film, *The Amorous Lotus Pan*. In addition, Chang was going to speak to the audience about the film, sing a couple of songs, and then engage in some cha-cha dancing with Bruce (who was an exceptional cha-cha dancer by all accounts). It was also announced that Bruce would be putting on a brief Kung Fu demonstration after the show. To Chang's fans, it was a wonderful opportunity to see her in person. To certain martial artists within Chinatown, however, it represented an opportunity to see if Bruce Lee's Kung Fu was all that it was cracked up to be.

Diana Chang's popularity ensured the theater was at full capacity. *The Amorous Lotus Pan* was well received by the crowd, and, when Chang's show ended, a few patrons began to file out of the theater. The majority stayed. A show of a different sort was about to begin.

By this time in his life, Bruce Lee had but three things he wished to communicate during his public martial arts demonstrations: first, that most Chinese martial arts were largely ineffective; second, that his method of Kung Fu was superior; and third, that he had just opened a school in Oakland and was accepting students (and payment). And this was the message he had prepared to deliver once again at the Sun Sing Theater that evening. After a few words of introduction to the crowd, Bruce walked out on the stage. And this is where any clarity regarding what happened next ceases.

MUDDY WATER

Type "Bruce Lee, Wong Jack Man" into a search engine and a host of surprising headlines will come up: "The Brawl That Almost Broke Bruce Lee," "Bruce Lee's Toughest Fight," "Did Bruce Lee Lose to Wong Jack Man?" and "The Time Bruce Lee Was Challenged to a Real Fight." It is truly bizarre that of all the fights that Bruce Lee would engage in throughout his life, this one should have been made so much of. There have been a number of articles written in martial arts magazines about the fight, and every biography of Bruce Lee references it. Entire books have been devoted to it: Rick Wing's *Showdown in Oakland: The Story Behind the Wong Jack Man — Bruce Lee Fight* and Charles Russo's *Striking Distance: Bruce Lee & the Dawn of Martial Arts in America*. A feature film was produced about the scrap (*Birth of the Dragon*), and another movie (*Dragon: The Bruce Lee Story*) portrayed Bruce's adversary chasing him all the way to Thailand to fight and attacking him with a regularity that rivaled that of Cato Fong's attacks on Inspector Clouseau in *The Pink Panther* series. And yet, as far as fights go, it was neither man's finest moment.

The two martial artists did indeed fight, and both sides have at various times controlled the narrative regarding what happened.[1] In one version, Wong contacted Bruce by letter requesting a beimo, and then, on the agreed-upon date, showed up with a small group of martial artists at Bruce's school in Oakland to fight him. In the other version, Bruce issued a challenge from the stage of the Sun Sing Theater to any martial artist in San Francisco to come and fight with him. In the former, Wong Jack Man was the instigator of the fight; in the latter, Bruce was.

On Bruce Lee's passing in 1973, a huge and unanticipated interest in him immediately sprang up. In short order, an offer was extended to Linda Lee to write a biography of her late husband. This she did, and in 1975 her book *The Life and Tragic Death of Bruce Lee* was published in the UK, while a North American version of it was released under the title *Bruce Lee: The Man Only I Knew*. Even Bruce's students were encouraged to write books on Bruce and his art. His assistant instructor at his Los Angeles school, Dan Inosanto, wrote a book entitled *Jeet Kune Do: The Art and Philosophy of Bruce Lee*, which was published in 1976. In both Linda's and Inosanto's books, Wong Jack Man didn't come out of his fight with Bruce looking very good at all.

Wong's Kung Fu students then became angry, believing their master to have been defamed. They decided to take Wong's case public through the martial arts press. Wong's student Michael Dorgan[2] wrote an in-depth account of the Lee-Wong fight based on Wong Jack Man's side of the story. It was an effort to set the record straight while also shoring up Wong's reputation after the hit it was believed to have taken in the books. Dorgan painted Bruce Lee as the instigator of the whole affair in his article, "Bruce Lee's Toughest Fight," published in *Official Karate* magazine in 1980. He wrote: "Lee had boasted during a demonstration at a Chinatown theater that he could beat any martial artist in San Francisco and had issued an open challenge to fight anyone who thought he could prove him wrong."[3] Wong's version of the encounter now known, the matter died down for another thirteen years.

But then, in 1993, Universal Studios dredged it up again when it released the biopic *Dragon: The Bruce Lee Story*. The film did Wong no favors, having his character appear as a bloodthirsty racist who in one scene attacks Bruce from behind, injuring Bruce's back with a vicious sidekick. Once again, and quite understandably, Wong's students took offense.

Ten years later, in another effort to undo the damage to his teacher's reputation, Rick Wing, a student of Wong's and the man who would later become the chief instructor of Wong's school in San Francisco,[4] self-published an e-book on the fight entitled *Showdown in Oakland: The Story Behind the Wong Jack Man — Bruce Lee Fight*. Despite being published thirty-three years after Dorgan's article, the thesis was the same, particularly when it came to who was responsible for starting the fight: "He [Bruce Lee] then said that he was better than any martial artist in San Francisco, and would welcome the challenge of anyone who could prove him wrong. If anyone needed to be shown his skill, they could come to his studio and see for themselves. Others recall him saying that he was better than any man in San Francisco, or that he could best anyone in the city."[5]

But did he? According to the earliest accounts published on the matter, Bruce Lee denied saying any such thing from the stage of the Sun Sing Theater: "[Wong] somehow received information that Bruce had announced on stage that he would challenge anyone from the local Chinese community. The man initiated the fight with Bruce and wanted to show Bruce that the local Chinese were angry about his proclamation. Bruce insisted that he did not announce such a challenge."[6] And while Wong might well have "received information" that Bruce had issued such a challenge, the reality was that Wong hadn't attended the Sun Sing Theater on the night of Bruce's demonstration, and so could not have heard Bruce say anything — good, bad or otherwise.

As Bruce was the person who gave the demonstration at the theater, and the one who spoke to the crowd immediately afterwards, presumably he knew exactly what he did and didn't say. Indeed, in an interview given in 2017, Wong Jack Man revealed that Bruce had told him the same thing at his studio prior to their fight: "I asked him if he had issued a challenge at the Sun Sing Theater. He told me no, that he had not issued a challenge on stage."[7]

But perhaps Bruce was covering his own tracks. After all, a man issuing challenges to fight any and all comers wouldn't be seen as the highest example of martial virtue, but rather a brash punk looking to establish himself as the top dog (or "kung-fu cat," to use Bruce's terminology)[8] in the Bay Area. Such charges would be leveled at Bruce not only by others,[9] but even by himself[10] throughout his lifetime. But the issue at play wasn't whether Bruce Lee had once been a punk capable of issuing such a challenge, which he certainly was, but simply whether or not he issued a challenge to fight anyone in San Francisco from the stage of the Sun Sing Theater.

David Chin, who played no small role in setting up the fight between Bruce and Wong, said in his earliest account on the matter that "when I went with Wong and others to Oakland, the original intent was to discuss and learn more about martial arts (because Bruce once mentioned on stage that if any local Chinese were interested to discuss and learn about martial arts, they were welcome to visit his academy)."[11]

This early statement again indicates that Bruce had not issued a challenge to every martial artist in San Francisco to fight him, but rather to "visit his academy" if they were interested "to discuss and learn more about martial arts." According to the online Cambridge Dictionary, the term "discuss" means "the activity in which people talk about something and tell each other their ideas or opinions."[12] It has never been used as a synonym for "a challenge to fight," unlike, say, the term "compare." But then, Chin wasn't at the Sun Sing Theater either, so he also hadn't heard anything that Bruce had said from the stage of the Sun Sing. Perhaps, like Wong, he had been misinformed on the matter.

And so, apart from Bruce and David Chin's testimony, we are left with only one other early account. A "Long time reader" of the *Chinese Pacific Weekly*, who, fortunately, was in attendance at the Sun Sing Theater that fateful night, wrote a letter to the editor of the newspaper about what he heard Bruce say from the stage: "I personally was in the cinema and heard what he said. I believe he just meant you could come for a visit."[13]

The earliest accounts of what Bruce Lee said from the stage of the Sun Sing Theater, then, affirm that he invited his audience members to visit his school in Oakland to "discuss" martial arts and/or "learn" (i.e., become a student) of his art. He did not say "he could beat any martial artist in San Francisco," nor did he issue "an open challenge to fight anyone who thought he could prove him wrong." It's important to remember that Bruce's only reason for moving to Oakland was to open a Kung Fu school. He was recently married, and a baby was on the way, so his sole focus was on making money. His recent spate of demonstrations (which included Alameda, Long Beach, Los Angeles, and the one at San Francisco's Sun Sing Theater) were undertaken for no other purpose than getting the word out about his new school and drumming up business from the neighboring communities. Consequently, and despite what would be claimed many years after the fact, the evidence clearly indicates that Bruce did not challenge anyone from the San Francisco Kung Fu community to come and fight with him.

THE FAILED DEMONSTRATION HYPOTHESIS

However, for Wong's apologists to sell the story that Bruce had issued a challenge, there had to be a motive for him to do so. After all, this was completely out of character for Bruce — at least in terms of it being part of any demonstrations he had given up until this point. Something had to have set him off. He wouldn't simply challenge audience members to fight for the hell of it. However, none of the earliest Chinese newspaper accounts of the incident indicate Bruce having had any problems during his demonstration at the Sun Sing Theater that evening.

But as the years passed, an amazing phenomenon occurred: people's memories evidently got sharper rather than duller, and this was particularly the case for the San Francisco Chinatown contingent. Indeed something *did* happen that set Bruce Lee off that night, it was claimed. His demonstration, one he had given without any problem whatsoever in any of his previous performances against top martial artists, simply didn't work for him on this night. Consequently the audience jeered him and he became flustered and issued his challenge. Unfortunately, the memories of the people who provided their anecdotes about this occurring have failed to find common ground regarding what precisely it was during Bruce's demonstration that went awry.

One anecdote advanced by Wong's supporters was that Bruce attempted his famous one-inch punch on a volunteer from the audience and, for some unexplained reason, he couldn't execute it successfully. According to Wong Jack Man's student Rick Wing, the volunteer from the audience was Kenneth Wong, who was a student in Choy Lay Fut Kung Fu under Chan Bing, who in turn was a student of Lau Bun, an accomplished martial artist and enforcer for one of the tongs in San Francisco's Chinatown.[14] Wong Jack Man, however, would later say the man who was on stage with Bruce that evening was a "friend" of Bruce's, the White Crane Kung Fu instructor George Long.[15] In author Charles Russo's account, it is indeed Kenneth Wong who appears on stage, but he doesn't thwart Bruce's one-inch punch, but successfully (and repeatedly) blocks Bruce's speed punch.[16] Matthew Polly repeats Russo's account.[17]

Clearly there are some problems with these contradictory stories. Moreover, there is no evidence that Bruce ever failed in demonstrating his speed punch or one-inch punch, so there is considerable reason to conclude that this hypothesis was advanced solely to make Bruce appear to be the aggressor in the affair by supporters of his adversary, and to doubt that any of these scenarios occurred at all.

INSULTING THE CHINESE MARTIAL ARTS HYPOTHESIS

Much has been made by authors and Bruce Lee historians of the fact that Bruce had denigrated the traditional Chinese martial arts in his public demonstrations, and that this was the underlying issue that led to this particular encounter. It may well be true. However, it must be pointed out that a Kung Fu instructor putting down other Kung Fu styles in order to advance his own certainly wasn't a new or even a surprising phenomenon in the world of Chinese martial arts. Indeed, it has been common practice by proponents of different Kung Fu styles ever since those styles were created,[18] and for the same reason: business.

The old Kung Fu masters of San Francisco's Chinatown were well aware of this and accepted it; they'd seen it happen before in China, in Hong Kong, and, more recently, in America. New schools would open up with some hotshot instructor who claimed that what he was offering his students was better than what any of the older, more established schools were offering. Sometimes such an instructor would get an initial surge in student enrollment owing to the novelty that his approach represented, but then his members would thin out, his income would diminish, and his school would close. Such ephemeral occurrences only made the established Chinatown schools look better and stronger by comparison. In time, most of the students of the new instructor would find their way back to Chinatown, pay their dues, and the traditional Kung Fu classes would go on as usual.

James Lee was a perfect example of this. He had studied with Wong Tim Yuen in San Francisco, then decided to make a go of it on his own. He ultimately ended up teaching out of his garage to only a handful of students. The fact that he had recently partnered up with a university dropout from Seattle and opened a new school in Oakland wasn't going to change anything. The pattern would repeat itself. Without the support of the Chinatown community (youth centers, businesses, churches, schools and tongs) to drive students in a Kung Fu school's direction, any new enterprise was doomed before it started. It was simply the way of things.

And this was precisely why there had been no pushback from the San Francisco Kung Fu community against the content of Bruce's recent series of demonstrations. As long as he was running his business outside the borders of San Francisco, the community simply didn't care. Once again, they would simply wait until the thunder stopped and this particular rain cloud had moved on, just like all the others that had come and gone before. At least that had been the plan.

That plan changed when Bruce ventured onto the stage of the Sun Sing Theater in San Francisco and invited anyone in the crowd who was interested to cross over the Bay Bridge and check out his new school in Oakland. He had crossed a line. He was clearly attempting to draw potential students and their money (money that otherwise might have gone into the pockets of other Sifus in Chinatown) out of San Francisco. His offense, then, to the Chinatown Kung Fu teachers hadn't been that he'd disrespected the traditional Chinese arts during his sales pitches, rather it was that he had somehow worked up the nerve to come onto their turf and attempt to cut into their business. Bruce may not have known the full implications of what his sales pitch meant to the Kung Fu teachers in Chinatown, but, even if he did, he probably wouldn't have cared. He needed money and business was business.

The Kung Fu teachers in Chinatown weren't having it; they wanted Bruce's new school (read: rival business) shut down.[19] If the martial arts instructors in Alameda, Long Beach and Los Angeles were okay with Bruce Lee taking money out of their pockets, that was *their* problem. It wasn't going to happen in San Francisco. One of the Chinatown instructors that immediately had a problem with what Bruce had done was Chan Bing, the Choy Lay Fut teacher. He was incensed by the young man's brazenness.[20] However, Chan didn't want either his school or his master, the venerated Lau Bun, to be seen to be involved in the affair,[21] so he sought out someone else who he knew would take care of the matter for him. And that man was David Chin.

THE MIDDLEMAN

David Chin was born in Sun Wei city in Guangdong, a Chinese province about seventy-five miles west of Hong Kong. His father, Chin Chong, taught him Hop Gar Kung Fu when David was just seven years of age. By the time he turned thirteen, David and his family had immigrated to America, settling in Stockton, California, and while there he dabbled in various Kung Fu styles such as Choy Lay Fut, Hung Gar, and Buddha's Palm. But it was the art of Tai Chi that hooked him.[22] Indeed, it was this passion that gained Chin admittance into the Soft Arts Academy (Gee Yau Seah) in San Francisco's Chinatown. It was from this "Tai Chi Social Club," as Charles Russo called it, that the plan to bring down Bruce Lee was hatched.

It was an odd place for such a desire to take root, as Bruce had never publicly criticized the soft arts of China; indeed, it was his defense of these soft styles of Kung Fu that led to his being challenged by Yoichi Nakachi in 1960. It's also unclear why David Chin was willing to insinuate himself into the Chinatown proceedings. He hadn't attended the Sun Sing Theater on the night Bruce gave his demonstration, so all he could have possibly learned about it was from hearsay, which, as we've seen, was riddled with contradictions.

Still, Chan Bing's wish to have him involved, particularly given Chan's connection to Lau Bun, may have been reason enough. It was brought to Chin's attention that someone needed to be brought forth — somebody who was fast, skilled and not afraid to step up to a martial artist of Bruce Lee's caliber. Chin was realistic enough to recognize that he didn't fit the bill. But, as he looked around the Soft Arts Academy, his eyes eventually came to rest upon a newcomer to San Francisco's Chinatown, a man who was both a Tai Chi practitioner and a Northern Shaolin stylist. That man was Wong Jack Man.

WONG JACK MAN

Wong Jack Man was twenty-two years old and working as a waiter in Chinatown's Great Eastern Café. The restaurant was owned by Lau Yee Sing, who was David Chin's Tai Chi teacher. When Lau found out that his waiter was also a Tai Chi practitioner, he invited him to join the Soft Arts Academy and teach some Tai Chi classes. "When

I first arrived in San Francisco," Wong later recalled, "I taught at a social club for what you might call the 'big shots' of Chinatown, who were interested in Tai Chi Chuan and other traditional Chinese martial arts."[23] But Wong had ambitions of his own: "I was asked by my teachers, Yim Sheung Mo and Ma Kin Fung, to spread the Northern Shaolin, Taijiquan [Tai Chi Chuan] and Xingyiquan to America and the world."[24] In other words, Wong desperately wanted to open his own Kung Fu school.[25] And, as it was common practice for a student to kickback some of the money he made to his teacher, Wong's plan of spreading his teachers' martial arts in America was a way to both earn a living and pay respect (read: money) back to the ones who had taught him the craft that he was now planning to trade upon.

According to an article published in the *Chinese Pacific Weekly* newspaper in 1964, Bruce Lee was believed to have done the same thing with regard to Yip Man:

> Bruce started learning martial arts when he was young; he was once a child star. He went overseas to study, learned Kung Fu and Wing Chun. He was a student of Yip Man. With Bruce's fame and expertise, both Yip Man and Bruce's father received financial benefits.[26]

While there is no evidence that Bruce ever sent one penny of what little he earned to either his father or Yip Man, it was generally believed that most Chinese immigrants to America did send money back home because that had always been the Chinese way, an application of the Chinese proverb *yam shui si yuen*: when you drink the water, remember its source.

Both of Wong's teachers had studied under the famous Northern Shaolin master Gu Ruzhang and were members of the prestigious Ching-wu School, which, from its inception, had been very much a commercial enterprise.[27] Of course Ching-wu was not alone in this respect; all instruction in any Kung Fu style was a business first and foremost, and each instructor charged as much as the market would bear for instruction in his method. Money then, like now, greased the wheels of the martial arts industry and allowed them to roll slowly but steadily into the twentieth century. And, without exception, Wong Jack Man, Bruce Lee, Lau Bun, T.Y. Wong, Chan Bing, David Chin and Lau Yee Sing each wanted their share of it.

David Chin liked the fact that Wong Jack Man had ambition. He could work with that. And given that Chin's Tai Chi teacher was not only Wong's boss, but also, in Wong's eyes, a "big shot" in Chinatown, he was also a man who could help spread the word necessary for Wong to realize his Kung Fu school ambitions and honor his teachers back in Hong Kong. Chin realized that these factors provided him sufficient leverage to approach the young man and exert some influence over him.

First, Chin praised his fellow Soft Arts Academy member (and younger Tai Chi brother) for his fighting ability. "They were impressed by my skills," Wong would later recall.[28] But Tai Chi alone wasn't going to be enough to take down Bruce Lee. Chin moved on to express admiration for Wong's skill in the Northern Shaolin style. "People were impressed," Wong said, "because they had never seen the Northern Shaolin system, which is both powerful and acrobatic. It includes high kicks, big leaps, aggressive long-range attacks and whirling, circular blocks."[29]

The bird seed having been laid out, Chin introduced a new subject. Wong wouldn't be told that Bruce merely invited those who were interested to visit his studio in Oakland to discuss martial arts; that wouldn't rouse any sense of moral indignation in him. Instead, he was told that a young and arrogant martial artist by the name of Bruce Lee had recently insulted the martial artists in San Francisco's Chinatown, calling them "old tigers with no teeth," and, even more insultingly, he claimed that his Kung Fu system was superior to all other traditional Chinese martial arts.[30] To cap things off, Wong was told that Bruce had "issued a public challenge to anyone who thought he was better than him" from the stage of the Sun Sing Theater.[31]

"The Chinatown martial arts community decided it needed to respond," Wong recalled, "and that I was the best-qualified person to exchange skills with Bruce Lee."[32] Wong was savvy enough to see the bigger picture of what was being presented to him. The men who could make his dream of opening a Kung Fu school a reality would look favorably upon any man who took care of the Bruce Lee problem for them, particularly if he could do so without involving the masters (or students) of the more established schools in San Francisco's Chinatown. Wong had nothing to lose by agreeing to fight Bruce on their behalf. Or so he thought.

CHALLENGE LETTERS

Having secured Wong's agreement, David Chin next conferred with Chan Bing.[33] It was decided that a letter should be written to Bruce issuing a challenge. According to the *Chinese Pacific Weekly* newspaper, Bruce received not one but two letters from Wong Jack Man, both of which were challenges to fight.[34] Bruce evidently ignored the first letter and so it was decided that a second letter should be sent. However, to ensure that Bruce received the letter it would not be entrusted to the U.S. postal service, but be hand-delivered. Upon receiving the second letter Bruce wrote Wong back to say he wasn't interested in having a match in San Francisco, but if Wong really wanted to fight, he would be willing to fight him at his studio in Oakland.[35] Bruce's reply, according to Wong's student Michael Dorgan, was what set the fight in motion: "The reason he [Wong Jack Man] showed up at Lee's school . . . is because a mutual acquaintance had hand-delivered a note from Lee inviting him to fight. The note was sent, says Wong, after he had requested a public bout with Lee."[36]

David Chin is the "mutual acquaintance" referred to by Dorgan, but he was more an acquaintance of Wong's than Bruce's. Chin admitted to being the one who delivered Wong's second letter to Bruce and he was also the person who delivered Bruce's reply to Wong. According to Chin, the letter he delivered to Bruce was placed in a sealed envelope, which he carried on his person as he left the Soft Arts Academy in Chinatown and drove east across the Bay Bridge into Oakland. Thirty minutes later he pulled up at 4157 Broadway, the location of Bruce Lee's Kung Fu studio. He parked the car, walked to the door of the studio, knocked, and stepped inside.[37]

Bruce was seated behind a desk just to the side of the door reading a Chinese martial arts novel when Chin entered. Linda Lee was standing nearby.

"Are you Lee Siu Loong ["Lee Little Dragon" — Bruce's marquee name in Chinese]?" Chin asked.

"Yeah, you're looking for me?"

"I have a letter for you."

Bruce held out his hand and Chin handed him the letter. Bruce pulled out the document and scanned its contents. He then looked up at Chin. "Okay, that's no problem." Reaching into his desk drawer, Bruce pulled out a single sheet of paper and a pen. He quickly jotted down his reply, placed it in an envelope, and then handed it to Chin. "I accept the challenge," he said matter-of-factly. "But you come to *my* school. I'm not going anywhere."

Chin nodded and returned to his car. Once back in San Francisco, he presented Bruce Lee's letter to Wong Jack Man.

Wong read its contents and said, "We go over there then."

"It was not a friendly atmosphere," Chin would later recall. "The challenge was real."[38]

THE RIGHT TO TEACH NON-CHINESE

In 1975, some eleven years after the fight took place, Linda Lee would claim that Wong's letter to Bruce (which she described as a "scroll") said that if Bruce "lost the challenge, he was either to close down his Institute or stop teaching Caucasians."[39] She would later repeat this claim in the 2000 Warner Bros. documentary *Bruce Lee: A Warrior's Journey*,[40] and it was corroborated by Bruce Lee's friend and assistant instructor at his Seattle school, Taky Kimura:

> One of the things that got Bruce into a little bit of dissension with his Chinese peers over was that . . . Gung Fu or Kung Fu, or whatever you want to call it, was existent in this country ever since way back in the early 1900s, but nobody ever heard of it because the Chinese kept it to themselves. They didn't want to teach outsiders because they knew that that was going to be bad. So, even at that point they felt like, "Hey, you should teach the Chinese but, for Christ's sake, don't teach anybody else, because it's going to cause us trouble in the long run." And Bruce's whole theory was, "Hey, I don't care what color you are, if you show me that you have sincerity of heart I'm going to teach

you." Even up here [in Seattle] there was some, the elders in the community, [who] were probably a little bit concerned that he was teaching outsiders, you know? I think that they felt like he was kind of doing something that was a betrayal, but there was nothing made of it up here to my knowledge. But when he went down there [Oakland], the elders in the community took it a little bit more [seriously] than they did up here.[41]

Indeed. Even the Chinese newspaper in San Francisco felt obliged to mention that Bruce had "accepted foreign students. He ended up with many students; they are all blue- or green-eyed young people."[42]

But writing some forty-nine years later, Rick Wing, a student of Wong Jack Man, maintained that Bruce's teaching non-Chinese was never an issue to the San Francisco Chinatown community, and thus not a topic that was broached in the letters that Wong wrote to Bruce: "The letter did not mention Lee's right to teach non-Chinese. [Chan Bing] himself, after all, already had non-Chinese (i.e., white) students in his studio, and other Sifus in Chinatown had already taught non-Chinese. The teaching of non-Chinese was, quite simply, a non-issue."[43]

This is not historically correct. While Chan Bing would allow non-Chinese students into his own studio, he didn't have a studio when the fight was being set up in 1964. In fact, Chan would not open a studio of his own until 1967, three years after Wong and Bruce had fought.[44] In 1964, Chan was still operating out of Lau Bun's Wah Keung studio, and all students and instructors in Lau's school followed Lau's rules — Kung Fu was not to be taught to non-Chinese.[45] Consequently, when the letter to Bruce Lee was drafted, it is quite likely that Chan Bing, out of respect to Lau Bun's policy, made sure to include a statement to the effect that Bruce teaching foreigners was not acceptable.[46]

Long-time Oakland resident and *Black Belt* Hall of Fame martial artist Leo Fong, who was in touch with both Bruce and James Lee during this period (in addition to knowing most of their opponents), believes the fight occurred because both men were manipulated by a third party: "It was instigated by David Chin, a troublemaker, who went back and forth saying one thing to Wong Jack Man and then to Bruce saying 'Wong Jack Man said this.' Bruce finally got pissed off and said, 'Bring the bastard over here!'"[47]

There is some evidence that Bruce Lee also believed Chin to be responsible for stirring up the trouble between him and Wong. The *Chinese Pacific Weekly* reported that, "Bruce said this so-called fight was caused by some misinformation that [Wong] received from a third party."[48] Whoever the catalyst was behind setting up this fight was irrelevant at this point. The wheels were now fully in motion.

CHAPTER TEN

RUMBLE IN OAKLAND

"Most important of all, you must have complete determination. The worst opponent you can come across is one whose aim has become an obsession. For instance, if a man has decided that he is going to bite off your nose no matter what happens to him in the process, the chances are he will succeed in doing it."

— Bruce Lee (*New Nation* [Singapore], 1972)

On a mild night in October 1964,[1] Wong Jack Man, David Chin, Chan Keung (another member of the Soft Arts Academy),[2] along with Ronald Wu, Martin Wong and Raymond Fong (three friends of Chin's),[3] piled into Chin's Pontiac and drove to Oakland to confront Bruce Lee.

Wong Jack Man, dressed in his black Kung Fu uniform,[4] was deadly serious; very little was said during the eleven-mile car ride to Bruce Lee's studio.[5] "It was a deserted part of town," Wong would later recall, "and we arrived at exactly 6:00 p.m. His school was an empty storefront with no business sign."[6] The six men remained seated in the car for a few minutes. Another of Chin's friends, Bill Chen, was said to be arriving soon with two friends to watch the match.[7]

As the men waited, Wong pulled out a pair of studded leather bracelets and fastened them to his wrists. Each bracelet was between two and three-and-a-half inches wide with rows of small metal studs protruding throughout the length and width.[8] These not only provided supplemental wrist support for blocking and striking, but also were particularly dangerous things to hit somebody with. The bracelets were certainly not part of the standard uniform of a Northern Shaolin or Tai Chi practitioner.[9] For a man who possessed "kicks of blinding speeds and crushing power," as his student Michael Dorgan would later claim, but who, it was also said, would not use his kicks in this fight because he thought they were too dangerous,[10] Wong evidently had no compunction about the damage he could do to his opponent by strapping on a pair of these bad boys. "I was surprised; I didn't expect it," Chin would later recall.[11] Wong then pulled the sleeves of his Kung Fu jacket over the bands to conceal them from view[12] and stepped from the car.

Bill Chen and his two friends arrived on the scene. Chin and his crew exited the car and walked over to speak with the new arrivals. After a brief discussion, Chin, Wong, Chen and one other man broke from the group and headed toward the studio. Their plan was to meet with Bruce and set down the rules of the engagement. The remaining five members of the party remained outside for the time being. All told, there were nine people from San Francisco's Chinatown who had made the trip to Oakland that evening to lend moral support to Wong Jack Man.

Waiting inside the studio were Bruce, his wife Linda, James Lee and another of Bruce's Oakland students, George Lee (no relation). When George saw David Chin's car pull up in front of the studio, he went out the back door to see if anybody else was coming. He would wait outside for the duration of the encounter.[13] James wasn't taking any chances either; knowing that the Chinatown martial artists had connections to the Hop Sing Tong, he went to the desk by the front door, where he'd placed a revolver.[14] A challenge match was the type of thing that could go off the rails quickly, and James wanted to be prepared. When he saw the four men approaching, he walked to the front door of the studio and let them in.[15] He then closed the door and returned to stand with Linda next to the desk.

Once inside, the four men[16] looked around the studio. It wasn't impressive. "Lee's studio was about thirty feet long and twenty feet wide, with few chairs or stools, like an empty store," Wong recalled.[17] Formerly a garment shop, the front door of the building was recessed back from two showcase windows. A wall with two doors was situated about fifteen feet in from the front door, serving to divide the room into two sections, and a rear door in the back led outside. Hardwood flooring ran the length and breadth of the unit.[18]

When they entered the studio, Bruce was writing something out with chalk on a blackboard. His back was turned to the men, as if he were oblivious to their having entered. He continued writing, making them wait, then slammed the chalk down on the lip of the blackboard.[19] The noise shattered the calm in the studio. Bruce now turned and advanced toward the four men. He was dressed casually in a pair of jeans and a white tank top.[20]

Seeking to prevent the fight starting before the rules were established, David Chin stepped forward to signify his position as the overseer of the match. As the two combatants had never met face-to-face, Chin began by formally introducing Wong Jack Man to Bruce Lee. The two martial artists shook hands.[21] That would mark the end of any civility between the two parties that day.

Bruce now assumed control of the room.

"Did *you* directly witness me announce a challenge?"

"No, I didn't," Wong replied. "Nevertheless, I had indirectly heard about this. Therefore, I have to teach you a lesson!"[22]

Bruce gestured toward David Chin. "You've been killed by your friend. He's going to ruin your life."

Wong said nothing.

"Is this what you want?" Bruce asked.

"Well, no, this is not what I want — but I'm representing these people."

Bruce shrugged. "Okay, then."

Linda Lee recalled that "this had an extraordinary effect on Wong Jack Man and his supporters. Obviously, they had imagined that Bruce was a paper tiger — that faced with an actual challenge by a skilled practitioner like Wong Jack Man, he would simply chicken out. They went into what I can only describe as a huddle." While Wong and his men were talking, the five men who had been waiting outside now entered the building. As soon as they were inside, James Lee walked to the front door and bolted it shut.[23] The Chinatown contingent now outnumbered Bruce's by a ratio of nine-to-three (not including Linda), and he wanted to ensure that no one else would be coming in to alter the odds any further.

Wong Jack Man approached Bruce. "The intention of our visit was to have a friendly sparring match."[24]

"We just want to discuss martial arts," added David Chin.[25]

"I don't do *friendly sparring matches*," Bruce replied cooly. "I want a match with a definitive result!"[26]

"We are just going to spar," Wong reiterated. "We'll follow the universal standard rules in a match: no poking the eyes, no grabbing the throat or kicking the groin . . ."

"You came to *my* school to challenge me and now *you* want to set the rules? I'm not standing for any of that! You've come here with an ultimatum and a challenge hoping to scare me off. *You've* made the challenge — so *I'm* making the rules. So far as I'm concerned, it's no-holds-barred. It's *all out*."

Wong and his supporters had to know that a real fight was what they had asked for in their letters. Even if Bruce Lee had issued a challenge to fight anyone from any Kung Fu school in Chinatown, his invitation had not been for a "friendly" sparring session. And why, if David Chin's statement is to be believed, would Wong strap on a pair of studded bracelets to "discuss martial arts?" Perhaps the belief was that if Bruce witnessed Wong perform a couple of forms from Northern Shaolin, or even faced him in some light sparring, it would cause Bruce to back down, apologize, and, ideally, perhaps close shop and move away. In truth, a sparring session was about all that Wong Jack Man was capable of. There exists no record of him ever having been in a real fight before this time.[27]

Regardless of what any of the Chinatown contingent might have thought beforehand, it was now obvious to everyone in the room that a real fight was about to go down.

Bruce motioned for Wong to step forward to face him in the center of the room.[28] The onlookers moved to the periphery.[29] The tale of the tape for the bout was:

- Bruce Lee, twenty-three years old, five feet seven-and-a-half inches tall, and weighing approximately 135 pounds.

- Wong Jack Man, twenty-two years old, five feet ten inches tall, and weighing approximately 135 pounds.[30]

Wong Jack Man bowed his head slightly[31] and then assumed the traditional stance of Northern Shaolin.[32] Bruce raised his hands in the Wing Chun ready position.[33] For a brief moment he might have experienced a slight case of déjà vu recalling his rooftop fight with Robert Chung, who was also a Northern Shaolin exponent. But this time around Bruce would not have Wong Shun Leung in his corner. There were no timekeepers, no referees — and no rules. There also was no one designated to announce the start of the fight, so Bruce took that role upon himself.

"Bam!" A lead vertical fist strike from Bruce landed flush on Wong's orbital bone, which snapped his head back.[34] Bruce followed up with a series of straight punches,[35] just as he had in his previous fights against Robert Chung and Yoichi Nakachi. However, those opponents had remained flat-footed during their fights with Bruce; Wong, in an effort to recover from the impact of Bruce's first punch (and also to get away from the onslaught of strikes now coming at him at full throttle), began to backpedal — quickly.[36] As Bruce attacked, he let out loud yells or war cries[37] that further unsettled his opponent.

Wong recalled: "He started to make these loud, horrifying sounds — like a ghost screaming is the only way I can describe it. I never heard sounds like that before in my life, and they were scaring everyone in the room. He continued to swear, yell and utter the terrifying sounds as he repeatedly tried to attack my eyes, throat and groin in between throwing straight punches at my chest."[38]

The punches and the war cries kept on coming. Wong would later estimate that "Bruce used his fists about sixty times and kicked about twenty-five times. Bruce also used eye jabs."[39] With Bruce pressing the attack, Wong realized that his backpedaling wasn't gaining him enough space to defend himself or launch any effective counterstrikes.[40] It was at this point that he turned and began to run, hoping to put some distance between himself and Bruce.[41]

Spying an open door in the partition wall, Wong ran toward it with Bruce, still punching at him, in hot pursuit.

David Chin and some of the others in Wong's crew stepped forward as if to stop the fight, which clearly wasn't going as well for their man as they had envisioned. James Lee yelled out to them to let the fight continue.[42]

Wong charged through one of the two doors in the partition wall with Bruce still on his heels. A moment later, the two men passed through the other door in the wall, reemerging into the main room of the studio.[43]

The fight continued on in the same fashion in which it started, with Bruce throwing rapid-fire chain punches and Wong moving as fast as possible in the opposite direction. Wong tried to fire back as best he could, throwing his arms back towards Bruce in a circular pattern in an attempt to hold him off. Certain of these techniques grazed Bruce's forehead and neck, leaving scratch marks.[44] Bruce pressed forward, his punches still coming in volleys, with Wong backpedaling towards the front door of the studio.[45]

Bruce sensed that he was rapidly running out of energy,[46] and this filled him with a sense of panic — which, in turn, pumped a final shot of adrenaline into his system. Like nitrous on an engine, he exploded forward[47] and took Wong to the ground.[48] A very narrow window had now opened: if Bruce couldn't end the fight within the next thirty seconds, he would be completely out of gas.[49] If Wong was still fresh, or at least fresher than Bruce was, the tide could turn — dramatically.

Bruce began to punch down at his supine opponent; some would later claim that these punches connected,[50] while others would claim that Wong deflected them.[51]

"*Lei fook mh fook ah?*" (Do you yield?) Bruce yelled between punches. "I yield, I yield!"[52]

Wong's associates moved in and separated the fighters.[53] As soon as Bruce stood up, Wong, in what would prove to be his last (perhaps only) offensive move of the encounter, attempted to sweep Bruce's legs out from underneath him.

In speaking to Taky Kimura afterward, Bruce said, "God damn it! While I was standing there and I was making him admit that he gave up, he tried to foot sweep me! He damn near got me; I was so damn tired. But I cracked him a few more times and that was the end of it."[54]

THE AFTERMATH

Wong Jack Man got to his feet, embarrassed and angry. He believed that the Chinatown contingent had misled him about Bruce Lee. "I learned from the fight not to trust what I hear from others," he would later recall. "I must analyze and research the truth and evidence before I act on it."[55]

For his part, Bruce was also angry — at himself: "The more I think of him to have fought me without getting blasted bad, the more I'm pissed off! If I just took my time, [but] anger screwed me up — that bum is nothing!"[56]

Bruce was also angry at himself for not having anticipated Wong's mobility, particularly his running away. Bruce's previous experience in fighting a practitioner of the Northern Shaolin style had seen his opponent rush straight toward him, which, of course, made Bruce's punches far more accurate and impactful. Wong had proven to be the exception to Bruce's long-held rule that every fight should be over quickly[57] — clearly, this was no longer something about which categorical rules could be made beforehand. It was also clear to him that he lacked the physical conditioning necessary for a protracted battle.[58]

Bruce and Wong Jack Man were united on one thing: their anger at David Chin, whom they now both believed to have been the instigator of the whole affair.[59] Wong said nothing, but Bruce turned to Chin and vented his spleen. "I shouldn't have beat up Wong Jack Man! I should have beat the hell out of *you!*"[60] Wong recalled that "Bruce was so angry that he cursed him [Chin], and that person became very frightened and nervous. All the people in the room were scared, and the tension was high."[61] Leo Fong would add, "I don't blame Wong Jack Man; the guy was a victim of circumstances. But David Chin had started the fight." Fong also recounted that, after Bruce yelled at Chin, "David got scared and took off."[62]

Wong Jack Man left the studio, followed by Chin's friends and fellow martial artists from San Francisco. The group split up, got in their cars, and headed back to Chinatown. The mood, according to Chin, was "sullen."[63] Neither Wong Jack Man nor Bruce Lee could have imagined that this encounter would be held up as one of the most significant fights in American martial arts history.

CHAPTER ELEVEN

PAYBACK

"There should be no *method* of fighting. There should only be tools to use as effectively as possible."

— Bruce Lee (*Washington Star*, 1970)

M any years after Bruce Lee's death, Wong Jack Man would claim that Bruce "threw away his system [Wing Chun] after the fight because it had not worked for him, and began developing his own system, Jeet Kune Do."[1]

Despite the claim, Bruce wasn't looking to discard Wing Chun immediately after his match with Wong. Indeed, the historical evidence indicates the opposite: that rather than pitching the art aside, he believed he was missing some element of it that might prove beneficial to his progress as a martial artist. At the very least, he wanted to learn more about the fighting application of the Wooden Dummy form — and he wanted Yip Man to teach it to him.[2]

This strong desire to further his training in the art, along with his wish (and familial obligation) to introduce his wife and infant son (Brandon, who was born on February 1) to his parents and siblings, led Bruce, Linda and little Brandon to board a plane and fly to Hong Kong in May of 1965.[3] He intended to stay there for the duration of the summer. Plenty of time to pick up a few pointers to sharpen his game.

APPROACHING THE MASTER

Shortly after his arrival, Bruce encountered an old friend from his early days at Yip's school, Hawkins Cheung. "I've come back to further my training in Wing Chun," Bruce said. "And I hope to learn more of the [wooden] dummy techniques from the old man [Yip Man]. Hopefully, Sifu will let me film him on 8mm, so that I may show my students in the U.S. . . . I'm on my way to see the old man now."[4] In truth, Bruce hoped that Yip would not only allow himself to be filmed performing the Wooden Dummy form, but also the first three empty-hands forms of Wing Chun: Sil Lum Tao, Chum Kiu and Biu Ji. He hadn't purchased a Super 8mm camera yet, as that would be putting the cart before the horse. But if Yip Man agreed to his request, Bruce planned to buy the highest-quality one he could find so that the films would be pristine.[5] He believed the films would be a great learning module for his assistant instructors in America, Taky Kimura and James Lee, providing them with a means to see the fundamentals of the Wing Chun art performed by its foremost master.

He was in for a rude awakening. Upon hearing the request, Yip Man flatly refused it. Bruce was only one of his pupils and Yip had never granted such a request to any of his students. To do so for Bruce would be to show favoritism, and that was something that the old master was not prepared to do.[6] Besides, the old man was no fool — he knew that Bruce intended to use the footage to assist him in teaching Wing Chun to the gwai lo, and he had no desire to have a movie made of himself demonstrating Wing Chun if it was for the purpose of teaching non-Chinese.[7] Certainly Bruce was aware of Yip Man's attitude on this matter; he had, after all, made Doug Palmer pretend he knew nothing of Wing Chun while in Yip's presence two years previously. But he was also aware that there was no point in pressing the issue with Yip; the Kung Fu master wasn't going to change his mind.

SPARRING THE STUDENTS

Despite Yip Man's refusal, or perhaps because of it, Bruce went to Yip's school to show the senior students how much his Kung Fu had improved — even without his knowing all of the intricacies of the Wing Chun system. He had a special motivation for doing so, as the senior students were not only responsible for having him kicked out of the school in 1958 but also had done their best to make Bruce's training while in the school a living hell. When practicing the sticking hands drill with Bruce and other newcomers to the art, the senior students had taken delight in roughing them up. "Those bastards enjoyed overpowering us," Bruce later recalled. "And as we weakened they used to slap us on our chest and face."[8] Seven years later, Bruce was now looking forward to giving them a taste of their own medicine.

Yip Man knew why Bruce had shown up at his school. Eager to see if and how Bruce had improved in his Kung Fu, he decided it might be best to have Bruce spar some of the students who were in attendance that day — rather than his most senior students, many of whom were now assistant instructors in the art. If Bruce made it past the students, then perhaps Yip would allow his instructors to try him on. Bruce nodded and moved to the center of the room. Yip had his pupils form a single line and then motioned for the lead student to step forth to face Bruce.

It couldn't have gone worse for Yip's disciple.

"The guy was so baffled by my moves," Bruce would later recall. "I kept moving in and out, letting go kicks and punches, never gave him a chance to recover his balance. I guess he got so frustrated because every blow I let go would have hit him if I didn't control it."

It was immediately apparent that this was not the same Bruce Lee many of them had known in 1958. Yip Man was impressed. He motioned for the next student in line to step forth. Once again, Bruce made the young man look foolish.

"The next guy was just as frustrated, because I kept throwing fakes and he kept biting. Once he got suckered and almost fell onto his face. I didn't even touch him."

Having effortlessly dispatched the two students, Bruce turned to face the assistant instructors in the room. Now it was *their* turn. To his surprise, not one of them was willing. "Those mothers, they chickened out," Bruce recalled some years later. "I sure would like to have sparred them. These were the same guys who gave me a bad time when I first studied Wing Chun. I was a skinny kid of 15 and these guys even then were already assistant instructors to Yip Man. Well I guess they saw enough and didn't want to make an ass of themselves."[9]

It's hard to know what Yip Man thought of this, though he no doubt recognized it for being the face-saving maneuver that it was. But he had a better idea. Rather than sparring, a better test of Bruce's skills in Wing Chun would be if he engaged in *chi sao*, the sticking hands drill of Wing Chun. After all, it would still allow contact, as it had been during sticking hands practice in the mid-1950s that the senior students had battered a younger Bruce around the studio floor. However, it would also determine how refined Bruce's defensive and tactile skills had become. For this exercise Bruce would need a talented partner, one who was exceptional in the practice of sticking hands. And Yip Man had an assistant instructor at his school that day who fit the bill and had no concerns about stepping up to engage with Bruce: Wong Shun Leung.

ENGAGING THE MASTERS

Wong was still the number one fighter in the Wing Chun system. He had lost just once in somewhere between sixty and one hundred beimo challenge matches,[10] and that was at a tournament in Formosa in 1957 where, according to Bruce, judging politics had been in play.[11] What Wong and Bruce were about to engage in was not a beimo, of course, but merely a training exercise that would allow both Wong and Yip to see how much Bruce had actually improved in Wing Chun.

Wong approached Bruce in the center of the room. The two men touched arms and went at it. To Wong's surprise, Bruce not only held his own, but was scoring on him during the encounter. This had never happened before — unless Wong wanted a student to score on him.[12] That Bruce could do so despite Wong's attempts to prevent it surprised his former teacher and made him smile. Wong was proud of him, and recognized just how hard he must have trained during the years he'd been away to bring his sticking hands skill up to such a high level.[13] Yip Man was similarly impressed; for Bruce to have dominated some of his students was one thing, but to hold his own in sticking hands against Wong Shun Leung was something else entirely.[14]

At this point Yip stood up and walked out onto the floor of his studio to perform some sticking hands with Bruce, who had to know this was coming. Yip saw something in Bruce's sticking hands performance that he wanted to experience directly. But as soon as they touched arms, Yip was disappointed; it was clear that Bruce was no longer trying. He had too much respect for Yip Man to attempt to assert himself against the master. He had his opportunities, no doubt some openings were deliberately provided by Yip, but Bruce continued to hold back. He felt that fighting back would have been disrespectful, particularly in front of Yip's students. Yip's disappointment now gave way to anger: he began to push Bruce hard, striking him as often as Bruce's defenses allowed, in an effort to get him to engage more meaningfully. It was to no avail.[15]

When his students left, however, Yip told Bruce to stick around. He wanted details as to what he had done to improve his skills so dramatically — particularly given that Bruce had been training on his own for the past several years. Bruce answered the master's questions and Yip took down notes of what he told him.[16] This made Bruce quite proud.[17] What happened next made him even prouder. Yip said he would allow Bruce to take photographs of him demonstrating the Siu Lum Tao form and various self-defense techniques of Wing Chun. This was music to Bruce's ears, as he had plans of writing a book on the art when he went back to the United States.[18] According to Robert Chan, Bruce's Hong Kong friend, "Yip Man didn't like to be photographed, but Bruce's request was the exception. Bruce was one of Yip Man's favorite students because of his dedication to the martial arts."[19]

CREATING A NEW KUNG FU

While the photos of Yip Man performing Siu Lum Tao would be incredible material for a book on Wing Chun, it had become obvious to Bruce that, in terms of his own progress as a fighter, learning all the forms and techniques of the Wing Chun system wasn't necessary. Learning the entire system would require him to spend considerable time on things like long pole and butterfly knife training — things that he could never envision himself using in a street fight situation. Besides, Siu Lum Tao, the first form of Wing Chun, was the most important form because it contained the lion's share of the art's empty-hand techniques.[20] Together with Bruce's knowledge of the techniques for fighting that Wong Shun Leung had taught him, sticking hands, trapping and what he already knew of the Wooden Dummy form, he had a pretty good base to build from. "I don't think that learning the whole system would have made much difference unless Bruce stayed in Hong Kong," Jesse Glover said. "It was the size of the people in the U.S., the lack of instruction, and his desire to surpass his seniors that made him change his approach to fighting. People have to realize that the brand of Wing Chun that Bruce found most useful were the techniques that the leading fighters in the clan actually used in fights."[21]

Whatever fighting principles Bruce lacked, he resolved to figure out on his own. Still, even a cursory review of Bruce's letters from Hong Kong to his assistant instructors in America during the summer of 1965 reveal that the art of Wing Chun remained front and center:

- "My style has now been formed. . . . Wing Chun principle is the nucleus (the most important foundation)."[22]
- "I'm having a Gung Fu system drawn up — this system is a combination of chiefly Wing Chun, fencing and boxing."[23]
- "Glad to hear you're [James Lee] practicing Sil Lum Tao and am especially happy to hear you understand that Sil Lum Tao is all the ways of the Wing Chun Hand [system] in a nutshell . . . anything for the betterment of Wing Chun."[24]
- "In my formation of a more complete Wing Chun I've added on an INDIRECT PROGRESSIVE ATTACK to the original chi sao [sticking hands], which is close quarter combat. Indirect Progressive Attack is the link to achieve chi sao. Indirect Progressive Attack is used against an opponent whose self-defense is tight and fast enough to deal with Simple Attacks like Straight Blast, Finger Jab, and Trapping Hit."[25]

The last letter is particularly interesting as it reveals that, rather than throwing away his Wing Chun because he no longer believed it was practical, Bruce had actually discovered a method to bridge the gap between himself and an opponent. This allowed him to employ his Wing Chun techniques against an opponent who did not rush in or who otherwise stood just outside of striking range.

TRUE REFINEMENT SEEKS SIMPLICITY

Contrary to Wong Jack Man's claim that Bruce threw away his Wing Chun after their fight and began developing his own system, it is important to note that Bruce had been in a continuously evolving process of martial evolution long before the two of them had locked horns in Oakland. Indeed, it could be argued that he had been modifying his Kung Fu ever since he was kicked out of Yip Man's school in the late 1950s. While still in living Hong Kong, he learned the forms of several Kung Fu styles from the instructor Siu Hon-San[26] and had even studied the fundamentals of Judo under Fung Ngai.[27] Upon arriving in Seattle, he learned forms from various Kung Fu styles from Fook Yeung[28] and also began investigating Western boxing, studying Jack Dempsey's drop step and vertical fist punching,[29] in addition to resuming his study of Judo under the instructorship of Shuzo Kato.[30] He further examined the footwork and attack principles of fencing after watching his older brother Peter in action.[31] This had been and would remain the continuum of evolution that Bruce Lee was on. According to Doug Palmer:

> When I had gone to Hong Kong with him [in 1963] he was still basically doing Wing Chun. And from that point forward, every time I came back on vacation from school, either Christmas vacation or summer vacation, and I went back to the old [Seattle Kung Fu] school, everything that had gone before was a subset of his expanded vision. His base was still Wing Chun, but it was more than that. He had, for example, incorporated what he called "broken rhythm," where he would throw a blow in kind of a rhythm, where it would seem to go one speed and then slow down and start again, and it would throw your timing off. Like a change-up [in baseball] kind of, but it was all one movement. And you would try to block it — and it wasn't there; it came in right after your block. I mean things like that, that were not part of Wing Chun, that he would kind of graft on but not graft on in an artificial way. I mean it was a very organic, functional [evolution] of what he was doing. And a lot of it came from other fighting styles.[32]

Given that Bruce doubled down on the central importance of Wing Chun in his personal Kung Fu system immediately after his fight with Wong Jack Man, even taking over 200 photos of Yip Man to write a book on the art, where did Wong — who never saw Bruce again after their match — get the idea that Bruce threw away Wing Chun and changed his methods as a direct result of their fight?

I suspect that the foundation of this misperception comes from a quote attributed to Bruce published in a special magazine devoted to him in 1974. In an article entitled "Bruce Lee: The Man, the Fighter, the Superstar," Bruce is quoted as saying: "I'd gotten into a fight in San Francisco with a kung-fu cat, and after a brief encounter the son-of-a-bitch started to run. I chased him and, like a fool, kept punching him behind his head and back. Soon my fists began to swell from hitting his hard head. Right then I realized Wing Chun was not too practical and began to alter my way of fighting."[33]

But did Bruce Lee ever say this?

The reason the quotation must be questioned is that Mitoshi Uyehara, the author of the article and the founder and publisher of *Black Belt* magazine, admitted to me in 1994 that most of the articles he wrote and published on Bruce contained quotes from interviews that never took place.[34] Therefore, most of the quotations attributed to Bruce that appeared in Uyehara's articles (which would include the one above) came solely from recollections of Uyehara, often under the noms de plume of Mitch Stom and Mike Plane.[35]

Uyehara has said he was comfortable concocting such quotes because he "knew Bruce so well."[36] That he knew Bruce well is not in question. That he possessed an unerring sense of recall when quoting him several years after the fact has to be. Another reason to doubt the validity of the above quote is that in 1988, fourteen years after it first appeared in print, this same quote was expanded from its initial two sentences to a whopping nine paragraphs in Uyehara's book *Bruce Lee: The Incomparable Fighter*.[37] How it was possible for Uyehara to recall nine paragraphs of verbiage from Bruce accurately from memory fifteen years after Bruce had died is quite a cerebral feat indeed. But even the two-sentence quote printed less than a year after Bruce's death contains problems. Why, for example, if the quote came from Bruce, would he say that his fight with Wong Jack Man took place in San Francisco when Bruce would have known full well that it occurred in his studio in Oakland? This is the type of factual mistake one would expect from somebody who wasn't there to witness it (such as Mitoshi Uyehara) — not from a direct participant in the event being spoken of.

It's clear that Bruce didn't abandon Wing Chun as a result of his fight with Wong Jack Man. However, it is also clear that he was no longer a slave to the style. His mission going forward was to use anything that worked in a fight. As his character Tang Lung would state some seven years later in the film *The Way of the Dragon*: "If it helps you to look after yourself when you're in a fix, then you should learn to use it. It doesn't matter where it comes from."

As simple as it sounds, and quite unbeknownst to Bruce, this new approach would be akin to an atomic bomb going off in the martial arts world.

CHAPTER TWELVE

THE LEGEND RISES

"Not every man can take lessons to be a good fighter. He must be a person who is able to relate his training to the circumstances he encounters."

— Bruce Lee (*New Nation* [Singapore], 1972)

By 1967, Bruce Lee was famous. Since returning from Hong Kong after the summer of 1965, he had co-starred as Kato in the short-lived ABC series *The Green Hornet*, which beamed him and his Kung Fu into living rooms all across North America each week. When the series was canceled, he opened a new Kung Fu school in Los Angeles, and frequently appeared in *Black Belt* magazine, which was the only martial arts publication in America at the time. He also began teaching private Kung Fu lessons to Hollywood's elite.

Academy Award–winning screenwriter Stirling Silliphant was among the first to sign up for private lessons:

> I was at one of those instantly-forget-the-name-of-the-host Hollywood parties and I heard someone talking about this fabulous Chinese martial artist named Bruce Lee. The story I heard was that Bruce had been invited to Las Vegas by Vic Damone, the singer. After his performance, Damone invited Bruce up to his suite. Vic had been very interested in Oriental martial arts, but was somewhat skeptical about their effectiveness as a form of combat. Vic expressed his opinion that a lot of the martial arts mystique was exaggerated.

A good tough street fighter, he insisted, could always beat a Karate man, especially an Asian, because Asians were smaller, thinner and just basically couldn't stand up to a big, tough American street brawler. Now Vic didn't say this out of prejudice, it's just that he really believed it.

At the time, Vic employed the services of two huge, armed bodyguards, one of whom held contempt for martial artists in general. Bruce studied the situation and arrived at a way of proving the effectiveness of martial arts without getting anyone hurt. "I'll tell you what we can do," Bruce said. "Put one bodyguard in front of the door. When I come through the door," he explained to the bodyguard, "stop me if you can." The other bodyguard Bruce placed about five feet behind the first man, and told him to put a cigarette in his mouth. "Let's assume that the cigarette represents your holstered gun," he continued. "Vic, when I come through the door I want you to begin counting to five. By the count of five I will be past the first bodyguard and will have knocked the cigarette from the mouth of the second bodyguard. The cigarette is equivalent to his gun. When he sees me come through the door, he should try to take it out of his mouth before I kick it out. Now, I'm at a disadvantage because I'm telling you all this in advance. If I succeed, then would you buy it as an acceptable example of what martial arts can do?" They all said, "Sure. Oh, boy! Yeah!"

Bruce then left the room. Meanwhile Vic said to his bodyguards, "Look, I don't want you to hurt him, cause he's small and he's Chinese. But I don't mind if one or both of you knock him on his ass. Give him a good shot and let's settle this matter once and for all." So, everyone's waiting, right? Suddenly there's a loud, wrenching explosion; not only does the door fly open but it's torn completely from the wall. Bruce kicked the son-of-a-bitch off its hinges! The door slams the first bodyguard so hard he's knocked violently out of the way with the door jammed in his face. Two seconds later — no more — the cigarette flies past the second bodyguard's nose. Bruce had kicked it from his mouth while he stood there frozen in place. Bruce turned and looked at Damone, who, eyes wide, was saying, "Holy Shit!"

Whether that story is true or not, I will never know. But that was the story I heard at the Hollywood party; in fact, it was a story that was circulating all over Hollywood at the time. And it was good enough for me. I decided Bruce was going to be my main man — the one I wanted to train with.[1]

The story, as over-the-top as Silliphant's recounting of it was, nevertheless had some truth to it. Bruce evidently did get into it with somebody in Las Vegas, although who it was and what happened depends on whom you talk to. When Bruce Lee biographer Matthew Polly interviewed Vic Damone, the singer told him that Bruce, Jay Sebring and he were in Las Vegas and heading out for dinner when they encountered Sammy Davis Jr.'s bodyguard, a huge man named John Hopkins. Hopkins waved at somebody who was behind Bruce. The sudden motion of his hand Bruce took to be an attempted attack, and he kicked out one of the bodyguard's legs, locked up his arms, bent him backwards, and was poised to finger-jab his throat when Damone called him off.[2]

Black Belt magazine publisher Mitoshi Uyehara, however, recalls that when he first heard the story shortly after the incident, the fellow Bruce fought was Frank Sinatra's bodyguard. He asked Bruce about whether the story was true:

One day I was talking to him. "Hey Bruce, what's this? I understand that you beat up Frank Sinatra's body-guard in Las Vegas." To me, I think it was wrong; Bruce did something wrong. I'm not sure. But anyway, all he told me was this: "No, it was Vic Damone. It wasn't his bodyguard, it was one of the guards at the casino. Yeah, all I did was just give him one kick to the jaw and the guy just flopped and I walked off." That's what he said, but he wouldn't go into detail. But I felt maybe it was Bruce's fault; maybe he aggravated someone. I'm not sure, but he would never go into detail.[3]

In any event, the rumors of Bruce's physical prowess soon gave way to firsthand confirmation. Future Academy Award–winning actor James Coburn signed up with Bruce for private lessons and was left awestruck after witnessing a demonstration of Bruce's kicking power:

I remember I got a brand-new heavy bag, about a hundred-pound thing, hung up with a big L-iron. Bruce thought it was a little too hard. "That's not really the right kind for you," he said, "but we'll work with it today anyway. Maybe I can soften it up a bit for you." So, he took a running sidekick at it — and broke the chain! I mean that thing hung on a seventy-five-pound chain and he broke that chain and broke a hole in the canvas! It flew up in the air and fell out in the middle of the lawn out there, busted and dilapidated. A brand-new bag. Wow![4]

BRUCE LEE VERSUS RYAN O'NEAL

When Blake Edwards, the Academy Award–nominated director of *Breakfast at Tiffany's* (and later the writer/director of the popular *Pink Panther* films), heard the stories circulating throughout Hollywood of Bruce's skill in the martial arts, he decided to invite him onto the set of his film *Wild Rovers* in hopes of witnessing it firsthand — and not in an abstract way. His intention, evidently, was to have Bruce stand up to a man who had been belittling the director on the set for several weeks. Never a tough man, Edwards had taken up the study of Kenpo Karate under Tom Bleeker, one of Ed Parker's black belts, to build up his confidence and sense of masculinity. The director even secured a job for Bleeker on the film as the stand-in for its star, Ryan O'Neal.[5]

The former star of the daytime television serial *Peyton Place*, and recent Academy Award nominee for his starring role in the movie

Love Story, O'Neal was considered a hot property in Hollywood. However, he had no use for the martial arts, and viewed Edwards's embrace of Karate as being nothing more than pretense, an exhibition of the director's insecurity. As if to underscore this belief, whenever O'Neal saw Bleeker on the set he baited him.[6] When Bleeker chose not to respond, O'Neal, like a high-school bully, made derisive comments to Edwards about his studying Karate.[7] O'Neal, however, wasn't just a blowhard, he was a boxer — and a good one. He'd been a two-time Golden Gloves competitor in the late 1950s, running up an impressive amateur record of eighteen wins and four losses, with thirteen knockouts.[8] In September 1967, he actually sparred so impressively in an exhibition bout with heavyweight boxing legend Joe Frazier that Muhammad Ali (who was seated ringside) marveled at his performance in the ring.[9]

Edwards was certainly not skilled enough to teach O'Neal to respect the martial arts, but he was hopeful that Bruce Lee was. When Bruce arrived on the set, Edwards took him directly over to meet O'Neal.[10] The two men greeted each other and soon the discussion turned to martial arts versus boxing. Lee's attitude at the time is well known. "If you put on a glove, you are dealing in rules. You must know the rules to survive. But in the street, you have more tools in your favor — the kick, the throw, the punch."[11] O'Neal didn't buy it.

Realizing only a sparring match would resolve matters, Bruce stood in front of the Golden Gloves veteran and threw down the gauntlet. "Try to hit me."[12]

O'Neal didn't need to be asked a second time. He did, indeed, try — but his punches found nothing but air. Bruce then unleashed a barrage of kicks and punches that drove the actor across the sound stage. O'Neal ran out of real estate and backed into a prop trailer. Bruce's barrage continued; he wasn't making full contact but enough that O'Neal covered up in what one observer described as a "rope-a-dope fashion."

"Enough!" O'Neal yelled out. "I've had enough!" He then laughed in disbelief. He would later say he believed he'd been struck no less than a hundred times in a matter of fifteen seconds.

But the encounter didn't end there. Blake Edwards picks up the story:

Bruce gave Ryan a kicking shield and set him up and told him to brace himself. Ryan's a pretty big guy. And Bruce launched himself; Ryan hit the trailer — went right into his trailer as I recall. Anyway, I understand that, after that, I don't know whether Ryan believes that was the thing that hurt his back, but he had some, I think, a ruptured disc or something like that. He was injured. And I always contended that it was that kick that did it. I mean, he was in mid-air![13]

O'Neal was not only hurt physically, but also completely bewildered by what he had just experienced. "God damn!" he exclaimed, "I've never been hit that hard by anything in my life!"[14]

TIME TO TRAIN

Bruce enjoyed teaching privately — and why wouldn't he? The money was spectacular. Compared to his Los Angeles school, where students paid fifteen dollars a month[15] for sixteen classes, usually taught by his assistant Dan Inosanto, if you wanted Bruce to train you personally it would cost you US$275 an hour.[16] It was an impressive sum for the time; adjusted for inflation, it's equivalent to $2,330 an hour in 2022.[17] If you wanted Bruce to train you for a week overseas, as Roman Polanski did in 1970 when he brought Bruce to Switzerland,[18] the cost was $1,000[19] ($8,474 in 2022)[20] — plus expenses. It didn't take long at those rates before Bruce was driving a new bright red Porsche, and had put a down payment on a 1,902-square-foot bungalow that sat on 13,504 square feet of posh Bel Air real estate.

More money meant more leisure time, and more leisure time meant more time to work on his physical attributes — and that he did. Bruce's workouts resembled those of today's mixed martial arts champions, only they weren't performed for only a few months leading up to a single bout; they were performed daily for a period of three years — nonstop. A peek into Bruce Lee's daytime diary for the month of January 1968 reveals some rather staggering data: in a mere thirty-one days he performed a total of 18,600 punches and 5,100 finger jabs. In addition, he made time for fifteen sessions where he worked on kicking and flexibility; twelve sessions of hitting the heavy bag and speed bag (this being apart from his punching and finger jab training); twenty-one sessions of isometric forearm work; nineteen sessions of isometric squat and stance work; 121 sets of sit-ups; 128 sets of side bends; 129 sets of leg raises; and almost ten hours of road work which incorporated both jogging and sprinting.[21] And that's just the tip of the iceberg, as this list does not include his additional sessions of weight training, calisthenics (warm-up exercises), skipping, sparring, supplemental forearm training, and teaching Kung Fu to students. His daytime diary entries for the rest of that year indicate a similar schedule.

As Bruce pushed himself in his workouts, he reached levels of physical ability that amazed all who knew him:

- George Lee, his student from Oakland, witnessed Bruce perform fifty chin-ups — with one arm.[22]
- Tae Kwon Do master Jhoon Rhee did a double take when he saw Bruce performing push-ups using only one finger of one hand.[23]
- Chuck Norris, the winner of Karate's triple crown for most tournament wins in 1969, had his eyebrows raised when Bruce knocked out fifty one-arm push-ups.[24]
- Heavyweight Karate champion Joe Lewis was impressed when Bruce took hold of a seventy-five-pound barbell and, standing up straight, pulled the barbell to his chest and then slowly pressed it out parallel to the ground until his arms were locked straight.[25]
- Pan Am Games Judo gold medalist Hayward Nishioka witnessed Bruce punch a focus mitt so hard it dislocated the arm of the man who was holding it.[26]
- Herb Jackson, his student from California, was left dumbfounded after he saw Bruce kick a massive three-hundred-pound heavy bag so hard that it broke the chain it was hanging from and sent the bag flying over twenty feet into the backyard.[27]

Bruce was determined to increase his speed, strength and (particularly after the Wong Jack Man fight) his endurance — any and all aspects of human dynamics that would better support his martial arts techniques.

PERFECTING MOBILITY

Bruce's perpetual training made him keenly aware of his body in a kinetic sense, which allowed him to express himself more totally and reflexively in fighting. Footwork and mobility became significant areas of emphasis, and he discovered that the quicker and more omnidirectional his footwork became, the more avenues of attack opened up. This was a toy that he wanted to play with — and he did. He experimented with balance and footwork not just during his martial art training sessions, but, as his student Richard Bustillo would recall, even during his roadwork:

> I ran with him one time and I didn't like the way he ran because when I run I like to relax and just jog. And what he used to do was he'd be jogging for a while, and then he'd be sprinting, and then he'd jog; then he'd run backwards and then he'd jog; then he'd do crossovers — left leg/right leg — and then he'd jog; he'd run in circles — and then he'd jog. And that's how he ran. That's *no fun* running! Man, that was a workout! He ran backwards for footwork and coordination because fighting is not "just like jogging"; sometimes you've got to move fast or turn or backpedal. That's how he applied it.[28]

This newfound mobility increased the potential weapons that Bruce could deploy. Different types of kicks, for example, became viable tools depending upon his angle of attack and what openings an opponent presented. This realization caused him to become fanatical about stretching,[29] with the result that his legs soon became as ambidextrous as his hands. His kicks became lightning fast and accurate, and could move from low to high — and anywhere in between — effortlessly. The new angles also allowed him to deliver different hand attacks, and so he found utility in the techniques of boxing: uppercuts, crosses, jabs and hooks. He practiced the bob and weave, the shuffle forward and backward — and lateral movement. Gradually, the heavy bag replaced the wooden dummy in his training.

JEET KUNE DO — VERSION 1.0

Along with his study and implementation of boxing techniques, Bruce took a deeper look into the art of fencing. He purchased books on the sport to thoroughly understand its principles, and to more closely examine its hand and foot techniques. He came away from his research and experimentation convinced that intercepting an opponent's attack was the height of efficiency and economy of motion in unarmed combat. Accordingly, he decided to change the name of his art from Jun Fan Gung Fu (Bruce Lee's Kung Fu) to Jeet Kune Do — the Way of the Intercepting Fist.[30]

Blocking was now discarded; Bruce believed that awareness, mobility and an intercepting offense were far superior to defensive techniques that depended on making contact with an opponent's limbs to block strikes and kicks.[31] He changed his fighting stance from the ready position of Wing Chun to one that resembled the posture of Western boxing, with the distinction that the heel of the rear leg was raised to allow for an explosive forward burst — not unlike how a sprinter's heel is raised just prior to starting a race. Such a stance, with bodyweight evenly distributed on both legs (rather than with the majority of the weight on the rear leg as in Wing Chun), made for quicker mobility. He adjusted his stance so that his strongest side was always closest to his opponent on the belief that if you were only presented with one opportunity to strike during an encounter, your most powerful weapons should be closest to the target.[32]

He doubled down on his study of the great Western boxers such as Muhammad Ali and Sugar Ray Robinson. He frequently projected films of these fighters into a mirror that reflected the moving images back onto a screen in reverse, so that Ali, for example, who fought from an orthodox stance (left hand and foot forward, right hand and foot back) was now moving from a southpaw position (right hand and foot forward, left hand and foot back).[33] He did this so that he could study the fighters' footwork and learn how their punching methods could be employed using his theory of keeping one's power side forward.

Bruce's already highly advanced skills continued to improve. "I got a second place in the Western U.S. Karate Championships," recalled Dan Inosanto. "I came back and started training with him and he said, 'You try everything you did so well in the tournament and I'll box you, using Western boxing with the left jab' — and he beat me just with his left jab."[34] One evening, film producer Fred Weintraub invited Bruce out for dinner and introduced him to the United States Senator John Tunney, whose father, Gene Tunney, defeated Jack Dempsey for the heavyweight boxing championship of the world in September 1926.

"Do you think you would have beaten my father?" Tunney asked.

"To tell the truth, I could beat anybody in the world," Bruce replied. "Of course, if I sat still and your father hit me — forget it. The question is: could he ever get close to me?"[35]

Bruce Lee was never one who wanted for confidence.

TRAINING THE KARATE CHAMPIONS

With his unique approach to unarmed combat, impressive physicality and rapidly growing celebrity status, Bruce was invited to perform at the major martial arts tournaments in America. The top three Karate tournament fighters at that time — Mike Stone, Chuck Norris and Joe Lewis — signed up with him for private training. According to Stone: "There were a lot of things I wanted to pick up to improve my sparring ability, such as his attitude of simplicity in self-defense. . . . Bruce had a tremendous amount to offer. . . . He was one of the most knowledgeable martial arts people I have ever met."[36]

With Bruce's coaching, Joe Lewis went on an absolute tear through the American Karate tournament circuit. "In those days, you had the All-American Championships, you had the United States National Championships, the International Championships, and the World Championships," Lewis recalled. "The first year I was with Bruce I won eleven consecutive Grand Championships without any losses — and that was unheard of back in those days. He even showed me how to get more out of the attributes that I possessed. He made me even faster."[37]

In 1972, Chuck Norris would go on Hong Kong television with Bruce and Bob Wall and say Bruce was his "teacher" and he thought he was "fantastic."[38] After Bruce's death, Norris recounted what it was like sparring Bruce: "The truth is Lee was a formidable opponent. . . . I totally enjoyed sparring and just spending time with him. . . . Lee was lightning fast, very agile and incredibly strong for his size."[39] While researching *Bruce Lee: Fighting Spirit,* author Bruce Thomas discovered that "[martial artist] Richard Bustillo and a Los Angeles policeman were both present at a sparring session between Bruce and Chuck Norris in which the karate champion was left 'red-faced.'"[40] Jon Benn, who co-starred with Norris in Bruce's film *The Way of the Dragon,* recalled having dinner with Norris one night when the pair encountered one another in Manila: "I bluntly asked him the biggest question on my mind: 'Tell me the honest truth, Chuck. Who would have won in the end if you and Bruce Lee really had faced each other in an all-out fight to the death?' Without a moment of delay, Chuck answered, 'Bruce, of course. Nobody could beat him.'"[41]

SPARRING THE MASTERS

Sparring became the lifeblood of his art,[42] and Bruce engaged in sparring sessions whenever martial artists were available and willing. He preferred black belts,[43] but would spar with anybody from any discipline.[44] This sharpened his ability to adapt and make on-the-fly adjustments in combat situations. If no one would come to him to spar, he would go to them. He called this "slumming,"[45] whereby he would venture out to martial art schools and ask the instructor if it was okay to spar with his more advanced students. George Dillman, a tenth-degree black belt in Ryukyu Kempo Tomari-te, remembered when Bruce showed up at his school in Reading, Pennsylvania, and asked if it was okay to spar his top students. "To him that was better than a tournament," Dillman said. "And he would fight all the students. . . . and he did very well with those students; he beat 'em up. Not badly, it was still 'point fighting,' but he would hit 'em."[46]

Perhaps out of curiosity, or perhaps to defend his art better than his students had, the Karate veteran stepped forth and challenged Bruce. "I said, 'I want to fight with you. I'll spar.'" Dillman was no slouch in Karate competition. He was a four-time national Karate champion (from 1969 to 1972), and during a nine-year competitive career he won a total of 327 trophies in fighting, forms, breaking and weapons.[47]

Bruce Lee shakes hands with Brother Edward Muss (the teacher who had recruited him for the school boxing team in 1958) on March 13, 1973. Bruce had returned to St. Francis Xavier's to present awards to the students. (Courtesy of St. Francis Xavier's College, Hong Kong)

Bruce Lee's student card from St. Francis Xavier's College.
(Courtesy of St. Francis Xavier's College, Hong Kong)

"The King of Talking Hands." Wong Shun Leung, Bruce Lee's primary teacher in Wing Chun and the man who directed him onto the path of practicality in martial arts.
(Courtesy of David Peterson)

Yip Man (1972–1983), Bruce Lee's first formal martial arts teacher and master of Wing Chun Kung Fu.
(Wikipedia)

The rooftop where Bruce Lee had his last beimo in Kowloon in 1958.
(Photo by John Little)

A citizen of the world. Many of the senior students of Yip Man resented Bruce Lee's success and his embrace of western fashion and lifestyle.
(Courtesy of Steve Kerridge)

Bruce with producer Raymond Chow, who was so impressed with Bruce's martial arts demonstration on Hong Kong's TV-B that he signed him for a two-movie deal that launched Bruce's career into the stratosphere.
(Courtesy of Steve Kerridge)

Bruce Lee (left) throws a kick at Bob Baker in the film *Fist of Fury* (1972). He would end up having a real fight on the set of this film. (Courtesy of Steve Kerridge)

Bruce with his co-star in *The Way of the Dragon*, Chuck Norris, who was one of the Karate champions who signed on with Bruce for private lessons in the late 1960s. (Courtesy of Steve Kerridge)

Bruce Lee (center) oversees some screen test choreography on the set of *Enter the Dragon* between Wan Kam Leung (left) and Wong Shun Leung (right) in 1973. (Courtesy of Alman Fung)

A comparison of stances. Bruce Lee's last private student, Ted Wong (left), and his highest-ranked student, Taky Kimura (right), demonstrate the stances Bruce employed in Jeet Kune Do (left) and Wing Chun (right) respectively. Seattle, 1998.

(Photo by John Little)

techniques. By understanding principles you can find your own way instead of being dependent on others for instruction or direction.

What happens if a person learns only principles? They become "intellectually bound". They get all tied up in theories and concepts, etc. To theorize on something is fine, but if you cannot manifest it, what good is it? The only way you can be sure a principle works is to put it to the test. In his writings concerning swordsmanship, Takuan Soho, the renowned Zen monk wrote:

There is such a thing as training in principle, and such a thing as training in technique. If you do not train in technique, but only fill your heart with principle, your body and hands will not function. Even though you know principle, you must make yourself perfectly free in the use of technique. And even though you may wield the sword that you carry with you well, if you are unclear on the deeper aspects of principle, you will likely fall short of proficiency. Technique and principle are just like the two wheels of a cart.

Technique and principle make up a "whole." The principles guide you to find the technique, and the technique should then illustrate those principles. So harmonize and unite both principle and technique in your training, and don't be "bound" by either one. ●

Bruce Lee pictured during a real confrontation he had on the set of "Enter the Dragon." His ability to not be bound by either techniques or combative principles allowed him the freedom to adapt — instantly — to each and every combative situation in a spontaneous and appropriate way. Incidentally, this particular encounter was over almost before it started with Lee's opponent not being able to land any technique, while Lee connected with a devastating side kick, a spinning back kick (not shown), a hook kick (above, left) and a punch (above right and below).

Bruce Lee was challenged to fight several times during the filming of *Enter the Dragon*. This sequence of photos captures moments from one of these altercations. (Magazine page courtesy of Multi-Media Communications Inc. and Curtis Wong)

Bruce in period costume during an experimental photoshoot at Golden Harvest Studios in 1972. (Courtesy of Steve Kerridge)

Twirling his nunchaku on the set of *The Game of Death*. Bruce Lee had intended to cast his former Wing Chun teacher Wong Shun Leung in this film, but Bruce died prior to being able to resume filming. (Courtesy of Steve Kerridge)

A star on the rise. After the runaway success of his first two films, Bruce Lee was able to form his own production company in Hong Kong.
(Courtesy of Steve Kerridge)

Ready for action. As he became more famous in Hong Kong, Bruce Lee had to be constantly ready to fight to defend his unspoken reputation as the "King of Kung Fu." (Courtesy of Steve Kerridge)

His pedigree evidently didn't faze Bruce. "He told me 'I can hit you four times before you can hit me once,'" Dillman recalled. The veteran Karateka doubted that would be possible. He quickly learned otherwise:

> So, I get in my fighting stance and all of a sudden — pow! His foot hits me upside the head. . . . He did it. By the time I got in my stance he had me hit. So, I mean, that's how fast he was. He was the first man that I [saw] who could use his hands, both of them, equally. We all strive for that. But I'm just telling you, if he hit you with a left, you weren't sure if it was a right [or] a left. He'd hit you with either hand and they both had the same power. And he could kick with either foot!

But Dillman wasn't alone. Any and all martial artists that Bruce Lee crossed paths with, from the black belts who attended his classes to the tournament champions, were invited to spar with him. And all who accepted his invitation came away bewildered by the experience:

- Jhoon Rhee, a tenth Dan in Tae Kwon Do, found that before he could even initiate a technique, Bruce was all over him: "You know what used to frustrate me? Bruce told me to attack him and before I could do anything, that son of a gun was right on me. I've been practicing martial arts for years and he stopped me right in my tracks every time."[48]
- Larry Hartsell, a former student of Ed Parker's Kenpo Karate who joined Bruce's school, recalled that, "I sparred him once. The minute we began I knew something was wrong. He just moved on me. He was beside me, or behind me, before I could even adjust. He'd tap my head to let me know he could score. He just tore down my ego. I remember thinking, 'Well, there goes six years of Kenpo right out the window.'"[49]
- Ken Knudson, a fifth Dan in Karate, and a man who defeated the American Karate legends Bill "Superfoot"

Wallace and Joe Lewis in competition, reported that "the power from Bruce's kicks and punches is bursting. He demonstrated a sidekick on me that moved me so fast that I felt as though my eyeballs were still where I was standing when he kicked me."[50]

- Leo Fong, a Golden Gloves boxer and black belt in Karate, put it succinctly: "I sparred with him and, man, it was like I was nothing."[51]
- Wally Jay, a black belt in Jiu-jitsu, agreed: "I saw him spar James Lee, but he was too good. Too good for me too."[52]

While Bruce Lee was wowing his sparring partners, his doctors were worried that his life was being placed needlessly at risk by his having neglected to do anything about his cryptorchidism. He'd ignored the condition of his undescended testicle for twenty-eight years. It hadn't proven to be a problem in terms of his growth, muscular development or fertility, but that wasn't what the doctors were concerned about. The older he became, the greater the risk of his developing testicular cancer.[53] The condition needed to be dealt with, and the sooner the better. And so, in March 1969, Bruce went under the knife at St. John's Hospital in Santa Monica for two surgeries: the first was to repair a minor hernia, the second to either lower his undescended testicle or surgically excise it and insert a prosthesis.[54] He was then ordered to rest and take it easy for a while. It's hard to know what degree of relief the surgery provided. No doubt the worry about cancer subsided, bringing some welcome peace of mind. But if that dark cloud had lifted, another one was forming on the horizon.

CHAPTER THIRTEEN

STANDING UP TO A BULLY

"I have no fear of an opponent in front of me. I'm very self-sufficient, and they do not bother me. And, should I fight — should I do anything — I have made up my mind that, baby, you had better kill me before [I get you]."

— Bruce Lee (Radio Hong Kong, 1971)

F or many years after Bruce Lee's passing, Karate champion Joe Lewis downplayed the prowess of his former teacher, particularly when it came to fighting. "I didn't get the feeling that [Bruce] was hungry about getting into a scrimmage line situation where he had to put his skills on the line and prove that he could really fight or spar," Lewis said.[1] On another occasion, Lewis put it more bluntly: "Bruce was not a fighter. He was an actor and a teacher."[2] Coming from a well-decorated Karate champion, such statements carried weight — even more so after Lewis went on to dominate the sport of kickboxing, running up a record of fourteen wins, four losses.[3] Lewis knew what it took to be a champion in the world of martial arts, both point style and full contact, and if he said Bruce Lee was leery of sparring with him and couldn't fight, who was going to argue with him?

FIGHTER WITH AN ATTITUDE

Joe Lewis, in Bruce Lee's words, was "kind of like the 'bad boy of Karate.' Many people look upon him as a bully."[4] He was a big man (six feet) and powerful (195 pounds, all of it muscle) who flattened just about anyone who was unfortunate enough to stand in front of him. Born in North Carolina, Lewis wrestled, lifted weights and later joined the marines. While stationed in Okinawa, he (incredibly) obtained his black belt in only seven months.[5]

When Lewis returned to the United States, he quickly became an absolute beast in Karate competitions, often leaving his opponents writhing on the floor in a crumpled heap. When he fought, he was ruthless and suffered no qualms about hurting an opponent. Fighting for the National Championship in 1967, his sidekick broke the ribs of sixteen-year-old Mitchell Bobrow during what was supposed to be a point Karate competition.[6] He further broke the ribs of his student and future business partner Bob Wall during a freestyle sparring practice.[7] His size and fiery demeanor had a way of psyching out many of his opponents even before their match began.[8]

While Lewis had won some major Karate tournaments before studying under Bruce,[9] he had also lost a few.[10] But soon his entire fighting approach changed, as noted by a reporter from *Black Belt* magazine:

> An example of a Lewis triumph with no holds barred and no quarter given was his resounding win at the National Karate Tournament in Washington, D.C. Here, Lewis was in rare form and apparently re-born with a new technique, incorporating Jeet Kune Do, and an ambition to conquer any opposition to his third straight karate championship in this arena. His usually surly disposition was put away in mothballs, so it seemed, for this tourney and he was in general good spirits throughout, no doubt sparked by his si-fu Bruce Lee who took extraordinary pride in his product. Lewis moved in and out of the battle with agility never seen before, and he pounded away at the opposition with such high caliber that the runner-ups seemed faint shadows against the Lewis in evidence here. When Lewis was awarded the crown, he humbly thanked his si-fu, giving him the credit for his improvement, something Lewis had never done before! It looked like a new Lewis on the mat.[11]

Mitoshi Uyehara recalled that it was Bruce's ability to read an opponent's weaknesses and intentions — and knowing precisely when to attack and with what weapon — that proved particularly helpful to Lewis's tournament successes:

> Bruce just told him what to do. He'd look at a Karate match and say, "Hey, all you have to do is as soon as he kicks just give him a reverse punch" — and that's what he told Lewis. Every time he goes in, Lewis would give the same punch and every time he was beating them out. All he did was give him one [punch] and that's it. And [Lewis] was winning all of the tournaments just with one punch — one technique, that's it. Bruce saw the flaw in Karate this way.[12]

Being able to accurately assess an opponent's strengths and weaknesses meant that Bruce also knew the Achilles' heels of the various champion martial artists he trained. Basketball superstar Kareem Abdul-Jabbar signed up with Bruce for private lessons in Jeet Kune Do. He became a better, more confident athlete, and when Bruce told him what to do in a sparring session against Joe Lewis, Abdul-Jabbar discovered to his surprise that he could easily hold his own against the world Karate champion: "I knew who Joe Lewis was. He had quite a reputation. So, I was a little nervous, you know, when Bruce just looked at me and said, 'Go ahead.' And I just learned a couple of techniques, but just from the defense that Bruce had showed me, and the use of a few techniques, Joe Lewis really had a problem in trying to attack me. He never did. That, too, [laughs] gave me a lot of confidence."[13]

Lewis studied under Bruce for the better part of two years and claimed he learned a great deal:

> He was a phenomenal master teacher. Mainly because of his ability to motivate people. Before you can motivate people, you have to first be able to relate to them and he knew how to make you feel visible, because if you don't feel visible, you're dead. And he knew how to

trigger your inspiration and once that inspiration was triggered, then the motivation started to flow. He knew how to reach inside of a person and could convince you to believe in yourself.[14]

Be that as it may, Lewis's ego was the equal of Bruce's. Over time, he began to resent having to share the championship spotlight with Bruce and his art:

Well, he was using me as his test tube to prove that Jeet Kune Do was the greatest fighting style going — and that Bruce Lee was the greatest trainer. Cause I was beating everybody's butt in those days, you follow me? And whenever I would go to some tournament like the International Championships or the National Championships, something like that, once in a while Bruce Lee would show up and when I'd win I'd invite him on stage and we'd take our pictures together and then the newspapers would come to me and Bruce would tell me what to say to the newspapers. I always made sure that I said something that would plug Jeet Kune Do, you follow me? I just went along with it. I didn't realize it was exercising a double standard there; he wanted to use my status as a fighting champion, to punctuate and amplify his credentials as a teacher.[15]

Lewis continued to take lessons from Bruce, but his resentment only grew. If he won a tournament, some might think that it was only because of what Bruce taught him. In other words, Lewis was only a by-product of the victory; a marionette that only danced well because of the talent of the man who pulled his strings from behind the scenes. Articles, such as the one that appeared in *Black Belt* magazine, only augmented Lewis's discontent. From Bruce's perspective, the tremendous success that Lewis enjoyed throughout 1968 and 1969 wasn't by *accident*; he had spent considerable time honing Lewis's skills and teaching him fighting tactics and strategies that Bruce had spent years cultivating. Yes, Lewis was good before he trained under Bruce, but he wasn't *this* good. Indeed, ever since coming under Bruce's wing, Lewis had left good at the starting line. Nevertheless, while competing in a Karate tournament in 1969, Lewis did something that would ultimately drive a wedge between the two men:

> I was at the International Championships, which in that day it was the major Karate tournament in the world. And let me get this straight: I was the defending champion, and that night when I walked up on stage to defend my title Bruce Lee is sitting ringside next to my wife. And the guy who was announcing me coming up on stage, the ring announcer, said "this is Joe Lewis." And he says, "Joe Lewis's instructor: John Korab" — instead of saying "Bruce Lee" he said "John Korab." And, instead of saying "Jeet Kune Do," which is Bruce's style, he said "Joe Lewis' style is Okinawa Te." Well, John Korab was the guy who taught me how to fight in Okinawa. And Okinawa Te, when I think of 'style" I don't think of fighting style, I think of the katas and all that stuff. So, when I said "Okinawa Te," I meant of all the katas, I think the Okinawa Te katas are prettiest and the most animal-like of all the katas. So, when I filled out a registration form earlier in the day it just said "Instructor," I put "John Korab;" it said "style," I put "Okinawa Te." Thinking no big deal. But I didn't think some guy was going to take that application and read it out to the audience that night! That pissed Bruce Lee off to no living end. He was really pissed![16]

BRUCE LEE VERSUS JOE LEWIS

Bruce may still have been pissed about it when one evening, he and three of his students, Herb Jackson, Ted Wong and Joe Lewis, headed into L.A.'s Chinatown and stopped by Bruce's school.[17] The school was closed, but since Bruce had the key, he opened the door, and the four men went inside. As all of Bruce's students engaged in full-contact sparring, there were boxing gloves, headgear and various other protective equipment at the school. Perhaps thinking about what happened when he coached Kareem prior to his successful sparring match with the Karate champion, Bruce told Herb to lace up the gloves and spar with Lewis. Unfortunately for Herb, he possessed none of Kareem's attributes; he wasn't seven foot two or a superb athlete, nor, at forty-seven, was he a young man. Lewis, by contrast, was in his prime. He was twenty-four years old, and the reigning national Karate champion.

The Lewis-Jackson sparring session was a pointless exercise from the start, and Lewis decided to put an exclamation point on the matter by smacking the five-foot-five man with an open-palm strike to his ear, which immediately dropped Herb to his knees. "I thought he popped my ear drum," Herb later recalled. "My ear was ringing for three weeks after that."

Bruce was looking on during the encounter and didn't like what he'd just witnessed. As Lewis was preparing to undo his gloves, Bruce told him to hold on a second. He walked over to a bench and reached beneath it where some sets of boxing gloves were kept. He picked up a pair and slipped them on his hands. He then motioned for Joe to meet him in the center of the floor.

Herb Jackson picks up the story: "And so, Bruce put on the gloves [and sparred with] Lewis, and Joe Lewis couldn't touch him. No way at all. *Could not touch him.* Bruce just popped him all over — he popped him in the face, all over, and Joe couldn't touch him. I'd love to have a film of that. He was the national Karate champion at that time, too. And later on, Bruce told me he put the gloves on with Lewis 'just to let Joe Lewis know that he didn't have all the answers.' And he let him know!"[18]

Kareem Abdul-Jabbar shared a similar sentiment with regard to Bruce's attitude toward the Karate champion:

> [Bruce] had fun just putting Joe Lewis down; just showing him that he wasn't going to beat everybody. That was his attitude, you know. He was very confident . . . Joe was too slow [for Bruce]. Joe's the type of guy that if you stand toe-to-toe with Joe, he'll beat

you down to the ground. But if you could box and move, make him have to invent a way to get in on you, he had problems . . . He [Bruce Lee] was having fun with Joe Lewis. Joe could never really figure out exactly what was going on. It was funny. It was kind of like how a matador deals with a bull. You know, I always got that feeling.[19]

Many years after that encounter, Joe Lewis recalled what it was like to stand in front of Bruce Lee:

For a guy who only weighed 138 pounds . . . he hit extremely hard. He could hit as hard as a heavyweight. He had real fast-twitch muscle fibers, something he's born with. He trained hard, he worked on a lot of his stabilizer muscles, and especially his speed; I always thought he was, like, the fastest guy who ever stood in front of me. He had an incredible, like, I call Zen-like level of consciousness. In psychology, we call it the "implicit level of consciousness." You didn't know when he was going to squeeze that trigger. And he always knew when you weren't ready. He had blinding speed, especially with his hands. I know that because he stood in front of me and he popped me a few times. So, I always told people, "I always knew how hard Bruce Lee could hit. I know how fast he was 'cause he nailed me." And I've always told people, "I know what real Jeet Kune Do is [laughs] because I got popped with it a few times."[20]

A PARTING OF THE WAYS

The sparring match was the beginning of the end of the relationship between the two martial artists. Fast forwarding to 1993, in researching an article on Bruce Lee's training methods for *Muscle & Fitness* magazine, I had arranged a telephone interview with Lewis. Along with some specific questions about his training under Bruce, I had some generic ones that I posed, such as "when was the last time you saw Bruce?" I wasn't prepared for his answer.

According to Lewis, Bruce and he had a major falling out at the end of 1969 and would never speak again.[21] The issue, he revealed, was that his wife had gone to Bruce and Linda's house to put some highlights in Bruce's hair. Upon her return, she told him that Bruce had made a pass at her.[22] Lewis, understandably, was irate. Without even bothering to change out of his suit and tie,[23] Lewis drove directly to the Lees' home in Bel Air. "I went up there to challenge Bruce," Lewis said.[24] Upon arriving, he stormed around to the rear of the house and knocked (perhaps pounded) on a screen door that led directly into the Lees' kitchen. Soon Bruce came to the door but didn't open it. He didn't have time to. Immediately Lewis started in on him concerning his wife's allegation. As it was a screen door, Bruce heard him loud and clear.[25] When Joe had finished his rather pointed accusation, Bruce offered a simple reply.

"You're an idiot."[26]

Bruce then called for Linda to come to the door.

"Joe, tell Linda what you just told me."

Lewis proceeded to do so.

Bruce then turned to Linda.

"Can you believe that?"[27]

Bruce and Linda were both angry and couldn't understand why Lewis would believe such a story.[28] "I was very gullible in those days," Lewis recollected. "I didn't know how to defend myself [verbally]. . . . I was in a trap, you know? My wife had set me up 'cause she wanted to dissolve the relationship, wanted the two of us to spend less time together. She was very jealous of the relationship — and she did a good job."[29] She did indeed, for Joe Lewis was now in a tough spot. If he was to apologize to Bruce and walk away it meant that he believed Bruce's denial, which meant that he thought his wife was lying — and that would spell trouble for his marriage. But if he dug in, it would mean that he believed his wife, which meant that he was accusing Bruce of lying — and this would infuriate Bruce, which, as the reader will know by now, was never a good thing.

When I asked Lewis what happened next, he became evasive.

"We just kind of had it out there."[30]

"How was it resolved?" I asked.

"Well, it was never really resolved," he replied.[31]

His answer struck me as odd. What did "have it out" mean, then? I knew that Bruce Lee was not in the habit of tolerating insults or refusing challenges. And Lewis had just stated that he went to Bruce's home specifically to "challenge" him. However, that was all Lewis would say on the matter.

A few days later I interviewed Bob Wall, who co-starred in Bruce's films *The Way of the Dragon* (1972) and *Enter the Dragon* (1973) and had known Bruce since the mid-1960s. He also had been a colleague and business partner of Joe Lewis. When I mentioned the nebulous conclusion to the anecdote Lewis had shared with me about his split with Bruce, Wall informed me that there was more to the story. "I got it firsthand," Wall said. "I heard it from Bruce and from Joe, so I know what happened. There's no question about it."[32]

Evidently, Lewis decided to side with his wife on the matter. Predictably, that's when things escalated. According to Wall:

> Bruce stood right in his face and said, "Let's get it on, motherfucker!" You're damn right — Bruce wouldn't back down from nobody, let me tell you something. Now Joe felt he could kick his ass, but the fact of the matter is it's the old saying that 'it isn't the size of the dog in the fight, it's the size of the fight in the dog in the fight.' And there was a *lot* of fight in Bruce Lee. Bruce was nobody's punk. In those days Joe was not a street fighter type; he didn't . . . he just kind of let it slide. It wouldn't have mattered if Bruce was ready to go or not, Joe wouldn't have, in my opinion, fought at that stage of his life. Today he would. But at that stage of his life he wouldn't have. But the fact is I know that he had to respect Bruce because Bruce was ready to go. And, like, "right now!"[33]

Lewis evidently opted not to engage and "let it slide" and headed home. When I asked him what the last words were that Bruce Lee ever said to him, he replied: "I think he called me a punk or something."[34]

Apart from Bob Wall, other martial artists that traveled in Bruce and Lewis's circle soon learned what happened between them. And when certain of Bruce's students heard the statements that Lewis would make in the decades after Bruce died, they simply looked at one another knowingly. Kareem Abdul-Jabbar would say, "Well, for whatever [Lewis] thought, he never seemed to be, like, too eager to have it happen, you know? To get in the ring with Bruce. He had one opportunity [to fight Bruce] and he won't . . . he doesn't talk about it."[35]

CHAPTER FOURTEEN

TOTAL MARTIAL FREEDOM

"I believe that the only way to teach anyone self-defense is to approach each individual personally. Each one of us is different and each one of us should be taught the correct form. By correct form I mean the most useful techniques the person is inclined toward. Find his ability and then develop these techniques."

— Bruce Lee (*Black Belt* magazine, 1968)

Heading into 1970, Bruce was continuing his training at a hectic pace. That is, until May of that year,[1] when, while performing a lower back exercise with a 125-pound barbell across his shoulders,[2] he suddenly felt a sharp pain in his lower back.[3] If the pain wasn't immediately overwhelming, it was progressive. Bruce fought through the discomfort into the summer,[4] but upon visiting a doctor, he learned he had damaged a sacral nerve in his lower back.[5] Surgery was discussed.[6] He received massages,[7] which seemed to help, and gave up "excessive stretching" and heavy weight training.[8] But the pain persisted, and by August it was worse.

It was decided that he'd better not do anything strenuous for a while, and he became bedridden for "quite some time."[9] According to his wife Linda: "The doctor warned him it meant lying on his back for a long time. Normally telling Bruce even to take it easy was like trying to tell a grasshopper not to jump, but when he set his mind to it, he could do anything. He stayed in bed for three months — enduring a period of great mental and physical pain, stress and financial problems. Altogether it was more than six months before he could resume even light training. But even during his recuperation his mind remained extraordinarily active."[10] Not able to train his body for the time being, Bruce switched gears and began to train his mind, working on aspects of psychology that would help him in fighting.

His friend Mitoshi Uyehara recalled an example of how Bruce sought to train his mental focus and awareness:

> When he would go to a restaurant, Bruce would pick out an individual and watch him. Every time the individual would make a move, such as shoving the food toward his mouth, Bruce would whisper "Ah." The idea was to be able to anticipate the person's movement. It was a kind of exercise in awareness and reaction. He would do this over and over, until he could predict when the person was going to put the fork into the food, for example. Bruce's idea, of course, was that in a fight, you had to anticipate. That was the key to success. As soon as his opponent would begin to make a move, Bruce would be on top of him. Before anyone could throw a punch, he'd be all over him.[11]

According to Bruce's student Larry Hartsell, even watching television became a training exercise for Bruce. "Something else he used to do to work on his reaction time," Hartsell recalled. "He would watch TV and when a camera cut or a scene would change he would punch out. He did this to train his visual awareness. That was his reaction drill every time he watched TV."[12]

Such mental discipline allowed him to better identify the precise time to land a blow on an adversary. According to his younger brother Robert, Bruce became so good at this that "he could predict when a boxer on TV was about to throw a right hook or a left cross. Just by looking, he'd know your thoughts."[13]

JEET KUNE DO — VERSION 2.0

During this down time, Bruce read whatever books he could find on any type of martial art, particularly ones that had well-settled principles of successful combat as their underpinning. Next, he analyzed the techniques of the various fighting arts in order to discern their strengths and, more importantly, their weaknesses — just in case he should ever have to fight a practitioner of one of these methods.[14]

During this down period, certain of his students from his Los Angeles school would drop by to try and keep his spirits up. "I took him down to a bookstore in Beverly Hills," recalled Larry Hartsell. "They had antique books. And he was looking at this one which was published in the 1700s: *Gentleman's Self-Defense*.[15] And they still had the old square hats on [in the illustrations in the book]. And it showed some of the kicks they used. And he paid, I think, about a hundred and fifty or two hundred dollars for that book, which was a lot of money back then."[16]

He also read extensively on resistance training, aerobics, flexibility, psychology and philosophy. He was particularly taken by the great minds of China, Japan and India. The philosophy that impacted him the most during this time was that of Jiddu Krishnamurti, particularly Krishnamurti's belief that truth, qua truth, can never be organized or ritualized:

> I maintain that Truth is a pathless land, and you cannot approach it by any path whatsoever, by any religion, by any sect. That is my point of view, and I adhere to that absolutely and unconditionally. Truth, being limitless, unconditioned, unapproachable by any path whatsoever, cannot be organized; nor should any organization be formed to lead or to coerce people along any particular path.
>
> If you first understand that, then you will see how impossible it is to organize a belief. A belief is purely an individual matter, and you cannot and must not organize it. If you do, it becomes dead, crystallized; it becomes a creed, a sect, a religion, to be imposed on others. This is what everyone throughout the world is attempting to do. Truth is narrowed down and made a plaything for those who are weak, for those who are only momentarily discontented. Truth cannot be brought down, rather the individual must make the effort to

ascend to it. You cannot bring the mountain-top to the valley. If you would attain to the mountain-top you must pass through the valley, climb the steeps, unafraid of the dangerous precipices.[17]

Such passages suggested to Bruce a new direction for martial art. He now recognized that for the better part of his adult life he had been attempting to find and organize what he believed to be the truth of martial art in order to teach it to others. He had first developed a system or way of Chinese martial arts (*The Tao of Gung Fu*), and, more recently, he created his new "way" of Jeet Kune Do (indeed, the "Do" in Jeet Kune Do translates as "way"). But now he saw that the ultimate truth of martial art could not be found in "ways" and styles, but through each individual looking inward and performing their own experimentation in order to learn their own strengths and weaknesses, and then working hard to maximize the former and minimize the latter.

His first formulation of Jeet Kune Do (the Way of the Intercepting Fist) was predicated on the "way" of interception. But what if a combat situation required striking *before* your opponent moved? There would be nothing to intercept. And what if, when an opponent attempted to kick or strike, instead of intercepting the attack with an attack of one's own, one simply moved back or to the side to evade the attack? Such options were valid, but they were denied to a practitioner of an art whose fundamental principle was interception. To Bruce's mind, the individual had to be free to initiate an attack or to adapt and respond immediately to whatever the fight situation called for at any given moment, like echo to sound. And awareness of what was happening every instant was necessary for a simultaneous response to a combat landscape that was constantly shifting and changing from second to second.

Awareness of the relationship between oneself and one's opponent was the key, which was a psychological phenomenon and could not be brought about by trying to conform to the postures of an external method. After all, what if your body type was such that certain techniques within a given style were awkward or not suitable for you? Should you continue trying to fit a square peg into a round hole? Or should you instead try to learn what your own aptitudes are and work from there? Bruce's student Kareem Abdul-Jabbar put it this way:

> He said if I were going to use, let's say, a Judo throw, it would be impractical stuff. Imagine me [at 7'2"] trying to get my hips underneath him [5'7½"] to throw him for a hip throw! He'd joke, "you're going to try and do that while I'm beating you down?" He'd be hitting me with something else while I was trying to get into position for the throw. And he was absolutely right.[18]

When Bruce became aware that his friend and student Leo Fong had been studying different martial arts, such as Judo, boxing, Choy Lay Fut and Sil Lum Kung Fu, he approached him and asked, "Why are you running around town training in all these methods?"

"I'm looking for the ultimate."

Bruce pressed his finger into Fong's chest. "Man, there's no ultimate style," Bruce said. "The ultimate is *inside of you*."[19]

Bruce Lee's art of Jeet Kune Do now became a non-method, a suggestion, a guideline to nudge the individual practitioner into discovering themself, and awakening all of their human attributes. It was a step in the wrong direction, therefore, to teach organized classes, where a curriculum was required and presented to students who were led to believe that progression in martial arts required a linear series of external levels to scale — beginner: so many techniques; intermediate: so many more techniques; advanced: even more techniques. What did any of this have to do with an individual learning the truth about which martial movements best suited them? And so, despite the loss of income such a move represented, Bruce decided to close all three of his Kung Fu schools. "Money comes second," he would tell student Daniel Lee in 1971. "That's why I've disbanded all the schools of Jeet Kune Do; because it is very easy for a member to come in and take the agenda as *the truth* and the schedule as *the way*, you know what I mean?"[20]

Going forward, and during those periods when his back pain subsided enough to allow him to practice, Bruce implemented his new vision of total martial freedom, learning to refine his strengths such as mobility and speed and to strike the instant that an opponent provided an opening. According to Jesse Glover, "At the end of Bruce's life, he was *beyond* technique. In a sense he was just fencing with his fists and feet. Whenever he saw a hole he just put something in it."[21] Bruce would describe it in this manner: "Here it is: if you can move with your tools from any angle, then you can adapt to whatever the object is in front of you. And the clumsier, the more limited the object, the easier for you to pot-shot it. That's what it amounts to."[22]

"AN ABSOLUTELY PERFECT FIGHTING MACHINE"

This was an entirely new approach to martial art and, once Bruce removed the self-imposed restrictions of his old approach, it served to make his movements even less predictable than they had been in the past — even to exceptionally skilled martial artists. When Bruce sparred a decorated grappler like Judo's Hayward Nishioka (a four-time national Judo champion and gold medal winner at the Pan Am Games), Nishioka recalled that his grappling skills never made it out of first gear: "As far as sparring with Bruce goes, he'd just play with us. I mean, I could move around but I could never match him. He was just too fast. *He was just too fast.* I mean, he'd go in and out and then you'd just be starting up and wondering, "What should I do?" He had the ability to figure out the timing of when to go in; he understands when you're breathing out and he goes in. He uses every possible means of attack."[23]

Bruce, of course, was aware of his own strengths and weaknesses, as well as those of the men he sparred with. He knew his strengths were in standing and striking — not on the ground. If someone grabbed hold of him, it was now a fifty-fifty matter, with the advantage typically falling to the bigger, stronger man. But if that man couldn't grab hold of him, the odds were more in his favor. Nishioka knew this, and, in a moment of frustration, brought it to Bruce's attention:

> I had confronted Bruce one time because, after a while,
> after getting beat up a lot because he was so good — I
> mean this guy could go in, tap your head, come out,
> while you were still starting your motors up — I said,

"Look, what would you do if I just lay down on the ground? I'm not going to stand up with you because I'd be a fool. If I was going to fight you, I'd lay down on the ground — what would you do then?" The corners of his mouth kind of went down and he kind of pursed his lips and said, "I'd just walk away." Then in the next sentence he said, "but don't get up!"[24]

Nishioka was so impressed with Bruce's abilities that he brought his physical education professor at California State University, Dr. Burt Seidler, over to Bruce's house. "I wanted him to see this phenomenon. I would talk about Bruce and he would never believe me," Nishioka recalled.[25] The professor was left in awe: "Bruce Lee was the most impressive human being I've ever met in my life. I've coached several NCAA wrestling champions and seen a lot of great athletes, but I've never seen anything like that man! I was awed. Mentally and physically he was an absolutely perfect fighting machine."[26]

Even those well-versed in street fighting were bewildered by Bruce's "now you see me, now you don't" approach to sparring. Typical was the case of Mark Komuro:

In early 1970, while working at *Black Belt* magazine, my boss, Mito Uyehara, introduced me to a little skinny Chinese guy named Bruce Lee. He was supposed to be "the greatest martial artist of all time." Yeah, right. I grew up in the inner city of Los Angeles and, believe me, I knew a tough guy when I saw one and Bruce Lee wasn't a tough guy. Maybe it was his accent or his attempts at being "hip," but I wasn't buying it. So, anyway, I asked him to show me some stuff. We squared off and he distanced himself a good fifteen feet away from me. I moved forward; he moved back. I asked him, "How are you going to do anything from way over there?" I suddenly felt two slaps to the middle of my forehead! And before I could do anything, Bruce was again fifteen feet away from me — laughing! "Hey, I wasn't ready," I said, slightly embarrassed. We moved around a little and then — bam! — the same thing happened. To this day I've never seen anyone who could move so fast.[27]

Another man who came away bewildered from an impromptu sparring session with Bruce was professional heavyweight boxer Joey Orbillo, an athlete who had swapped leather with legendary fighters such as Jerry Quarry, Manuel Ramos and Eddie Machen:

> Joe Lewis took me to a tournament that he was fighting in and Bruce Lee was sitting there. And I had this nice-looking girl — God bless her — anyway, and Bruce looked at me and said: "Joey Orbillo!" And I looked and said, "Kato!" And he said, "Hey!" And I left my girl and we went walking. We went outside, and I don't even know who won the tournament . . . it was at the Holiday Inn in Long Beach, and, to make a long story short, we went out and we [sparred]. We were in the parking lot. Everybody was — I mean, the place was about 3,000 people that were there, and Bruce Lee and I are out in the parking lot — sparring. Now you have to understand this was my first encounter with the man. And to me, fast was fast, but when you cannot see [the punches], what can you say? I mean, fast is fast, right? But if you're not seeing them — he was hitting me all over — I said "Wow!"[28]

While Bruce's speed was one thing. His fury was quite another. One martial artist that had the misfortune to experience both was Daniel Lee (no relation), a man who was not only a black belt in Kenpo Karate and a brown belt in Judo, but also the National Amateur Boxing Champion of China.[29] It was an experience he would never forget:

> I used to box a lot. And once when I was working out with Bruce at his home in Culver City he had a pair of big sixteen-ounce boxing gloves. Danny [Inosanto] was there and two other guys. Bruce said to me, "Hey

Dan, put the gloves on." I said, "Okay." Bruce said, "Let's play around a bit." And during the course of what was supposed to be a very light sparring session, I mean, Bruce wasn't being at all serious, my boxing reflexes took over and — boom! — I caught him with a shot. Immediately his face changed. He was surprised. And I could see him thinking, "How did he get me?" So, he had a total personality change, and he started to come at me viciously; he really meant business and was attacking me! I was going backwards trying to ward him off but he was nailing me, and, as this was in the kitchen, I soon ran out of room to retreat and I hit the counter and he unloaded a right cross to the side of my jaw and I went down. Afterwards, Bruce came to his senses and said, "Are you okay?" I said, "Yeah." Later he asked Dan Inosanto, "Was I rough on Dan?" Inosanto said, "You sure were!" It didn't knock me out but it shook me up quite a bit. And the next day I was out in the yard and my jaw suddenly locked open. I had to hit my own jaw in order to reset it. And, almost two years passed and I continued to have that problem. So, I went to a dentist and he took a jaw x-ray and said, "Mr. Lee, you have a little injury on your jaw." I said, "Yeah, I know that." It turned out to be Bruce's gift to me.[30]

Such was the skill set that Bruce Lee brought with him when he returned to Hong Kong to launch a film career that would shatter box office records and make him an international legend.

CHAPTER FIFTEEN

A FIGHT FAR FROM THE MADDING CROWD

"Remember that the power of the kick and punch comes from the correct contact at the right spot, and at the right moment with the body in perfect position, not from the vigor with which the kicks or blows are delivered as many people think."

— Bruce Lee (*Black Belt* magazine, 1968)

A t 4:00 p.m. on April 9, 1970, Bruce Lee stepped out from the wings on *Enjoy Yourself Tonight*, a popular Cantonese-language variety show that was broadcast live from Hong Kong's TVB studios. The host of the show, Joseph Lau, began the program with a sit-down interview with Bruce, during which the pair discussed Bruce's film work in the United States. He had recently appeared as a villain in the James Garner private eye flick *Marlowe*, and Bruce, together with the Hollywood A-lister James Coburn and Academy Award–winning writer Stirling Silliphant, had collaborated on a screenplay entitled *The Silent Flute*. Bruce expressed confidence that the project would soon be heading before the cameras. Since both Coburn and Silliphant were students of Bruce's Jeet Kune Do, it made for a perfect segue for Lau to move the discussion to the subject of fighting. Bruce was perfectly at home discussing this topic, of course, and his answers came quickly and easily — as did his criticism of the traditional Chinese martial arts, which was reflexive by now. This was old hat to those who attended his demonstrations or read his interviews in America, but in Hong Kong such a critique was novel and, in some quarters, alarming.

A demonstration of Jeet Kune Do followed. A local Karate expert, Lee Kam-kwan, was invited on the show to assist Bruce with his demo. He brought along several of his students, who also stepped onto the stage before the studio cameras. Bruce stood up, kicked off his sandals — and put on the performance of his life.

He began with a demonstration of speed in punching and kicking. His techniques were almost too quick to register on camera. Next came a demonstration of his kicking power. He first performed a sidekick on an air shield (an inflatable pad that was used as a training aid for practicing hitting and blocking in American football) that was held by one of the black belts — the impact from which sent the Karateka airborne for several feet, before he hit the ground and rolled another eight feet or so. The audience went wild with applause. Next, Bruce performed a series of one-armed push-ups using only the thumb and index finger of his right hand. A board-breaking demonstration followed, in which he snapped a board in half with his one-inch punch.[1] He capped off his performance that evening by sidekicking five one-inch boards held by one of the black belts. "In the demonstration," Bruce would later recall, "I had a person dangle five one-inch boards in the air, and I sidekicked them and broke four of them. It is much easier to break boards that are held securely by a person using two arms. It is very difficult to do when the boards are suspended in the air."[2]

It was a tour de force presentation and the studio audience, along with those watching at home, would talk about it for several months afterward. When the announcement finally arrived that a Hong Kong movie studio had inked Bruce Lee to a two-picture deal, it was almost expected. It was abundantly clear to the people of Hong Kong that Bruce Lee was the new "thing" in Chinese martial arts — the young, cool face of the future. They eagerly looked forward to the release of his first film, *The Big Boss*, and then filled the theaters to watch it — repeatedly — until it became the highest-grossing film in Hong Kong history.[3]

THE MARTIAL ARTIST AS MOVIE STAR

Kung Fu films were certainly nothing new in Hong Kong. There had been movie serials devoted to the action adventures of the Hung

Gar Kung Fu founder Wong Fei Hung, for example, since the late 1940s. These had proven incredibly popular with the Chinese movie-going public. Since then, *The Chinese Boxer*, directed by and starring Wang Yu, and *Vengeance*, directed by Chang Cheh and starring David Chiang (both released in 1970), had been box office hits, indicating a strong appetite for Kung Fu films in the region, as well as in the Chinese communities throughout Europe and North America. David Chiang[4] and Bruce (unlike Wang Yu)[5] were martial artists in real life, and the serious money their films were making opened the eyes of other martial artists in Hong Kong to the fact that devotees of Kung Fu — as opposed to just professional actors — could become movie stars in this exciting new genre. Fame and fortune had long been the dream of a good many Kung Fu practitioners, and now a direct path to these two goals had just opened up before them. But how could a martial artist get noticed by the producers of such films? One man, a Western boxer named Lau Dai Chuen, believed he had the answer.

FIGHTING FOR FILM ROLES

Since Chinese Kung Fu films were fiercely nationalistic, with the Chinese protagonist typically being oppressed by foreigners and fighting back using the national art of Kung Fu, Lau Dai Chuen saw a means of drawing the attention of producers to his pugilistic skills by wrapping them up in the flag of Chinese nationalism. He went to the Hong Kong press and publicly challenged Bruce Lee to a fight under the pretense of standing up for the Chinese martial arts. He seized on a statement that Bruce made during his appearance on *Enjoy Yourself Tonight* in which he criticized many of the Hong Kong Kung Fu practitioners for being more talk than action when it came to fighting.[6] Never mind the fact that Lau Dai Chuen was not a practitioner of Chinese martial arts himself, but rather Western boxing,[7] he believed the people of Hong Kong would appreciate that he was standing up for Chinese Kung Fu.

Lau aired his grievance in the local newspapers,[8] proclaiming that he was willing to fight Bruce Lee at any time and place of Bruce's choosing. Soon another challenge appeared in the Hong Kong press. This one came from Chan Sing-Biu, an instructor of Choy Lay Fut

Kung Fu. "I find this sort of thing really annoying," Bruce said. "I am not going to fight with anybody."[9]

FIST OF FURY

Bruce ignored both challenges and, by November of 1971, was busy filming his next picture for Golden Harvest Studios, *Fist of Fury*.[10] But the problem followed him onto the set. An extra that had been hired got in his face and challenged him to fight. It didn't last long. "Bruce sparred with him," Bruce's co-star Bob Baker would later recall, "but within a few seconds finished the kid off with a sidekick — end of the matter."[11]

The truth, however, was that the matter had just begun. Max Lee, who played one of Bruce's opponents in the film, recalled a conversation he had with Bruce while on a ferry ride to nearby Macau: "During the ferry trip . . . he said that a lot of people knew he could fight, so there were a lot of letters, phone calls, people with connections asking him to fight with them to see if he was really that good . . . I told him he didn't need to do this . . . I said it wasn't worth it, it didn't make good business sense to do it. It just wasn't necessary."[12]

While this was certainly true, Bruce's patience was beginning to wear thin. "These motherfuckers will come up to me shaking their fists and daring me to fight," he said. "You know, if they did this to me a few years ago, I'd knock them on their asses. But now I can't do it because these sons of bitches will go right to the newspapers and boast about how they had beaten me, even if I had kicked their butts in. If they get hurt, they'll sue me for sure because they think I got so much money. I can't win either way, so I try to keep my cool. But sometimes I'm tempted to whack 'em."[13] The action actor Bolo Yeung recalled, "Bruce Lee was angry. He knew these guys just wanted publicity. He told me, 'Every day the people are saying *fight me*! I cannot or else I'll be fighting every day.'"[14]

Unfortunately, Bruce's passivity did not stop the challenges from rolling in. Indeed, once word reached Lau Dai Chuen's ears that Bruce was making yet another Kung Fu film, he wrote a letter to the Hong Kong martial arts magazine *New Martial Hero* in a further attempt to goad Bruce into a beimo.[15] Once again, Bruce ignored the challenge. He had more pressing matters that needed to be dealt with.

While he and his family were now living in Hong Kong, he was still paying the mortgage on their Bel Air home back in the United States. Paying money for a house they were no longer living in was a problem that needed to be addressed. To this end, Bruce and Linda returned to California for a week in early January 1972 to finalize the sale of the property.[16] While at the house he received a telephone call from his student Daniel Lee, who wanted to touch base. During the conversation, the matter of Lau Dai Chuen's recent challenges came up:

> *Bruce Lee*: "Let's say if Lau Dai Chuen were man enough, instead of going to the newspaper, to walk up to me and slap me, well, that's the end of him! I mean, [laughs] I [haven't] yet been able to 'turn the other cheek,' man!"

> *Daniel Lee*: ". . . unlike ten years ago, when you would have said 'Okay, Lau Dai Chuen: pick the time!'"

> *Bruce Lee*: "*Pick the time?* I wouldn't 'pick the time,' I wouldn't even say anything! I would just show up right in front of his door waiting for him! That's all there is to it."[17]

ENCOUNTER IN A RESTAURANT

Not long after returning to Hong Kong, Bruce was having dim sum with several of the Golden Harvest stuntmen in the Hon Gung Restaurant when in walked Lau Dai Chuen. The men watched as Lau walked past them to another table. Soon, Lau took notice of Bruce and stared at him.

This upset one of Bruce's crew, Lam Chin Ying, who stood up and made his way directly to Lau's table. "Fight *me*! You fight me first — then you get to fight my Sifu [teacher]!"

Lau ignored him.

"You're not much of a fighter," Lam hissed. "Get up!"[18]

Lau paid no attention. Realizing that he was wasting his time, Lam made his way back to Bruce's group and fumed.

After finishing his tea, Lau stood up and walked over to Bruce's table. Bruce kept his eyes on him. Lau reissued his challenge.

Just as he had ignored the challenges by Yoichi Nakachi in Seattle until he recognized that he could no longer do so, Bruce now accepted the fact that Lau wasn't going to stop challenging him until he agreed to fight. "All right," Bruce replied. "But we'll fight somewhere where there are less people around."[19]

This stipulation prevented the fight from occurring right then and there, as the restaurant was full of people, and taking the matter outside onto the sidewalk would only have invited more witnesses to the encounter. But Bruce's specification was also a test to see if Lau really wanted to fight or whether his challenge efforts had been merely a ploy for publicity. After all, if no one was present to witness the fight, Lau couldn't trade on it. But as Lau's posture in the press had always been that he was simply standing up for Chinese Kung Fu, then a private match would suffice. To Bruce's surprise, Lau accepted the condition. The Bruce Lee–Lau Dai Chuen fight was going to happen.

A PRIVATE MATCH

Tang Sang, a chief detective with the Royal Hong Kong Police Force, was a student of Yip Man's since the mid-1960s. His passion for Chinese martial arts led him to found the Hong Kong Chinese Martial Arts Community (HKCMAC), which, as its name implies, served to promote Chinese Kung Fu. Along with several other senior Wing Chun students, Tang also helped Yip Man create the Ving Tsun (Wing Chun) Athletic Association, a school that exists to this day in Hong Kong.

One might be tempted to conclude that Detective Tang was a stand-up guy who was a huge supporter of the Chinese martial arts, but that was only one half of a rather complex psychology; the other half featured a somewhat darker side. He was, for example, less than exemplary in his duties as a law enforcement officer, earning a reputation as a man who was not above taking bribes from the triads.[20] However, the martial arts community in Hong Kong was willing to wink at this given all that he had done on its behalf. Consequently, Tang's name carried influence, which he put into play to arrange the fight between Lau Dai Chuen and Bruce Lee.

The match would be held at Tang's personal villa in Fanling, in Hong Kong's New Territories, eighteen miles to the north of Kowloon and far away from the city's plentiful and curious eyes.[21] On the designated day, Bruce drove from Kowloon to the Ma Mei Ha district of Fanling. Soon the driveway of the detective's private villa came into view.[22] Upon his arrival, however, Bruce was annoyed to discover that approximately twenty people were meandering about the property.[23] While this was far less than the number that would have shown up had the fight been staged in the city (particularly given that Lau's challenges had appeared in newspapers and the martial arts press in Hong Kong), it was still a far cry from the privacy Bruce had stipulated in agreeing to the fight, and which he had evidently been promised by Detective Tang.

THE FIGHT

What happened next is not clear. In one account, Bruce and Lau stepped into a boxing ring set up by Tang to train certain of the Ving Tsun Athletic Association fighters who were starting to enter full-contact matches at the time.[24] Another says both men were dressed in Western boxing attire.[25] Both of these reports seem highly unlikely, as squaring off in a ring or wearing Western boxing outfits would have been needlessly formal and highly out of character for Bruce, based on his previous fights. Also, this was a martial arts contest, not a Western boxing match. It seems far more likely that the two men simply faced off in the yard of Detective Tang's house before a small group of people that were either members of the HKCMAC or students from the Ving Tsun Athletic Association who had been invited there by Tang.

While there is a lack of consensus as to how the fight ended, there is absolute unanimity on how it started — Lau Dai Cheun rushed at Bruce employing the hand techniques from Western boxing that had brought him so much success in the ring. Bruce deftly avoided Lau's jabs, hooks and crosses through a series of bobs, weaves and slips.[26] Having now experienced Lau's speed and technique, Bruce's confidence grew.

Lau, on the other hand, still wasn't sure what Bruce had in his arsenal. Bruce's nickname in the Hong Kong press at the time was "three-kick Lee," a reference to his on-screen fight scenes in which he would take out the bad guys with three quick kicks — right, left, right.[27] Knowing this, Lau believed that Bruce would attempt to deploy his signature maneuver during their match, and so kept looking down at Bruce's feet, waiting for him to initiate it.[28] Evidently Lau had based his entire counteroffensive strategy upon this attack occurring, and he intended to answer it with a low leg sweep to Bruce's supporting leg.[29]

Unfortunately, the films Lau had been studying consisted solely of Bruce's Kung Fu movies, in which Bruce displayed flashy kicks and strikes that looked flamboyant on the big screen — but which were nothing at all like the techniques he used in his real fights. Taking notice of Lau's area of focus, Bruce quickly discerned his opponent's intent. Lau expected Bruce's first kick in the sequence to be a high hook or roundhouse kick, and so he leaned back slightly in anticipation.[30] Seeing his opening, Bruce darted forward and drove a lightning-fast punch into Lau's jaw.[31] He followed this up immediately with a sidekick that landed with a mammoth impact on Lau's chest, knocking him flat on his back, where he began writhing in pain.[32] The fight was over. According to Bolo Yeung, the entire contest lasted "maybe twenty seconds."[33]

Lau attempted to get back to his feet but found that his chest pain was too intense for him to push himself up. He grimaced and clutched at his chest as he fell back to the ground.[34] Several people now came forward to help him up.[35] Seeing that his opponent was seriously hurt, Bruce approached the injured fighter and said that he would cover any medical expenses that Lau might have to incur as a result of the match.[36] Moreover, just as he had after his fights with Yoichi Nakachi and Wong Jack Man, Bruce announced to Lau, Tang and all of the spectators that no one was to speak a word of the fight to anyone.[37]

The action now over, everybody left Tang's villa. Bruce returned to his home in Kowloon, and Lau, according to Golden Harvest production manager Chaplin Chang, ended up flying to Japan so that his hospitalization would not be discovered by the Hong Kong press.[38] Upon arrival at the Japanese hospital, Lau was treated for three broken ribs.[39]

Despite everyone's pledge to keep quiet about what they had witnessed, news about the match soon began to trickle out. "Word reached me while I was on the set of *Enter the Dragon*," recalled Bolo. "I asked Bruce if the story about the encounter was true. Bruce nodded grimly in the affirmative and told me, 'Keep it to yourself.'"[40] Bolo suspected that Chief Detective Tang was the one who had opened his mouth about it; after all, the match was at his villa.[41] However the information came out, it was piecemeal and fragmentary. Hong Kong broadcaster Ted Thomas said he heard rumors in 1972 about a fight involving Bruce, but thought it occurred in a nightclub. "Bruce was involved in a fight and half killed the guy but it was all covered up by — and I do stress this is a rumor — Raymond Chow, who had paid out a good deal of money to bury the whole thing. I don't think there was anything ever published about it."[42]

The less people knew about the incident the better as far as Bruce was concerned. The plan at this stage of his life was to become an international movie star, not the back-alley Fight Club champion of Hong Kong.

CHAPTER SIXTEEN

BAD PRESS AND GANGSTERS

"If somebody attacks you, your response is not Technique No. 1, Stance No. 2, Section 4, Paragraph 5. Instead, you simply move in like sound and echo, without any deliberation. It is as though, when I call you, you answer me, or when I throw something at you, you catch it. It's as simple as that, no fuss, no muss."

— Bruce Lee (*Black Belt* magazine, 1967)

Bruce Lee was now the biggest superstar in Hong Kong. His face peered out from the covers of countless magazines, he was a frequent guest on Cantonese-language talk shows, and, whenever he went out in public, he was followed by hordes of people, particularly young kids, who wanted to get an up-close glimpse of their hero.[1] Bruce Lee Mania was in full swing.

But Bruce's success wasn't applauded by everybody, particularly the senior students at Yip Man's school — the same ones who had been instrumental in having him kicked out of the institution fifteen years previously. To them, Bruce Lee remained persona non grata, an apostate who, rather than knuckling down and learning the complete Wing Chun system, had taken bits of the art and then built his own mongrel system around it.

In truth, Bruce's art of Jeet Kune Do diverged markedly from the Wing Chun that was taught in Yip Man's Ving Tsun Athletic Association: its stance was different, its footwork was different, the kicking was different, no forms were performed, and its striking attacks incorporated hooking or curved lines of attack, rather than just the linear striking pattern of Wing Chun. And yet, while you could take the boy out of the art, you couldn't take the art out of the boy. Not fully anyway.

Despite the creation of his own art, a chronological look over Bruce Lee's media materials from 1967 to 1972 reveals the actions of a man who was engaged in a public relations campaign on behalf of Wing Chun:

- In October and November 1967, after he'd created Jeet Kune Do, he was profiled in a two-part series in *Black Belt* magazine in which he publicly credited his martial achievement to Wing Chun.[2]
- In 1969 *Black Belt* published an article he wrote on the sticking hands exercise of Wing Chun.[3]
- In May 1971 he wrote a book on Wing Chun and oversaw the photography of the Sil Lum Tao and fighting sequences.[4]
- In September 1971 he appeared in the premiere episode of the TV series *Longstreet*, which aired nationally on the ABC network. In the episode he is shown performing the sticking hands exercise from Wing Chun.[5]
- In the summer of 1972, he gave the okay for his book on Wing Chun to be published. To help out his friend and student James Lee with his medical bills, he asked the publisher to list James as the author of the book.[6]
- In September 1972 he allowed photographs of himself demonstrating Wing Chun hand techniques with Yip Man to appear in an article published in *Black Belt* promoting the Wing Chun book.[7]

To Bruce, all of these things were an acknowledgment of the martial art that had so positively influenced him, in addition to being a tip of the hat to his old instructor back in Hong Kong.

To Yip Man's senior students, however, such press was a further example of Bruce Lee's apostasy; he had taken material that was proprietary to their art and put it out there for non-Chinese all across America to see. Despite the animus of these students, Bruce retained a fondness for both Wing Chun and Yip Man. While in Hong Kong, he always made sure that Yip's school received free tickets to his films. He gave Yip Man gifts and took him out for tea.[8] And, upon learning that Yip Man had become gravely ill, he reached out to the Yip family and offered to help in any way he could.

"When my father was ill," recalled Yip Chun, Yip Man's eldest son, "Bruce called us up several times. He told my brother that if there were any financial problems, he was willing to offer help. My father appreciated him very much. He especially liked his humble attitude in learning and his diligence. At later times, he used Bruce as an example to teach his students."[9] This was all well and good, but Yip Man's senior students simply didn't want to hear it.

THE DEATH OF YIP MAN

In early December 1972, Bruce flew to California with his production partner Raymond Chow to finalize negotiations between their new company, Concord Films, and Warner Bros. to make *Enter the Dragon.* He returned to Hong Kong a week later only to discover that his beloved teacher, Yip Man, had passed away and been buried during his absence. Not one Wing Chun student had seen fit to contact him and let him know that Yip had died. Yip Chun had thought to notify Bruce about his father's passing, but was prevented from doing so by one of his father's senior students.[10]

The students saw Bruce's willingness to teach foreigners as being expressly against Yip Man's wishes.[11] His having created his own martial art, his not mentioning either Yip Man or Wing Chun during his numerous Hong Kong radio and television interviews — these were interpreted as acts of betrayal. Even worse, his attitude reeked of America: he was born in America, he'd lived in America, he hung out with American movie stars, he dressed in American fashions, he spoke in American slang, his students were American, and he had just signed a deal to co-produce his next film with Warner Bros., an American movie studio. By contrast, Yip Man's way had always been nationalistic; his art of Wing Chun was to solely benefit the Chinese people, a principle which, to the senior students' way of thinking, Bruce had turned his back on. In truth, they were resentful of his success and fighting prowess, and the fact that their many attempts over the years to drive a wedge between him and Yip Man had failed.

CALLED OUT BY THE SENIOR STUDENTS

Bruce always viewed his Chinese heritage as a source of pride and hoped to introduce Kung Fu to the West in order to make other nations sit up and take notice of this aspect of Chinese culture. But to many members of the Wing Chun clan, his behavior was engineered to bring glory to himself as the primary beneficiary; any glory that his films and celebrity might bring to the Chinese people was a markedly downstream effect. Consequently, his adversaries were only too happy to point out to local newspapers that the Little Dragon had not attended his master's funeral in Hong Kong because he'd been too busy kissing up to Warner Bros. executives in America. One of Yip Man's senior students, Luo Yao, made the following statement to the Hong Kong press:

> I think the key issue is: did Bruce view himself primarily as a student of Yip Man and Wing Chun, or as the founder and grandmaster of Jeet Kune Do? This contradiction was not easy to resolve, so I think we have to keep in mind his own difficult position when Grandmaster Yip passed away. From my perspective, whether the relationship is between master and disciple or between friend and friend, when someone passes away, the traditional values my country holds dear demand one pay one's respects. Nevertheless, I don't blame or fault him for this, since I don't know what he was going through. If he had shown up for Sifu's funeral procession, then that would have simply been what was expected. As for the fact that he didn't, the key issue is what was in his heart.[12]

Another of Yip Man's senior students, Liang Xiang, commented:

> Though Bruce Lee started his own new school of martial arts, one cannot deny that the majority of his Kung Fu came from Wing Chun. So far as I know, my Sifu had a very high estimation of Bruce's skills and hard work in the world of martial arts. When Bruce Lee's father Lee

Hoi-chuen passed away, Sifu Yip attended his funeral. As for why Bruce Lee didn't show up when his own Sifu passed away, it's pretty hard to understand. As founder of Jeet Kune Do and a big movie star, perhaps it was just too inconvenient! Nevertheless, looking at it in human terms, and in terms of traditional master-disciple relationships, Bruce should have been there, no doubt.[13]

Even his private instructor in Wing Chun, Wong Shun Leung, expressed his disapproval:

> Bruce Lee was a student of Wing Chun. No matter what he himself might say, this is the undeniable truth. He was also my brother in studying Wing Chun under Yip Man. When we were young, we would cross arms with one another so often, we really knew each other very well. After he left for America, he would still keep in touch; only after he started his own school of martial arts did our relationship begin to grow a bit more distant. Perhaps he viewed his own skills as having arrived at a certain level. After returning to Hong Kong, he only called me a few times.
>
> As for the fact that he didn't show up for Sifu's funeral, this was definitely a breach in terms of the decorum of the martial arts world. I think people can't forget their "roots." After all, even if you break off on your own and start a great new martial art of your own, you'll never forget the foundations you built with your teachers. As for Bruce's behavior on this occasion, I don't know if perhaps he was going through a difficult time or felt awkward, but I still think he should have shown up or provided some expression of his sympathies. It is certainly very difficult for a person not to let fame get to him![14]

Wong's rebuke cut the deepest. Bruce was both angered and embarrassed by the public shaming. He telephoned the Yip household to explain himself and to apologize for having missed the master's funeral. According to Yip Chun: "Five days after my father's death, Bruce gave us a phone call. It was my brother Yip Ching who took the call. According to what I know, Bruce expressed that he had just come back from the States after signing a contract with Warner Bros., and that he felt sad when he heard that his teacher had passed away. He felt sorry for us and asked about the matter of commemorating my father. So, my brother told him all about it."[15]

A memorial service for Yip Man, not unlike a Celebration of Life, took place two days later, and Bruce made sure to arrive at the Ving Tsun Athletic Association an hour prior to the service to formally apologize to Yip's family.[16] As Yip Chun recollected:

> The service was held in our Wing Chun Institute. That night, soon after the meeting had started, Bruce came, accompanied by two friends. He stood in the midst of the hall before the picture of my father, he fixed his eyes on the picture for a while. Then he burned incense and bowed to his teacher. He was very courteous in doing all these. After that, he left behind two hundred dollars as a gift, and then he left . . . As a matter of fact, he did not owe my father anything, and my father showed no sign of dissatisfaction with him. Although Bruce did not come to the funeral, he had come to the meeting that night, and we should not be harsh on him.[17]

A RESENTMENT FESTERS

While Bruce had made his peace with the Yip family, an anger percolated below the surface. He had been in and out of Yip Man's memorial service quickly, having no desire to mix with the same students who had connived to have him kicked out of Yip's Wing Chun school and who shoved his mixed heritage in his face. Their comments in the press he could handle, but he had no intention of spending one second more of his time with them than the propriety of the service demanded. Wong Shun Leung, however, was a different story.

Wong's comments upset him, particularly his statement that Jeet Kune Do enjoyed a high standing solely because it stood upon the foundation of Wing Chun. While it was certainly true that Wing Chun played an important role in Bruce's development, Wong's comments failed to respect the fact that Bruce had spent thousands of hours, years in fact, on his own in unwavering study and diligent practice of unarmed combat. They ignored his research and incorporation of fencing principles and techniques, boxing footwork and strikes, and how hard he had trained — without any guidance from his Wing Chun brothers — to make his techniques faster and more powerful.

He'd also spent considerable time sparring the best martial artists that America had to offer, men who were much bigger than he was and incredibly athletic, the best of the best, any one of whom would have fed any of Yip Man's students their lunch (with the possible exception of Wong) had they the inclination. To say that Jeet Kune Do was no big deal and no different from Wing Chun was to spit on his life's work. Not to mention that a public reprimand from someone whom he deeply respected was a loss of face. It was a matter he intended to address — not publicly, but privately.

For his part, Wong Shun Leung, ever the straight-shooter, remained angry at Bruce for missing the funeral of his master, and he stood by his statements to the newspapers. He meant it when he said that fame had gone to Bruce's head. A storm cloud was brewing.

THE RISE OF A GANGSTER

Chan Wai Man was a legit gangster. He was born into an impoverished family in Guangdong, China, in 1943. By the time he turned twelve, his family had relocated to Hakka village in Tsuen Wan, in Hong Kong's New Territories. There, Chan was put to work in a spinning mill to earn money to help support his parents and siblings. As Bruce Lee did at a similar age, Chan soon took up the martial arts and joined a street gang.[18]

By the age of seventeen, he was a corrections officer at a Hong Kong prison. By nineteen he was promoted to the position of police officer in the anti-drug division of the Hong Kong Police Force, walking the streets and knocking heads with the underworld. "The 1960s and 1970s were the darkest period," Chan recalled, "with the most dance clubs, nightclubs, drug trafficking, selling MDMA (ecstasy pills), and gambling dens."[19] Soon, however, he switched allegiances and began to work *with* the triads, rather than against them, which resulted in his being fired from the police force.[20] He recalled, "Police were gangsters and gangsters were police. All worked together to make money, you see. In the seventies, eighties and nineties there were so many police officers who were triads."[21]

Chan made the transition from law enforcement officer to full-time triad smoothly, becoming a full member of one of Hong Kong's largest triad societies, the 14K. Indeed, he proved so good at collections on behalf of the mob that he was soon promoted to the position of "red stick," a title that was given to well-trained fighters who ran the enforcement operations of the triads. Chan had almost five hundred men working under him at one point, any one of whom would do his bidding at a snap of his fingers: "Every day I'd go out with ten to fifteen bodyguards. At that time, all of Tsim Sha Tsui [the core urban area in southern Kowloon] was *my* territory. Anybody who wanted to open a nightclub in Tsim Sha Tsui, all you needed was my consent. If not, we'd do you in. Back then, you couldn't call the police because when I collected your protection fee, the police got a cut too."[22] You didn't get to be an enforcer/collector for the 14K unless you were an exceptionally good fighter and exceptionally menacing, and Chan was both. He had won Western boxing championships and the Southeast Asian kickboxing championship,[23] and would later parlay his reputation into a career in Kung Fu and gangster films.

Chan had also been friends with Bruce since the pair were teenagers,[24] but the two had lost touch when Bruce moved away to the United States in 1959. With Bruce's movies making him *the* martial arts superstar in Hong Kong, Chan decided it was time to pay him a visit, both to reconnect and to see if Bruce lived up to the hype. He brought along the actor Chan Ling-chung (better known by his screen name Little Unicorn), who was also a long-time friend of Bruce's and may well have been responsible for reintroducing the pair. According to Chan, it was strictly a friendly visit. Perhaps so. But Chan was a genuine badass, an alpha male who never took an inferior position to anybody. Consequently, he hadn't been at Bruce's house long before the two were exchanging martial arts techniques.

Chan tried to impress Bruce with his kicking power by throwing a sidekick at an air shield held by Unicorn. Unicorn was pushed back a few feet from the impact. Bruce sidekicked the same air shield and Unicorn's feet left the ground. "Bruce Lee took three steps to kick the air shield," Chan recalled, "and Little Unicorn was like an arrow — boom! — he flew out! I've only seen this in the movies!"[25] Chan then challenged Bruce to a wrist-wrestling match — and lost quickly.[26]

Whatever impression the triad enforcer-cum-kickboxing champion had been trying to make on Bruce up until this point wasn't making much headway. Well aware of how interconnected the Hong Kong Police Department was with the triads, Chan knew of Chief Detective Tang Sang and Bruce's fight with Lau Dai Chuen.[27] But he also knew that Lau was only proficient in Western boxing, whereas Chan was not only a Western boxing champion but also a champion in kickboxing. Bruce, by contrast, hadn't been in a ring since he won a boxing match in 1958. This suggested to Chan that he would have little trouble getting the better of Bruce in a sparring match.

It would prove to be his third embarrassment of the evening. "I just moved a little bit and — boom! — his fist hit me in the face!" Chan recalled.[28] The blow evidently sent the triad enforcer sprawling to the floor.[29] The sparring match was over as quickly as it started. Chan was experienced enough to know what the outcome would have been had he pressed his luck any further that evening: "If I fought him, I'd lose to him. He could beat me easily . . . Bruce never fought in the ring but I did . . . [and yet] his skills were way better than me. That's the truth. He was way better than me."[30]

When asked years later if the triads had tried to move in on Bruce when he was at the peak of his fame (they would attempt this with Jackie Chan years later),[31] Chan denied it. "It's impossible," he replied. "No secret societies dared to provoke Bruce Lee to a fight at that time."[32] When asked if Bruce was the only person he would have been hesitant about fighting in real life, Chan's answer was honest and succinct: "Yes. Only an idiot would fight with him."[33]

PUTTING OUT THE TRASH

While the triads might have known better than to try their muscle against Bruce in Hong Kong, the "idiots" evidently didn't get the memo.

One evening, not long after the Lees had moved into a new house in the upscale district of Kowloon,[34] Bruce saw a man climb over the wall of his property and into his yard. This was no small feat, as the walls that surrounded the Lee home were made of brick and concrete and stood eight feet high, with broken glass and razor wire affixed to their tops.

Bruce yelled at the man, which made him stop in his tracks.

"How good are you?"[35] the man yelled back.

Bruce couldn't believe his ears. He would later tell his student Herb Jackson that "just the idea of someone coming on my property, where my family is, to challenge me, I got angry — I mean, *really* angry."[36] Bruce ran down the stairs and out into his front yard. His pace sped up as he approached the man, who by now was standing in the middle of his lawn. Before the interloper could do anything, Bruce skipped forward and sidekicked him as hard as he could.

"He told me that was the hardest kick he'd ever given anybody," Jackson recalled. "I know he would have had to have broken his ribs, because when Bruce kicked, you had to use special padding, like a telephone book or something equivalent to that, to protect yourself, otherwise he would break your ribs.[37] Bruce never told me what happened to the guy afterward; they let him out or sent him back over the wall or something."[38]

The ill-will Bruce was receiving in Hong Kong, both from his former Wing Chun brothers and those seeking to test his fighting abilities, was on the rise. He made it known that he would be moving back to the United States as soon as he finished up his movie commitments.[39] But he was about to discover that a film set offered no special solace or protection from reputation-seekers who were determined to take him down.

CHAPTER SEVENTEEN

ENTER THE EXTRAS

"It's really a smooth rhythmic expression of smashing the guy before he hits you, with any method available."

— Bruce Lee (*Miami Beach Sun*, 1969)

Bruce Lee wanted the films that he was starring in (and had started directing) in Hong Kong to become so successful that Hollywood would come calling. At that point, he could write his own ticket, return to America, and move on to the next stage of his revised master plan: to become the biggest movie star in the world. But the recent spate of challenges and home invasions had made him keenly aware that the success of his plan hinged entirely on his ability to deal with these threats — and this meant that he had to keep his martial arts ability well-honed.

To this end, he had equipment created for him in Hong Kong that, through negative reinforcement, refined the precision of his strikes. According to his co-star in *The Way of the Dragon*, Jon Benn:

> He had an electrical thing; I remember when you'd put your fist in it you would get a shock — unless you were very, very fast and could withdraw your hand before the electric charge could touch you. He had it made, and it was a very sharp piece of metal, so you had to be very careful when you put your hand in that you didn't touch the edge and cut yourself or get zapped. He could do it so fast — Bip! Bip! Bip! — and never once got a shock or touched the edge. He was very

accurate. I remember I stuck my hand in it one time and — Zap! — I wouldn't do that again! But he was in and out of that hole in the metal so fast! He'd just do it constantly. There were four holes in it of varying diameters and he would jab four fingers, three fingers, one finger — and he'd never miss.[1]

He took to using an electronic muscle stimulation machine, which emitted volts of electricity resulting in muscle contractions of varying levels of intensity. This allowed his muscles to be exercised while he was reading a script, a book, or conducting business over the phone. The wires that came out of the machine were attached to small pads of various sizes that were affixed to the muscles he wished to exercise. "He used electrostimulation with little pads that would contract the muscles — for power," Bolo Yeung recalled. "He'd put the pads on his upper and lower back, he'd put them on his quadriceps and attempt to kick against the contraction. He'd put them on his abdominals — everywhere."[2]

Bruce's co-star in *Enter the Dragon*, John Saxon, recalled that "Bruce also had this strange fishing net hanging from two walls in the back of his house with round pads embedded within it. He told me to step aside, and then he grabbed the side of the net and shook it hard until the net flowed back and forth on its own. He then jumped in the air, kicking and punching the pads as the net waved toward his position. Seeing this firsthand was pretty amazing! Bruce was ahead of his time with training aids and way ahead of his time in how he trained his physicality."[3]

As cutting edge as Bruce's physical training was, it paled in comparison to what Bolo observed him doing to enhance his mental focus and awareness:

> One day I went to his house and his wife told me to go upstairs. I couldn't believe what I saw. I dared not enter until he opened the door to call me in. Bruce was sitting behind his desk with a wired ring around his head. My first thought was he must be *chi jo sin* [mentally ill]. He said, "I am training my nervous system to

transmit reactions faster. It is for *san sau mang chit* [agile body and hands]. Your eye sees someone make a move toward you and your eye nerve directs the brain's central nervous system and your brain's nervous system directs your hand or arm or foot to block or kick or strike. This takes time. Too much time. I wanted to train to have it happen faster.

"How to do this? I tried many experiments. It is very abstract. I finally figured out that a person's reflexes are fastest when he is sleeping. When he is almost completely relaxed. The more relaxed you are, the faster the reflexes are. When a person's external and internal systems are relaxed, the nervous transmission is the fastest. When you know this, you can possibly recreate this condition. How? During sparring you are very tense and cannot relax. What to do? You must want to sleep! You must get yourself into a condition that is the equivalent of sleep even when you are sparring or fighting.

"I invented a machine that teaches me to do that . . . I strap this on my head and I have two [cassette] recorders. I can make the sounds from each recorder louder or softer. One tape has very loud sounds — automobile traffic, airplanes taking off, gongs and drums. The other tape is the sound of water slowly dripping — very rhythmic and hypnotic. I switch on both and mix the sounds, but turn the quiet sound louder than the noisy one. Slowly I decrease the dripping water and bring up the loud noises. But I can still hear the hypnotic sound no matter how loud the sound of an airplane gets. I have complete concentration on the dripping water no matter what. Internally, I can hear it. I can hear this sound — tap, tap, tap.

"In my pictures, watch my expression before a fight. Watch the close-ups. You watch carefully. My expression is different from the others. Others have their eyes wide open, tense. Gnashing teeth, fists clenched. My expression is wanting sleep. You look carefully."[4]

His new mind/body training would soon be put to the test.

ENTER THE DRAGON

By mid-March 1973 the cameras had been rolling on *Enter the Dragon* for just over a month and a half. Bruce was in charge of the choreography and, given the importance of this film to his career plan, he wanted its climactic battle sequences to be nothing short of spectacular.[5] Whereas in his second film for Golden Harvest, *Fist of Fury*, audiences had witnessed him single-handedly facing down a dojo packed with twenty-five black belts, for the finale of *Enter the Dragon* Bruce envisioned a massive brawl involving well over a hundred men.[6] This number far outstripped Golden Harvest's supply of stuntmen, and, because the studio staff was also limited, they simply didn't have the manpower to vet everybody who showed up to appear as extras in the film. As a result, an inordinate number of gang members, many itching to make a reputation for themselves, found their way onto the outdoor sets, and this meant that more challenges would soon be coming Bruce's way.[7]

THE UNPROTECTED STAR

Anything that can cause delays in the making of a film inevitably costs production companies large sums of money, enough to put a film way over budget. Consequently, the production team for *Enter the Dragon* should have seen to it that the star of their movie was insulated from challenges to fight on set. A broken bone, a sprained ankle or a bruised face could set back the production by several weeks, perhaps months. But Golden Harvest's associate producer Andre Morgan had a more cavalier attitude: "There were challenges from young martial artists. There were several fights, yeah. It was no big deal, because it wasn't a fight to the death. They'd get out there, and it was like a couple of boxers sparring for a couple of rounds. Nobody got seriously hurt. Yeah, you know, half in jest and half seriously. It happened a couple of times up on the sound stages when you're doing big action scenes."[8]

Given that no one from the production company took steps to protect Bruce, it is not surprising that he was challenged on the set. What is surprising, however, is that they passively stood back and watched no fewer than four fights take place.[9]

THE FIRST FIGHT

Twenty-nine-year-old Ahna Capri, the actress who played Tania, the exotic hostess of Han's Island in the film, was using her new Super 8mm camera to capture some of the sights on the outdoor set. The set was dressed to look like an arena in an outdoor martial arts tournament, but was really the multi-tiered tennis courts of the powerful Hong Kong attorney Lo Man Wai. Lo's expansive estate included a large mansion on the southwestern shore of Hong Kong Island that overlooked scenic Tai Tam Bay.

Meandering about the set, Capri set her camera rolling when American Karate champion Jim Kelly did some light sparring with Shotokan and Goju Ryu Karate expert Peter Archer. On top of the stone wall behind them sat a group of extras watching the Karate practitioners performing their techniques. They wore light brown Karate outfits to signify they were guards on the island. Capri approached Bruce Lee and Bob Wall, the latter a member of Karate's first World Championship team in 1970. Capri asked the pair if they wouldn't mind sparring for her camera. Despite Wall's martial pedigree, it is obvious from the footage that he simply had no answer for Bruce's speed, as Bruce was able to score at will, driving Wall backwards time and again.[10] The impromptu sparring match concluded, Capri put down her camera and prepared to film her next scene.

And that's when the problems began.

"You're a movie star — not a martial artist!" somebody shouted.[11]

Bruce looked at the extras on the stone wall. One of them smirked, but it didn't look like anything negative was going to happen. Bruce walked over to confer with Henry Wong, a cinematographer hired by Warner Bros. to shoot some behind-the-scenes footage for a featurette on the making of the film that would later be used for promotional purposes.

"I don't believe you can do it!" the extra called again.[12] His friends chortled at his moxie.

Bruce ignored him.

"You're just an actor for the movies!"[13]

Bruce paused his conversation with Wong.

"You're not much of a fighter — it's easy to see your martial art isn't any good!"[14]

Bruce faced the extra. "Oh, really? Well, come on down and we'll settle it."[15]

Urged on by his friends, the extra jumped down from the wall and sauntered over to where Bruce was standing. Nothing more was said. The fight began.

Bob Wall recalled:

> What was funny was that there was a certain amount of hostility coming out of the guy — but not Bruce. Bruce was very mellow, like, you know, he wasn't concerned about anybody. And the guy really started trying to hurt Bruce. I mean you could see that it wasn't a respectful, little starstruck kid doing a fight; this kid was a gang-banger type of guy from Hong Kong. He was trying to take Bruce's head off. And he was a damn good martial artist. He was fast, he was bigger than Bruce, and he was strong! I remember my reaction was, a minute or so into it, that Bruce's whole demeanor changed. His eyes got more focused, and you could see him going from happy-go-lucky — because Bruce was really full of life and love and a happy, funny guy; he was making you laugh most of the time — and he went deadly serious, for Bruce. Because he realized that this guy was not kidding; he was trying to hurt him.[16]

Bruce's footwork helped him avoid the extra's assault. "Bruce just kept moving so well, this kid couldn't touch him," Wall said. "But he was trying, and he came really close to hurting Bruce a couple of times. Then, all of a sudden, Bruce got him."[17]

Two rapid-fire kicks hit the man flush in the face, and he fell back against a wall.[18] Bruce's Wing Chun training now surfaced. "Bruce just methodically took him apart," Wall recollected. "He slammed the kid into a rock wall, then trapped him with his right knee and left hand. He took the kid's hand, punched in, just touched his cheek, brought his hand back, and said, 'See, you're mine.' He had the kid locked up! He couldn't move."[19]

Shih Kien, the veteran Chinese actor who played Lee's adversary Han in the film, saw the extra pinned to the stone wall by Bruce, who had his right fist cocked and ready to strike. It seemed to him that Bruce hesitated, perhaps thinking his adversary had had enough,[20] but then he suddenly pulled the trigger and delivered two quick punches to the man's face.[21] Blood was now flowing freely from the challenger's nose and mouth.[22] But then Bruce changed gears. "He made the kid fight until he couldn't move a muscle," Wall said. "And then he talked to him and said, 'This is like a lesson for you. I want you to understand.' Bruce was doing it like a lesson! He told him, 'Look, your stance is too wide; you were doing this.' And then the kid shook his hand and said, 'You really are a master of the martial arts,' and he climbed back up on the wall. . . . Bruce not only punched the kid out, but he didn't hurt him doing it. I was very impressed."[23]

The matter now concluded, Bruce got a drink of water and walked out to shoot the next scene.[24]

"Bruce just let him fly back up on the wall," Wall would later say. "But he let him know in no uncertain terms that they were totally mismatched. You see, Bruce was a world-class martial artist, and there are a lot of black belts walking around thinking there's no difference between a world-class martial artist and a black belt. But there is a *big* difference. Bruce was the real deal."[25]

While Bruce's grace under fire had impressed Bob Wall, John Saxon, the actor who played Roper in the film, was mortified by what he witnessed. "I remember wondering if it was at all necessary."[26]

Necessary or not, the lesson Bruce taught the extra did put a temporary stop to the challenges. However, after a week or so, the insults and the challenges returned. "The classic challenge would be to tap your foot three times in front of Bruce," director Robert Clouse recollected. "For the most part Bruce would laugh it off. A few would persist by becoming increasingly insulting."[27]

THE SECOND FIGHT

Henry Wong continued with his filming duties, capturing activities on set and scenic shots of the hills and Hong Kong harbor that the editors at Warner Bros. could incorporate into their promotional featurette. Upon his return to the set after one of these excursions, Wong filmed something completely unanticipated.

Bruce was typically among the last to leave after a day of shooting, and Wong approached him to strike up a conversation. An extra came up to them and asked if Bruce would be willing to take a moment to show him how to execute a particular kick. Wong picked up his camera. "I took a 16-millimeter movie of this," he recalled. "Bruce spent a lot of time with this extra because Bruce was good that way. He taught when he could."[28] Once he was confident that the extra had it down, Bruce nodded his approval and said that he had to get going. To both his and Wong's surprise, however, the extra suddenly became belligerent.

"No!" he exclaimed. "I want to show you what I learned!"

Bruce explained, politely but firmly, that he had to get going.

The extra shook his head. "No — we fight!"

Bruce wasn't interested, but the extra now pressed harder. "Your skill in Kung Fu isn't real!"[29]

Bruce laughed. "If *I* do not have real Kung Fu, I don't think you will have it."[30] He waved the man off.

"You're a coward!" the extra shouted.

A few of the crew members paused what they were doing to see what would happen. Wong wasn't sure if he should keep his camera rolling or not. After all, footage of two people calling each other names (even if one of them was Bruce Lee) wasn't something that was usable in a promotional film.

The mother of the extra showed up and tried to pacify him. It didn't work.

Sensing that there was only one way this was going to end, Bruce nodded and the extra approached him.

"How should we play?" the extra asked.

"*Fight.* That is the way we *play.*"[31]

The extra indicated that this was fine with him.

Bruce now became angry.[32] With a shout, he sent out a quick hook kick, which caught the extra flush in the lower abdomen.[33] "I only used a small part of my energy," Bruce would later recall, "yet he did not know how to defend himself. He fell back against the setting board."[34]

Recovering slightly, the extra ran at Bruce, only to be met with a second kick, which connected firmly with his chest. That one hurt.

"He looked bad. He did not make a sound," Bruce recalled.[35] "Later, other fighting actors came. They wanted to beat him. So, he apologized for his fault. Seeing his appearance, I did not want to hurt him again. I let him go."[36]

While Bruce may not have wanted to hurt him again, other members of the cast had other ideas. Perhaps looking to endear himself to Bruce, or trying to put an end to these challenges to the star of the film, one of the "fighting actors," Bob Wall, now inserted himself violently into the proceedings.

"Hey, *me!*" he motioned to the extra. "Me come in!"[37] Wall then delivered a vicious sidekick to the man's ribs,[38] which doubled him over. Bruce had not been trying to hurt the extra, but Wall had something else on his mind entirely.[39] "Come on!" Wall yelled, and then delivered a second, even more powerful, sidekick to the extra's ribcage.[40] The young man crumpled.

Bruce didn't witness Wall's assault on the man. He'd left the area beforehand and was elsewhere on the set.[41] Meanwhile the extra was in such agony that some of the crew members that had watched the beatdown thought they should check on him. After a cursory inspection, they quickly went to Bruce and told him that they thought the man's ribs were broken.[42] The young man needed medical attention, but the extra's mother couldn't afford it. Bruce gave her 20,000 Hong Kong dollars (approximately US$4,000) and told her to take her son to the hospital.[43] Wong captured all of this on film — whether the people at Warner Bros. who were ultimately responsible for editing the promotional film would have any use for it was up to them.

As the young man was being driven away, Bruce turned to Wong and asked him for the footage. He wanted it destroyed. Wong refused. He told him he couldn't give it to him; the film contained many other things he had shot on set that day that Warner Bros. might need.[44] Bruce wasn't pleased by Wong's response. However, he also knew there was nothing he could do about it. As it turned out, after clipping out ten minutes of footage from the five or so hours that Wong would end up filming, all of the unused footage was thrown away — including the segments that contained the on-set fights. After Bruce's death, Golden Harvest Studios contacted Wong and told him to name his price for the footage he shot, but by then the footage was gone.[45]

THE THIRD FIGHT

Madalena Chan, the executive assistant to the producer on *Enter the Dragon*, was on the set when Bruce had his third fight with an extra. Cameraman Henry Wong also witnessed it. Their story came to light during an interview conducted with Chan and Wong for a documentary on Bruce Lee produced in the 1990s. The producers of the documentary had arranged for the pair to film their segment on the tennis court of the American Club, which was presented as if it were the tennis court where the fight took place. Asked about the fight, Chan recalled, "There was this kid who said, 'I'll bet you anything I'm faster than you are.' And Bruce said, 'Okay, if you're betting me, let me help you out.'" At this point, she said, Bruce drew a large circle on the ground to serve as a ring for the encounter. Henry Wong's eyes widened when she mentioned this. "Oh, yeah. I remember that!" he exclaimed.[46]

Bruce told the extra, "I'm going to let you try and hit me three times. If you knock me out of the ring, I lose. But I'm going to hit you back one time."[47]

The extra agreed to the terms and came out swinging, but each kick and punch missed its mark, as Bruce either slipped or side-stepped the blows with ease. Never once was he in danger of being moved or knocked outside of the circle. Once the man's three attempts were over, Bruce motioned to the extra. "Okay. My turn." Then, like a scene out of the 1971 movie *Billy Jack*, Bruce pointed to a spot on the left side of the extra's face. "I'm going to hit you right here," he said. "Are you ready?"

"What do you mean—"

Before the man could complete his question, Bruce struck him exactly where he said he would — on the left side of his face. And just like in the *Billy Jack* movie, there wasn't a damn thing the extra could do about it.

Whether Bruce hit him with a punch or a kick has never been confirmed. Whatever it was, Chan said the extra lost his teeth.[48]

Director Robert Clouse would later recall, "I didn't believe he had been hit until he opened his mouth and revealed it was full of blood."[49]

The set of *Enter the Dragon* had become a war zone. With gang members hired as extras looking to make a name, and Bruce Lee's unwillingness to back down from a challenge, any scene involving extras yielded the potential for violence to break out. Certain of the actors in co-starring roles in the film were growing uncomfortable with the number of triads that were showing up on the set. Jim Kelly, for example, despite having won the world middleweight title at the 1971 Long Beach International Karate Championships, was unnerved by their presence: "I thought the teenage gangs in the U.S. were tough but they are real tame compared to those in Hong Kong. The gang, I think they are called 'Triads,' is vicious. They not only stab their victims to death but even cut their heads off."[50]

THE FOURTH FIGHT

Despite the trepidation of his co-stars, Bruce Lee remained unfazed. While he was discussing a forthcoming scene with production assistant Andre Morgan, another gang member decided it was time to make his move. It would prove to be a foolish (and ultimately fatal) mistake. "Between shots we were sitting down chatting when this kid called out to Bruce: 'I don't think you're so fast, I think it's all trick photography,'" Morgan recalled. "Bruce ignored him and he went on with the conversation and the kid called out again: 'You're a phony! They speed up the cameras![51] No one's that fast . . . I'll challenge you!'"[52]

Bruce's failure to respond only emboldened the gang member. He stepped away from his group. "I've seen you perform a lot of Jeet Kune Do on the screen — I want to see it in real life!"[53]

According to Linda Lee, "Bruce was a moody person. Some days he would be in a bad mood or a good mood. On this particular day he didn't feel like a hassle . . . Bruce just didn't want to go any further with it."[54]

"What is Jeet Kune Do?" the man asked.

Without looking up, Bruce raised his voice and asked, "Do you want to see?"

"Yes!" the man replied. "I want to see!"[55]

"Do you know anything about Jeet Kune Do?"

The man turned and smiled back at his friends. "I know as much as I need to know."[56]

"Come here."[57]

The extra walked over. One of the man's friends yelled out: "You're fast but you have no power!"[58]

Bruce assumed the on-guard stance of Jeet Kune Do, ready to release himself into action upon the first opening that presented itself. The extra sneered at Bruce[59] and launched his attack.

"The kid is going for broke, charging in using his best Kung Fu," Morgan recalled, "and Bruce is just standing there sidestepping."[60] Bruce was now playing with his adversary like a cat with a mouse;[61] he wasn't looking to hurt the man (he knew how costly that could be after his second fight with an extra), but, according to Clouse, "Bruce would lash out two or three times, not trying to kill him, but to 'mark' him. Draw blood, as it were."[62] Two quick punches that were less than full force did just that, hitting the challenger directly in the face and cutting his mouth.[63]

The extra, seeing the blood, now became enraged. He leapt forward with a kick toward Bruce's face.[64]

Bruce simply moved his head and the kick fell short of its intended target.[65] His temper flashed and he responded with a kick of his own, which hit the extra flush in the mouth,[66] sending several of his teeth flying[67] and knocking the challenger to the ground.[68]

The man was out of it, "almost unconscious."[69] According to the *China Mail* newspaper: "When he recovered and seemed anxious to have a crack at Lee, he was dragged away by several members of the camera crew. He was apparently uninjured, and refused to give his name. Onlookers thought he may have been a boxer from a local sect."[70]

DAMAGE CONTROL

Someone contacted the local press, perhaps in the hope of payment in exchange for a hot tip about Bruce Lee being in a real fight. Soon two reporters turned up on the set to get the scoop. Fearing any negative publicity, the top brass at Golden Harvest immediately came forth to put a softer spin on the affair. Producer Raymond Chow told reporters that the fight was actually "a friendly match. The young man just wanted to see how Bruce fought off the screen. It was just a little fight and there were no hard feelings between the two of them."[71] Twenty-nine years later, long after Andre Morgan had left the employ of Raymond Chow, he continued to downplay the fight:

> It wasn't battle-to-the-death nonsense. Bruce was fast and he was good and he knew what he was doing. And he knew that if he had to humble a kid, he could do it because he was so fast. No, that was the spirit of the times. Martial artists like to *do* martial arts. And they *do* spar. But they aren't out there calling each other out for the final shootout at the O.K. Corral every day . . . Yeah, the [fight] with the kid on the tennis court set I guess was the most serious, but I can tell you Bruce was playing with the kid. Aww, come on, it was like the difference between slapping a kid in the face a couple of times or hauling off and decking him. He was playing with him. He was teasing him . . . But it never became *vendetta time*. It's nonsense.[72]

While the fight may not have been a "battle to the death," it had fatal repercussions. The next day the extra's body was found floating face down in Victoria Harbor.[73] He had been stabbed to death.[74] Bruce later learned that a group of his supporters jumped the man because he had dared to insult their hero.[75] Perhaps that was what happened. However, the challenges on the set of the film had clearly gotten out of hand, and it's quite possible that someone who had a stake in the matter decided that something needed to be done to bring them to an end. It certainly wouldn't have been a difficult job to find a street gang in Hong Kong that was willing to kill a man. And while Jim Kelly was intimidated and John Saxon disgusted, for Bruce Lee, violence and death now represented just another day at the office.

CHAPTER EIGHTEEN

THE FINAL MATCH

"A good martial artist should be able to strike and kick from all angles and, with either hands or legs, take advantage of the moment."

— Bruce Lee (*Black Belt* magazine, 1968)

Not long after *Enter the Dragon* finished filming, Bruce Lee placed a phone call to Wong Shun Leung. He wanted to re-establish contact with his former teacher, and to resolve any problems that had arisen between them as a result of his missing Yip Man's funeral. He called under the pretense of wanting to pop by to take some photographs of Wong's Kung Fu school. Wong, perhaps still angry with him, refused. He said his family had been home all week and he'd promised to take them out of the city to spend some time in the countryside outside of Kowloon.[1] Wong recognized that he was being petty. "Later, I regretted this decision," he recalled. "We were old friends. At least I should have let him take some photographs."[2]

AN OLIVE BRANCH IS EXTENDED

Bruce called Wong again, this time to invite him to appear in his next film.[3] He told Wong he was planning to resume production on *The Game of Death*, a movie he had started filming in 1972 but had been put on pause when he had the opportunity to make *Enter the Dragon*. In *The Game of Death*, he envisioned his character battling his way to the top of a multi-level pagoda, each floor guarded by a martial artist of a particular style. What better way of honoring his former teacher and his art than by having Wing Chun's greatest living exponent, Wong Shun Leung, play the role of a guardian of one of these levels? Of course, Wong's character would be defeated by Bruce's in the film, but that didn't mean the fight scene couldn't be choreographed to make it a close battle — close enough that no one would come away from watching it thinking that Wong was anything less than one of the greatest martial artists in the world. Besides, if Wong accepted the role, it would add further credibility (not that he needed it, in Hong Kong at any rate) to Wong's reputation as the premier Wing Chun man in Asia.

Of all the martial artists Bruce could have offered the role to, that he chose Wong Shun Leung was certainly a flattering gesture. Wong recognized this and agreed to meet Bruce at Golden Harvest Studios to try out certain of his Wing Chun techniques on camera to see if they would make for good viewing.[4] It was a necessary formality, as Wing Chun, being an in-close fighting art, might not appear as dramatic or spectacular on camera as certain other martial arts. Bruce understood this, but thought he was now camera-savvy enough to make the art look good on screen, to showcase its strengths. He had, after all, incorporated elements of Wing Chun in his previous three films to good effect[5] and he was certain he could replicate this, if not expand on it, with Wong Shun Leung. As Bruce's gesture gave respect to Wong, his former teacher was appreciative and consented to shoot the screen test as a favor to his former student.[6] Wong also brought along his senior student Wan Kam Leung[7] to observe how Bruce, who by this point in time was the most famous martial artist and celebrity in Asia, was openly acknowledging Wong's skill and reputation.

AN UNEASY FEELING

When Wong and Wan arrived at the studio, Bruce took them and another martial artist, Joey Chen, to one of the Golden Harvest sound stages. The production company had not yet removed Han's "chamber of horrors" from the *Enter the Dragon* set, and it was there they recorded the test footage. Bruce had his cameraman film Wong sparring with Chen, performing sticking hands with Wan Kam Leung and then reacting to a punch that Bruce threw. It all looked good.

Wong, however, noticed something strange. As the lights on the set were quite bright for filming, he noticed there was something markedly "off" about Bruce's eyes. "At once, I had an uncomfortable and unlucky feeling in me," Wong would later recall. "His eyes showed something which was very familiar to me. I seemed to have seen that somewhere before."[8] Wong decided he needed a break from the heat of the sound stage; he walked outside and lit a cigarette. As he smoked, he wracked his brain about where he had previously seen the look that he'd just seen in Bruce's eyes. And then it came to him: "Finally, I found the answer. I saw that phenomenon in my aunt's eyes two months before she passed away. Then I was still a small boy, but, because my family had many doctors, I also had some medical knowledge, and was more careful in observing physiological phenomena. I saw that the black and white in Bruce's eyes were not clear."[9]

Not long afterward, Bruce came outside and asked how Wong was doing. Wong immediately turned the question back on him. "Do you feel tired?"

Bruce was surprised by the question, and shook his head in the negative.

"I see that the color of your eyes is different. Is it because you have stayed in a foreign land for a long time?"

"No, I don't see any difference."[10]

Wong said nothing more about it, but the experience left him feeling uneasy.[11]

Bruce explained that *The Game of Death* would resume shooting sometime after *Enter the Dragon* launched in August, and that he would watch the test footage when it came back from the lab and let Wong know how it turned out.

CLEARING THE AIR

While the offer to appear in *The Game of Death* brought Bruce and Wong together again, it didn't provide an opportunity for the two to clear the air. Bruce was still smarting from Wong's comments to the Hong Kong press about how Bruce had shown disrespect for his teacher by failing to attend Yip Man's funeral, and how Jeet Kune Do was built upon the back of Wing Chun Kung Fu.[12] While Bruce never denied the debt his art owed to Wing Chun, he wanted Wong to know that Jeet Kune Do was unique, a distinctly different approach to unarmed combat.

In particular, Jeet Kune Do was an art that emphasized mobility. This opened up more avenues for attack, allowing for the deployment of more offensive weaponry, particularly kicking techniques. Mobility further enabled a fighter to adapt instantly to any offensive maneuver initiated by his opponent.[13] The stance for Jeet Kune Do allowed for considerable versatility and movement, turning a fighter into a "rolling arsenal" (to borrow a phrase used to describe the "Black Beauty," the car that Kato drove in *The Green Hornet* TV series). By contrast, the ready position of Wing Chun required the fighter to be rooted for generating maximum power in one's strikes, which in Bruce's view limited mobility and, thus, offensive options.

In April of 1973, finding himself with some free time on his hands for the first time in months, Bruce Lee decided it was time he and Wong brought their differences to the surface. According to Wan Kam Leung:

> One day [a few months before Bruce's death], I was training with Sifu at our kwoon [Kung Fu school] when the phone rang. It was Bruce. He asked Sifu whether he was interested to come over to his house and have a chat. Sifu said, "Why not?" I asked Sifu whether it was convenient for me to accompany him there. Sifu said it didn't matter, and we'd just pay Bruce a casual visit. Thus, we took a cab there. By the time we reached the destination, Bruce, who was waiting for us, saw us from his windows and quickly ordered his servant to open the gate. Then, Bruce came over and gave Sifu a big hug. Sifu tapped Bruce's shoulder twice as an acknowledgment before we all sat down in the hall.[14]

The three men shared tea and, after the small talk had run its course, the topic turned to martial arts.

"Combat demands an all-roundness," Bruce said.

Wong nodded. "I do not object to this statement. But now that you have reached such a high state, don't you think that you need to take away the useless things that are in you? In combat, if your weakness is exposed, it may become a deadly blow."[15]

That was an insult. For years, Bruce had emphasized that martial artists must "hack away the unessential" from their arts.[16] Indeed, he taught this very principle to his students. What Wong was suggesting was that he hadn't followed his own doctrine, that there were still a lot of "unessential" things that Bruce had neglected to "hack away" from his art.

Bruce disagreed and felt obliged to show his two guests that there were no weaknesses in his technique for anyone to expose. To illustrate, he brought the two Wing Chun advocates to the back of his house, where the bulk of his martial arts training equipment was. He wanted his former teacher to be impressed by his skill but, more importantly, he wanted to prove to Wong Shun Leung that Jeet Kune Do was not Wing Chun.

Wan was impressed that Bruce's training area had so much equipment. In Wong's Kung Fu school, as in Yip Man's, there were only some wall-mounted punching pads and a wooden dummy. Bruce had a staggering amount of training equipment in his home — in his personal gym there was a huge, chromed, eight-station Marcy Circuit Trainer, with multiple weight stacks. There was a stationary bicycle and a rowing machine. At the back of the house, under a makeshift awning made of fiberglass, were a heavy bag and speed bag, a small padded box that was attached to bungee cords, and a leg-stretching cable that was fed through a pulley mounted on the ceiling. What particularly caught Wan's attention were several pairs of women's nylons, each of which had a tennis ball in the middle. The nylons were then stretched so that the top part of the nylon was attached to the ceiling and the bottom part to the floor.

"Why so?" Wong asked, gesturing toward the nylons.

"Because of the elasticity. It helps to train your reflexes, flexibility and mobility as you move and punch and dodge and jab at the same time."[17]

Bruce also had what Wan described as an "air-pressure booster," which produced a strong discharge of air whenever you punched at it, requiring you to punch harder to break through the cushion of air and hit the target.[18]

Bruce then walked over to where three small balls were hung from the ceiling by thin strands of fishing line. He suddenly leapt into the air and kicked each of the balls individually before landing back on the ground.

"The balls were very bouncy," Wan recalled. "There were no regular patterns of where they were moving from, either from the front, back, left or right. So it was not easy to manage. But Bruce was cool and was able to handle them with ease. He was, indeed, really fast and accurate."[19]

Bruce then told Wong about his fight on the set of *Enter the Dragon* with the extra who doubted that his Kung Fu was legitimate. He related how, a few days after this fight, he had almost been involved in another altercation while he was jogging along Waterloo Hill Road. "I passed by a construction site," Bruce said. "This time a construction worker asked me whether I would fight with him. So, I jumped over a plank and stood before them. I asked them, 'Who wants to fight?' However, no one answered, so I scolded them."[20] Bruce then went into a string of curse words in Cantonese, indicating what he said to the construction crew.

Wong laughed upon hearing them. "Certainly, you didn't fight with them."[21]

Bruce shook his head. "In the end, they bowed their heads and apologized for their actions. They said that they were only joking with me. Seeing this, I didn't care about them and continued to do my running."[22]

Wong knew without Bruce drawing him a picture what he was communicating. Bruce would fight anyone — any place, any time — who thought, or said publicly as Wong had done, that his Jeet Kune Do was not authentic.[23]

AN INVITATION TO BEIMO

Bruce invited the two men up to his study on the second floor of the house. It was a large room with several chairs, a large desk and an expansive library filled with books on almost every style of martial arts. Shortly after entering, Wong and Bruce resumed their conversation about fighting. Bruce asked for Wong's opinion of his striking ability. Wong was dismissive; in his opinion Bruce was faster at withdrawing his fists and kicks than he was at launching them. The critique made no sense to Bruce, who countered that his punches and kicks hit and withdrew with equal speed.[24] Bruce then extended an invitation to Wong that had been brewing for a long time: he offered to spar with him.

"If it is only for interest and research, it will be fine. But if it is a competition beimo I will not do it."

Wong had been out of the challenge match game for some time at this point, and now focused on teaching others the art of Wing Chun. He had nothing to prove by sparring, as his record stood for itself. Besides, whenever Wong engaged in beimo, someone usually got hurt. Having a fight with Bruce Lee simply wasn't on his agenda.

To Bruce's mind, a light sparring session would suffice. "Okay," he replied.[25] And with that, both men stood up and walked to an open area in the study.

Now it had come down to the comedown. The only way that Bruce could prove to Wong that his Jeet Kune Do was a real and practical martial art — and something vastly different from the cinematic performances Wong had seen Bruce give on the big screen — was by sparring with him. However, just as when they had engaged in sticking hands practice in 1965, Bruce had no intention of going all out on Wong.[26] For his part, Wong also knew the difference between a sparring match and a fight, and acted accordingly. Neither man would hurt each other, but it was understood that both would try to make contact.[27] It was Wing Chun's greatest fighter versus Jeet Kune Do's creator — and Wan Kam Leung had a front-row seat.

THE MATCH BEGINS

Wong Shun Leung was wearing slacks and a yellow, long-sleeve Montagut shirt. Bruce Lee was shirtless and wearing track pants.[28] Wan marveled at Lee's physique; his body fat levels were lower than a professional bodybuilder's, and the muscles of his torso were highly defined and stood out in bold relief.[29] Both men assumed their fighting positions.[30]

Wong assumed the ready position of Wing Chun — left arm extended, palm up and pointing toward Bruce's nose, his right hand close to his left elbow with the fingertips pointed toward the ceiling. He stood square to his opponent.

Bruce Lee assumed the on-guard position of Jeet Kune Do. His stance resembled that of a southpaw boxer: his right forearm was lowered, the fist pointing toward Wong's chest, and his left hand was held up to protect his jaw. Bruce placed his right foot forward — his power side — with his left heel just off the ground and his body turned slightly to the side. His weight was distributed evenly between his front and rear legs, so as to allow for a quick move in any direction, depending on what openings Wong might offer him.

Wong inched closer.

Bruce watched, ready for any sudden attack — and he didn't have to wait long.

Wong went on the offensive, launching a kick at Bruce's right shin.

Bruce instantly drew his lead leg behind him so that Wong's kick missed its mark. It was a shuffle motion, which resulted in Bruce's left leg now becoming his lead leg. As he did this, he lashed out with a punch toward Wong's throat.

The move impressed Wong. "He was experienced," Wong later recalled. But so was Wong. He raised his hands to block Bruce's punch; Bruce adapted by redirecting his strike to Wong's chest. It made impact just as Wong unleashed a finger jab at Bruce's throat, causing Wong to come up short. Both men paused.

Bruce smiled. "You want to hurt my knee? You are smart. Fortunately, I'm accustomed to this trick. Okay, let's try again."

Both men reset. Wong again took the classic Wing Chun stance, but this time Bruce assumed no stance whatsoever. Instead, he kept his feet in motion, moving in, out and laterally, bouncing lightly on the balls of his feet. The upturned hand of Wong's lead arm followed his every move.

Bruce leapt forward with another punch, which Wong deflected with his hand while moving backwards out of range.

Wong suspected that Bruce was trying to trick him with the punch and then seize upon Wong's counteroffensive.[31] But, thus far, the seasoned beimo fighter wasn't taking the bait. According to Wan: "Sifu used his favorite center lines to attack and close the gaps by moving in fast, forcing Bruce to move sideways and then backwards. However, Bruce was able to avoid all Sifu's punches very easily. Bruce's . . . stance was amazingly agile too. Maybe he was training all the time, that's why his reactions were fast. And when he retreated or moved, all his steps seemed very coordinated and swift."[32]

Bruce continued using his right hand to jab, while Wong moved his head from side to side, staying just out of range. Wong then darted to his right and attacked from a different angle. This surprised Bruce, particularly since the attacks of Wing Chun were typically linear, back and forth. However, Bruce adapted instantly, and as Wong launched a punch toward his chest, Bruce opened his hand and, using a right hook, struck Wong lightly but firmly with an open palm across the face.

At this point, Bruce began to mix some kicks into his attacks, which connected with Wong's arms with some authority.

Wan recalled: "I was really impressed by Bruce's superb kicking ability. His kicks were very sharp and speedy. He was able to kick anywhere on the upper parts of your body, even at close range."[33]

Wong blocked some of the kicks, but Bruce's speed and power made this difficult. Wong quickly realized that the smarter course was to shuffle backwards and out of Bruce's kicking range. He didn't remain out of range long, however. He suddenly rushed towards Bruce employing angular attacks, shifting his footwork and mixing up his hand techniques.

Wan Kam Leung was watching two master chess players plying their trade. "Due to space constraints, they moved carefully yet very fast and nimbly. In fact, Sifu was more eager to take Bruce down, but Bruce was able to tackle all his attacks and fought back with his fast kicks."[34]

Wong threw a vertical fist punch with his left arm, but Bruce deflected the strike away from his body. Wong was impressed. "He was experienced and understood the weakness of Wing Chun," he recalled, "so he used this method." Wong then struck out with a right-handed finger jab toward Bruce's throat, but just shy of the strike making contact, he felt Bruce's fist on his chest. Bruce sprang back out of range and the two men stared at each other.

"Leung, I hit you first — do you agree?"

Wong laughed. "You're right; your hand hit first," he admitted, but then pride entered the picture. "[But] who hit the other isn't the most important thing. It's the power of the strike that matters. My defending hand had dissolved most of your strike's power.

"It's true that if you had hit me with full power, you might have knocked me down. But if your power is reduced, then your strike wouldn't have the same impact, while my hand could have struck your throat. If we had really fought, you know who would have been hurt the most."

Both men laughed and hugged each other.[35]

"Ha! Your hands are still as fast as before and you are still very precise in your center line," Bruce said. He was legitimately impressed.

"Of course. I've told you already — and don't forget I'm your Sihing [elder Kung Fu brother]."[36]

Bruce smiled. "But I moved faster and shunned your attacks many times."

"You avoided once, but you can't avoid all the time."

Both men laughed again.[37]

It's an odd thing, peculiar to the combat sports, that if two fighters give a good account of themselves in a match, no matter what ill will the combatants might have had toward one another prior to the fight, it dissolves immediately afterward. In this way new friendships are often made and old friendships strengthened. Such was the case on this day. And while the men were now laughing, both were glad the match was over, and the water had now passed under the bridge.

Although it was supposed to be a friendly match for the sake of interest and research, Wan Kam Leung referred to it as a beimo.[38] Granted, neither man was really fighting, but there was an underlying aggression to the contest that made it more than simply a friendly match. Wong, for example, had twice taken aim at Bruce's throat, and Bruce, despite pulling back the throttle on his techniques, landed his kicks with enough authority to inflict heavy punishment to Wong's arms. More telling, Bruce had slapped Wong's face, punched him twice and kicked him repeatedly. Wong, even by his own admission, hadn't landed a blow.

Many years later, Wan Kam Leung would reflect on the match: "Honestly speaking, Bruce's skills and physical condition outclassed Sifu . . . to be fair, Bruce's kick was really fast and astonishing. If they were in real fight, I doubt Sifu was able to take him down. Of course, they were sparring and not in real fighting. So, they did reserve their strength and power."[39] Given that Wan was one of Wong's top students and, one would assume, would take his teacher's side in the matter, his statement is rather hard to refute.

THE CIRCLE COMPLETES ITSELF

The sparring session over, Bruce Lee, Wong Shun Leung and Wan Kam Leung left for a nearby coffee shop where Bruce and Wong resumed their discussion about the martial arts. Wong said he had been impressed with Bruce's Jeet Kune Do, and particularly by the mobility that Bruce showed. Bruce was pleased to hear this, as it meant their match had revealed to Wong that Jeet Kune Do had something to it that demarcated it from Wing Chun. It was important, Bruce believed, to be flat-footed when delivering a blow but mobile the rest of the time, because it opened up angles for attack. Mobility required keeping your heels off the ground, as opposed to being firmly rooted as in the Wing Chun stance. Such mechanics made for quicker moves in and out from the target.[40]

According to Wan, Wong Shun Leung agreed and adapted Bruce's recommendation into his training.[41] "After his sparring with Bruce," Wan recalled, "Sifu was inspired. He made some modifications to the [Wing Chun] training programs by introducing modern scientific training methods. For instance, improving the body stamina . . . everyone in our academy then started jogging like Bruce in order to be equipped with a better physical condition during the fight. We also emphasized the development of explosive power and mobile footsteps, as well as using various training equipment to improve our training."[42]

Wong Shun Leung had taught Bruce Lee his most formative lessons in Kung Fu, and Bruce completed the circle by sharing with his teacher the insights into fighting that he'd developed from traveling down the path that Wong first set him on sixteen years previously. The information would prove helpful to Wong and future generations of his students.[43] Wong, like Bruce, had never been a slave to the old ways, and his version of Wing Chun was always open to any method that might improve it.[44] Both men benefited from each other's knowledge despite their prior differences. There was too much history between them for it to be otherwise. And too much respect.

Bruce and Wong now stood up and shook hands. "You should come and visit me again when you are free," Bruce said.[45] The two men said goodbye, and Bruce left the coffee shop and headed home. It was the last time that Wong Shun Leung and Bruce Lee saw each other. Wong and Wan returned to Wong's school, where they discovered the extent of the damage Bruce's kicks had done:

> We returned to our kwoon [and] I discovered Sifu's arms were all bruised and swelled. Luckily, Sifu's long-sleeve Montagut shirt covered his arms and no one noticed his bruises. Sifu said he used Wing Chun's Tan Sau [open palm block] to disperse Bruce's kicks, but Tan Sau could only "Tan" the upper five inches and lower five inches of his legs. Bruce's kicks still hit Sifu's arms badly, and the places which were hit all turned black and blue. I had to use the medicated oil to help him rub on the bruises.[46]

In a sense, the bruises were something to remember his former student by. A memento from Bruce Lee's last match.

EPILOGUE

"If I tell you I'm good, probably you will say that I'm boasting. But if I tell you I'm no good, you know I'm lying."

— Bruce Lee (Radio Hong Kong, 1971)

B y the time Wong Shun Leung's bruises healed, Bruce Lee was dead. He was taken down, ultimately, by something inconclusive and frequently speculated upon. Over the decades since his passing, numerous scribes and authorities have claimed his death to be the result of everything from an overdose of cortisone[1] to heat stroke,[2] drinking too much water,[3] to epilepsy.[4] A coroner's inquest was held in Hong Kong, which concluded that his death was most likely due to a hypersensitivity to the ingredients (specifically meprobamate) in a prescription headache tablet.[5] An autopsy revealed that Bruce died from a rapid swelling of the brain that came on sometime between the late afternoon and early evening of July 20, 1973. As to what triggered it, the answer remains unsettled.

I've been contacted many times over the decades by people who claimed to "really know how Bruce Lee died." But the truth is they didn't, and neither do I. I've been involved in researching everything I could get my hands on about Bruce Lee ever since I was twelve years old, and have spoken with those who knew him best and were with him on the day he died — and I've got nothing. Whatever the catalyst was that started the fatal swelling of his brain, once it was underway it presented Bruce Lee with a fight that, for once, he could not win. His passing left behind a wife and two children, and denied the world all of the art he still had within him to share.

WHAT MIGHT HAVE BEEN

It is interesting to speculate on what would have become of Bruce Lee if he somehow survived July 20, 1973. Most certainly he would have starred in more films, and the superstardom and financial success that he had worked so feverishly for would have been his for the taking. Even before his death, the pre-release buzz about *Enter the Dragon* had already spilled out from Hollywood and was circulating among the major studios and producers. During the final months of his life, Bruce found himself flooded with offers to star in motion pictures from all points of the compass.

Academy Award–winning producer Dino De Laurentiis offered him one million dollars to appear in a film.[6] Another Academy Award–winning producer, Carlo Ponti, also wanted to bring Bruce to Italy to make a movie.[7] Warner Bros., knowing what they had in *Enter the Dragon*, had by this point sent Bruce a dozen scripts, hopeful that he would agree to signing on for five of them — for which they were willing to pay him or his wife US$150,000 a year for as long as either of them lived.[8] In 2023, that would be a little over a million dollars. Run Run Shaw, Hong Kong's answer to Cecil B. DeMille, threw his hat into the ring, offering Bruce half a million dollars (US) to star in a film for Shaw Brothers Studios — but Bruce thought Shaw would quadruple that offer.[9] And then there was a proposition from importer Andy Vajna, who had acquired two movie theaters in Hong Kong and wanted desperately to produce several films starring Bruce Lee.[10] In addition, Vajna's friends in the film world back in his native Hungary were willing to offer Bruce a starring role in two films which, if he accepted, would make him the highest-paid actor in the world.[11] Hanna-Barbera, the cartoon company that gave the world *The Flintstones*, *Yogi Bear* and *Scooby-Doo*, wanted to meet with Bruce to pitch him on their creating a cartoon series based on his persona.[12]

And then there was the matter of the on-again/off-again film, *The Silent Flute*, based on a script written by Bruce, James Coburn and Stirling Silliphant. Bruce was slated to play no less than five roles in the film, whose script perfectly expressed his philosophy of martial arts (or at least what that philosophy was in 1970). However, things had cooled between the writing partners over the past two years, and Bruce had moved on from the project.[13]

Silliphant, however, hadn't been willing to let the fire go out. If anything, he was even more enthusiastic about making the picture, particularly after he'd been invited to a private advance screening of *Enter the Dragon* at Warner Bros., along with some other Hollywood bigwigs. One of them was Sy Weintraub, the former owner of Panavision and one-time head of CBS Television. Weintraub could see that, going forward, any film with Bruce Lee in it was money in the bank. And Bruce Lee and James Coburn together, along with Silliphant's contributions to the script, well, that was a smash hit waiting to happen. After the screening, Weintraub approached Silliphant, adamant that he should get Bruce back on board with *The Silent Flute* as soon as possible. To this end, Weintraub phoned Bruce during the last week of his life to tell him that both he and Silliphant would be flying to Hong Kong that coming weekend to do (and pay) whatever was required to get his signature on a contract. Bruce had agreed to hear them out.[14]

These were all serious offers, and serious lifestyle changers. Millions (perhaps tens of millions) of dollars would soon be heading into Bruce Lee's Bank of America account, including his percentages on the back ends of these films. Bruce had long wanted to be a multi-millionaire,[15] and he was now finally poised to fulfill this dream. There is no doubt that Bruce Lee's immediate future would have revolved around making movies, money and easing into the superstar lifestyle.

A NEW SCHOOL

And then there was the matter of Jeet Kune Do, his martial art. What would have become of it had Bruce Lee lived? He had closed his three formal martial arts schools in Seattle, Oakland and Los Angeles in 1970, causing some to speculate that his interest in teaching his martial art had waned or, at the very least, been superseded by his career in film. Perhaps that was true — for a time. But while in Los Angeles two months prior to his death, Bruce dropped by the offices of *Black Belt* magazine to have lunch with his friend and student Mitoshi Uyehara, and, according to the former publisher, some big news was coming from Bruce Lee. Uyehara said Bruce was planning on opening a brand-new martial arts school — a large one with three different instructors of three very different arts:

Bruce said, "You know what I want?" I said, "What?" He said that he wanted to have like a studio; a gym. And then what he wanted to do, he said, "I want you to come in. I want you to hold a class in Aikido [a Japanese martial art]; I'll teach Jeet Kune Do; and I want Hayward [Nishioka] to start teaching Judo. And then we all sit down and have a session and we all talk about, you know, the different arts and whatnot." And [laughs] that was his goal . . . that's what he wanted to do. He said, "I just want to see how Judo works, how Aikido works, and then [I'll] teach, and then we all put it together and see what will happen."[16]

Had Bruce Lee lived to accomplish this, it would certainly have lent credence to the disputed claim that he was the father of mixed martial arts (MMA). His school would have featured the full-contact, reality-oriented street art of Jeet Kune Do, the geometrical precision of Aikido and the grappling of Judo. Perhaps the school would have spread — with Bruce Lee's soaring popularity it would have been almost impossible to prevent — and MMA would have arrived on the world stage some two decades before it did. At the very least, it would have (for the first time) brought diverse martial arts together under one roof for students to study — not as separate methods, with ranks, belts and formal regimentation, but as different approaches and techniques that might prove useful to the individual student. Something for everyone, but in the spirit of the individual determining their own attributes and limitations and seizing upon those elements that best suited them.

ASSESSING BRUCE LEE'S FIGHTING STATUS

Was Bruce Lee only a paper tiger (or dragon, as it were)? A man who looked like a fighter in movies but who in real life was anything but? Surely, the answers to these questions have been settled. Was Bruce Lee the greatest fighter of all time? In the final analysis, it is a meaningless question. Who among us has the necessary omniscience to answer it? There have been millions of fighters from all over the world that history has not seen fit to report on in the millennia that preceded Bruce Lee's birth. Should they be excluded from consideration because they happened to fight prior to the arrival of the sporting press? And, if we base our decision solely on those fighters from the twentieth century onward, what would be the criteria when there are so many different disciplines? Boxing is hands only; grappling allows no striking or kicking, whereas kickboxing allows no grappling; and mixed martial arts has an abundance of particular rules — no eye jabs, throat strikes, rabbit punches, biting or groin kicks, with three-to-five minute rounds and one-minute rest periods in between rounds, and a referee to stop a one-sided match and the option to "tap out" before any real harm comes to someone. Bruce Lee can't even be considered in such a discussion because he refused to put limits on his fighting options and didn't view fighting as a sport.

We do know, however, that whenever Bruce Lee fought, he won. When he sparred professional boxers, gold medal–winning grapplers and world champion Karate practitioners, they couldn't touch him — but he could strike them at will. Whoever it was that could beat Bruce Lee never crossed his path while he was alive. And we also know that those who competed at the highest level in various disciplines had nothing but glowing things to say about him:

Boxers

- **Muhammad Ali** (three-time heavyweight boxing champion): "He was truly one of a kind. I wish now that I could have met him because I really liked his style. He was way ahead of his time."[17]
- **Roberto Duran** (lightweight, welterweight, light middleweight and middleweight champion): "I don't, as a rule, compare kickboxers or Karate people but, in my opinion, I think Bruce Lee was the best."[18]
- **George Foreman** (two-time heavyweight boxing champion): "In his weight class, he [Bruce Lee] would have been a boxing champion."[19]
- **Sugar Ray Leonard** (welterweight, junior middleweight, middleweight, super middleweight and light heavyweight champion): "He was very spontaneous in his movement

and everything he did was for a reason. He didn't move to just be cute. He moved for a reason — to get in line, to get in position, to throw something, to position himself. Everything was for a reason. He had such ability to outperform anyone. No matter what size, no matter how strong."[20]

- **Leo Fong** (Golden Gloves and AAU boxing champion): "I would assess Bruce, as martial artists go, as being ahead of his time. Even if he was here today he would still be ahead of his time."[21]

- **James DeMile** (Air Force heavyweight boxing champion): "Well, Bruce, 135 pounds, against Jim DeMile, 225 pounds, or Ed Hart, 240–250 pounds — a professional boxer who could kill you with either hand — or Jesse Glover, super athlete, Judo, Karate. All of us were street fighters — Bruce could beat us all, and I don't mean it would be a struggle. I mean he could beat us all and we didn't have a chance."[22]

- **Ed Hart** (professional boxer): "Jesse told him I used to be a boxer and he said, 'Oh,' in a very interested way. And Jesse said to me, 'I bet you can't hit Bruce.' He said [to Bruce] 'Ed's got pretty fast hands; he moves pretty fast.' And Bruce said, 'Well, try to hit me.' So I was going to throw a very quick left jab and just touch him on the side of the face, you know? Well, I can throw a left jab so quick that the average guy can't even see it. So, when Bruce said 'go ahead and hit me,' I was absolutely confident that I could hit him. And he was standing there with his hands down, sort of half grasping each other, in front of his belt, you know? And I said, 'Aren't you going to get your hands up?' He said, 'No, I'm ready.' And I thought, 'Shit, this is going to be child's play.' So, I stood there and looked at him for a second and he looked at me. And I went WIFFT! And — SLAM! — my hands were trapped into my chest and he had a knuckle up against my throat. And I said, 'SHIT!' I don't know how he did it. I thought nobody could be that fast, you know? And Jesse was laughing. Bruce was just chuckling. And I walked around in circles slapping my thighs and saying, 'How the hell can you do that?'"[23]

Kickboxers

- **Don Wilson** (eleven-time professional kickboxing world champion): "Bruce Lee was a martial arts genius. I suppose that's not a very radical view. Most rational martial artists would agree without argument."[24]

- **Benny Urquidez** (six-time world kickboxing champion): "Let's get this straight: I love Bruce Lee. His philosophy and what he did for martial arts, the man was completely unique."[25]

- **Larry Hartsell** (full-contact Karate fighter and grappling master): "When I was home on leave [from the army] in 1966/1967 he came by the school [Ed Parker's school]. I sparred with him and he beat me so bad. I was stationed in Alaska and that's all I did was workout and train with this Hawaiian martial artist. But he just moved; started moving on his toes and I couldn't get close to him. He just played with me; touched me — boom! — touch me, move. I weighed 230 then. Well, I asked him to become his student after that."[26]

- **Chan Wai Man** (kickboxing and boxing champion, Hong Kong): "Pound for pound, I don't think anyone could beat him, either in Hong Kong or internationally."[27]

Karate Champions

- **Chuck Norris** (International, All American, U.S. Karate, New York World Professional Middleweight Champion): "I learned a lot from him. He was a very knowledgeable individual; his whole life was the martial arts. They'll never find somebody as good as him."[28]

- **Mike Stone** (U.S. national Karate champion): "He would have done extremely well in competition; if anything, he would have [been] much too fast for a lot of the officials. He was that skillful."[29]

- **Joe Lewis** (multiple winner of national and world Karate championships and world heavyweight kickboxing titles): "If he is not the greatest martial artist of all time, then he is at least the number one candidate."[30]

- **Ernest Lieb** (world Tae Soo Do lightweight division champion): "Although I have won forty-two karate tournaments, I do not consider myself a match for him. His speed surpasses most of the black belts I know."[31]
- **Louis Delgado** (East Coast versus West Coast Karate champion): "I have never seen anyone like Bruce Lee. I have met and sparred with several Karate men, but Bruce has been the only one who has baffled me completely. I am completely in awe when I fight with him."[32]
- **Fred Wren** (two-time grand champion of the U.S. Karate Championships): "I have never met anybody with more ability in fighting and knowledge than Mr. Lee."[33]
- **Jim Kelly** (world middleweight Karate champion): "There's a lot of stuff that people aren't saying about Bruce and his abilities. It's like a code of silence, and people aren't saying how good he really was because they're protecting their friends and their own reputations and tremendous egos. On film, as a martial artist, Bruce was the greatest. He had soul. He had rhythm. He had style. And there's not a martial artist today who's doing films that has any of that. I'm not saying they're no good, I'm just saying that Bruce was incredible. There may never be another martial arts film star who will be equal to Bruce. I would bet my life that Bruce would have done very, very well in tournament competition. As a matter of fact, I doubt there was anyone in the world who could have beaten him."[34]
- **Bob Wall** (world Karate champion): "Bruce Lee was simply a world-class martial artist. He could have been lightweight world champion had that been a goal of his. He was just phenomenal: hit like a heavyweight, lightning speed, phenomenal footwork, excellent condition, excellent defense. And very intelligent. I mean he was a tough guy. He had *all* the world champions' respect, I'll assure you of that."[35]

Mixed Martial Artists
- **Conor McGregor** (featherweight and lightweight UFC champion): "I have no doubt he would have been world

champion in MMA, no doubt. . . . He's fluid, he's loose, he's fast. His movement is fluid, it's efficient, it's functional."[36]

- **Georges St-Pierre** (welterweight and middleweight UFC champion): "Bruce Lee changed my life. He always said, be the perfect nemesis of your opponent. If he is a wrestler, strike him. If he is a striker, wrestle him. Fight him out of his comfort zone. I believe I was a champion in my sport not because I was the best, it was because I was able to transform myself into the perfect nemesis of my opponent. Bruce Lee said 'be like water,' and that's what I was. It was all there in his philosophy."[37]

- **Kenny Florian** (UFC fighter): "Bruce was so far ahead of his time; he wanted to learn everything. Whatever worked from the different martial arts he used, and whatever didn't work he threw out."[38]

- **Anderson Silva** (middleweight UFC champion): "I would like to have known him and to have had lessons with him. But to risk a fight with Bruce Lee? No."[39]

- **Eddie Bravo** (Abu Dhabi Combat Club Submission Wrestling world champion): "The real Bruce Lee was even more fascinating than the movie Bruce Lee. He truly had an open mind, and he broke through the chains of tradition in martial arts. He had so many powerful quotes. He was like Buddha, but as a martial artist."[40]

- **Rickson Gracie** (multiple champion in Vale Tudo and Pride, co-founder of Gracie Jiu-Jitsu): "Even back then, he was already doing things and explaining like in today's world. He was open to new things. Everything he spoke was the true essence of martial arts . . . Bruce Lee was a great martial artist."[41]

- **Roy Nelson** (The Ultimate Fighter heavyweight champion): "Bruce was a true visionary recognizing the need for integration of various martial arts into one in order to form a true and realistic martial art. Bruce Lee saw the need for MMA."[42]

- **Michelle "Karate Hottie" Waterson** (Invicta FC atomweight champion): "He was a true pioneer to the MMA world. When it was taboo to mix different arts, he ventured outside the box and intertwined different styles that suited him!"[43]

- **Scott Coker** (former Strikeforce CEO and current president of Bellator MMA): "Bruce Lee was the greatest martial artist of all time. He was clearly fifty years ahead of his era."[44]

- **Dana White** (president of the Ultimate Fighting Championship): "The Gracies were the founding fathers of the actual UFC, but I think the sport of mixed martial arts was started by Bruce Lee."[45]

Grapplers

- **Hayward Nishioka** (four-time national AAU Judo champion, Pan Am gold medalist): "He, by far in the physical realm, was the best that I've ever seen."[46]

- **Gene LeBell** (two-time national AAU Judo champion): "He was the top martial artist of his era, no doubt about it. How can you rate anybody higher? The reason that he's a hero is that he was the first; he was an innovator. He's the George Washington of martial arts. He was by far the best of his time at what he did. Bruce Lee was an innovator and there aren't that many innovators in the martial arts. Many martial artists are heroes but Bruce Lee was a god."[47]

- **Wally Jay** (Small Circle Jiu-Jitsu): "I've seen a lot of good martial artists in my time, even great ones. But Bruce was at least one or two levels above the best. He could have beaten any of the champions."[48]

- **Jesse Glover** (fourteen-time Pacific Northwest Judo champion): "These guys who talk about their strength and their relationship with Bruce, like, 'Yeah, I'm a big guy and I'm strong and he's small,' they forget that a guy like Bruce could just blind you. Not to mention the fact that Bruce could hit harder than hell. But let's concede to them for a moment that their size means something; he could still take their eyes out and there wouldn't have been anything they could have done with him. These guys have too much ego. They can't get beyond their own stuff. Bruce Lee is like Michael Jordan when he was on top, or he was like Muhammad Ali when he was in his prime, or somebody who kind of stood above everyone else in a series of activities. It's not that the other guys weren't good, it's that this guy was *great*. Bruce could move faster and hit harder than any martial artist in this country, and there was a strong possibility that he hit harder and moved faster than any martial artist in the world. One comment that sticks in my mind is the absurd claim that Bruce 'would have been among the top five lightweight tournament fighters if he were to compete today.' The truth is that Bruce would have defeated any of the people competing in this country and perhaps anyone in the world — of any size."[49]

Given the expertise of these people, it's highly unlikely that they were deceived when it came to Bruce Lee. Interestingly, statues have been erected to celebrate Bruce's memory in mainland China, Hong Kong, the United States and Bosnia. No fighter in history has had such unanimous and international respect bestowed upon him. To date, no statues have been erected anywhere to those Bruce Lee fought or sparred with, which tells us something.

For those of us who watched his films repeatedly in theaters throughout the 1970s, our initial perceptions about Bruce Lee's fighting ability were correct. His naysayers simply haven't done their research. Bruce Lee fought anyone who challenged him and sparred the best his era had to offer — and never lost.

And that, in the final analysis, is the only meaningful measure of his fighting ability that is necessary.

A SNAPSHOT OF BRUCE LEE'S FIGHTING AND SPARRING RECORD

Key

UD = Unanimous Decision

KO = Knockout

TKO = Technical Knockout (fight is stopped by an outside party as a result of one combatant being unable to defend himself or the fighter is unable to continue)

S = Submission

* = Matches that we know about

FIGHTING

Year	Age	Art Employed	Venue	Opponent(s)	Result
1952 (?)	12	Tai Chi	Unknown	(1) Unknown	Loss
1955	15	None	Hong Kong street	(2) Street gang members	Win (KO)
1957	17	Wing Chun	Sham Shui Po	(1) Ax-wielding man	Win (KO)
1958	17	Boxing	St. Francis Xavier's	(1) Edward Muss	Win (UD)
1958	17	Wing Chun	St. George's School	(1) Gary Elms	Win (UD)
1958	17	Wing Chun	Unknown	(1) Kung Fu practitioner	Win (TKO)
1958	17	Wing Chun	Mirador Mansions	(1) Robert Chung	Win (KO)
1959	18	Wing Chun	Kowloon teahouse	(1) Handsome Fo	Win (TKO)
1960	19	Wing Chun	Seattle drive-in	(5) Unknown	Win (KO)

Year	Age	Art Employed	Venue	Opponent(s)	Result
1960	19	Wing Chun	Seattle	(1) Japanese fighter	Win (KO)
1960	19	Wing Chun	Seattle poolhall	(2) Unknown	Win (KO)
1960	19	Wing Chun	Montana honky-tonk	(2) Unknown	Win (KO)
1960	19	Wing Chun	Kokusai Theater	(3) Unknown	Win (KO) ·
1960	19	Wing Chun	Ruby Chow Restaurant	(1) Cook with knife	Win (KO)
1960	19	Wing Chun	Seattle YMCA	(1) Yoichi Nakachi	Win (KO)
1963	22	Jun Fan Method	Nathan Road	(1) Unknown	Win (TKO)
1964	23	Jun Fan Method	Oakland school	(1) Wong Jack Man	Win (TKO)
1968	27	Jeet Kune Do	Las Vegas	(1) Casino security guard	Win (KO)
1971	30	Jeet Kune Do	Golden Harvest Studio	(1) Unknown	Win (KO)
1972	31	Jeet Kune Do	Fanling	(1) Lau Dai Chuen	Win (TKO)
1972	31	Jeet Kune Do	Cumberland Road	(1) Chan Wai Man	Win (TKO)
1972	32	Jeet Kune Do	Cumberland Road	(1) Unknown	Win (KO)
1973	32	Jeet Kune Do	Tai Tam Bay	(1) Unknown gang member	Win (S)
1973	32	Jeet Kune Do	Tai Tam Bay	(1) Unknown gang member	Win (KO)
1973	32	Jeet Kune Do	Tai Tam Bay	(1) Unknown gang member	Win (TKO)
1973	32	Jeet Kune Do	Tai Tam Bay	(1) Unknown gang member	Win (KO)

Record: 34–1

SPARRING*

Opponent	Outcome	Opponent	Outcome
Jesse Glover	Win	Wally Jay	Win
Ed Hart	Win	James Lee	Win
Leroy Garcia	Win	Jim Kelly	Win
James DeMile	Win	Hayward Nishioka	Win
Ryan O'Neal	Win	Mark Komuro	Win
Jhoon Rhee	Win	Joe Lewis	Win
Larry Hartsell	Win	Joe Orbillo	Win
Dan Inosanto	Win	Wong Shun Leung	Win
George Dillman	Win	Daniel Lee	Win
Ernest Lieb	Win	Herb Jackson	Win
Ken Knudson	Win	Ted Wong	Win
Louis Delgado	Win	Bob Bremer	Win
Yip Man student # 1	Win	Richard Bustillo	Win
Yip Man student # 2	Win	Chuck Norris	Win
Leo Fong	Win	Bob Wall	Win

Record: 30–0

Combined Records (fighting and sparring): 64–1

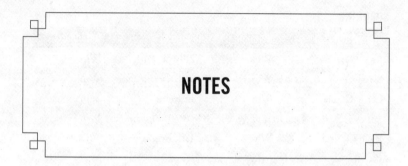

NOTES

PROLOGUE

1. "In the week ending 6 May 1973 (around the time *Enter the Dragon* was being wrapped up) the *Kung Fu* TV series starring David Carradine was the No. 1 show on US television, attracting a regular audience of 28 million viewers." Thomas, Bruce, *Bruce Lee: Fighting Spirit*, Frog Ltd., Berkeley, California, 1994, p. 235.

2. "The Hong Kong film industry attained international crossover commercial success in 1973 when *Five Fingers of Death* secured the number one box office spotlight during its first week of limited theatrical release in the United States." From the article "Restoring the Transnational from the Abyss of Ethnonational Film Historiography: The Case of Chung Chang Wa" by Aaron Han Joon Magnan-Park, *Journal of Korean Studies*, Vol. 16, No. 2 (Fall 2011), p. 249.

3. Bob Wall quoted in the article "A View from The Wall" by Jim Whitmore, *Deadly Hands of Kung Fu*, February 1977, pp. 36–37. Wall neglected to mention that he had been partners with Joe Lewis in running a Karate school in California and, at the time he made such comments, was partnered with Chuck Norris in the school. Norris was also starting out on what would prove to be an incredibly successful career in film, which was tremendous advertising for their school and Wall was simply doing his part to promote Norris at the expense of Bruce.

4. Chuck Norris quoted from an interview with David Brenner on *Nightlife*, November 19, 1986, at youtube.com/watch?v=j331wiSUhVo&t=2s.

5. Joe Lewis quoted from the online interview "Legendary Joe Lewis: I Never Lost My World Full Contact Karate/Kickboxing Titles to Anyone" by Tim Tal at bzfilm.com/talks-interviews/exclusive-interview-with-the-great-joe-lewis/.

6. Sylvester Stallone quoted from the online article "Sylvester Stallone on 'Rocky II' Sparring Partner Roberto Duran" by Jack Beresford at ultimateactionmovies .com/sylvester-stallone-interview-rocky-ii/.

7. From the online article "'Rocky IV' at 35: Sylvester Stallone Was in the ICU After a Dolph Lundgren Punch Actually Connected" by Ryan Parker at hollywoodreporter .com/movies/movie-news/rocky-iv-at-35-sylvester-stallone-was-in-the-icu-after -a-dolph-lundgren-punch-actually-connected-4097952/.

8. "By the early 1970s more than 1,200 tae kwon do instructors were reportedly teaching in the U.S." From the online article "The History of Karate in America" by Emil Farkas at usadojo.com/the-history-of-karate-in-america/.

CHAPTER ONE: THE CONCRETE JUNGLE

1. Goldman's books were largely trashed by the press for their negativity. For example, in his review of *Elvis* for the *Village Voice*, rock critic and Elvis scholar Greil Marcus wrote "The real significance of Goldman's *Elvis* is its attempt at cultural genocide . . . The torrents of hate that drive this book are unrelieved." From the article "Lies About Elvis, Lies About Us," by Greil Marcus, *Village Voice* (*Voice Literary Supplement*), December 1981. Lucy Sante, in her critique of *The Lives of John Lennon* for *The New York Review of Books*, wrote that "Goldman's background research was either slovenly or nonexistent." From the article "Beatlephobia" by Lucy Sante, *The New York Review of Books*, December 22, 1988.

2. Albert Goldman, "The Life and Death of Bruce Lee, Part II," *Penthouse*, February 1983.

3. "Mr. Goldman's article ends with a conclusion smacking of racism when he says, 'Bruce Lee put balls on four million Chinamen.' Bruce would be furious at such an implication. He was a man who honored and respected his forebearers. Bruce recognized the greatness of the Chinese people throughout history. To say Bruce 'put balls on four million Chinese' is not only racist, it is a childish, ludicrous falsehood." Dan Inosanto letter to Bob Guccione, *Penthouse*, March 6, 1983, published in the book *Absorb What Is Useful (A Jeet Kune Do Guidebook: Volume Two)*, Action Pursuit Group, Burbank, California, 1982, pp. 157–158.

4. Per: countryeconomy.com/demography/population/china?year=1973.

5. "Cryptorchidism, or an undescended testis, is a common congenital anomaly in children, occurring in 1%–4% of full-term and 10%–30% of preterm male neonates." *Asian Journal of Andrology*, May–June 2019; 21(3): 304–308. Published December 18, 2018, online at doi: 10.4103/aja.aja_106_18.

6. "The draft authorities took away his student deferment and when he returned to Seattle in September 1963, he was ordered to report for a medical examination. Some 10 or 12 University of Washington fellows had to report at the same time. Only two of them could be described as really fit and athletic — Bruce and a football player; and both failed! Bruce . . . was categorized as 4-F! In view of his tragic death, I think it as well to set the record straight here. It has been reported that Bruce was turned down because his arches were too high. In fact, his complaint was an undescended testicle." Lee, Linda, *The Life and Tragic Death of Bruce Lee*, A Star Book, W.H. Allen & Co., Ltd. London, 1975, p. 62.

7. Bruce Lee quoted from an interview with Alex Ben Block, *The Bruce Lee Audio Series, Volume II:* "Bruce Lee: The Alex Ben Block Interview," Little-Wolff Creative Group, Calabasas, California, 1995.

> *Alex Ben Block*: "So, what do you feel your nationality is?"
> *Bruce Lee*: "'American,' of course, because I hold a U.S. passport. And as soon as I finish with all these films in Hong Kong, I would like to move back to the States and just stay there."

8. Lee, Linda, *The Life and Tragic Death of Bruce Lee*, p. 29. Note: The spelling of Bruce's Chinese name is "Lee Jun Fon" on his Immigration and Naturalization Service records from 1941, but as Bruce would render "Fon" as "Fan" in his adult years, I have kept his spelling for consistency throughout the text.

9. "Later the name was changed to Lee Yuen Kam when it was realized that the Chinese characters were similar to his late grandfather's." Linda Lee quoted in Lee, Linda, *The Life and Tragic Death of Bruce Lee*, p. 29. See also: "The Chinese characters were changed slightly a few months later, says Grace Li, because the Chinese pictographs were the same as his late grandfather's. Although in the West the sameness in names would be an honor, the name had to be changed for Eastern superstitious reasons." Block, Alex Ben, *The Legend of Bruce Lee*, Dell Publishing Co., Inc., New York, 1974, p. 17.

10. Block, Alex Ben, *The Legend of Bruce Lee*, p. 17.

11. Block, Alex Ben, *The Legend of Bruce Lee*, p. 17.

12. While answering questions for the U.S. Department of Justice Immigration and Naturalization Service on March 29, 1941, Ho Oi Yee answered that her and Lee Hoi-chuen's first son, "Lee Teung, died when he was a little over three months old at Hong Kong." Document on file at the National Archives at San Francisco.

13. "Because their first son had died in infancy, any boy born afterward had to be given girl's clothing, a girl's nickname, and a pierced ear to trick the boy-hunting devil." Polly, Matthew, *Bruce Lee: A Life*, Simon and Schuster, New York, 2018, pp. 41–42, Kindle edition.

14. "When Bruce was born he was given a girl's nickname, 'Little Phoenix,' as a diversionary tactic, and his ears were pierced to further confound the evil ones." Clouse, Robert, *Bruce Lee: The Biography*, Unique Publications, Burbank, California, 1988, pp. 3–4. See also: "At home he [Bruce Lee] was always called 'Small Phoenix' — a feminine name. Mrs. Lee had lost a son only thirteen months earlier [Linda is mistaken here, as the child that was lost was the Lee's first son, Lee Teung, in 1938; Peter Lee was born thirteen months before Bruce, on October 23, 1939, and so no child died around the time that Peter Lee was born] and according to Chinese tradition when future sons are born in a family, they are usually addressed by a girl's name in order to confuse the spirits who might steal away his soul. He also had one ear pierced to distract the gods." Lee, Linda, *The Life and Tragic Death of Bruce Lee*, pp. 29–30. See also: "And when the birthday cake came out with candles on it, and after Bruce blew out the candles I realized that written on the birthday cake was 'Little Phoenix.' And I realized that [at his home] he was not called

'Little Dragon.' But later on, I found out that 'Little Phoenix' was the female side of the 'Dragon.' . . . And Bruce's family was very superstitious and got Bruce's ear pierced when he was born and also gave him a female name, 'Little Phoenix,' to confuse the evil spirits so that this spirit would not take this child away." William Cheung quoted from the documentary *The Grandmaster & The Dragon: William Cheung and Bruce Lee*, fsharetv.co/movie/the-grandmaster-& -the-dragon:-william-cheung-&-bruce-lee-episode-1-tt2063811#.

15. William Cheung quoted from the documentary *The Grandmaster & The Dragon: William Cheung and Bruce Lee*.

16. Most reports of the film indicate that Bruce Lee was only three months old when he was brought before the cameras for this film. However, Tan Hoo Chwoon, in his book *Bruce Lee in His Greatest Movie: The Orphan*, writes: "Less than one month after he was born on November 27, 1940, in San Francisco, Bruce Lee was bundled off to the film set by ace director Kwan Man-ching to appear in the movie *Golden Gate Girl* . . . The Lees stayed on in the States till mid-January 1941 before they tossed and tumbled across the high seas on a six-week voyage back to Hong Kong and arrived in late February 1941, by which time Bruce was on the brink of his third month, thus calling into question the widely documented account that he appeared in *Golden Gate Girl* (which was shot in San Francisco) when he was three months old." Chwoon, Tan Hoo, *Bruce Lee in His Greatest Movie: The Orphan*, Noel B Caros Productions, Singapore, 1998, p. vii.

17. The film was written and edited by the famous Chinese filmmaker Kwan Man Ching, who would later claim in his memoirs that he had also directed it for either the Grandview Film Company or the Golden Gate Production Company (there is some conflict here). Lost Films website: lost-films.eu/films/show/id /4109.

18. Women Film Pioneers Project at Columbia University, web.archive.org/web /20161221000604/https://wfpp.cdrs.columbia.edu/pioneer/esther-eng-2/.

19. For the Hong Kong release date, please see Hong Kong Cinemagic website: hkcinemagic.com/en/movie.asp?id=9597.

20. Bruce Lee quoted from the video "Bruce Lee: Screen Test February 4 1965" at youtube.com/watch?v=k2BKNDc48N4&t=13s:

> *Off-camera interviewer*: "And you worked in motion pictures in Hong Kong?"
> *Lee*: "Yes, since I was around six years old."

21. Per the online article "Bruce Lee's Forgotten Child Star Start: Before *Enter the Dragon* and Breaking into Hollywood, the Martial Arts Actor Was Hong Kong's 'Little Dragon Li' After Landing His First Role as a Baby" by Douglas Parkes at scmp.com/magazines/style/celebrity/article/3167557/bruce-lees-forgotten-child -star-start-enter-dragon-and.

22. Chwoon, Tan Hoo, *Bruce Lee in His Greatest Movie: The Orphan*, pp. vii–ix.
23. "Bruce Lee Has 10 Masters! Rare News on Bruce Lee's Kung Fu Training," from the magazine *Bruce Lee: His Unknowns in Martial Arts Learning*, Bruce Lee Jeet Kune Do Club, Hong Kong, 1977, pp. 14 16.
24. Yutang, Lin, *The Wisdom of Laotse*, Random House, New York, 1948, p. 47.
25. The number 108 has a long and extensive mystic history, and is considered sacred in religious traditions such as Buddhism, Hinduism and Jainism. In Buddhism, for example, this number results from multiplying the six senses (smell, touch, taste, hearing, sight and consciousness) by the three experiences (pain, pleasure, neutrality) by the two locations of the source (internal or external) and then by the three tenses (past, present and future): This results in 108 feelings or emotions (6 x 3 x 2 x 3 = 108). (Gunaratna, Henepola, *The Four Foundations of Mindfulness in Plain English*, Wisdom Publications, Somerville, Massachusetts, 2012, p. 86.) Zen priests wear a ring of prayer around their wrists that contains 108 beads; in the *Lankavatara Sutra*, the Buddha is asked 108 questions, the Buddha gives 108 statements of negation (Suzuki, Daisetz, Teitaro, *The Lankavatara Sutra*, published online at lirs.ru/do/lanka_eng/lanka-nondiacritical.htm, sections 1 and 2). As most Chinese martial arts trace their origins back to the Shaolin Temple (a Buddhist temple) in southern China, the number 108 has been worked into certain Chinese Kung Fu styles as having a mystical or symbolic significance. There are, for instance, considered to be 108 pressure points in the body (Subramaniam PhD., P., [general editors] Dr. Shu Hikosaka, Asst. Prof. Noringa Shimizu, & Dr. G. John Samuel, [translator] Dr. M. Radhika [1994], *Varma Cuttiram: A Tamil Text on Martial Art from Palm-Leaf Manuscript*. Madras: Institute of Asian Studies, pp. 90 & 91); there are 108 locking hand techniques in Eagle Claw Kung Fu (Leung, Shum, and Chin, Jeanne, *The Secrets of Eagle Claw Kung Fu: Ying Jow Pai*, Charles Tuttle Publishing, Boston, 2001, p. 15), and both the Yang Tai Chi Chuan Long form and the final version of the Wooden Dummy form in Wing Chun consist of 108 movements. (From the article "108 Steps: The Sino-Indian Connection in the Martial Arts," by Joyotpaul Chaudhuri, *Inside Kung Fu*, January 1991.)
26. All details about Lee's unsuccessful attempt to use the Tai Chi Chuan he had learned in a fight is drawn from the article "Bruce Lee Has 10 Masters! Rare News on Bruce Lee's Kung Fu Training," from the magazine *Bruce Lee: His Unknowns in Martial Arts Learning*, Bruce Lee Jeet Kune Do Club, Hong Kong, 1977, pp. 14–16. Perhaps as a result of this altercation, Lee no longer believed in the fighting effectiveness of the so-called "internal arts," such as Tai Chi. Indeed, when his *Enter the Dragon* co-star John Saxon expressed interest in studying Tai Chi while in Hong Kong, Bruce attempted to discourage him. According to Saxon: "I had become interested in things like Tai Chi and some of these more esoteric Chinese internal arts. And he scoffed at them usually. And he said, 'Oh, come on with that stuff!' He called it a 'mind trip' or a 'head trip' or something like that." John Saxon interview with the author, March 22, 1996.

27. Wang, Robert, author of the book *Walking the Tycoon's Rope*, quoted from the Radio Television Hong Kong program, *Asian Threads*, podcast.rthk.hk/podcast/item.php?pid=363&eid=22299&lang=zh-CN.

28. As per William Cheung's recollection in Cheung, William, *Mystery of Bruce Lee*, Bruce Lee Jeet Kune Do Club, Hong Kong, 1980, p. 16.

29. William Cheung quoted from the documentary *The Grandmaster & The Dragon: William Cheung and Bruce Lee*.

30. Including *Golden Gate Girl* (1941), by the time of his birthday on November 27, 1953, Lee had appeared in the following eight films: *The Birth of Mankind* (1946), *Wealth is Like a Dream* (1948), *The Kid* (1950), *The Guiding Light* (1953), *A Mother's Tears* (1953), *Blame It on Father* (1953), *A Myriad Homes* (1953) and *In the Face of Demolition* (1953).

31. William Cheung quoted from the documentary *The Grandmaster & The Dragon: William Cheung and Bruce Lee*.

32. Wang, Robert, author of the book *Walking the Tycoon's Rope*, quoted from Radio Television Hong Kong program, *Asian Threads*.

33. From the online article "Bruce Lee & William Cheung: The Early Years," posted on William Cheung's website: wingchunacademy.wordpress.com/2011/03/14/bruce-lee-william-cheung-the-early-years/.

34. Clausnitzer, Rolf, *My Wing Chun Kung Fu Journey: From Bruce Lee to Wong Shun Leung*, self-published, Amazon Publishing, 2020, pp. 140–141, Kindle edition.

35. Bruce Lee quoted in *The Best of Bruce Lee* magazine, Rainbow Publications, Los Angeles, 1974, p. 14.

36. Chan, Shun-hing, and Leung, Beatrice, *Changing Church and State Relations in Hong Kong, 1950–2000*, HK University Press, Hong Kong, 2003, p. 24.

37. As reported in Polly, Matthew, *Bruce Lee: A Life*, p. 768.

38. Bruce Lee quoted in the article "Is the Green Hornet's Version of Gung Fu Genuine?" *The Best of Bruce Lee* magazine, p. 14.

39. "The man who had first taught him [Kung Fu] was from the Hung style. Bruce showed me some pictures of the man and he appeared to be a tough individual. He was about five foot ten inches tall and weighed over two hundred pounds. Bruce said that the man was a good teacher, and that he had learned a lot from him about the Hung and other styles. One picture that Bruce had of the man showed him practicing his footwork on two-foot-high stakes that were driven into the ground. Another picture showed him practicing footwork on small bottles that were spread out in a form pattern. The top of the bottles didn't leave the man much margin for error, but Bruce said that he had seldom seen the man fall from the bottles as he went through his practice sessions. Bruce showed me some books that the man had sent him on Chinese Jiu Jitsu. He said the man was highly skilled in the use of these joint and wrist locks, and that he had taught a few of them to him before he had left Hong Kong. Bruce said that in those early days he had a strong feeling for the Hung style because of its reputation for strong footwork and punching. . . . He never talked openly about

his reasons for giving up the practice of the Hung style, but he hinted that one time things had not gone well for him in a fight. This experience had caused him to seek out a method which he could better apply." Jesse Glover, quoted in Glover, Jesse, *Bruce Lee: Between Wing Chun and Jeet Kune Do*, self-published, Glover Publications, Seattle, 1976, pp. 20–21.

40. Both of Yip Man's sons confessed as much to me when I interviewed them in 2009 and 2012. Yip Chun, the eldest of Yip Man's children and eighty-five years old at the time, told me: "Not just Wing Chun, but all southern style Chinese Kung Fu history, have this situation: a lot of history but no written record. So, history passed down is by master educating student, and that student, telling their student. One generation to one generation, some add a little, some omit a little, some tell fragments like in a fictional novel. So, what happened back then, and what we know today will have differences. Wing Chun has two accounts. One account is the original master was Yim Wing Chun, who learned this art from Ng Mui, and passed the art down the generations. The second account was from Emperor Yung Jing period, Tan Sow Ng who passed down the art. Some believe one, some the other account, but looking at facts, it is hard to say because there is no official record. So, when we consider the history, it is that of the master, of the master of Yip Man, Leung Chan. Leung Chan collected the art from the people of that era which all were related to Wing Chun. From that era, he took elements from these sources, and formed the art of Wing Chun we see today. Leung Chan didn't take many disciples, he only taught two people. One was his own son Leung Bik. The other was his one student Chun Wah-shun. Yip Man initially learned from Chun Wah-shun, but then met Leung Bik in Hong Kong, and proceeded to advance his study. After he mastered the art, he then continued to pass on Wing Chun." Yip Chun interview with the author, August 12, 2009.

41. "According to [Bruce], Yip Man had once killed another Gung Fu man with one punch when the man had refused to leave his school after Yip Man had refused the man's challenge. The incident had occurred long before Bruce became one of Yip Man's students, but he said that he found the story easy to believe because of the awesome punching power that his teacher possessed . . . This was told to me in the latter part of 1959, when Yip Man was in his early sixties." Glover, Jesse, *Bruce Lee: Between Wing Chun and Jeet Kune Do*, p. 15.

42. Wong Shun Leung quoted from the online article "Bruce Lee and His Friendship with Wong Shun Leung" at wongvingtsun.co.uk/wslbl.htm.

43. "Bruce's parents didn't like Bruce to learn any martial art because they thought that martial art always linked up with the triads." William Cheung quoted from the documentary *The Grandmaster & The Dragon: William Cheung and Bruce Lee*. See also: "Bruce's father wanted all of his children to be scholars, and he didn't hold with the likes of Gung Fu. Bruce told me that in Hong Kong Gung Fu men didn't have the same status as martial artists of other Asian countries. He said that in Hong Kong most Gung Fu men were considered to be little

more than thugs." Jesse Glover, quoted in Glover, Jesse, *Bruce Lee: Between Wing Chun and Jeet Kune Do*, p. 20.

44. "But through months of persuasion, eventually Bruce got the grant for learning martial art." William Cheung quoted from the documentary *The Grandmaster & The Dragon: William Cheung and Bruce Lee*. "The fact that Gung Fu was looked on by so many people with disfavour was the primary reason that Bruce did not tell his father that he was practicing Wing Chun. Bruce told his father that he was going to music practice whenever he went to Gung Fu. He had a great deal of respect for his father, and he would have quit Gung Fu in a second if his father had ordered it." Jesse Glover, quoted in Glover, Jesse, *Bruce Lee: Between Wing Chun and Jeet Kune Do*, p. 23.

45. Wong Shun Leung quoted from the article "Bruce Lee and His Friendship with Wong Shun Leung."

46. "When I introduced Bruce to Yip Man, from the first sight, he already liked Bruce because he saw a few movies of Bruce's previously and he wanted to accept Bruce as a student." William Cheung quoted from the documentary *The Grandmaster & The Dragon: William Cheung and Bruce Lee*.

47. Duncan Leung, a contemporary of Bruce Lee's in Yip Man's school, wrote that: "He [Yip Man] charged eight dollars per month . . . Eight Hong Kong dollars was considered a large sum of money then, when workers made fifty or sixty dollars a month." Ing, Ken, *Wing Chun Warrior: The True Tales of Wing Chun Kung Fu Master Duncan Leung, Bruce Lee's Fighting Companion*, Blacksmith Books, Hong Kong, 2010, pp. 1398–1405, Kindle edition. Linda Lee writes that the amount Bruce paid Yip Man was "twelve Hong Kong dollars a lesson." Lee, Linda, *Bruce Lee: The Man Only I Knew*, Warner Paperback Library, New York, 1975, p. 37.

48. With the rare exception of a son or daughter learning a martial art from a parent, Chinese martial arts have always had a commercial component: "It is often incorrectly assumed that the commercialization of Chinese martial arts is somehow a modern, Western evil; it is not. Chinese martial arts have always been a business and have always had a very obviously commercial aspect to them. And the Jingwu did much to increase their commercialization. It was with the Jingwu that Chinese martial arts became a product that could be marketed. The Jingwu also encouraged other businesses to buy advertisements in Jingwu publications and help support the program — businesses that included beer companies, tobacco companies, and insurance companies." Kennedy, Brian, and Guo, Elizabeth, *Jingwu: The School That Transformed Kung Fu*, Blue Snake Books, Berkeley, California, 2010, pp. 16–17. (Worthy of note: The Jingwu school officially opened in 1909 in Shanghai, and would later be popularized in the Bruce Lee movie *Fist of Fury*.)

49. Yip Man quoted from the article "Interview with Wing Chun Grandmaster Yip Man," published in *New Martial Hero* magazine #56, Hong Kong, 1972, naamkyun.com/2012/03/interview-with-wing-chun-grandmaster-yip-man/:

Yip Man: "In olden days, people were very strict concerning the teacher/student relationship. Before they admitted a student, they had to know the character of this would-be student very clearly. This is what is called 'to choose a right student to teach.' Secondly, it also depended on whether the student could afford to pay his school fees or not . . . The fact is, not too many people could afford to pay for such a high school fee. For example: at the time I paid, the red packet for the 'Student-admitting Ceremony' had to contain 20 taels of silver. And I had to pay 8 taels of silver each month as my school fee."

New Martial Hero: "How much was 20 taels of silver worth, in terms of your living standards?"

Yip Man: "For 20 taels of silver you could marry a wife, say if you did it economically. Also, with no more than one and a half taels of silver you could buy 1 picul [around 60kg] of rice . . . That was why, at that time, most of the people who learnt Kung Fu were rich people. These people could leave their jobs and live in the old temples in deep mountains for training. It is not the same as today when people can easily learn Kung Fu anywhere."

50. It is by no means clear how old Bruce Lee was when he began his training in Wing Chun. According to the Lee family (including Bruce) he began his training in Wing Chun in 1953 when he was thirteen years old: "I began learning Gung Fu at 13 because I wanted to learn how to fight." Bruce Lee quoted in the newspaper article "Bruce Lee, Chinese Movie Star, Speaks to Garfield Seniors," by Cindy Thai, unidentified Seattle newspaper article, circa 1962. See also:

Alex Ben Block: "At what age did you begin studying the martial arts?"
Lee: "How old when I started?"
Alex Ben Block: "Yes."
Lee: "Thirteen."
(Bruce Lee quoted from "Bruce Lee: The Alex Ben Block Interview," August 1972, Little-Wolff Creative Group, Calabasas, California, 1995.)

See also: "At thirteen, he met Master Yip Man, leader of the [Wing Chun] School of Gung Fu, and since then he has devoted himself to that system." Publisher James Yimm Lee in his "About The Author" section in Lee, Bruce, Chinese Gung Fu: The Philosophical Art of Self-Defense, Oriental Book Sales, Oakland, 1961, p. 1; see also: "He [Bruce Lee] learned the martial arts when he was 13 years old." Grace Lee interview, "Good Night America," with Geraldo Rivera, 1976, youtube.com/watch?v=atur4sJN96s; and: "At that point in time Wing Chun was the 'in' thing. Wing Chun is a system of martial art, of Chinese

Kung Fu, that believes in economy; straight punches and things like that. And to him at that point [it] was the most logical approach for protection. So, he decided to talk to this old gentleman by the name of Yip Man, who later became his instructor. He was around 13 or 14." Robert Lee interview, "Good Night America," with Geraldo Rivera, 1976, youtube.com/watch?v=atur4sJN96s. However, despite having to concede that Bruce Lee would know how old he was when he started his training in Wing Chun, certain other facts indicate he was older than he recalled. For example, Hawkins Cheung said he met Lee when the latter came to St. Francis Xavier's College (in 1956, when Lee was sixteen) and that the two of them started Wing Chun together shortly thereafter. (From the article "Bruce Lee's Hong Kong Years," *Inside Kung Fu*, November 1991.) Perhaps more telling is the fact that Wong Shun Leung, Lee's senior in Wing Chun, started his training in Wing Chun at the age of eighteen in 1953:

> *Qi Magazine*: "When did you first start practicing Wing Chun Kuen and what made you start?"
> *Wong Shun Leung*: "When I was 17 or 18 years old I started learning Wing Chun [1952 or 1953, as Wong was born in 1935]."
> (Wong Shun Leung quoted from an article in *Qi Magazine*, published online at web.archive.org/web/20070928072440/http://vingtsunupdate.com/index.php?option=com_content&task=view&id=82&Itemid=76.)

To get a sharper point put on this, I asked David Peterson, one of Wong's top students, how old his teacher was when he began learning Wing Chun and was told: "He definitely started in 1953 and was around 18 years of age." (David Peterson, Facebook message to the author on July 24, 2021.) Given that Wong was senior to Lee, and learned the art and had already established his reputation in beimo matches throughout Hong Kong by the time Lee had signed on at Yip Man's school, it seems most likely that Lee started his training in Wing Chun in and around 1956 at approximately fifteen or sixteen years of age.

51. "The Bruce Lee Story" by Yip Chun, published in *The Star* newspaper, Hong Kong, March 17, 1973.

52. The incident as recalled by Bruce Lee's brother Robert and La Salle College students Pau Siu Hung and Dennis Ho is recounted in Polly, Matthew, *Bruce Lee: A Life*, pp. 46–47.

CHAPTER TWO: THE "UPSTART"

1. "Bruce Lee was successful because he was determined. He studied at Dai Kok Chuy, near Yip Man's home. He would get out of school at three p.m., carrying his schoolbag, walking and practicing Kung Fu while he walked. So, this is what led to him being so successful. He was very dedicated." Yip Chun interview with

the author, August 2009. See also: "He would be walking along and doing Huen Sao, or Lop Sau or Biu sau strikes as he walked. And even sometimes when he was eating, he would be doing something with the other hand. And when he was walking in the streets sometimes he carried two dumbbells and doing rolling punches. So that's why Bruce was progressing so well." William Cheung quoted from the documentary *The Grandmaster & The Dragon: William Cheung and Bruce Lee*.

2. "At home, he could not sit through a meal without pounding away with alternate hands on a stool beside him, to toughen his hands and strengthen his muscles." Lee, Linda, *Bruce Lee: The Man Only I Knew*, p. 42.

3. "From as soon as he [Bruce] started he would never come up and ask for new technique." William Cheung quoted from the documentary *The Grandmaster & The Dragon: William Cheung and Bruce Lee*.

4. William Cheung quoted from the documentary *The Grandmaster & The Dragon: William Cheung and Bruce Lee*.

5. William Cheung quoted from the documentary *The Grandmaster & The Dragon: William Cheung and Bruce Lee*.

6. Wong Shun Leung on Bruce Lee, from the online article "Bruce Lee and His Friendship with Wong Shun Leung."

7. Rolf Clausnitzer's anecdote from the article "Wing Chun Memories" by David Peterson, *Inside Kung Fu*, March 1994.

8. Rolf Clausnitzer's quote from the article "Wing Chun Memories" by David Peterson, *Inside Kung Fu*, March 1994.

9. The Robert Lee anecdote is recounted in the article "In the Shadow of a Legend," *Black Belt*, August 1974.

10. Robert Lee quoted from "An Interview with Bruce Lee's Brother, Robert Lee" by Andrew Heskins at easternkicks.com/features/an-interview-with-bruce-lees -brother-robert-lee.

11. Leung Pak Chun's anecdote, quoted in Thomas, Bruce, *Bruce Lee: Fighting Spirit*, p. 25.

12. Bruce Lee's incident with the Tai Chi master as reported in Uyehara, Mitoshi, *Bruce Lee: The Incomparable Fighter*, Ohara Publications Inc., Santa Clarita, California, 1988, p. 8.

13. The incident and dialogue from Bruce Lee's interaction with Wong Shun Leung and Master Li is drawn from Wong Shun Leung's account of the affair in "Bruce Lee and His Friendship with Wong Shun Leung."

14. "Yip Man had a very good sense of humor," William Cheung says. "He liked to give his students nicknames, and he would take a long time to dream them up. Like Wong Shun Leung was called 'Wong Ching Leung,' which means that he's like a bull. I was called 'Big Husky Boy.' And Bruce was nicknamed 'Upstart.'" William Cheung quoted from the online article "Yip Man: Wing Chun Legend and Bruce Lee's Formal Teacher" by *Black Belt*, August 12, 2013, at blackbeltmag.com/yip-man-wing-chun-legend-and-bruce-lees-formal-teacher.

15. "'Because he progressed so quickly, he became a threat to some of the seniors,' says Cheung. Yet according to custom, a Kung Fu student was supposed to remain humble and subservient to his seniors. To do otherwise was considered a direct combat challenge. Since Lee only respected the knowledge and fighting abilities of Yip Man and Yip's appointed instructors, he refused to comply with the arrogant whims of his seniors. Instead, he would challenge and defeat them easily." From the online article "Bruce Lee & William Cheung: The Early Years." See also: "Bruce progressed very fast, and because he trained very hard and, within a few short years, he was already giving a lot of the senior students trouble in the friendly sparring." William Cheung quoted from the documentary *The Grandmaster & The Dragon: William Cheung and Bruce Lee.*

16. "My father appreciated him [Bruce Lee] very much . . . my father showed no sign of dissatisfaction with him." Yip Chun quoted from "The Bruce Lee Story," published in *The Star* newspaper, Hong Kong, March 17, 1973. See also: "Quietly, Yip Man was proud of Bruce, even before he became a popular Kung Fu star. There was a friendship between Yip Man and me, Bruce and me, Bruce and Yip Man." From the online article "Bruce Lee & William Cheung: The Early Years."

17. Under oath, with lawyers and immigration officials present, Grace Lee answered the following questions:

> *Question*: "Are both of your parents full blood Chinese persons?"
> *Grace Lee*: "My mother is English."
> *Question*: "Has your mother any Chinese blood?"
> *Grace Lee*: "No."
> (National Archives and Records Administration in San Bruno, California, 1941.)

18. "Then they found out that he had a little bit of European blood in him (his mother is half German)." William Cheung quoted from the online article "Bruce Lee & William Cheung: The Early Years."

19. ". . . at that time, there was still rules that Kung Fu wasn't allowed to be taught to Caucasian or other nations." William Cheung quoted from the documentary *The Grandmaster & The Dragon: William Cheung and Bruce Lee.*

20. "And by accident, some of the senior students found out that Bruce wasn't a full-blooded Chinese. His mother was actually half German and half Chinese. That made him three quarters Chinese. So, they ganged up to put pressure on Yip Man to get Bruce kicked out of the school." William Cheung quoted from the documentary *The Grandmaster & The Dragon: William Cheung and Bruce Lee.*

21. William Cheung quoted from the article "A Grandmaster Remembers Bruce Lee" at cheungsmartialarts.com/wp-content/uploads/2021/12/A-Grandmaster-Remembers-Bruce-Lee.pdf?v=3e8d115eb4b3.

22. "The fact that Bruce was kicked out of Wing Chun school . . . Bruce never forgave them." William Cheung quoted from the documentary *The Grandmaster & The Dragon: William Cheung and Bruce Lee.*

23. "And what Sifu [Wong Shun Leung] taught us was that Yip Man and Bruce Lee's father were already quite familiar with each other. They had both come from the same area of Foshan, and with Bruce Lee's father being a very famous performer in the opera school and Yip Man being a lover of art and culture, they had connections in the past. And, apparently, they used to have tea together in Foshan when they were younger men." David Peterson interview with the author, September 15, 2012.

24. "Now Yip Man of course was no longer the wealthy man he was in China; he was living from week to week on what he got as an instructor of Wing Chun. And he was in that profession not by choice but by necessity. So, he thought about it, thought it over for a while and apparently came to the decision that it was better to lose one student than lose perhaps a dozen students. And so, what he did was take Wong Shun Leung off to one side and explain the situation and ask him if he'd take care of Bruce Lee's instruction. And Sifu [Wong Shun Leung, David Peterson's teacher] willingly agreed 'cause he liked Bruce Lee and they seemed to get along well. So, what then happened was that Bruce Lee would go to train at Wong Shun Leung's father's home in the afternoons, after he would finish school. And that relationship lasted a good 18 months or so before Bruce Lee finally left for America." David Peterson interview with the author, September 15, 2012.

25. These would be the first three sets, or forms, of Wing Chun Kung Fu; namely, Sil Lum Tao, Chum Kiu and Biu Jee.

26. Wong Shun Leung, quoted from the documentary *Wong Shun Leung: The King of Talking Hands*, produced and directed by John Little, 2016, © David Peterson.

27. "Even Yip Man himself would not practice the Wooden Dummy form consistently . . . his movements were always changing. Beyond the first sixty movements of the Wooden Dummy form, Yip Man kept switching around the movements and sequences. Let me try to explain it in this way: a really good fighter is able to forget all the movements, to just use his skills. Because in the Wing Chun point of view, it's not about using certain set movements. For example, the exercise of Chi Sau drills us to develop our reaction; we're not thinking about any specific methods for hitting our opponent. Even though, after the first sixty movements of Wooden Dummy form, in my eyes the techniques/sequences of myself and my Wing Chun brothers may be different, but the basic principles are still the same. Keep in mind, a long time ago, Yip Man was a very rich man. He never considered that he would [one day] have to teach Kung Fu for a living. So, he did not force himself to remember every individual move. I have seen that some students always take notes. That's because the students who take notes are intending to be a teacher. For myself, in learning martial arts, I have

to *experience* things [instead of taking notes]." Wong Shun Leung, quoted from the documentary *Wong Shun Leung: The King of Talking Hands*.

28. Wong had replied that "everyone is Si-Hing Dai (Cantonese for "brothers in Kung Fu"); if they're willing to come learn, it's a good thing. There's no reason to reject them." "Interview Wong Shun Leung (Ving Tsun) about Bruce Lee" at youtube.com/watch?v=w8qg1R4d-Q4.

29. "Interview Wong Shun Leung (Ving Tsun) about Bruce Lee."

30. "Interview Wong Shun Leung (Ving Tsun) about Bruce Lee."

31. Bruce Lee's letter to Wong Shun Leung, dated January 11, 1970, can be viewed online at jkd.com.hk/Chi/Photo_Gallery/images/wong_letter_big.jpg or on Wikipedia at en.wikipedia.org/wiki/Wong_Shun-leung. It was first made public in the book *Reminiscence of Bruce Lee* by Wong Shun Leung, Bruce Lee Jeet Kune Do Club, Hong Kong, 1978, and can be seen on exhibit at the Ip Man Tong in Foshan, China.

32. Sid Fattedad quoted in Clausnitzer, Rolf, *My Wing Chun Kung Fu Journey: From Bruce Lee to Wong Shun Leung*, p. 135, Kindle edition.

CHAPTER THREE: FIGHTING FOR ST. FRANCIS

1. "Brother Edward who had a reputation for being strong and something of a boxer himself . . ." Brother Gregory Seubert quoted from "Brother Gregory of SFXC Recalls Bruce Lee" (Part Two), Bruce Lee Club Channel, at youtube .com/watch?v=77uvKCIIxLM.

2. "According to Alvin Wong, who was a form two student, [at SFX] then and there, Bruce told the school the reason he accepted Brother Gregory's invitation [to present the athletic awards to students at St. Francis Xavier's in 1973] was that he had once got caught fighting in the school washroom by Brother Edward, but he hadn't been punished. Instead Brother Edward encouraged Bruce to make good use of his gift in another arena, the inter-school boxing tournament, which used to be dominated by Westerners from International schools for children of expatriates in the then British colony." From the online video "Bruce Lee SFXC The Return of the Dragon to Saint Francis Xavier's College, 13th March 1973 Second Edition (26th March 2017)" at youtube.com/watch?v=ILGto6xvNcM.

3. Recollection of Sid Fattedad, published in Clausnitzer, Rolf, *My Wing Chun Kung Fu Journey: From Bruce Lee to Wong Shun Leung*, p. 134, Kindle edition.

4. "I looked down there and saw somebody doing pull-ups. And I was counting — 1, 2, 3, and I reached 50. And Bruce was doing all these pull-ups on this bar down there. And after 50 I stopped counting, but Bruce continued to do pull-ups beyond 50." From the video "Brother Gregory of SFXC Recalls Bruce Lee (Part Two)."

5. Brother Edward Muss, quoted in Felix, Dennis, and Ateyo, Don, *Bruce Lee: King of Kung Fu*, Straight Arrow Books, San Francisco, 1974, p. 16.

6. "I was teaching Bruce Lee how to fight with boxing, and he fought in the way of Wing Chun." Wong Shun Leung quoted from the documentary *Wong Shun Leung: The King of Talking Hands*.

7. Hong Kong newspaper account (name of paper unknown), March 30, 1958.

8. "The whole class was there. In fact, there must have been a hall full of students there." Sid Fattedad quoted in Clausnitzer, Rolf, *My Wing Chun Kung Fu Journey: From Bruce Lee to Wong Shun Leung*, p. 134, Kindle edition.

9. Hong Kong newspaper account (name of paper unknown), March 30, 1958.

10. Hong Kong newspaper account (name of paper unknown), March 30, 1958.

11. Unless otherwise indicated, the report of the match is drawn from the recollections of eyewitnesses Rolf Clausnitzer and Wong Shun Leung as reported in the documentary *Wong Shun Leung: The King of Talking Hands*.

12. Both Wong and Clausnitzer describe Bruce Lee as assuming a *bai jong* or "ready position" stance as taught in Wing Chun Kung Fu. All photos of Bruce taken during the 1950s in which he is assuming this stance show that he held his right hand forward and left hand back.

13. Robert Wang quoted from the program *Asian Threads* on Radio Television Hong Kong, podcast.rthk.hk/podcast/item.php?pid=363&eid=22299&lang=zh-CN.

14. Rolf Clausnitzer quoting Bruce Lee in the documentary *Wong Shun Leung: The King of Talking Hands*.

15. Lee's diary entry is taken from Lee, Linda, *The Life and Tragic Death of Bruce Lee*, p. 40.

16. Robert Lee quoted in Clouse, Robert, *Bruce Lee: The Biography*, Unique Publications, Burbank, California, 1988, p. 19.

CHAPTER FOUR: BATTLE ON THE ROOFTOP

1. "If someone practices any martial art, then that person must become stronger and more durable than someone who hasn't practiced. So, if you are punched you are able to take a lot more punishment than a normal person. I have been hit many times, as have all of the great martial artists that I know of. So, we are not supermen, but we can take a lot more. Any martial artist who says that he doesn't get hit is lying to himself." Wong Shun Leung quoted from the article "Interview with Wong Shun Leung and Barry Lee" at wingchunlexicon.com/interview-with-wong-shun-leung-and-barry-lee/.

2. "After this boxing championship, Bruce Lee fought twice again. Bruce Lee fought with other martial art styles. There was a time when I wasn't around. This time Bruce Lee's opponent wasn't a tough fighter." Wong Shun Leung, quoted from the documentary *Wong Shun Leung: The King of Talking Hands*.

3. "Bruce invited me to be his trainer. Because of our close relation, I eventually granted his wish." Wong Shun Leung quoted from the online article "Bruce Lee and His Friendship with Wong Shun Leung."

4. Unless otherwise indicated, all dialogue and actions from the fight are drawn from Wong Shun Leung's recollection as presented in the documentary *Wong Shun Leung: The King of Talking Hands*; Lang Ngan, "Bruce Lee's Real Fighting Account 15 Years Ago," published in the Hong Kong magazine *Superstar of the Generation — Bruce Lee*, 1973, reproduced at tapatalk.com/groups/bruceleelives tributeforum/bruce-lee-rooftop-fight-t3663.html and Wong Shun Leung quoted from the online article "Bruce Lee and His Friendship with Wong Shun Leung;" and Bruce Lee's diary entry for May 2, 1958, in Lee, Linda, *Bruce Lee: The Man Only I Knew*, p. 44.

5. Glover, Jesse, *Bruce Lee: Between Wing Chun and Jeet Kune Do*, p. 23.

CHAPTER FIVE: CROSSING THE TRIADS

1. Doug Palmer interview with the author, August 2, 1993.

2. William Cheung's memory of the occupants of the Lee family home, from the online article "William Cheung and Bruce Lee Story," at karateforums.com/william-cheung-and-bruce-lee-story-vt2268.html.

3. Per William Cheung, from the documentary *The Grandmaster & The Dragon: William Cheung and Bruce Lee*.

4. Robert Lee interview with the author, June 5, 1996.

5. Robert Lee interview with the author, June 5, 1996.

6. Yip Man quoted from "Wong Shun Leung: The Legend Behind the Legend, Recalling the Life of Bruce Lee's Teacher" by David Peterson, and Wong Shun Leung quoted from the online article "Bruce Lee and His Friendship with Wong Shun Leung."

7. Wong Shun Leung quoted from the documentary *Wong Shun Leung: The King of Talking Hands*.

8. Information about *The Orphan* is drawn from Chwoon, Tan Hoo, *Bruce Lee in His Greatest Movie: The Orphan*, pp. xvi–xvii.

9. The account of the altercation in the tearoom and the threat on Bruce Lee's life by the triad gang is drawn from the account presented in Lee, Chow-Kan (who was Bruce Lee's cousin), and Wong, Tak Chiu (a Bruce Lee historian in Hong Kong), from the chapter entitled "Secret Assassination from The Underworld," *Forever Superstar Bruce Lee*, Hong Kong, 2000.

10. "It was a good time for Bruce to leave Hong Kong when he sailed off to America. He had made quite a few enemies and some of them were talking about killing him." Peter Lee quoted in Block, Alex Ben, *The Legend of Bruce Lee*, p. 24.

CHAPTER SIX: COMING TO AMERICA

1. "[Jesse Glover] had a tattoo on the back of one hand, as I recall between his thumb and index finger, which someone told me was a 'pachuco' tattoo [a cross with dots signifying crimes committed, used by Chicano gangs in

California] . . . Leroy Garcia told me recently that Jesse was indeed exposed to Chicano gang culture in East L.A., becoming a 'gang-banger' for a while." Palmer, Doug, *Bruce Lee: Sifu, Friend and Big Brother*, Chin Music Press Inc., Seattle, 2020, pp. 43, 57.

2. "Bruce asked if I knew anything about other martial arts, and I told him that I had done a little boxing in the Air Force." Glover, Jesse, *Bruce Lee: Between Wing Chun and Jeet Kune Do*, p. 14.

3. Jesse Glover quoted in Bax, Paul, and Smith, Steve, *Disciple of the Dragon: Reflections of Bruce Lee's Student, Jesse Glover (Disciples of the Dragon Book 2)*, self-published, Amazon Publishing, 2019, pp. 68–69, Kindle edition. See also: "Jesse was a second-degree black belt in Judo. He won 14 Pacific Northwest [Judo] championships in a row as a brown belt." Ed Hart interview with the author, August 1993.

4. Ed Hart interview with the author, August 1993.

5. Jesse Glover interview with the author, September 1993.

6. Yip Chun quoted in Chun, Yip, *116 Wing Tsun Dummy Techniques as Demonstrated by Grandmaster Yip Man*, technical advisor Leung Ting, Leung Ting Publication & Distribution, Hong Kong, 1981, p. 109.

7. It's true that there was one gentleman, Fook Yeung, who lived in Seattle and was a martial arts practitioner of some experience. He had impressed Bruce with his knowledge of the various Chinese Kung Fu styles, which fed into Bruce's desire to create the ultimate Chinese Kung Fu super system. Fook had taught Bruce several forms from different Kung Fu styles, including one from the Praying Mantis system. In exchange, Bruce shared with Fook some of the basic movements of Wing Chun that he had learned in Hong Kong (Glover, Jesse, *Bruce Lee: Between Wing Chun and Jeet Kune Do*, p. 65). However, Yeung also worked full time and simply wasn't available to train with Bruce for several hours each day.

8. Jesse Glover claimed that James DeMile was a boxing champion while in the United States Air Force. Glover, Jesse, *Bruce Lee: Between Wing Chun and Jeet Kune Do*, p. 3.

9. James DeMile quoted from an interview in the May 1995 issue of *Combat* magazine.

10. James DeMile quoted from the video "Bruce Lee Vs Pro Fighters: 'He Could Beat Us All, We Had No Chance'" at youtube.com/watch?v=_Yf-Cpvvucs.

11. Greg Luke quoted from the online article "Young Bruce Lee, Part I: Street Brawling and Cha-Cha Dancing in Seattle" by Billy Potts, November 19, 2020, at zolimacitymag.com/young-bruce-lee-part-i-street-brawling-and-cha-cha-dancing-in-seattle-chinatown/.

12. Greg Luke quoted from the online article "Young Bruce Lee, Part I: Street Brawling and Cha-Cha Dancing in Seattle."

13. Betty Lau quoted from the online article "Young Bruce Lee, Part I: Street Brawling and Cha-Cha Dancing in Seattle."

14. Annie Galarosa quoted from the online article "Uncovering Bruce Lee's Public

School Years" by Devin Israel Cabanilla at iexaminer.org/uncovering-bruce
-lees-public-school-years/.

15. Information about Ruby Chow, her restaurant and its patrons is drawn from the
online article "Young Bruce Lee, Part I: Street Brawling and Cha-Cha Dancing
in Seattle."

16. Judge Mark Chow quoted from the online article "Young Bruce Lee, Part I:
Street Brawling and Cha-Cha Dancing in Seattle."

17. Lee Hoi-chuen's and the Chow family's desire to have Bruce Lee returned to
Hong Kong is taken from the online article "Young Bruce Lee, Part I: Street
Brawling and Cha-Cha Dancing in Seattle."

18. "Leroy [Garcia] taught Bruce how to shoot and gave him his first gun (a .25
automatic) for a birthday present. Bruce told me later that he was target shooting
at pigeons out of his window at Ruby Chow's. He was surprised to learn that this
was not permissible behavior in the city. The first time that Leroy took Bruce
out to shoot was incredibly funny. Bruce had Leroy's nine-inch barreled .357
Magnum strapped to his side, was holding a 30–06 in his hand and had a cowboy
hat on his head. Bruce was an excellent shot and could score good patterns at
75 yards with a handgun." Glover, Jesse, *Bruce Lee: Between Wing Chun and Jeet
Kune Do*, p. 66. See also: "Between Leroy and I, because of our 'gun-related'
backgrounds he and I taught Bruce how to shoot pistols, revolvers, rifles, and
shotguns. Bruce totally loved it. I loaned Bruce one of my own guns, a very small
'antique' Colt .25 caliber semi-automatic pistol with black handle-grips, and he
carried that piece for at least a couple of years . . . Bruce loved to shoot, and
therefore we would often go shooting together. He really liked to practice quick
drawing and shooting at cardboard targets that were the same size and shape as
a man." Skip Ellsworth quoted in Bax, Paul, *Disciples of the Dragon: Reflections
from the Students of Bruce Lee*, first edition, self-published, Outskirts Press Inc.,
Denver, 2008, p. 53; and: "Bruce liked to fire guns. He and Leroy Garcia used to
do a lot of shooting." James DeMile quoted in Bax, Paul, *Disciples of the Dragon:
Reflections from the Students of Bruce Lee*, p. 118.

19. Skip Ellsworth quoted from Bax, Paul, *Disciples of the Dragon: Reflections from
the Students of Bruce Lee*, pp. 51–52, and Skip Ellsworth interview with the
author, August 1993.

20. "He worked out like a fanatic; he'd work out six or seven hours a day every day."
Ed Hart interview with the author, August 1993.

21. Glover, Jesse, *Bruce Lee: Between Wing Chun and Jeet Kune Do*, p. 53.

22. Jesse Glover interview with the author, September 1993.

23. From the online article "Young Bruce Lee, Part I: Street Brawling and Cha-Cha
Dancing in Seattle."

24. From the online article "Uncovering Bruce Lee's Public School Years."

25. "Bruce spent two to four hours practicing on the [wooden] dummy every day
and the sharpness of his attack was due, in part, to this training. . . . After
work, Bruce would come down to my house and we would work out for a

couple of hours." Glover, Jesse, *Bruce Lee: Between Wing Chun and Jeet Kune Do*, pp. 17–18. See also: "We trained, like, four or five hours every day, and what was interesting about the group was that we weren't there as a *martial* group. We were just guys who liked to fight and get together and, like, were very physical." James DeMile, from an interview in *Combat*, May 1995.

26. "[Bruce] Lee kept a trash can filled with gravel; the jagged stones were for punching. 'His knuckles were so calloused that if you were ever to get hit by them, it would probably have been like getting hit by some big old hunk of wood,' says Brien Chow." From the online article "Young Bruce Lee, Part I: Street Brawling and Cha-Cha Dancing in Seattle."

27. Trisha Mar quoted from the online article "Young Bruce Lee, Part I: Street Brawling and Cha-Cha Dancing in Seattle."

28. Glover, Jesse, *Bruce Lee: Between Wing Chun and Jeet Kune Do*, p. 17.

29. Glover, Jesse, *Bruce Lee: Between Wing Chun and Jeet Kune Do*, p. 17.

30. Skip Ellsworth interview with the author, August 5, 1993.

CHAPTER SEVEN: ELEVEN SECONDS OF MAYHEM

1. From the bio of Soke Yoichi Nakachi, online article at spiritforcekarate.yolasite .com/expanded-history-nakachi.php.

2. From the online article "Shinpu-Ren Lineage: Yon Pon Gun" at prescottkarate .com/shinpu-ren-lineage-yon-pon-gun.html.

3. Information on Yoichi Nakachi's rank in Shinpu-Ren Karate is taken from the online article "Soke Yoichi Nakachi" at spiritforcekarate.yolasite.com/expanded -history-nakachi.php.

4. From the online article spiritforcekarate.yolasite.com/expanded-history-nakachi .php, and the online article "Shinpu-Ren Lineage: Yon Pon Gun."

5. For information on Nakachi being trained in Judo, see the online article "Soke Yoichi Nakachi." Jesse Glover also told me: "I'd known [Nakachi] from Judo and he was a Judo black belt, too." Jesse Glover interview with the author, September 1993.

6. Jesse Glover interview with the author, September 1993.

7. According to Glover: "The year was 1960 and few Americans had heard of Gung Fu, but everyone knew what Judo was, and we were banking on it being the drawing card." Glover, Jesse, *Bruce Lee: Between Wing Chun and Jeet Kune Do*, p. 39.

8. All information about the Judo and Kung Fu demonstration unless otherwise noted is drawn from Jesse Glover's interview with the author, September 1993.

9. Glover, Jesse, *Bruce Lee: Between Wing Chun and Jeet Kune Do*, p. 42.

10. Glover, Jesse, *Bruce Lee: Between Wing Chun and Jeet Kune Do*, p. 42.

11. Glover, Jesse, *Bruce Lee: Between Wing Chun and Jeet Kune Do*, p. 42.

12. Cowles, Joseph, *Wu Wei Gung Fu*, self-published, circa 1981, p. 11.

13. Glover, Jesse, *Bruce Lee: Between Wing Chun and Jeet Kune Do*, p. 42.
14. There is some confusion as to how long Nakachi's taunting of Bruce went on. Jesse Glover told the author it went on for "a long time," Ed Hart indicated that it went on for "two weeks," and Skip Ellsworth said it was more than a week. However, they are all agreed that the demonstration on Friday, October 28, 1960, had triggered the fight that would occur, and Bruce Lee's daytime diary entry indicates that the fight itself took place on Tuesday, November 1, 1960 (see "Bruce Lee's contest diary exposed! 11 seconds KO Japanese Karate Black Belt Challenger" at daydaynews.cc/en/constellation/314599.html). Consequently, the time between the demonstration and the fight was only four days. As two of those days would have fallen on a weekend, no interaction between Nakachi and Bruce would have taken place in Edison Technical School; the evidence indicates that the taunting/interaction occurred for a (school) day and a half.
15. Cowles, Joseph, *Wu Wei Gung Fu*, p. 11.
16. All dialogue and action pertaining to the fight between Bruce Lee and Yoichi Nakachi unless otherwise noted is drawn from the accounts that Ed Hart and Jesse Glover shared with the author in August and September 1993, respectively, as well as Glover's book *Bruce Lee: Between Wing Chun and Jeet Kune Do*, pp. 43–45.
17. "Nakachi switched studies to Olympic College in Bremerton, and started to teach at the 'Y' in downtown Seattle (5 nights a week). He taught at a health club in the downtown area as well." From the online article "Soke Yoichi Nakachi."
18. Ed Hart interview with the author, August 1993.
19. Ed Hart interview with the author, August 1993.
20. The author was told this by both Ed Hart and Jesse Glover.
21. "Bruce made everybody there swear to secrecy — all his people, right? But I think the other guys [Nakachi's friends], they're the ones that started talking about it. Soon everybody knew about it." Jesse Glover interview with the author, September 1993.
22. Ed Hart interview with the author, August 1993.
23. "Later we learned that Bruce had cracked the man's skull around his eye and down into his cheek bone." Jesse Glover quoted in Bax, Paul, and Smith, Steve, *Disciple of the Dragon: Reflections of Bruce Lee's Student, Jesse Glover (Disciples of the Dragon Book 2)*, pp. 34–35.
24. Bruce was mistaken about Nakachi being only a first-degree black belt. According to the online article "Soke Yoichi Nakachi": "In 1948, when the ban on martial arts was lifted, the open practice of Shinpu-ren resumed. By this time, at the age of 16, Nakachi had his 2nd degree black belt."
25. Bruce Lee's diary entry for November 1, 1960, is reproduced online at daydaynews.cc/en/entertainment/314599.html.
26. Jesse Glover interview with the author, September 1993.

CHAPTER EIGHT: FAMILY, GUNS, AND BUSINESS

1. Doug Palmer interview with the author, August 2, 1993.
2. Doug Palmer interview with the author, August 2, 1993.
3. Doug Palmer interview with the author, August 2, 1993.
4. Doug Palmer interview with the author, August 2, 1993.
5. Glover, Jesse, *Bruce Lee: Between Wing Chun and Jeet Kune Do*, p. 52. In Jesse's quote from his book he says, "Auh Hing" [William Cheung]. However, in his second book, he indicates that he was mistaken and that the person he referred to as Auh Hing was, in fact, Wong Shun Leung: "Bruce often spoke of Wong's skills and exploits when he first came to the U.S. and I wrote about him in the first book under the name of Auh Hing. . . . Bruce also said that he had learned a great deal from Wong's teachings and that most of his hand techniques were an outgrowth of this instruction." Glover, Jesse R., *Bruce Lee's Non-Classical Gung Fu*, self-published, Glover Publications, Seattle, 1978, p. 2.
6. "When he first came to Seattle, Bruce told me that he was the sixth best person in the Wing Chun style, and his greatest desire was to become number one. His major problem in accomplishing this goal was how to become more skillful than the five people who were above him by using the same techniques that they used. He realized that these people had taken years to reach their skill levels, and that he was going to have to develop modifications that circumvented their classical techniques." Glover, Jesse, *Bruce Lee: Between Wing Chun and Jeet Kune Do*, p. 52.
7. Bruce Lee quoted from a dialogue he had that was recorded by his student Daniel Lee, a copy of which was given to the author by Daniel Lee. It is available online at youtube.com/watch?v=1UtUgOgRrXA.
8. All information about the actions and dialogue about Bruce Lee's encounter on Nathan Road are drawn from Doug Palmer's recounting of the event when interviewed by the author, August 2, 1993.
9. Jesse Glover interview with the author, September 1993.
10. Bax, Paul, *Disciples of the Dragon: Reflections from the Students of Bruce Lee*, first edition, Outskirts Press, Inc., Denver, 2008, p. 26.
11. James DeMile quoted in Bax, Paul, *Disciples of the Dragon: Reflections from the Students of Bruce Lee*, p. 110.
12. Jesse Glover interview with the author, September 1993.
13. Unless otherwise indicated, all dialogue and descriptions of Lee's dispute with DeMile are drawn from DeMile's statements on his Facebook page, which were republished online at tapatalk.com/groups/bruceleelivestributeforum/james-w-demile-and-bl-falling-out-t3474.html, and from Bax, Paul, *Disciples of the Dragon: Reflections from the Students of Bruce Lee*, p. 114.
14. "We [Glover and Howard Hall] talked to [James] Lee for three hours [in 1959]. He told us that he was a brown belt in Judo." Glover, Jesse, *Bruce Lee: Between Wing Chun and Jeet Kune Do*, p. 11.

15. "TY Wong was the Hop Sing Tong's go-to enforcer for whenever U.S. servicemen on shore leave got too rowdy while carousing the neighborhood's Forbidden City nightclubs." From the online article "Doing Research (6): Working the Beat — One Journalist's Efforts at Perfecting the Fine Art of Hanging Out" by Charles Russo, at chinesemartialstudies.com/2016/05/05/doing-research-6-working-the -beat-one-journalists-efforts-at-perfecting-the-fine-art-of-hanging-out/. For the tongs being associated with criminal activity see: "By the early twentieth century, Tongs were found in nearly every major American city. Eventually incorporating prostitution, gambling, drug trade, and racketeering, Tongs became the preeminent Asian organized crime network in the country." From the online article "The Tongs of Chinatown: 'I Was There' — A Conversation with Bill Lee" by Michael Zelenko at foundsf.org/index.php?title=The_Tongs_of_Chinatown; for an overview of the criminal history of the Hop Sing Tong, see "Chinese Mafia — Hop Sing Tong/ Raymond 'Shrimp Boy' Chow" at youtube.com/watch?v=5eGGvxPGeXI.

16. "Years later, [Bay Area martial artist Leo] Fong laughs the whole misunderstanding off as trivial: 'Jimmy fell out with TY Wong over just $10. They got real upset with each other over that. Can you imagine?'" From the online article "James Yimm Lee and T.Y. Wong: A Rivalry that Shaped the Chinese Martial Arts in America" by Charles Russo at chinesemartialstudies.com/2016/09/01/james-yimm-lee-and -t-y-wong-a-rivalry-that-shaped-the-chinese-martial-art-in-america/.

17. "I studied the sil lum style, which featured such forms as 'A Dragon and Tiger in Conference' and 'Nine Dragons at Sea.' I wasted three and a half years performing kata. Not once during those years did I see the students spar. We were told that this type of training would eventually lead to deadly 'internal strength.' I realized later that the whole repertoire was just a time-killing tactic to collect the monthly fee. In disgust, I quit practicing this particular sil lum style." James Lee quoted in Lee, James Yimm, *Wing Chun Kung Fu: Chinese Art of Self-Defense*, Ohara Publications Inc., Santa Clarita, California, 1972, p. 5. Regarding the date of the split, there appears to be some confusion. According to Charles Russo, the split occurred in 1961: "At some point in late 1961, James Lee stormed out of the Kin Mon Physical Culture Studio in San Francisco's Chinatown, effectively breaking off his tutelage under Sil Lum master TY Wong." (From the online article "James Yimm Lee and T.Y. Wong: A Rivalry that Shaped the Chinese Martial Arts in America" by Charles Russo.) Given that the book in question, *Chinese Karate Kung-Fu: Original 'Sil Lum' System for Health & Self Defense* was self-published by James Lee and is dated January 1, 1961, this would certainly be plausible. However, Jesse Glover Inc., writing on this same topic some forty years before Russo, recalled speaking with LeRoy Porter, a former student of James Lee, in 1959: "Judo greenbelt . . . LeRoy Porter . . . had been one of [James] Lee's students while living in California . . . we talked for a long time about James Lee. LeRoy told me that Lee had studied under a professor Wong in San Francisco. He said that Lee had learned a great many forms at Wong's school, but that he

had become concerned about their application in a fight and had finally ventured out on his own." (Glover, Jesse, *Bruce Lee: Between Wing Chun and Jeet Kune Do*, p. 8.) A few weeks after this, Glover and two friends traveled to Oakland to visit with James Lee and recalled James speaking about the split between him and Wong, saying: "He told us . . . that he had gotten most of his Gung Fu training at a school in San Francisco. He said that he had grown tired of doing forms and had turned to the development of his own method, which was a combination of a number of different styles." (Glover, Jesse, *Bruce Lee: Between Wing Chun and Jeet Kune Do*, p. 11.) It's important to remember that Glover met James Lee *prior* to his meeting Bruce Lee, which took place in 1959, while the pair were on their way to Edison Technical School. So, perhaps James Lee had stopped attending Wong's Sil Lum classes a full year prior to the book royalties becoming an issue.

18. Lee, James Yimm, *Wing Chun Kung Fu: Chinese Art of Self-Defense*, p. 7.

19. "Bruce did [the book] because James Lee told him [he] had written some books, and he had made quite a bit of money off them and he thought Bruce could make about five grand if he wrote a book and Bruce needed the money. That's why he wrote the book." Jesse Glover interview with the author, September 1993.

20. Jesse Glover interview with the author, September 1993.

21. Lee, Bruce, *Chinese Gung Fu: The Philosophical Art of Self-Defense*, Oriental Book Sales, Oakland, 1961, p. 1.

22. ". . . Lau Bun and TY Wong. Both men were enforcers for the Hop Sing Tong", having been recruited for their martial abilities many years earlier upon arriving to town. . . . Their schools emerged out of these roles, beginning with Lau Bun's Hung Sing in the late 1930s (though originally known as Wah Kuen) and then TY's Kin Mon a few years later in the early 1940s. Both practiced medicine, played music, and operated Lion Dance teams that were heavily involved in neighborhood festivals and holidays." From the online article "James Yimm Lee and T.Y. Wong: A Rivalry that Shaped the Chinese Martial Arts in America" by Charles Russo.

23. Lee, Bruce, *Chinese Gung Fu: The Philosophical Art of Self-Defense*, p. 1.

24. "It [the book] must have been a thousand copies he had printed, because he told me the thing generated five grand and he sold the book for five bucks a copy." Jesse Glover interview with the author, September 1993.

25. Bruce Lee's letter to Pearl Tso, dated September 1962, in Little, John (editor), *Bruce Lee: Letter of the Dragon*, Tuttle Publishing, Boston, 1998, pp. 60–65. The letter is also reproduced in its entirety on the Lee Estate website: brucelee.com /podcast-blog/2018/10/17/120-letter-to-pearl.

26. Linda Lee Cadwell quoted in Polly, Matthew, *Bruce Lee: A Life*, p. 138.

27. Taky Kimura interview with the author, 1994.

28. "Gung Fu, the ancestor of karate, jiu-jitsu, etc., is one of the oldest known forms of self-defense and can well be called the concentrated essence of wisdom and profound thoughts on the art of combat. With a four-thousand-year-old background, Gung Fu has never been surpassed in comprehensiveness and

depth of understanding." Lee, Bruce, and Little, John (editor), *The Tao of Gung Fu*, Tuttle Publishing, Boston, 1997, p. 21.

29. "There are two schools of Gung Fu . . . one is the 'hard school' which concentrates on speed, coordination, and physical power, like cracking bricks and stones with bare hands. The other school, the 'soft school,' advocates gentleness and unity of mind and body — firmness is concealed in softness. Gung Fu is not preoccupied with breaking bricks and smashing boards, such as Karate. We're more concerned with having it affect our whole way of thinking and behaving. The American is like an oak tree — he stands firm against the wind. If the wind is strong, he cracks. The Oriental stands like bamboo, bending with the wind and springing back when the wind ceases, stronger than ever before." Bruce Lee quoted from a newspaper interview "Mike Lee Hope for Rotsa Ruck: U Introduced to Gung Fu," by Weldon Johnson, *Seattle Times*, circa 1961.

30. Bruce Lee's letter to Pearl Tso, dated September 1962, in Little, John (editor), *Bruce Lee: Letters of the Dragon*, pp. 60–65. The letter is also reproduced in its entirety on the Lee Estate website: brucelee.com/podcast-blog/2018/10/17/120 -letter-to-pearl.

31. Lee, Bruce, and Little, John (editor), *The Tao of Gung Fu*, p. 150.

32. Lee, Bruce, *Chinese Gung Fu: The Philosophical Art of Self-Defense*, p. 84.

33. Lee, Bruce, *Chinese Gung Fu: The Philosophical Art of Self-Defense*, p. 6.

34. Conze, Edward (ed.), *Buddhist Texts Through the Ages*, Philosophical Library, New York, 1954, pp. 296–298.

35. Ed Parker quoted in Block, Alex Ben, *The Legend of Bruce Lee*, p. 47.

CHAPTER NINE: TURF WAR IN CHINATOWN

1. The author is obliged to point out that martial arts instructors and their students are a notoriously clannish group. In fact, the author has yet to encounter one who doesn't believe their art to be the best, or their instructor to be the deadliest person on the planet. Few, if any, students of a Karate or Kung Fu instructor believe that their teacher is capable of losing a fight. Moreover, students of the same teacher more often than not will bicker among themselves as to who among them practices their teacher's art *correctly*, and that most, if not all, of their teacher's other students "don't get it." It is a phenomenon that is peculiar to the martial arts; one typically doesn't observe this attitude among students of other arts such as painting or music. And so, the reader is forewarned that a person looking to discover the truth about a fight that occurred well over half a century ago, involving two teachers of two different martial art styles, is tasked with sifting through a welter of conflicting opinions issued from representatives of both sides (and contrasting these with newspaper accounts and documents in which the encounter is referenced) in order to arrive at any semblance of what really transpired.

2. Michael Dorgan is a long-time devotee of the "soft arts," principally, Xing-I and Yang Style Tai Chi, although, according to his website, he also learned Northern Shaolin Kung Fu. His bio states that "I moved to San Francisco from the Midwest in 1978 primarily to learn Chinese martial arts. The teacher I found there was Wong Jack Man, and from his students and other martial artists I began to hear whispers of an epic fight he had had with Bruce Lee" (taichisanjose.com /articles-bruce-lee-toughest-fight). His devotion to his teacher is unquestionable; despite a varied martial arts background (including earlier training in Okinawan Karate and Tae Kwon Do), and his extensive training in Tai Chi and Xing-I, two of the three articles on Dorgan's website are devoted to Wong Jack Man.

3. From the article "Bruce Lee's Toughest Fight" by Michael Dorgan, *Official Karate*, July 1980.

4. "Master Rick L. Wing has studied the Northern Shaolin Style ever since he was a young boy. He learned directly at the hands of the master, Shifu Wong Jack Man, for decades and attended more classes with his teacher than any other student. Rick was an extremely dedicated and apt pupil, learning well all that his teacher taught him. Upon his Shifu's retirement from the martial world in December of 2005, Shifu Rick assumed the mantle of Chief Instructor of Shifu Wong's San Francisco school, the Ching Mo Athletic Association." From the online bio of Wing at shaolinlomita.com/masters/master-rick-wing/.

5. Wing, Rick L., *Showdown in Oakland: The Story Behind the Wong Jack Man — Bruce Lee Fight*, self-published, Amazon Publishing, 2013, p. 2581, Kindle edition.

6. *Chinese Pacific Weekly*, December 17, 1964.

7. Wong Jack Man quoted from an online interview with his student Michael Dorgan at Michael Dorgan's website: taichisanjose.com/wong-jack-man -interview. The interview is also available on the EBM Kung Fu Academy website: kungfu.net/interview.html, and on the "Northern Shaolin" Facebook page at facebook.com/groups/632811690133144/posts/4583215048426102/?comment _id=4588661554548118.

8. "I'd gotten into a fight in San Francisco with a kung-fu cat." Bruce Lee quoted from the article "Bruce Lee: The Man, the Fighter, the Superstar," by Mitoshi Uyehara in *The Bruce Lee Memorial Issue*, Rainbow Publications, Los Angeles, California, 1974, p. 23.

9. "In Chinatown, I'd hear how unhappy they were about Bruce. They'd call him a wise punk." Ed Parker quoted in Block, Alex Ben, *The Legend of Bruce Lee*, p. 47.

10. "You know, I was such a smart-assed punk . . ." Bruce Lee quoted in Uyehara, Mitoshi, *Bruce Lee: The Incomparable Fighter*, p. 8. See also: "I was a punk and went looking for fights." Bruce Lee quoted in *The Best of Bruce Lee* magazine, p. 14.

11. David Chin quoted in the *Chinese Pacific Weekly*, January 7, 1965.

12. See dictionary.cambridge.org/dictionary/english/discussion.

13. "Long time reader" quoted from his letter to the editor as published in the *Chinese Pacific Weekly*, January 14, 1965.

14. Wing, Rick L., *Showdown in Oakland: The Story Behind the Wong Jack Man — Bruce Lee Fight*, pp. 731–736, Kindle edition.

15. Wong Jack Man online interview.

16. Russo, Charles, *Striking Distance: Bruce Lee & the Dawn of Martial Arts in America*, University of Nebraska Press, Nebraska, 2016, pp. 2470–2478, Kindle edition.

17. Polly, Matthew, *Bruce Lee: A Life*, pp. 149–150.

18. "Over a period (18th [to] early 20th Century) limited employment opportunities and the lack of social acceptance resulted in a movement by some to legitimize the practice of martial arts [in China]. Following the example set by herbalists and bone setters, martial artists attempted to establish themselves as members of the "Kung" or artisan class. They began to open schools ("Mo Gwoon" in Cantonese dialect). . . . Even though a would-be instructor was seeking to legitimize himself and gain general acceptance, he simultaneously desired to maintain the respect of his peers. The quickest and by far the most popular method of doing this was to issue an open challenge and defeat several local fighters before opening one's school. Until it was declared illegal by the Nationalist government in 1928, it was relatively common in southern China to see an instructor fight all challengers in public duels with no rules and no restrictions. These duels often resulted in serious injury or even death but they were viewed as necessary to demonstrate that an instructor was worthy of opening a school. Another popular method of making a name for oneself was to challenge an already established instructor in hopes of defeating him and taking over his school." From the online article "A Brief History of Chinese Kung-Fu: Part 2" by David A. Ross at fightingarts.com/reading/article.php?id=477. Moreover, one martial arts master putting down a rival master and his school is the plot of virtually every single Kung Fu movie that came out of Hong Kong during the 1970s.

19. "Bruce read the scroll which appears to have been an ultimatum from the San Francisco martial arts community. Presumably, if Bruce lost the challenge, he was either to close down his Institute or stop teaching Caucasians." Lee, Linda, *Bruce Lee: The Man Only I Knew*, pp. 71–72. If true, then Bruce's school (i.e., the rival business) was the point of contention.

20. There is an animus towards Bruce Lee that exists to this day among certain students from the Chan Bing lineage of Choy Lay Fut Kung Fu. A post on kungfumagazine.com, from a second-generation student of Chan's, passes on some additional hearsay comments regarding Kenneth Wong blocking Bruce's speed punch: "[After Bruce Lee's demonstration] anyways, they went back to bing chan and told him what happened, and bing chan asked one question . . . 'did you hit him back?' Kenneth [a student of Chan's] said NO. From what i hear is that bing chan got hella ****ed about kenneth waisting his time by just blocking, he should have laid into bruce [Lee]," kungfumagazine.com/forum/showthread.php?39874-Lau-Bun-Stories/page5.

21. "Sifu Bing Chan was also supposed to go and watch the match [between Bruce Lee and Wong Jack Man], but in actuality he did not go, though I do not know why." Wing, Rick L., *Showdown in Oakland: The Story Behind the Wong Jack Man — Bruce Lee Fight*, p. 1063.

22. From the online article "Keeping Kung Fu Secrets Grandmaster David Chin: Grandmaster David Chin's Legacy of Hop Gar Rebels and Guang Ping Tai Chi Revolutionaries." Note: This is in conflict with Rick Wing's account that "[David Chin] at that time [1964] was an avid practitioner of Fut Ga, having studied it for most of his teenage years." Wing, Rick L., *Showdown in Oakland: The Story Behind the Wong Jack Man — Bruce Lee Fight*, pp. 969–974.

23. Wong Jack Man online interview.

24. Wong Jack Man online interview.

25. "Well, I'm going to open a kwoon," Wong Jack Man quoted in Polly, Matthew, *Bruce Lee: A Life*, p. 152.

26. *Chinese Pacific Weekly*, November 26, 1964.

27. See Chapter One, endnote 48.

28. Wong Jack Man online interview.

29. Wong Jack Man online interview.

30. "What provoked the fight was Bruce Lee's arrogance and his insulting treatment of other martial artists. He trashed the teachers in Chinatown, calling them 'old tigers with no teeth' and lectured them about his Wing Chun system being far superior to their traditional Chinese martial arts." Wong Jack Man online interview.

31. Wong Jack Man online interview.

32. Wong Jack Man online interview.

33. "In the coming weeks a letter was drafted. Wong Jack Man sat down at the Jackson Street Café after finishing his shift waiting tables, joining David Chin and Bing Chan." Russo, Charles, *Striking Distance: Bruce Lee & the Dawn of Martial Arts in America*, p. 2498.

34. "According to Bruce, he did not invite the man [Wong] to a fight; it was the man who initiated it (Bruce then took out two letters to show). The first letter showed the fight location . . . which Bruce refused. The man then sent a second letter and Bruce invited the man to meet up at his martial arts academy." *Chinese Pacific Weekly*, December 17, 1964.

35. "He refused to come to San Francisco, but wrote a note inviting me to his school in Oakland with the date and time to meet." Wong Jack Man online interview.

36. From the article "Bruce Lee's Toughest Fight," by Michael Dorgan, *Official Karate*, July 1980. Forty-seven years after this article, Dorgan would interview his teacher Wong Jack Man again, and Wong's recollection would be virtually the same: "A letter was written and hand delivered to Bruce at his Oakland school inviting him to discuss what happened at the Sun Sing Theater and to exchange martial arts skills with me." Wong Jack Man online interview.

37. Unless otherwise indicated, all details and dialogue between Bruce Lee and David Chin are drawn from Chin's interviews as excerpted and presented in Wing, Rick L., *Showdown in Oakland: The Story Behind the Wong Jack Man — Bruce Lee Fight*, pp. 1082–1095, and Polly, Matthew, *Bruce Lee: A Life*, pp. 152–153.

38. David Chin quoted in Polly, Matthew, *Bruce Lee: A Life*, p. 154.

39. Lee, Linda, *Bruce Lee: The Man Only I Knew*, pp. 71–73.

40. "In Oakland, he received a challenge from the San Francisco Chinese martial arts community. And the challenge read that Bruce, if he were to be defeated in this challenge, would have to cease teaching Caucasian or non-Chinese students." Linda Lee quoted in the documentary *Bruce Lee: A Warrior's Journey*, produced and directed by John Little, Warner Bros., Burbank, 2000.

41. Taky Kimura interview with the author, 1994.

42. *Chinese Pacific Weekly*, November 26, 1964.

43. Wing, Rick L., *Showdown in Oakland: The Story Behind the Wong Jack Man — Bruce Lee Fight*, p. 1058, Kindle edition.

44. "Still, there is wide agreement that Chan Bing was one of the first instructors in the San Francisco Chinatown area to accept large numbers of Western students when he opened his school in 1967." From the online article "Through a Lens Darkly (62): Chan Bing's Choy Li Fut Students, 1967," by benjudkins at chinesemartialstudies.com/2019/10/20/through-a-lens-darkly-62-chan-bings-choy-li-fut-students-1967/.

45. "Lau Bun was fiercely loyal to his community, and . . . refused to teach Kung Fu to non-Chinese individuals." From the online article "Lives of Chinese Martial Artists (5): Lau Bun — A Kung Fu Pioneer in America" at chinesemartialstudies.com/2013/02/20/lives-of-the-chinese-martial-artists-5-lau-bun-a-kung-fu-pioneer-in-america/.

46. "Lau Bun school was majorly involved in not allowing Bruce Lee to teach the Gwai Lo . . . Even more surprising to hear was the late Bing Chan (my Sifu's first Sifu) was the one who wrote up the declaration to bruce lee telling him why he shouldn't be teaching Gwai Lo, and if it doesn't stop, a match was to be set up in which Wong Jack Man ended up fighting him." From the online article at kungfumagazine.com/forum/showthread.php?39874-Lau-Bun-Stories/page5. See also Linda Lee's recollection above (endnotes 19 and 40). Whether or not Chan Bing would include a statement in the letter being drafted about Lee teaching non-Chinese, it is clear that he had a problem with Bruce and was involved up to his elbows in the composition of the letter: "Bing Chan also encouraged the men in their endeavor, not that they needed much encouragement since they were fairly intent on what they were going to do anyway, but he did offer a healthy dose of verbal and moral support." Wing, Rick L., *Showdown in Oakland: The Story Behind the Wong Jack Man — Bruce Lee Fight*, p. 1034.

47. Leo Fong interview with the author, August 12, 2021.

48. *Chinese Pacific Weekly*, December 17, 1964.

CHAPTER TEN: RUMBLE IN OAKLAND

1. A reference to the fight appearing in the *Chinese Pacific Weekly*, November 26, 1964, says news of the fight had first been published in a newspaper "about a month ago," indicating that the encounter occurred in late October 1964.

2. The number of people with David Chin that night (and their names) are from Russo, Charles, *Striking Distance: Bruce Lee & the Dawn of Martial Arts in America*, pp. 2553–2561, Kindle edition.

3. "I got a ride to Bruce's school with an acquaintance. Four of his friends were also in the car, but I didn't know them." Wong Jack Man online interview.

4. "I was wearing my traditional black Kung Fu uniform." Wong Jack Man online interview.

5. "Yet for all the bluster in Chinatown that day, the ride over was unusually quiet." Russo, Charles, *Striking Distance: Bruce Lee & the Dawn of Martial Arts in America*, pp. 2553–2561.

6. Wong Jack Man online interview.

7. Wing, Rick L., *Showdown in Oakland: The Story Behind the Wong Jack Man — Bruce Lee Fight*, p. 1225.

8. As per an advertisement for "spiked/studded wrist bands" in *Black Belt*, July 1982, p. 87.

9. In none of the photos of Wong Jack Man demonstrating his art are such bracelets present. For Wong wearing spiked wrist bracelets see: "Prior to the fight, Wong had strapped on a pair of leather wrist bracelets studded with metal spikes." Polly, Matthew, *Bruce Lee: A Life*, p. 156.

10. "Northern Shaolin had armed Wong with kicks of blinding speeds and crushing power. But before the fight, recalls [William] Chen, 'Sifu Wong said he would not use his kicks; he thought they were too dangerous.'" From the article "Bruce Lee's Toughest Fight" by Michael Dorgan, published in *Official Karate*, July 1980.

11. David Chin quoted in Polly, Matthew, *Bruce Lee: A Life*, p. 156.

12. "Wong wore long-sleeves to cover it." David Chin, quoted in Polly, Matthew, *Bruce Lee: A Life*, p. 156.

13. "Well, I was outside the school when it took place. Wong Jack Man had a whole group of guys when he went in." George Lee quoted in Bax, Paul, *Disciples of the Dragon: Reflections from the Students of Bruce Lee*, first edition, self-published, Outskirts Press Inc., Denver, 2008, p. 136.

14. For James Lee having a revolver see Russo, Charles, *Striking Distance: Bruce Lee & the Dawn of Martial Arts in America*, p. 2553.

15. "Jimmy Lee opened the door for them." Wing, Rick L., *Showdown in Oakland: The Story Behind the Wong Jack Man — Bruce Lee Fight*, p. 1219.

16. "Three other Chinese accompanied Wong Jack Man." Lee, Linda, *Bruce Lee: The Man Only I Knew*, pp. 71–73.

17. Wong Jack Man quoted from the *Chinese Pacific Weekly*, January 28, 1965.

18. Wing, Rick L., *Showdown in Oakland: The Story Behind the Wong Jack Man — Bruce Lee Fight*, p. 1145.

19. Bill Chen's account is presented in Wing, Rick L., *Showdown in Oakland: The Story Behind the Wong Jack Man — Bruce Lee Fight*, pp. 1219–1230. Note: Given that Linda Lee claimed that Wong Jack Man entered the building with three other Chinese men (one of whom we know to be David Chin), and that the remaining group of men from San Francisco's Chinatown would enter the studio after the rules of the match had been discussed, the fact that Bill Chen recalled Lee writing on a chalkboard before the introductions got underway indicates that he had to be among the first group of men that entered the building with Wong.

20. Unless otherwise indicated, all dialogue from the two parties prior to the fight is drawn from the accounts of Linda Lee, Allen Joe, David Chin and Wong Jack Man as presented in Lee, Linda, *Bruce Lee: The Man Only I Knew*, pp. 71–73; Linda Lee quoted in the documentary *Bruce Lee: A Warrior's Journey*; Russo, Charles, *Striking Distance: Bruce Lee & the Dawn of Martial Arts in America*, pp. 2546, 2569 and 2577; Wing, Rick L., *Showdown in Oakland: The Story Behind the Wong Jack Man — Bruce Lee Fight*, p. 1288 and pp. 154–155; "Bruce Lee's Toughest Fight" by Michael Dorgan, published in *Official Karate*, July 1980; Wong Jack Man online interview; and Allen Joe interview with the author, April 1994.

21. "At first, Chan introduced Wong to Bruce. They shook hands . . ." *Chinese Pacific Weekly*, January 28, 1965.

22. "When the man [Wong] arrived at Bruce's academy, Bruce asked the man if he had directly witnessed Bruce announcing the challenge; the man stated that he did not. Nevertheless, the challenger said he indirectly heard about this and therefore had to give Bruce a lesson!" *Chinese Pacific Weekly*, December 17, 1964.

23. "Bruce's assistant locked the door." Wong Jack Man quoted from the *Chinese Pacific Weekly*, January 28, 1965.

24. Wong Jack Man quoted from the *Chinese Pacific Weekly*, January 28, 1965.

25. David Chin quoted from the *Chinese Pacific Weekly*, January 7, 1965.

26. Wong Jack Man quoting Bruce Lee from the *Chinese Pacific Weekly*, January 28, 1965.

27. "As for Wong's offensive capabilities, they have apparently never been tested." "Bruce Lee's Toughest Fight" by Michael Dorgan, *Official Karate*, July 1980.

28. "Bruce stood in the middle of the academy and invited [me] to come forward." Wong Jack Man quoted in *Chinese Pacific Weekly*, January 28, 1965.

29. "After the other people stepped to the side, Bruce asked me to come to the center of the room." Wong Jack Man online interview.

30. For the ages of the fighters see: "Bruce Lee was a year older than me. He was born on November 27, 1940 (23) and I was born on December 1, 1941 (22). I never met him or heard of him while I was in Hong Kong." Wong Jack Man online interview; see also: "Bruce Lee's Toughest Fight" by Michael Dorgan, *Official Karate*, July 1980.

31. "Wong then walked to the middle of the room towards Lee, gave a slight bow of his head . . ." Wing, Rick L., *Showdown in Oakland: The Story Behind the Wong Jack Man — Bruce Lee Fight*, p. 1288.

32. "Wong adopted a classic stance . . ." Lee, Linda, *Bruce Lee: The Man Only I Knew*, p. 73.

33. "Lee's open and extended hands . . ." Wing, Rick L., *Showdown in Oakland: The Story Behind the Wong Jack Man — Bruce Lee Fight*, p. 1288.

34. Wong Jack Man would claim that Bruce's first strike was a finger jab towards his eyes. "My quick instincts," Wong would remark, "blocked him from doing damage to my eyes, though he ended up scratching me with his fingernail above my eye" (Wong Jack Man online interview). Unfortunately, no one else who was present saw it that way. David Chin, for example, told Matthew Polly that Bruce's first strike was a "sun punch," the English translation of the Chinese name for the vertical fist strike of Wing Chun (Matthew Polly citing an interview conducted by phone with David Chin on May 14, 2014, and published in Polly, Matthew, *Bruce Lee: A Life*, p. 534); Chin would repeat this to author Charles Russo: "Bruce didn't hesitate to seize on the opening and execute it, but instead of a mere tap to the head, he darted in and delivered a sharp punch to Wong's temple, just narrowly missing his eye" (Russo, Charles, *Striking Distance: Bruce Lee & the Dawn of Martial Arts in America*, p. 2619). According to the earliest account of the fight "Bruce said . . . he beat the challenger with one hit right at the start . . ." (*Chinese Pacific Weekly*, December 17, 1964).

35. "Bruce, who at the time was still using his Wing Chun style, produced a series of straight punches." Lee, Linda, *Bruce Lee: The Man Only I Knew*, p. 73; "There were flurries of straight punches and repeated kicks at his groin, adds Wong." "Bruce Lee's Toughest Fight" by Michael Dorgan, published in *Official Karate*, July 1980; "By [David] Chin's account Bruce employed low kicks to close in and then advanced with a flurry of punches." Russo, Charles, *Striking Distance: Bruce Lee & the Dawn of Martial Arts in America*, p. 2619.

36. "A minute later, with Bruce continuing the attack in earnest, Wong began to backpedal as fast as he could." Lee, Linda, *Bruce Lee: The Man Only I Knew*, p. 73; "Wong Jack Man backed off, and Bruce Lee kept coming in. He kept coming with rotary punches." David Chin quoted in Polly, Matthew, *Bruce Lee: A Life*, p. 156; "I had to step backward to avoid his attacks." Wong Jack Man online interview.

37. Given that the year was 1964, Bruce Lee's war cries were not yet the high-pitched, catlike sounds that he would become famous for in movies such as *Fist of Fury* and *Enter the Dragon*, but more like the eerie, sharp yells that can be heard in the video of his screen test for "Number One Son" (1965), *The Green Hornet* TV series (1966) or in the movie *Marlowe* (1968).

38. Wong Jack Man online interview.

39. Wong Jack Man quoted in *Chinese Pacific Weekly*, January 28, 1965.

40. "I also had to create distance so I could attack him using my long-range techniques to counter his attacks." Wong Jack Man online interview.

41. "Bruce also said. . . . The man became afraid and ran." *Chinese Pacific Weekly*, December 17, 1964; David Chin recalled that "Wong tried to run away . . . His back was facing Bruce." Polly, Matthew, *Bruce Lee: A Life*, p. 156; "For an instant, indeed, the scrap threatened to degenerate into farce as Wong actually turned and ran!" Lee, Linda, *Bruce Lee: The Man Only I Knew*, p. 73; "But Bruce told me this guy literally turned on his heels and ran. He said, 'I was chasing him around the room there.'" Taky Kimura interview with the author, 1994; "Wong Jack Man ran scared like a rabbit . . . That is what Bruce told me on the phone after the running fiasco." Facebook message from Leo Fong to the author on August 12, 2021.

42. "Within a minute, Wong's men were trying to stop the fight as Bruce began to warm to his task. James Lee warned them to let the fight continue." Lee, Linda, *Bruce Lee: The Man Only I Knew*, p. 73.

43. David Chin told Matthew Polly, "They went in one side and came out the other. . . . After Wong came back out from the room, he was front-facing Bruce Lee again." (Polly, Matthew, *Bruce Lee: A Life*, p. 156.) Linda Lee corroborated Chin's account, but claimed that they went in and out of the open doors several times: "Oh yes, he [Wong Jack Man] ran. He ran and he ran. There were two doors leading into a backroom kind of thing and he ran in one door and out the other and in one door and out the other. They went around two or three times." (Linda Lee Cadwell quoted in Polly, Matthew, *Bruce Lee: A Life*, p. 156 and footnote on p. 534.)

44. Bruce Lee's friends and students would learn of the scratches he suffered in the fight, but were unclear as to what caused them and where he was struck. Jesse Glover, for example, would recall speaking with Bruce in February 1966 and learning of the fight: "But this guy apparently could move, because Bruce said he was chasing the guy, the guy was running, almost running away from him, but as he was running he was kind of flinging his arms back, I guess in some kind of weird, circular eye-strike kind of thing. It wasn't getting Bruce's eyes but it was scratching him across the forehead." (Jesse Glover interview with author, September 1993.) Leo Fong was given a similar account the day after the fight by Bruce: "When Wong Jack Man ran, he was swinging his arms backward, and his fingernails scraped Bruce on the neck. That was the only injury he sustained." Leo Fong quoted in Bax, Paul, *Disciples of the Dragon: Reflections from the Students of Bruce Lee*, p. 145. George Lee confirmed Fong's account: "I noticed Lee had a scratch on his neck." George Lee quoted in Bax, Paul, *Disciples of the Dragon: Reflections from the Students of Bruce Lee*, p. 136.

45. "Now approaching a frenzy, he [Lee] pressed in on Wong with blasts of 'chain punches.'" David Chin's account in Russo, Charles, *Striking Distance: Bruce Lee & the Dawn of Martial Arts in America*, p. 2627. See also: "[Bruce told me that] he did nothing but straight punches, going around and around, all the way up

to the front of the school, and then his opponent yielded." Allen Joe interview with the author, April 1994.

46. "Bruce said, 'I couldn't catch him. I was running out of breath.'" Taky Kimura interview with the author, 1994.

47. "And then he said he started running out of gas and he just sort of willed himself to move with one big surge." Jesse Glover interview with the author, September 1993.

48. "Bruce chased him and took him down," *Chinese Pacific Weekly*, December 17, 1964; ". . . and he caught the guy, hit him, knocked him down. . ." Jesse Glover interview with the author, September 1993; "But Bruce pounced on him like a springing leopard and brought him to the floor." Lee, Linda, *Bruce Lee: The Man Only I Knew*, p. 73; "Bruce finally got a hold of him and took him down to the floor." Cadwell, Linda Lee, quoted from the documentary *Bruce Lee: A Warrior's Journey*; "'Finally,' he said, 'I got him down.'" Taky Kimura quoting Bruce Lee, interview with the author, 1994.

49. Based on his interviews with David Chin and Bill Chen, Rick Wing concluded: "The time from Wong's foot hitting the raised part of the floor to the fighters being separated was about ten to twenty seconds." Wing, Rick L., *Showdown in Oakland: The Story Behind the Wong Jack Man — Bruce Lee Fight*, p. 1484.

50. "He [Bruce] began pounding him into a state of demoralization." Lee, Linda, *Bruce Lee: The Man Only I Knew*, p. 73.

51. "Wong also used circular arm motion to ward off Lee's strikes." Wing, Rick L., *Showdown in Oakland: The Story Behind the Wong Jack Man — Bruce Lee Fight*, p. 1468.

52. "Bruce chased him and took him down, holding a fist and asking, 'Surrender?' The man said 'Yes, yes.' Bruce then stopped. The other twelve people who came with the challenger all came to separate them." *Chinese Pacific Weekly*, December 17, 1964. See also: "'Is that enough?' shouted Bruce. 'That's enough!' pleaded Wong in desperation." Lee, Linda, *Bruce Lee: The Man Only I Knew*, p. 73; Leo Fong was told by Lee the next day: "So, finally, Bruce stopped him and got him in the corner, and was about ready to lower the right hand on him and then the guy said 'I give up. I give up.'" Leo Fong quoted from an online video interview at dailymotion.com/video/x2qmb8c; "From there, he [Wong Jack Man] said he gives up." David Chin quoted in the online article "Bruce Lee vs. Wong Jack Man: Fact, Fiction and the Birth of the Dragon" by Charles Russo, vice.com /en/article/d7my3v/bruce-lee-vs-wong-jack-man-fact-fiction-and-the-birth-of -the-dragon; "Bruce was recently challenged by G[ung] Fu man from Hong Kong — took place at the gym — the other man had to give up after about 2 minutes with a black eye, swollen lips, etc." James Lee quoted from a letter he wrote to Gene Snelling Jr., North Carolina, circa 1965, from oakauctions.com /Important__Bruce_Lee__James_Yimm_Lee__Archive_rela-LOT6591.aspx.

53. "The other twelve people who came with the challenger all came to separate them." *Chinese Pacific Weekly*, December 17, 1964; "The others decided to separate them to prevent further escalation." *Chinese Pacific Weekly*,

January 7, 1965; "[Chin] approached the men to separate them." *Chinese Pacific Weekly*, January 28, 1965. See also: ". . . and we stopped the fight. . ." David Chin quoted in the online article "Bruce Lee vs. Wong Jack Man: Fact, Fiction and the Birth of the Dragon."

54. Taky Kimura quoting Bruce Lee in an interview with the author, 1994.

55. Wong Jack Man online interview.

56. Bruce Lee letter to James Lee, August 7, 1965, reproduced in Little, John (editor), *Bruce Lee: Letters of the Dragon*, p. 100.

57. "In those days he used to say, 'Well, you don't need to be totally fit because you're not going to make a fifteen-round fight out of it. You put him out right now.'" Taky Kimura interview with the author, 1994. See also: "In the old days he didn't worry about it [endurance] because the matches didn't . . . last very long." Doug Palmer interview with the author, August 2, 1993.

58. Jesse Glover recalled: "I did talk to Bruce after the match and he described what had happened and what he had learned from the fight. What he learned was that some people could retreat from an attack with the same speed that he could launch an attack. This showed him the need to greatly increase his cardiovascular fitness and his punching power." Jesse Glover interview, published in *Knowing Is Not Enough: The Official Newsletter of Jun Fan Jeet Kune Do / Bruce Lee Educational Foundation*, Spring 1999, Vol. 3, No. 1, p. 4. See also: "But I think he got in one match where the opponent moved backwards real quick [laughs]. He had to chase him through several rooms before he finally caught the guy and foot swept him or somehow knocked him down and, as Bruce told the story, he was breathing very hard; he said, 'You give up?' You know, and the guy said, 'Yeah.' And he said, 'I'm glad he did because I didn't have the strength to [laughs] throw another punch at that point.' I mean he realized that physical conditioning was, you know, important too." Doug Palmer interview with the author, August 2, 1993.

59. "Bruce knew that the person who hand-carried the letter to him [i.e., David Chin] had set us both up." Wong Jack Man online interview.

60. Leo Fong quoting Bruce Lee from an online video interview at dailymotion. com/video/x2qmb8c.

61. Wong Jack Man online interview. See also: "It was a rather tense situation." David Chin quoted from *Chinese Pacific Weekly*, January 7, 1965.

62. Leo Fong quoted from a video interview online at dailymotion.com/video /x2qmb8c.

63. David Chin quoted in Russo, Charles, *Striking Distance: Bruce Lee & the Dawn of Martial Arts in America*, p. 2635.

CHAPTER ELEVEN: PAYBACK

1. Wong Jack Man online interview.

2. "Bruce Lee returned to Hong Kong and paid a visit to his Sifu, imploring Yip Man to teach him the art of 'Dismantle Wooden Man' (chai Zhuang),

meaning 'breaking it down.' 'Drill Wooden Man' (shang Zhuang) is the practice of the 108 techniques with the Wooden Man. It is relatively easy, and many Wing Chun practitioners are conversant with these. 'Dismantle Wooden Man,' however, is the actual application of the techniques — fighting with the Wooden Man. It is extremely difficult and is known only to a few of Yip Man's formal disciples. Bruce Lee knew 'Drill Wooden Man,' but had not been taught how to dismantle, which is the actual application aspect. Many Wing Chun practitioners either don't have an instructor who can and will train them in this; the majority do not even realize the essential component they are missing. But Bruce Lee did. He was aware of this gap in his martial arts education. He knew that without learning 'Dismantle Wooden Man,' the mastery of applied fighting techniques of Wing Chun was illusory." Ing, Ken, *Wing Chun Warrior: The True Tales of Wing Chun Kung Fu Master Duncan Leung, Bruce Lee's Fighting Companion*, pp. 1901–1910, Kindle edition.

3. Bruce Lee's letters written during this time to Taky Kimura and James Lee date from May 10 to August 16, 1965. These letters are published in Little, John (editor), *Bruce Lee: Letters of the Dragon*, pp. 111–133.

4. Hawkins Cheung quoting Bruce Lee from the article "Bruce Lee's Hong Kong Years" by Hawkins Cheung, *Inside Kung Fu*, November 1991. See also: "I'll find out about the wooden dummy the first chance I get; I think the dummy will help you in sharpening your skill." Bruce Lee letter to Taky Kimura, June 7, 1965, published in Little, John (editor), *Bruce Lee: Letters of the Dragon*, p. 57.

5. "Am going to buy a nice 8mm movie camera (already got a projector and screen) and shoot the 3 forms of Wing Chun, having my instructor as the demonstrator." Bruce Lee letter to Taky Kimura, August 29, 1965, published in Kimura, Taky, *Regards from The Dragon: Seattle*, compiled and edited by David Tadman, Empire Books, Los Angeles, California, 2009, p. 41.

6. "Grandmaster Yip Man refused him saying 'I can't promise you that, for the reasons that firstly, you were not the only student I admitted, secondly, I had never promised any one of my students for such a request. If I accept your proposal, what should I say to my other students?'" Yip Chun quoting his father Yip Man in Chun, Yip, *116 Wing Tsun Dummy Techniques as Demonstrated by Grandmaster Yip Man*, p. 110. Yip Chun would go on to claim that Bruce Lee offered to buy his father a flat in Hong Kong in return for his teaching what he wanted to learn about the wooden dummy form and being allowed to film him performing Siu Lum Tao — a claim that is preposterous on its face. To begin, Bruce Lee couldn't afford a flat for himself and his family at this point in his life (while in the United States he and his wife and child were living with James Lee), let alone for Yip Man. Moreover, according to Wong Shun Leung, Yip Man didn't have a set-ending series of movements for the wooden dummy form and often improvised its ending, so there was no codified or fixed final section of the wooden dummy set for him to teach or explain to Bruce. And, finally, Bruce already knew how to perform the Siu Lum Tao form, and had done so

daily for the past eight or nine years. The idea that he would mortgage his future to Yip Man, in exchange for making a home movie of Yip demonstrating a form that Bruce already knew, seems highly unlikely. According to Yip Man student Duncan Leung, the reason that Bruce Lee told him for Yip refusing his request was because Yip believed himself to be too old and lacked the stamina. He suggested that Bruce ask one of his private disciples to teach him. "But Bruce had too much pride to learn from anyone but Yip Man." Duncan Leung quoted in Ing, Ken, *Wing Chun Warrior: The True Tales of Wing Chun Kung Fu Master Duncan Leung, Bruce Lee's Fighting Companion*, p. 1917, Kindle edition.

7. "My father reminded [Bruce] that . . . the techniques of Chinese Kung Fu should not be taught freely to foreigners (it was typically Chinese traditional thinking of the old Kung Fu masters)." Yip Chun, *116 Wing Tsun Dummy Techniques as Demonstrated by Grandmaster Yip Man*, p. 109. This is corroborated by Hawkins Cheung: "I found out that the 'old man' refused his request to be filmed doing the dummy set. I knew that the 'old man' was very Chinese tradition minded." Hawkins Cheung quoted from *Inside Kung Fu*, November 1991. See also: "Throughout all of his life Yip Man did not own any property and even though Bruce Lee had offered to pay him to tape him doing the Siu Lim Tao form in order to use it as teaching material back in the U.S., he refused. He rejected that offer." Yip Chun interview with the author August 12, 2009.

8. Bruce Lee quoted from the article "Bruce Lee: The Man, the Fighter, the Superstar" by Mitoshi Uyehara, *Black Belt Magazine's Best of Bruce Lee #2*, Rainbow Publications, Inc., Burbank, California, 1975, pp. 24–25.

9. The account of Bruce Lee sparring with Yip Man's students is taken from Uyehara, Mitoshi, *Bruce Lee: The Incomparable Fighter*, p. 78.

10. As most of Wong Shun Leung's beimo matches were held behind closed doors, there is no official record of how many matches he engaged in. Wong's student John Smith recalled, "He had more than sixty documented real-time fights that were organized, where people placed bets. And he always came out a winner. That's not to say that he was never scarred or hit; there were scars on his face, there was blood involved. It was a real fight that he was involved in." John Smith quoted in the documentary *Wong Shun Leung: The King of Talking Hands*. Bruce Lee believed the number of Wong's fights was well north of sixty, telling Jesse Glover that "Bruce told me that when he left Hong Kong [Wong Shun Leung] had already won well over a hundred fights against the city's best Gung Fu men." Glover, Jesse, *Bruce Lee: Between Wing Chun and Jeet Kune Do*, p. 22.

11. There is some controversy as to how Wong Shun Leung lost his match at the Taiwan–Hong Kong–Macau Open Chinese Kung Fu Competition held in Taiwan on November 22, 1957. The Wikipedia biography of Wong says he was knocked out by his opponent from Taiwan as a result of receiving a powerful kick to the jaw (en.wikipedia.org/wiki/Wong_Shun-leung). However, Wikipedia provides no source for this. Another account has him merely knocked down by a kick: "The regulations had one rule which stipulated: 'If a competitor is

able to knock down or throw down his opponent to the floor (if the elbow does not touch the ground it is not counted as a knockdown) he receives 3 points'; another rule stipulated 'In a single match of three minutes (and, according to rumor, was later reduced to two minutes) the one who strikes harder and strikes the opponent more times is awarded two points.' That meant that no matter how many times a competitor struck the opponent in a round, the points would never be as many as if he threw the opponent once. For those who were unfamiliar with jiujitsu or shuai jiao, it was an obvious disadvantage. It was said that 'The King of Sparring' Wong Shun Leung when faced off with the Taiwanese 'King of Kicks' Wu Ming Jer, Wong maintained a furious attack, but because the opponent's head and body were protected, he was not cowed. However, in the end, Wong was kicked by Wu and fell down, which gave the opponent three points, and led to Wong losing the match" (from the online article "A Brief History of Lei Tai Fighting in Hong Kong" by Bernard Kwan at benotdefeated bytherain.blogspot.com/2015/06/a-brief-history-of-ring-fighting-in.html). However, Bruce Lee would view a movie of the tournament that had been released in Hong Kong theaters in 1958, and, in speaking with Wong afterward, his account (which he related to Jesse Glover in 1959) was that "the match was held in a twenty-foot circle. Attacks to the eyes and groin were banned and both contestants had to wear gloves. A match could be won by scoring points, forcing the opponent to quit, or by knocking the opponent out. [Wong's] opponent wouldn't stand and fight, and [Wong] kept chasing him from the ring. [Wong's] opponent sensed that he didn't have a chance, and decided to get sneaky. When he was returning to the center of the ring after being driven out of bounds, he pointed at something behind [Wong], and shouted "Look out!" When [Wong] turned to see what he was being warned about, the opponent let go with a kick. Bruce said that [Wong] partially blocked the kick, but not enough to prevent his opponent from scoring a point, and winning the match. After the match, [Wong] had walked up to the man and called him a coward and a sneak. He challenged him to fight, and slapped his face when he refused. When [Wong] found that he couldn't goad the man into a fight, he turned and walked away. Bruce said that the reason that [Wong] was scored on was because of his bad habit of leaving his elbows apart. No one in the Wing Chun clan was strong enough to force [Wong] to close his elbows, and it led to a bad habit that Bruce felt had lost [Wong] the match." Glover, Jesse, *Bruce Lee: Between Wing Chun and Jeet Kune Do*, p. 24.

12. "Bruce had already taken himself to another level of martial art with his speed and power. So, he decided to do some Chi Sau [sticking hands] with Wong Shun Leung alone, you know. And he actually gave Wong Shun Leung a very hard time because his speed and power was dominating the whole exercise." William Cheung quoted from the video "Grandmaster William Cheung on Meeting Bruce Lee" at youtube.com/watch?v=NzRU21NBYRA. See also: "The second time that Bruce returned from Hong Kong [1965] he told me that he had

stuck hands with [Wong Shun Leung] and that he was able to push him around at will. Bruce said that his teacher had watched them play, and that [Wong Shun Leung] had commented after it was over that Bruce, if he kept improving, might soon be as good as himself. Bruce said that he had looked at Yip Man after [Wong Shun Leung] had made his comment, and Yip Man had given him a look that told him that he was already as good and maybe even better." Glover, Jesse, *Bruce Lee: Between Wing Chun and Jeet Kune Do*, pp. 52–53. Rolf Clausnitzer's recollection of Wong (see note 13) indicates that Bruce was scoring on Wong. It must be emphasized that this was not a fight or a contest, and that neither man was going full out; Wong Shun Leung was not in the habit of throttling his students but helping them to progress, and Bruce Lee respected Wong too much to try and assert himself aggressively against him, particularly in front of Yip Man and the rest of the Wing Chun class.

13. "There was one evening when Wong started talking about how Bruce had visited Hong Kong some months previously and they had ended up doing a bit of Gau Sau (hand sparring). And Wong was saying he was so impressed with the way that Bruce had improved over time and that his Gau Sau was now very, very good and that he was starting to score and getting through on Sifu [Wong Shun Leung]. And he was finding it difficult to handle Bruce. And I think it's a mark of sort of Wong's honesty and humility to actually say that. And I found that quite impressive." Rolf Clausnitzer quoted in an interview for the documentary *Wong Shun Leung: The King of Talking Hands*. See also the recollection of Wong Shun Leung's student, David Peterson: "It was very hard to get stories out of [Wong Shun Leung] about Bruce Lee; you pretty much had to pry them out of him. But other people around him were very proud of the fact that he played a role in Bruce Lee's career. But if you put it to sifu, 'Aww, you're responsible for Bruce Lee being what he was!' He always said, 'Nope. Not me. Bruce Lee was as good as he was because he worked very hard. It was all credit to Bruce Lee. All I did was point him in a few directions; give him a bit of advice.'" David Peterson quoted from the documentary *Wong Shun Leung: The King of Talking Hands*.

14. According to an article published in *New Martial Hero* magazine in 1971, Wong Shun Leung and Bruce Lee would go at it again during a banquet hosted by Yip Man: "There were stories about Bruce fighting with other people, but most were just baseless rumours. Very few people know that Bruce did have a fight with a Wing Chun brother in a washroom! The story was that Bruce had returned to Hong Kong from the US and attended a banquet hosted by Wing Chun Grandmaster Yip Man. All attendees were former Wing Chun students ('brothers'). Bruce had a disagreement with a brother named Wong about a particular technique, 'bong sau.' Bruce believed it should be executed in a certain manner to make it more offensive, but Wong disagreed. Both argued and neither backed down. The debate ended with a situation of letting 'actions speak louder than words.' Since Yip Man was present and they were

'brothers', neither wanted to cause a scene, nor be observed by the others. As such, it was determined that the best place to settle the disagreement would be in the washroom. They winked at each other, left their seats and went to the washroom. Both men later returned to their seats. Bruce looked relaxed and talked as if nothing had happened, but Wong was very quiet. The other Wing Chun masters present, such as Lok Yu and Tong Shan easily figured out who won the challenge." *New Martial Hero* magazine, July 1971. Given that there is no evidence that either Wong or Bruce made any attempt to refute the article (and both were in Hong Kong when it was published), we have no reason to conclude that the story isn't true.

15. "Bruce said that when he stuck with his teacher he felt that he could finally score on him, but held back out of respect. Yip Man was happy that Bruce respected him enough not to press him, but he still resented his not trying and he knocked him about the room." Jesse Glover's recollections of what Bruce Lee told him about the incident as published in Glover, Jesse, *Bruce Lee: Between Wing Chun and Jeet Kune Do*, p. 53.

16. "After they had finished practicing Yip Man asked Bruce to sit down and tell him all the new things that he had learned about fighting." Glover, Jesse, *Bruce Lee: Between Wing Chun and Jeet Kune Do*, p. 53. See also: "While Bruce was slaughtering his students, the old man kept taking notes. 'You know, the old man was really smart. He knew I had superior techniques and wanted to know everything about them. He even kept me after the session so he could ask more questions. He was really impressed . . . wanted to incorporate my movements and techniques to Wing Chun.'" Bruce Lee quoted in Uyehara, Mitoshi, *Bruce Lee: The Incomparable Fighter*, p. 78.

17. "Bruce said that Yip Man's request was a real honor and it made him proud to be in possession of something his teacher wanted." Glover, Jesse, Little, John (editor), *Bruce Lee: Between Wing Chun and Jeet Kune Do*, p. 53.

18. "By the way, we've finished the shooting of the whole set of sil lum tao [the first form of Wing Chun] and many other [techniques], demonstrated by my Sifu Yip Man. Over 130 photos have been taken and when we're through there will be way over 200. These pictures will prove to be valuable when my book comes out as never before [has] the Wing Chun master, Sifu Yip Man ever been on photograph. He is 66 now, I think, and years after that these photos will be the only set." Bruce Lee letter to James Yimm Lee, July 29, 1965, published in Little, John (editor), *Bruce Lee: Letters of the Dragon*, p. 58.

19. Bruce Lee's friend Robert Chan quoted in Polly, Matthew, *Bruce Lee: A Life*, p. 387, Kindle edition.

20. "Sil Lum Tao is all the ways of the Wing Chun Hand [method] in a nutshell." Bruce Lee letter to James Lee, August 13, 1965, published in Little, John (editor), *Bruce Lee: Letters of the Dragon*, p. 63. See also: "Siu Lim Tao [Sil Lum Tao] is the foundation and the basis of Wing Chun Kung Fu. So, even the foundation of anything is of utmost importance. If you don't have a good foundation, no

matter how hard you train, how long you train, you still won't reach the highest level." Yip Chun interview with the author, 2012. See also: "Siu Lim Tao form is so important to Wing Chun that you couldn't learn Wing Chun properly without this form." David Peterson quoted from the documentary *The Art of Wong Shun Leung: A Ving Tsun Journey*, produced and directed by John Little, © 2016 David Peterson. See also: "The most important [form] is Siu Lim Tao. All of the important things come from Siu Lim Tao." Lun Gai (first-generation student of Yip Man) interview with the author, 2012.

21. Jesse Glover quoted in Bax, Paul, and Smith, Steve, *Disciple of the Dragon: Reflections of Bruce Lee's Student, Jesse Glover (Disciples of the Dragon Book 2)*, pp. 27–28, Kindle edition.

22. Bruce Lee letter to Taky Kimura, June 7, 1965, published in Little, John (editor), *Bruce Lee: Letters of the Dragon*, p. 57.

23. Bruce Lee letter to James Lee, July 31, 1965, published in Little, John (editor), *Bruce Lee: Letters of the Dragon*, pp. 60–61.

24. Bruce Lee letter to James Lee, August 13, 1965, published in Little, John (editor), *Bruce Lee: Letters of the Dragon*, p. 63.

25. Letter from Bruce Lee to James Lee, July 31, 1965, published in Little, John (editor), *Bruce Lee: Letters of the Dragon*, p. 59.

26. "After Bruce had learned Wing Chun boxing, he came to ask me to teach him some Kung Fu. I chose to teach him the second set of boxing forms of Ching-wu school — Kun-lik-kune. I chose this because it is easier to learn, since it is short. Later, when he wanted to learn some more Chinese Northern Kung Fu, he came to me again. So, I taught him some fundamental training methods in Chinese Northern Kung Fu. Chinese Northern Kung Fu is more well-developed in the use of kicks. Chinese Northern Kung Fu has wider actions. Later I taught him a set of Jumping-step-boxing. . . . This kind of boxing is a basic boxing form of Northern Mantis Kung Fu. Its characteristics are jumps, swift movement and the circular horizontal kick. But Bruce was very smart. He learned it in six or seven lectures. So, I taught him a set of Jeet-Kune, the fourth set of the basic boxing forms of Ching-wu school." Siu Hon-San, quoted in the article "Meeting one of Bruce Lee's Masters, Sifu Siu Hon-San," published in *Bruce Lee: His Unknowns in Martial Arts Learning*, Bruce Lee Jeet Kune Do Club, Hong Kong, 1977, pp. 36–37.

27. Fung Ngai was a third dan in Judo who studied directly under the art's founder, Jigoro Kano, in Japan. "Upon his return from Japan, he began to teach Judo in Hong Kong, offering tuition at the Hong Kong University and the YMCA building in Tsim Sha Tsui, where he incidentally met a young Bruce Lee, who would frequently visit the building to study English as well as learn Judo from Fung Ngai before leaving for the States in 1959." Fung Ngai would later play the role of the chief Judo instructor in Lee's film *Fist of Fury* (1972). According to Fung Ngai: "At that time I was teaching Judo at the Hong Kong YMCA when Bruce first became my student. But by the time he had returned to Hong Kong

when we made *Fist of Fury*, he had way surpassed me." As reported in Kerridge, Steve, and Chua, Darren, *Bruce Lee: The Intercepting Fist*, section "Bushido Boss," On the Fly Productions Ltd., England, 2020.

28. "Although Fook Yeung was primarily a Southern Mantis man, he knew a lot about other styles. Bruce was teaching him basic Wing Chun in exchange for Fook Yeung's teaching him a variety of forms from different styles." Glover, Jesse, *Bruce Lee: Between Wing Chun and Jeet Kune Do*, p. 65.

29. "Reading books on boxing and watching televised matches led Bruce to realize the importance of the knockout punch. Bruce's favorite boxer in those days was Jack Dempsey, mostly because of his aggressive style and tremendous punching power. One of Bruce's favorite books was Dempsey's approach to boxing. In the book Dempsey talked about the development of punching power using the drop step. Bruce incorporated many of Dempsey's ideas in his punching development." Jesse Glover quoted from the article "Jesse Glover: Bruce Lee's First Student," *Inside Kung Fu*, Jesse Glover, August 1989, pp. 41–42. See also: "I mean he used to watch boxing movies all the time; he had a library of some of the best boxers — Sugar Ray Robinson, Archie Moore, Dempsey; he learned how to hook from [watching] Dempsey. And he learned that from boxing films. And other things too; slipping, etc., etc., he learned from boxing." Doug Palmer interview with the author, August 2, 1993.

30. "Bruce's martial arts interests were not restricted to Gung Fu. He learned a lot about Judo from Fred Sato and myself, and he once enrolled in a formal Judo class at the University of Washington under Shuzo Kato, who was a U.S. national champion and one of my earlier Judo teachers. . . . The Judo techniques that Bruce liked best were the foot sweeps and trips that could be easily fitted into his Gung Fu." Glover, Jesse, *Bruce Lee: Between Wing Chun and Jeet Kune Do*, p. 49.

31. Peter Lee was a world-class fencer and had competed in the 1958 British Empire and Commonwealth Games in Cardiff, Wales. Per: thecgf.com/results /athletes/46459. See also: "Bruce modified his Wing Chun close with some things that he took from fencing. He studied all of the fencing books that he could get his hands on and worked out the fastest possible close. Once he was sure of the basic move he practiced it thousands of times until he could do it better than anyone in the world. One example of Bruce's closing speed was the way that he could get in on his brother Peter with a straight fencing lunge. Peter was that British Commonwealth fencing champion, but he was unable to stop Bruce's straight lunge." Jesse Glover, from Glover, Jesse, *Bruce Lee: Between Wing Chun and Jeet Kune Do*, p. 53. See also: "Lee developed a keen interest in Peter's fencing. In fact, Peter taught Bruce a good bit of epee and foil at home. Lee was most fascinated with the footwork that he saw in fencing, and sought to improve his own fighting by incorporating that footwork into his martial arts. Peter introduced Bruce to the writings of famous fencing master Aldo Nadi,

whose books he studied in depth." From the online article "Bruce Lee — The World's Most Famous Fencer?" by Igor Chirashnya at academyoffencingmasters .com/blog/bruce-lee-the-worlds-most-famous-fencer/.

32. Doug Palmer interview with the author, August 2, 1993.

33. Bruce Lee quoted in the article "Bruce Lee: The Man, the Fighter, the Superstar," by Mitoshi Uyehara, *The Bruce Lee Memorial Issue*, Rainbow Publications, Los Angeles, California, 1974, p. 23.

34. Mitoshi Uyehara interview with the author, 1994:

> *Mitoshi Uyehara*: "You know the articles I used to write on Bruce?"
> *Q*: "Yeah."
> *Mitoshi Uyehara*: "Most of them I didn't even interview him."
> *Q*: "No?"
> *Mitoshi Uyehara*: "No, because I knew him so well. So, I just put it together . . . like, I used 'Mike Plane'?"
> *Q*: "Right."
> *Mitoshi Uyehara*: "Yeah, that's me."
> *Q*: "Is that right?"
> *Mitoshi Uyehara*: "Yeah, and the other one — Mitch Stom? That's me, too."
> *Q*: "That's you? So, were those ones just done from your head or did you have a tape recording of it?"
> *Mitoshi Uyehara*: "No, I just used different names because I didn't want to use my same 'M. Uyehara' all the time, so I used to say, 'Ah, I'll use Mitch Stom.' I didn't want to even be known."
> *Q*: "[laughs] Mitch Stom, I'll have to remember that."
> *Mitoshi Uyehara*: "I tried to write the way I thought I knew him. And that's how I wrote the whole book on him."

35. Mitoshi Uyehara interview with the author, 1994.

36. Mitoshi Uyehara interview with the author, 1994.

37. See Uyehara, Mitoshi, *Bruce Lee: The Incomparable Fighter*, p. 15.

CHAPTER TWELVE: THE LEGEND RISES

1. Stirling Silliphant quoted in the article "One-On-One with Stirling Silliphant," by John Corcoran, published in *Martial Arts Legends*, January 1993.

2. Polly, Matthew, *Bruce Lee: A Life*, pp. 220–221.

3. Mitoshi Uyehara interview with the author, 1994. Uyehara also published what Bruce had told him about the fight in his book *Bruce Lee: The Incomparable Fighter*, p. 18.

4. James Coburn quoted in Lee, Linda, *Bruce Lee: The Man Only I Knew*, p. 104.

5. "Ryan at that time was making a film for me, a western, and my [Karate] teacher [Tom Bleeker] was Ryan's stand-in." Blake Edwards interview with the author, April 8, 1996.

6. "[Ryan O'Neal] kind of, with a sense of humor — at least an attempt at a sense of humor — kept maligning Karate and all of that. And he kept constantly baiting Tom, my teacher." Blake Edwards interview with the author, April 8, 1996.

7. ". . . and occasionally kind of making funny remarks in my presence, because he knew that I was involved in taking Karate from Tom [Bleeker]." Blake Edwards interview with the author, April 8, 1996.

8. "O'Neal trained to become a professional boxer, competing in two Golden Gloves championships in Los Angeles in 1956 and 1957. He had an impressive amateur fighting record — 18 wins to 4 losses, with 13 knockouts." From "Biography" article at biography.com/actors/ryan-oneal.

9. "I can tell by the way he's [Ryan O'Neal's] moving, the way he's getting out of the way. Usually, when boys are playing like this they just pat each other, but he's really moving and if Frazier wasn't as good as he was, he couldn't get out of the way." Muhammad Ali commentating on the Ryan O'Neal versus Joe Frazier sparring match; video available on youtube.com/watch?v=6ilMU8yR Cyo&t=143s.

10. "And Ryan [was] in those days a considerable boxer. And he's very handy with his fists. He's a tough kid. . . . And one day I invited Bruce over to the set and I told Bruce about Ryan. And I introduced them." Blake Edwards interview with the author, April 8, 1996.

11. Bruce Lee quoted from the newspaper article "The Man with A Stomach Like a Brick Wall," by John Hardie, the *Hong Kong Star*, November 1971.

12. Unless otherwise noted the account of Bruce Lee's impromptu sparring match with Ryan O'Neal is drawn from the article "Bruce Lee: Before and After the Praise" by Tom Bleeker, *Black Belt*, January 1979.

13. Blake Edwards interview with the author, April 8, 1996.

14. "Bruce Lee: Before and After the Praise," by Tom Bleeker, *Black Belt*, January 1979.

15. "I think they [the students' fees] were $15 per month. Can't swear to it." Steve Golden (Bruce Lee's Chinatown school student), Facebook message to the author on September 16, 2021.

16. See Bruce Lee's business card with rates at pinterest.ca/pin/bruce-lees-rate-card -for-private-tuition-as-well-as-his-group-classes-this-is-one-of-the-many-items -of-removable-memorabilia-in-the-treas—243053711112825413/.

17. Per the inflation calculator of DollarTimes at dollartimes.com/inflation/inflation .php?amount=275&year=1967.

18. Bruce flew to Switzerland to train Roman Polanski for at least ten days per his letters to his wife Linda from Gstaad during the month of February 1970 as published in Little, John (editor), *Bruce Lee: Letters of the Dragon*, pp. 128–131.

19. See Bruce Lee's business card with rates at pinterest.ca/pin/243053711112825413/.

20. Per the inflation calculator of DollarTimes at dollartimes.com/inflation/inflation .php?amount=1000&year=1967.

21. From Bruce Lee's daytime diary entries for the month of January 1968 in Little, John (editor), *Bruce Lee: The Art of Expressing the Human Body*, Tuttle Publishing, Boston, 1998, pp. 186–202.

22. George Lee interview with the author, March 1994.

23. Jhoon Rhee interview with the author, August 1993.

24. "Bruce took off his T-shirt, and I marveled again as I always did every time I saw his physique; he had muscles on muscles. As I sat and enjoyed the peace and quiet in the yard, Bruce counted off one-hand push-ups. After about fifty, he stopped and turned his attention to me." Chuck Norris quoted from Norris, Chuck, *The Secret Power Within: Zen Solutions to Real Problems*, Little, Brown and Co., Boston, 1996, p. 69.

25. Joe Lewis interview with the author, July 1993. Bruce Lee's student Larry Hartsell witnessed him perform this same feat of strength "with about eighty pounds, which he held out in front of him for two to three minutes." Larry Hartsell interview with the author, July 12, 1994.

26. Hayward Nishioka interview with the author, July 1994.

27. "We were training martial arts/Jeet Kune Do in Bruce's backyard and taking turns punching and kicking different pads and shields. When it came time to work out on Bruce's special giant red 300-pound punching bag, we would all take turns hitting it. . . . That bag was so heavy, that whatever power kicks or punches we would put into it, it barely moved a few inches. That bag was stuffed with at least a couple thousand rags or more; using any other materials would have made it too bulky and lumpy. It was handcrafted and stitched very securely, so it could take a significant impact from all the punching and kicking and whatever that whacked it. Just the size of it and standing next to it was unreal and surreal. No one had ever seen anything like it before. . . . So, after we all had our chance at hitting the bag, it was then Bruce's turn to punch, kick and utilize his physical arsenal against that behemoth monster. . . . He then ran at the bag as fast as possible, doing his famous trademark scream and hitting the bag like a freight train. The force of Bruce's kick broke the chain that held the bag to his roof outside and the bag flew about 25 feet, exploding with all the rags and packing inside it. All of us stood there in shock and awe with our mouths open. Bruce just looked at us and laughed, and walked away." Herb Jackson quoted from the article "The Amazing Feats of the Little Dragon" published in *Bruce Lee Forever Fanzine*, Nov./Dec. 2022, pp. 23–25. As incredible as such a feat reads, Jon Benn (who co-starred with Bruce Lee in *The Way of the Dragon* and never met Herb Jackson) reported witnessing Bruce do the exact same thing to a three hundred-pound bag while in Hong Kong in 1972: "On one occasion, I watched several would-be tough guys play around with a 300-pound punching bag that hung by a strong chain. One of them would hit it a few times, causing it to move an inch or two. Next, someone else would

kick it, and at most, it might move ten inches. Then Bruce decided to intervene. 'Stand back,' he warned. Seconds later, he ran at the bulky bag and hit it with a fierce flying sidekick. Damn! The bag flew up to the ceiling and broke in half. Stuffing from its innards flew everywhere, dropping down all around us, like an unprecedented Hong Kong snowstorm. As often happened, Bruce looked slightly astonished by his destructive force. 'Oh, my God,' he said, staring at the eviscerated punching bag. 'I am so sorry. Forgive me.' All the eye-witnesses to the display, including me, felt deeply impressed." Jon Benn, from his memoir *Remembering Bruce Lee: And Jon Benn's Other Adventures* by Jon T. Benn, Blacksmith Books, 2013, pp. 17–18.

28. Richard Bustillo interview with the author, June 1994.

29. "The only routines he did steady were the stretching routines he'd go through before a workout, before he would start fighting or training." Herb Jackson interview with the author, June 1993; "James Coburn and I went to India with him on *The Silent Flute* [film]. We were on a research and reconnaissance trip. All the time we were there, Bruce would be kicking or stretching or punching or moving. He was like a cat. But when he was still, he was still. He was always aware of his body and of his art, and that's all he lived for. He was the most dedicated man I've ever known in my life." Stirling Silliphant quoted from the article "Bruce Lee as Seen Through the Eyes of Movie Executives," published in *The Bruce Lee Memorial Issue*.

30. "I call it Jeet Kune Do just because I want to emphasize the notion of deciding at the right moment in order to stop the enemy at the gate." Bruce Lee quoted from the article "Me and Jeet Kune Do" by Bruce Lee, first published in an unidentified Taiwan newspaper in 1972 and republished in the special publication *Bruce Lee: Studies on Jeet Kune Do*, Bruce Lee Jeet Kune Do Club, Hong Kong, 1976, p. 26.

31. "Bruce felt that blocking was a wasted step in self-defence. He could intercept you before you even got started. In fact, even if you did get started he could intercept you. He was that fast." Ted Wong interview with the author, June 1, 1993. This fact makes the following anecdote of Chuck Norris's rather inexplicable: "One day during a workout at Bruce's home, I scored on him constantly despite his attempts to block my kicks. . . . 'No matter how much I tried I was unable to block your kicks,' he said. 'What am I doing wrong?' 'You tried to speed your blocks up,' I said. 'And your timing was off.'" Chuck Norris quoted from Norris, Chuck, *The Secret Power Within: Zen Solutions to Real Problems*, pp. 68–69. While this is certainly an interesting story, it makes little sense. In 1967, which was when Norris was training with Bruce, blocking had been discarded from Bruce's art. See: "Blocking is considered the least efficient." Bruce Lee quoted in Little, John (editor), *Jeet Kune Do: Bruce Lee's Commentaries on the Martial Way*, Tuttle Publishing, Boston, 1997, p. 159. If Bruce's art (which Chuck was taking lessons in) did not incorporate blocking, why, then, would Bruce attempt to block a kick from Norris — repeatedly — and then

admit to him that he couldn't block his kick, and inquire what he could do to block better? In the author's opinion, Norris concocted the entire scenario, as blocking, per se, was not something Bruce either believed in or practiced in his training during the time that Norris was training with him.

32. "Bruce was really big into boxing. In fact, he reversed the normal left lead boxing stance because he felt that you should put your best [strongest] foot (and hand) forward." Dan Inosanto quoted from Inosanto, Dan, and Sutton, Alan, *Jeet Kune Do: The Art and Philosophy of Bruce Lee*, Know Now Publishing Company, Los Angeles, California, 1976.

33. "He used to watch Muhammad Ali and other boxing films through a mirror to simulate a right-hand lead." Dan Inosanto quoted from Inosanto, Dan, and Sutton, Alan, *Jeet Kune Do: The Art and Philosophy of Bruce Lee*. See also: "He [Bruce Lee] loved boxing, he'd watch Muhammad Ali in a mirror to see him as a southpaw. He had every movie of Muhammad Ali in Super 8mm, Dempsey too. He'd watch Dempsey bob and weave." Leo Fong interview with the author, June 1994.

34. Dan Inosanto quoted in the article "Bruce Lee in the 1980s," published in *Fighting Stars*, August 1983.

35. Fred Weintraub quoting the conversation between Bruce Lee and John Tunney in Dennis, Felix, and Atyeo, Don, *Bruce Lee: King of Kung Fu*, p. 27.

36. Mike Stone quoted from the article "Bruce Lee as Seen Through the Eyes of Fellow Martial Artists," *The Bruce Lee Memorial Issue*, pp. 56–57.

37. Joe Lewis interview with the author, July 1993.

38. "Chuck Norris, the American karate champion who recently did a movie with Bruce called *The Way of the Dragon*, readily admitted to millions of people watching TV in a recent interview in Hong Kong that Bruce was his 'teacher,' and he considers him to be 'fantastic.'" Bruce Lee quoted from an audio recording entitled "An Objective Evaluation of the Combative Skill of Bruce Lee by Those Who Know What It Is," published in the book *Bruce Lee: Artist of Life*, edited by John Little, Tuttle Publishing, Boston, 1999, p. 479. This quote is from an audio recording made by Bruce Lee for an intended article about his martial art of Jeet Kune Do. He evidently intended it to be a promotional piece to be published in the Hong Kong press and did not wish to be indicated as the author of the piece, and so referenced himself in the third person. See also: "When these two champions [Chuck Norris and Bob Wall] arrived in Hong Kong, they admitted before two million spectators [viewers] that Bruce was their teacher." From the article "Norris Asked Angrily, 'What Is Wrong with Karate?' Bruce Talked with Him for a Whole Night," published in "Bruce Lee Memorial Monthly No. 1" by Bruce Lee Jeet Kune Do Club, Hong Kong, 1976.

39. Chuck Norris quoted from the article "Chuck Norris Versus Bruce Lee" by *Black Belt* magazine at blackbeltmag.com/chuck-norris-vs-bruce-lee.

40. Thomas, Bruce, *Bruce Lee: Fighting Spirit*, p. 278.

41. Jon Benn, quoted from his memoir *Remembering Bruce Lee: And Jon Benn's Other Adventures*, p. 36. See also: "Chuck Norris told me one time that if they ever got in a real fight, he knew Bruce would beat him. And so, they realized that he was the best there was at the time and, of course, they had different styles and all that, but Chuck was quite sure that he didn't want to get in a real fight with him." Jon Benn interview with the author, December 1994.

42. "No amount of idealistic land swimming will prepare you for the water. . . . The best exercise for swimming is swimming. The best exercise for Jeet Kune Do is actual sparring." Bruce Lee quoted from the article "In Kato's Gung-Fu Action Is Instant" by Maxwell Pollard, *Black Belt*, November 1967.

43. "If I find a black belt who likes to spar, I charge nothing because I really enjoy the company." Bruce Lee quoted in the article "Is *The Green Hornet*'s Version of Gung Fu Genuine?" by Maxwell Pollard, *Black Belt*, October 1967. See also: "It is more enjoyable to teach those who have gone through conventional training. They understand and appreciate what I have to offer. When I find an interesting and potential prospect, I don't charge him a cent." Bruce Lee quoted from the article "In Kato's Gung-Fu Action Is Instant."

44. ". . . my students and associates . . . are a wonderful group of matured, groovy people from all branches of un-rhythmic art, street fighters, boxers-kickers, etc., etc." Bruce Lee letter to William Cheung, January 20, 1969, Little, John (editor), *Bruce Lee: Letters of the Dragon*, p. 171. See also: "It doesn't matter if they are Western boxers, tae kwon do practitioners or wrestlers, I will teach them as long as they are friendly and will not get uptight." Bruce Lee letter to Wong Shun Leung, January 11, 1970, Little, John (editor), *Bruce Lee: Letters of the Dragon*, p. 241.

45. Per Leo Fong: "To further his research, Bruce liked to visit other martial arts schools so that he could see their techniques and training methods in person but also to test his new ideas. Bruce called this 'slumming.'" Interview with Leo Fong at usadojo.com/wp-content/uploads/2017/02/fma-Digest-Special-Edition -Leo-Fong.pdf.

46. All information on Bruce Lee sparring George Dillman and his students is quoted from the videos "George Dillman on Bruce Lee" at youtube.com /watch?v=J7cGj2RbfdE and "George Dillman Bruce Lee" at youtube.com /watch?v=g_wg6TS-lPQ.

47. Per information from George Dillman's website at dillman.com/about.asp.

48. Jhoon Rhee interview with the author, August 1993.

49. Larry Hartsell quoted from the article "Bruce Lee: The Little Dragon Remembered," published in *Inside Kung Fu*, September 1985.

50. Ken Knudson quoted from a survey taken by *Black Belt* magazine and published under the title of "An Objective Evaluation of the Combative Skill of Bruce Lee by Those Who Know What It Is" in Little, John (editor), *Bruce Lee: Artist of Life*, p. 211.

51. Leo Fong interview with the author, June 1994.

52. Wally Jay interview with the author, September 1993.

53. "As he grew older, the concern for testicular cancer would have been considered, and, if it was an undescended testicle it would have been removed." Urologist Dr. Anthony Drohomyrecky interview with the author, June 22, 2021.

54. "In March of 1969 Bruce was admitted to St. John's Hospital in Santa Monica, where surgeons removed the undeveloped testicle that had remained undescended since birth and repaired a hernia." Bleeker, Tom, *Unsettled Matters*, Gilderoy Publications, Lompoc, California, 1996, p. 59. Note: It is not altogether clear what the surgery was or even what Bruce's actual medical condition was. In speaking with urologist Tony Drohomyrecky about the procedure, the author was informed that no surgeon would lower a testicle that was undescended, particularly if the patient was twenty-eight-years of age, as it wouldn't flourish in the scrotum and would remain considerably smaller than the other testicle. And, according to Dr. Drohomyrecky, if the testicle was removed, then there would have been only one testicle in the scrotum after the procedure; if the testicle had simply been lowered, there would have been two testicles of vastly different sizes in the scrotum. However, during Lee's autopsy, the coroner indicated that both testes were of normal size (Polly, Matthew, *Bruce Lee: A Life*, p. 563). So, this compounds the matter. Dr. Drohomyrecky indicated that another possibility might have been that Bruce Lee had a retracted testicle (not an undescended one), which would have been normal in size, but that during times of stress or at other times, might ascend into his lower abdomen — and that this could have been adjusted surgically. As Lee was said to have had a hernia repaired at the same time as his surgery, it does (Drohomyrecky believes) lend credence to his testicle having been undescended and that the two surgeries were performed at the same time.

CHAPTER THIRTEEN: STANDING UP TO A BULLY

1. Joe Lewis interview with the author, July 1993.

2. Joe Lewis quoted from an interview on Bruce Lee Divine Wind Forum: bruceleedivinewind.com/joelewis.html. See also: "[Bruce was] a little Chinese actor, not a fighter (who has no professional fight record)." Joe Lewis quoted from the online interview "Legendary Joe Lewis: I Never Lost My World Full Contact Karate/Kickboxing Titles to Anyone."

3. "Joe Lewis's competitive career in kickboxing and PKA full-contact karate ended with a combined record of 14 wins and 4 losses. The PKA World title record was 4 wins 4 losses." From the online article "Joe Lewis: Legendary American Kickboxer" by USAdojo at usadojo.com/joe-lewis/.

4. Bruce Lee quoted from Little, John (editor), *Bruce Lee: Artist of Life*, pp. 485–486.

5. "A Martial Arts Legend's Four Greatest Career Moments" by Herb Borkland at wakousa.org/wp-content/uploads/2015/02/march-joe-lewis.pdf.

6. "The first time I faced Joe, he broke one of my ribs." Mitchell Bobrow quoted in the article "Tales of American Karate," *Black Belt*, January 1992. That Bobrow is

sixteen-years of age, see: "Lewis beats first Mitchell Bobrow, only 16 years old ..." at karate-in-english-lewis-wallace.blogspot.com/2008/03/joe-lewis-karate-and -full-contact.html.

7. "A few months after Bob first saw Norris in action, Bob met and began training with Joe Lewis. . . . 'The first thing Joe did was to break my rib,' Bob laughed recalling the incident. 'He was tough, but that's what it took for me to learn how to be a good fighter. . . . I was the first person to make black belt under Lewis.'" Bob Wall quoted from the online article "Off the Wall with Bob Wall" by Terry Wilson at usadojo.com/off-the-wall-with-bob-wall/. See also: "Many people look upon him [Joe Lewis] as a bully. Well, he did break a few ribs; in fact, when Bob Wall, one of his students, who also appeared in Bruce's *The Way of the Dragon*, first met Joe in a freestyle sparring, three of Bob's ribs were broken by a sidekick by Joe Lewis." Bruce Lee quoted from Little, John (editor), *Bruce Lee: Artist of Life*, pp. 485–486.

8. "Tanaka refused to fall for Lewis' usual 'psyching' act ..." From the article "The Top 10 Karatemen in the United States," *Black Belt Yearbook 1968*, p. 31. See also: "Joe Lewis reports that he's had it when it comes to tournaments. . . . Next stop: movies! Why not . . . Young, good looking (so he says) and single. . . . But Joe, you can't 'psych out' an audience." From the article "Off the Gi" by D. David Dress, Managing Editor, *Black Belt*, September 1968, p. 43.

9. On May 7, 1966, he was declared the Grand Champion at the U.S. Nationals in Long Beach, California; he won the World Karate Championship in Chicago and the Northwest Karate Championships in Washington. On June 24, 1967, he won the Henry Cho Tournament in New York; he won the Nationals again by defeating John Wooley (Joe Lewis's tournament record from the article "USA Karate Story: Chuck Norris, Joe Lewis, Bill Wallace" at karate-in-english-lewis -wallace.blogspot.com/2008/03/joe-lewis-karate-and-full-contact.html).

10. Lewis had been disqualified in 1964 while competing in the Okinawa Championships (karate-in-english-lewis-wallace.blogspot.com/2008/03/joe-lewis -karate-and-full-contact.html); on July 31, 1966, he lost to Allen Steen in the finals at the Internationals Karate Championships in Long Beach, California (karate-in-english-lewis-wallace.blogspot.com/2008/03/joe-lewis-karate-and -full-contact.html); on May 19, 1967, he lost in the California State Karate Championship to Ralph Castellanos (karate-in-english-lewis-wallace.blogspot. com/2008/03/joe-lewis-karate-and-full-contact.html); in 1967 he lost to Chuck Norris in the Tournament of Champions (*Black Belt*, June 1967); he lost again to Chuck Norris at the All American Championships in New York (*Black Belt*, October 1967); he lost to Ron Marchini at the Pacific Coast Invitational Karate Tournament (*Black Belt*, November 1967); and on June 29, 1967, he lost yet again to Chuck Norris at the Internationals (*Black Belt*, November 1967).

11. From the article "Top 10 Karatemen in The United States" [Lewis was voted Number Two that year, behind Chuck Norris] in *Black Belt Yearbook 1968*, pp. 30–31.

12. Mitoshi Uyehara interview with the author, August 1993. See also: "[Lewis's] favorite techniques were lightning-quick side thrust kicks, backfist strikes, and reverse punches. These three techniques invariably destroyed his opponents, and he won most of his matches by relying on those moves." From the article "Retrospect: The Development of Sport Karate in the 60s (Part II)" by Alex Sternberg (as told to Gary Goldstein), *Black Belt*, July 1981. See also: ". . . all a man really needs to become a champion is a good hand technique and a good kicking technique, or two real good hand techniques." Joe Lewis quoted from the article "Candid Interview With The Real Joe Lewis," *Professional Karate*, Fall 1973.
13. Kareem Abdul-Jabbar interview with the author, August 1993.
14. Joe Lewis interview with the author, July 1993.
15. Joe Lewis interview with the author, July 1993.
16. Joe Lewis interview with the author, July 1993.
17. All information on what led up to the sparring match between Bruce Lee and Joe Lewis is from Herb Jackson's interview with the author, June 1993.
18. Herb Jackson interview with the author, June 1993.
19. Kareem Abdul-Jabbar interview with the author, August 1993. Evidently, Bruce Lee felt the same way: "Lewis doesn't have the ability to hit solidly on elusive objects." Bruce Lee letter to Leo Fong, reprinted in Bax, Paul, *Disciples of the Dragon*, first edition, self-published, Outskirts Press Inc., Denver, 2008, p. 146.
20. Joe Lewis quoted from the video "According to Joe Lewis, Bruce Lee Was by Far the Greatest" at youtube.com/watch?v=1X2byotY220.
21. Joe Lewis interview with the author, July 1993:

> *Question*: "When was the last time you spoke to Bruce?"
> *Joe Lewis*: "Probably the latter part of 1969."

22. "I was married at the time and my wife did not want me . . . she was very jealous of my and Bruce's relationship. So, she went up to his house one day to put some highlights in his hair. And she came back and told me that Bruce had made a pass at her — which wasn't true. But, dumb me, I believed it." Joe Lewis interview with the author, July 1993.
23. "I went up there to . . . I was wearing a suit and tie, as a matter of fact . . ." Joe Lewis interview with the author, July 1993.
24. Joe Lewis interview with the author, July 1993.
25. "I didn't even walk into his house — just talked to him through the screen door at the back of his house." Joe Lewis interview with the author, July 1993.
26. "He thought I was an idiot." Joe Lewis interview with the author, July 1993.
27. Joe Lewis quoting the doorway dialogue between he and Bruce Lee. Joe Lewis interview with the author, July 1993.
28. "Bruce and Linda were kind of upset with me because they couldn't understand why I would even believe such a story to begin with." Joe Lewis interview with the author, July 1993.

29. Joe Lewis interview with the author, July 1993.
30. Joe Lewis interview with the author, July 1993.
31. Joe Lewis interview with the author, July 1993.
32. Bob Wall interview with the author, July 1993.
33. Bob Wall interview with the author, July 1993.
34. Joe Lewis interview with the author, July 1993.
35. Kareem Abdul-Jabbar interview with the author, August 1993.

CHAPTER FOURTEEN: TOTAL MARTIAL FREEDOM

1. Bruce Lee's daytime diary entry for Sunday, May 31, 1970: "Back problem." As shown in the documentary *Bruce Lee: A Warrior's Journey*.
2. "One morning he decided to experiment with a 125-pound weight, placing the weight on his shoulders and bending over from the waist while keeping his back straight." Lee, Linda, *Bruce Lee: The Man Only I Knew*, p. 15.
3. "I don't think he fully appreciated how strenuous this exercise is for he suddenly felt a terrible pain in the lower part of his back." Lee, Linda, *Bruce Lee: The Man Only I Knew*, p. 15. See also: "Anyway I hurt my lower back from 'tons and tons of exercises' — a sort of pinching nerve when pressed." Bruce Lee letter to Bob Baker, June 17, 1970, posted online at entertainment.ha.com/itm/movie-tv-memorabilia /documents/bruce-lee-handwritten-letter-signed-bruce-written-to-bob-baker -informing-him-to-forget-about-sending-stuff-as-excessive-in/a/7241-89425 .s?ic16=ViewItem-BrowseTabs-Auction-Archive-ThisAuction-120115.
4. "Since it [the pain in his back] doesn't really hinder me too much, I keep up my endurance work." Bruce Lee letter to Bob Baker, June 17, 1970.
5. "The doctor told him he had damaged a sacral nerve and would never do his kung fu kick again." Lee, Linda, *Bruce Lee: The Man Only I Knew*, p. 15.
6. "It might necessitate surgery." Bruce Lee letter to Bob Baker, August 17, 1970.
7. "Your massages and experience in back problems have helped greatly in my long way back to normal activity." Bruce Lee letter to Bob Baker, September 10, 1970, posted online at entertainment.ha.com/itm/movie-tv-memorabilia/documents /bruce-lee-handwritten-letter-signed-bruce-written-to-bob-baker-regarding -baker-s-help-in-lee-s-back-recovery/a/7241-89431.s?ic16=ViewItem-BrowseTabs -Auction-Archive-ThisAuction-120115.
8. ". . . but [I] lay off heavy lifting and excessive stretching. It bugs me though." Bruce Lee letter to Bob Baker, June 17, 1970.
9. "I did not write because since I last saw you, my back has worsen[ed]. It has become serious and I've been in bed for quite some time. The pain is there for over three months." Bruce Lee letter to Bob Baker, August 17, 1970.
10. Lee, Linda, *Bruce Lee: The Man Only I Knew*, p. 15.
11. Mitoshi Uyehara quoted from the article "Bruce Lee: The Final Years," published in *Fighting Stars*, October 1976.
12. Larry Hartsell interview with the author, July 12, 1994.

13. Robert Lee quoted in Block, Alex Ben, *The Legend of Bruce Lee*, pp. 94–95.

14. "... when I see a Japanese martial artist, I can see the advantage and the disadvantage of his style. In that sense, I am relating to him." Bruce Lee quoted from an interview with Alex Ben Block published in Little, John (editor), *Bruce Lee: Words from a Master*, Contemporary Books, Chicago, 1999, p. 65. See also Bruce Lee's list of the strengths and weaknesses of various martial arts which was compiled during this period as published in Little, John (editor), *Jeet Kune Do: Bruce Lee's Commentaries on the Martial Way*, pp. 40–45

15. Hartsell may have been mistaken on the actual title of the book and its date of publication, which the author believes was *Every Gentleman's Manual: A Lecture on the Art of Self-Defense* by Pierce Egan, published by Sherwood and Bowyer, Strand, London, 1845.

16. Larry Hartsell interview with the author, July 12, 1994.

17. Jiddu Krishnamurti quoted from his speech "Truth Is a Pathless Land," August 3, 1929, at jkrishnamurti.org/about-dissolution-speech.

18. Kareem Abdul-Jabbar interview with the author, August 1993.

19. Leo Fong interview with the author, June 1994.

20. Bruce Lee quoted from a dialogue he had with his student Daniel Lee over the phone in 1971 that was recorded by Daniel Lee. From a copy given to the author by Daniel Lee in 1994. See also other statements from Bruce during this same conversation: "When there is a Way, man, therein lies the limitation. And when there is a circumference, it traps. And if it traps, it rottens. And if it rottens, it is lifeless." And "Man [the species] is constantly growing. And when he is bound by a set pattern of ideas or way of doing things, that's when he stops growing."

21. Jesse Glover quoted in Bax, Paul, and Smith, Steve, *Disciple of the Dragon: Reflections of Bruce Lee's Student, Jesse Glover (Disciples of the Dragon Book 2)*, p. 192.

22. Bruce Lee quoted from a dialogue he had with his student Daniel Lee over the phone in 1971 that was recorded by Daniel Lee. From a copy given to the author by Daniel Lee in 1994.

23. Hayward Nishioka interview with the author, December 1993.

24. Hayward Nishioka interview with the author, December 1993.

25. Hayward Nishioka interview with the author, December 1993.

26. Dr. Burt Seidler interview with the author, June 11, 1998.

27. Mark Komuro interview with the author, 1996.

28. Joe Orbillo quoted from his talk at the Jun Fan Jeet Kune Do Nucleus Seminar, San Francisco, January 11, 1997, youtube.com/watch?v=iw6W1MMKm4o.

29. "'Shanghai was a very international city, so he went to a YMCA to learn boxing,' says his son, Robert Lee. 'At the time, I don't think Chinese martial arts were that well-structured, and my father had a very orderly mind, so the more structured nature of boxing appealed to him.' Daniel Lee was so good at boxing that he continued to train after the war, and in 1948 he won the National Amateur

Championship of China." Robert Lee quoted in *Black Belt Fightbook*, May 1, 2016, at pressreader.com/usa/black-belt/20160501/281530815117210.

30. Daniel Lee interview with the author, July 1994.

CHAPTER FIFTEEN: A FIGHT FAR FROM THE MADDING CROWD

1. A poor-quality video that was shot on 8mm film during Bruce Lee's appearance reveals this sequence and can be viewed at youtu.be/2Ii-gumUQIQ.

2. Bruce Lee quoted from an interview with Alex Ben Block, published in Little, John (editor), *Bruce Lee: Words from a Master*, p. 69. Lee would joke with Raymond Chow that he was never doing a demonstration like that again: "As he would tell me later, it was one of his best demonstrations ever. Because he can't really do it every time you threw a board in the air by dropping [it]. You [must] jump up and kick it and break it. He said he won't do it again live. So, I knew it was very special." Raymond Chow interview with the author, June 12, 1996.

3. "The film, having bossed the local screens for 19 days, outgrossed the last record holder, *The Sound of Music*, by about $800,000." From the article "The Big Boss Takes a Record Profit," *China Mail*, November 19, 1971.

4. "I studied Hung Kuen, the Tiger and Crane style. Liu Chia-liang, the action director of many kung fu films, trained us. I was not that good, neither a senior nor a junior. I don't train now — I'm getting old. But I practice every day for exercise." David Chiang quoted in the online article "Kung Fu Master of Shaw Brothers' Golden Era Still Shines," by Alex Choi Ingamells at bangkokpost .com/life/arts-and-entertainment/435642/kung-fu-master-of-shaw-brothers -golden-era-still-shines.

5. "Despite receiving no formal martial arts training, Jimmy Wang Yu predates Bruce Lee as Hong Kong's first action hero." From the online article "Profile: Jimmy Wang Yu" by Ben Johnson at kungfumovieguide.com/profile-jimmy -wang-yu/.

6. "You returned to Hong Kong and appeared on a television station for an inter-view. You criticized [that] our Hong Kong Martial Arts practitioners 'Gung Sao' (talk fighting) more than 'Gau Sau' (actually fighting). You said there must be more 'Gau Sau' then there would be progress, and you were willing to compare techniques with our practitioners of the Hong Kong Martial Arts community, etc." Lau Dai Chuen quoted in his letter, published in Kerridge, Steve, and Chua, Darren, *Bruce Lee: The Intercepting Fist*, section "A Challenging Situation."

7. "As for me, I've also attained the western boxing champion[ship] in Hong Kong four times consecutively." Lau Dai Chuen quoted in his letter, published in Kerridge, Steve, and Chua, Darren, *Bruce Lee: The Intercepting Fist*. See also: "This fellow [Lau Dai Chuen] was the Asian boxing champion and had loudly protested Bruce Lee's status in the martial arts world. Mr. Lau is before a boxer. He's a winner in Asia. A champion. Good boxer." Bolo Yeung interview with the author, November 1993. However, Hong Kong's *New Martial Hero* magazine indicated

that in addition to Western boxing, Lau had also studied Cha Kuen, a northern style of Kung Fu: "The Mongolian Cha Keun boxer and bantamweight champion Lau Tat-Chuen has attempted to challenge Bruce Lee. His letter of the challenge stated Lee offended the Hong Kong martial art community in his television interview and as such gave reason to request a friendly fight." Article from *New Martial Hero* magazine, circa November 1971, reprinted in Kerridge, Steve, and Chua, Darren, *Bruce Lee: The Intercepting Fist*, section "A Challenging Situation."

8. "The one person [Lau Dai Chuen] challenged him every day in the newspaper. He wanted to fight with Bruce Lee. Every day in the newspaper." Bolo Yeung interview with the author, November 1993.

9. Bruce Lee quoted in the article "The Big Boss Takes a Record Profit," *China Mail*, November 19, 1971.

10. As per Bob Baker's journal entry for November 21, 1971: "Yesterday [November 20] was the first day on the movie set. We took a lot of pictures, still pictures for movie posters and newspapers, it was fun!" published online at entertainment.ha.com /itm/movie-tv-memorabilia/documents/robert-baker-journal-making-fist-of -fury-with-color-fight-scene-snapshots-from-the-set/a/7241-89466.s?ic16 =ViewItem-BrowseTabs-Inventory-BuyNowFromOwner-ThisAuction-120115.

11. Bob Baker quoted in Kerridge, Steve, and Chua, Darren, *Bruce Lee: The Intercepting Fist*, section "A Challenging Situation."

12. Max Lee quoted from the video "Remembering Bruce Lee — Max Lee" at youtube.com/watch?v=Nu6g42YFoFM.

13. Bruce Lee quoted in Uyehara, Mitoshi, *Bruce Lee: The Incomparable Fighter*, p. 22.

14. Bolo Yeung interview with the author, November 1993.

15. The editorial on Lau Dai Chuen's letter to the editor of *New Martial Hero* is reproduced in Kerridge, Steve, and Chua, Darren, *Bruce Lee: The Intercepting Fist*, section "A Challenging Situation."

16. "I and the kids will be coming back in January to take care of leasing the house and storing furniture and sending things to Hong Kong. Then we will be coming back to work for 6 months to a year maybe longer." (Linda Lee letter to Bob Baker, December 17, 1971, at entertainment.ha.com/itm/movie -tv-memorabilia/documents/linda-lee-handwritten-letter-signed-bruce-linda -written-to-bob-and-bev-baker-regarding-bruce-s-completion-of-jing-mo-moon -/a/7241-89448.s?ic16=ViewItem-BrowseTabs-Inventory-BuyNowFrom Owner-ThisAuction-120115). The letter indicates that Linda and the children were returning to California to tie up the matters with the house. However, as Bruce Lee says in his phone conversation with Daniel Lee that he was in Bel Air at his house sorting through things and references the moving company, it is evident that he made the return trip to the United States with Linda.

17. Bruce Lee quoted from a dialogue he had that was recorded by his student Daniel Lee in 1971, a copy of which was given to the author by Daniel Lee in 1994.

18. Tony Liu, an actor who was among the stuntmen with Bruce at the restaurant that day, quoted from the online article "Bruce Lee's Real Fight with Lau

Dai-Chuen: Truth or Fake?!" at wingchunnews.ca/bruce-lees-real-fight-with
-lau-dai-chuen-truth-or-fake/.

19. "Lau Dai Chuen walked up to Bruce Lee during a banquet that they both
happened to be at and challenged Bruce Lee. This is of course after months of
taunting Bruce in the newspapers etc. etc. Bruce Lee agreed to the challenge,
but said they should fight somewhere where there were less people around."
Lam Ching Ying quoted from an interview with Joe Hung, a famous novel
writer in Hong Kong (audio courtesy of Paul Li).

20. "As a chief detective during the sixties and early seventies, Tang Sang was regu-
larly accepting 'tea money' from local gangsters (*hak sai wui* — black societies).
It was not uncommon for police, especially those in a high-ranking position to
accept these bribes — corruption was a standard operating procedure for the
Royal Hong Kong Police Force in the sixties and seventies." From the online
article "Tang Sang" at en-academic.com/dic.nsf/enwiki/5668864.

21. "So, in Hong Kong, there's the police number one. He wanted to see Bruce
Lee fighting. And then he spoke to Bruce Lee and the other guy, Lau, that
nobody would know. Who is the winner? Nobody would know. You understand? And a big house. So, nobody can see [the fight]." Bolo Yeung interview
with the author, November 1993; "This was at the time of the Colonial era . . .
police powers were great. A plain-clothes detective, Mr. Chang was there, but
not on police duty . . . but as Chairman of the Hong Kong Chinese Martial
Arts Association. Mr. Chang was a friend of Bruce's and with his power and
authority, arranged a fight at an undisclosed villa in the New Territories (in
HK). Bruce didn't want it made public." From the online article "Bruce Lee's
Real Fight with Lau Dai-Chuen: Truth or Fake?!"; "A secret bout was staged
at a private villa in Hong Kong." From the online article "Bruce Lee Real
Fight with Western Boxing Champion Lau Dai Chuen" at wingchunnews.ca
/bruce-lee-real-fight-with-western-boxing-champion-lau-dai-chuen/; "Among
the many challenges, the most famous was that of Lau Dai-Chuen. The secret
bout was held at a private villa." From the video "Bruce Lee's Challenger talks
of Bruce's death 1973" citing the report of a witness and published in *Huang
Chun Leung Martial Arts* magazine (2008) at youtu.be/IUPDC04-rqY; "Liu
Chi Keung, one of the founders of the Hong Kong Chinese martial arts association, told me that he witnessed the fight at Tang's home in Fanling. From
what he told me, I had the feeling that there was some time between the
decision to have the fight and the actual fight itself." Alex Richter interview
with the author, September 3, 2021.

22. "His [Tang Sang's] villa was in Fanling in a section called Ma Mei Ha . . . At
that time there was no quick rail from Kowloon up to that part of the New
Territories, so it would've been a bit of a trip for anyone going there in the early
'70s." Alex Richter interview with the author, September 3, 2021.

23. "There was about 20 persons witness his fight." From the online article "Bruce
Lee Real Fight with Western Boxing Champion Lau Dai Chuen." See also:

"Bruce and Lau came out . . . to an audience of twenty or more." From the video "Bruce Lee's Challenger talks of Bruce's death 1973."

24. "The other hearsay was that Tang had a boxing ring in his backyard which he had used to help train up some of the Wing Chun fighters who were going into full-contact contests at that time. Supposedly the fight happened in that boxing ring, but again there's no real solid corroboration on any of these details." Alex Richter interview with the author, September 3, 2021.

25. "Bruce and Lau came out in Western boxing attire . . ." From the video "Bruce Lee's Challenger talks of Bruce's death 1973."

26. "At the beginning [Lau Dai Chuen] was boxing and Bruce Lee is slipping, bobbing." Bolo Yeung interview with the author, November 1993; "Lau rushed in with a flurry of punches. Bruce jumped and dodged, his hands in front of his face like a seasoned boxer." From the video "Bruce Lee's Challenger talks of Bruce's death 1973"; "Lau Dai-Chuen thought he could use Western boxing with Cha fist against Bruce's Jeet Kune Do." Tony To, publicity manager for Golden Harvest Studios, quoted from the online article "Bruce Lee's Real Fight with Lau Dai-Chuen: Truth or Fake?!"

27. "He was called, nicknamed by the cast in Bangkok [where Lee was shooting *The Big Boss*, his first film for Golden Harvest Studios] as 'three-kick Lee' . . . because he can kick three guys virtually within two seconds, things like that. He became famous with that name for a long, long time." Raymond Chow interview with the author, June 12, 1996.

28. Bruce Lee's friend, the stunt person and actor Lam Ching Ying, mentioned that Lau was focusing on Lee's legs during two separate interviews: "Because Bruce Lee's nickname in the press was 'three-kick Lee,' Lau Dai Chuen was fixated and staring at Bruce Lee's legs the whole time. This was a signal to Bruce that Lau Dai Chuen did not know anything about martial arts." Lam Ching Ying quoted from an interview with Joe Hung, a famous novel writer in Hong Kong (courtesy of Paul Li); "Lau was watching Bruce Lee's leg when the fight was about to start. This is because Bruce Lee was well-known for his lightning kicks." Lam Ching Ying quoted from the online article "Bruce Lee Real Fight with Western Boxing Champion Lau Dai Chuen."

29. "Therefore, Lau was thinking to sweep Bruce's leg before he was able to kick and attack him." Lam Ching Ying quoted from the online article "Bruce Lee Real Fight with Western Boxing Champion Lau Dai Chuen."

30. "When Lau's offensive stopped, he leaned back a little and tried to sweep Bruce's leg." From the video "Bruce Lee's Challenger talks of Bruce's death 1973."

31. "When Bruce and Lau Dai Chuen met, it was over with one punch." Chan Wai Man quoted from an audio series called Paths of Little Dragon that was released in 2008 on Commercial Radio in Hong Kong (courtesy of Paul Li); "Bruce gave him one punch and the fight was over." Lam Ching Ying quoted from an interview with Joe Hung, a famous novel writer in Hong Kong (courtesy of Paul Li).

32. "Bruce, with a quick instep, intercepts the sweep with a crushing sidekick to Lau's chest. Immediately ending the match." From the video "Bruce Lee's Challenger talks of Bruce's death 1973"; "A friend of mine came back after one round and said, 'It's over' . . . with one kick, Bruce ended the fight. He was just too fast (laughing)." Tony To, publicity manager for Golden Harvest Studios, quoted from the online article "Bruce Lee's Real Fight with Lau Dai-Chuen: Truth or Fake?!"

33. "And then, maybe 20 [seconds later], Lee threw one kick — Bam! [and the fight was over]" Bolo Yeung interview with the author, November 1993.

34. "Lau, unable to stand, and caressing his chest, showed excruciating pain on his face." From the video "Bruce Lee's Challenger talks of Bruce's death 1973."

35. "Several men came into the rope circle ring to carry him out." From the video "Bruce Lee's Challenger talks of Bruce's death 1973."

36. "Bruce then pulled out his check book and wrote a check out in the fallen boxer's name in order to pay the hospital expenses necessary to stitch the man back up." Bolo Yeung interview with the author, November 1993; "Bruce kindly paid for Lau's medical treatment." From the video "Bruce Lee's Challenger talks of Bruce's death 1973." See also: "It was only after his death that I heard about one challenge fight Bruce had to take on. This story I believe because the guy was known, although I don't remember his name now. He repeatedly challenged Bruce, even went through the media which forced Bruce to accept. The guy was a master in his own right, yet he lasted only a few seconds. He was injured and Bruce gave him quite an amount of money for him to go to Japan to treat so people in Hong Kong wouldn't see him in bad shape." Chaplin Chang quoted from the interview at bruceleedivinewind.com/chaplinchang .html.

37. "Since then, Lau has tried to keep his loss a secret. Witnesses also complied to the secrecy of the fight, so the matter has not been confirmed." Tony To, publicity manager for Golden Harvest Studios, quoted from the online article "Bruce Lee's Real Fight with Lau Dai-Chuen: Truth or Fake?!"

38. Chaplin Chang online interview.

39. "Lau Dai-Chuen later learned that three of his ribs were broken." From the video "Bruce Lee's Challenger talks of Bruce's death 1973."

40. Bolo Yeung interview with the author, November 1993.

41. "Apparently, the police chief didn't keep the secret very private." Bolo Yeung interview with the author, November 1993.

42. Ted Thomas interview with the author, published in Little, John (editor), *Bruce Lee: Words from a Master*, p. 50.

CHAPTER SIXTEEN: BAD PRESS AND GANGSTERS

1. Kareem Abdul-Jabbar recalled, "When Bruce went out in Hong Kong, it was like Michael Jackson going out in public. We drove around in his car a

little bit, and the kids, you know, at the street corners, would go nuts and start screaming, pointing at the car." Kareem Abdul-Jabbar interview with the author, August 1993.

2. "I would like to stress the fact that though my present style is more totally alive and efficient, I owe my achievement to my previous training in the Wing Chun style, a great style. It was taught to me by Mr. Yip Man, present leader of the Wing Chun Clan in Hong Kong where I was reared." Bruce Lee quoted in the article, "In Kato's Gung Fu Action Is Instant," by Maxwell Pollard, *Black Belt*, November 1967, pp. 16–17.

3. "The 'Chi Sao' of Wing Chun" by Bruce Lee, published in *Black Belt Yearbook 1969*, pp. 25–32.

4. "Spent two tiresome, tiresome days with Ted and James shooting pictures at *Black Belt* for the Wing Chun book, total 14 hours of shooting. We are not finished yet, but will have to shoot again on the weekend of the 5th of June." Bruce Lee letter to Bob Baker, May 25, 1971, posted online at entertainment .ha.com/itm/movie-tv-memorabilia/documents/bruce-lee-handwritten-letter -signed-bruce-written-to-bob-baker-regarding-a-shoot-for-black-belt-magazine -promoting-mentor-jame/a/7241-89442.s?ic16=ViewItem-BrowseTabs-Inventory -BuyNowFromOwner-ThisAuction-120115].

5. The episode (as of March 2023) is available to watch on YouTube at youtube .com/watch?v=1_C6wKGL_ug (the Chi Sao segment appears at 25:16).

6. Lee, J. Yimm, and Lee, Bruce (technical editor), *Wing Chun Kung Fu: Chinese Art of Self-Defense*, Ohara Publications Inc., Santa Clarita, California, 1972. "In the summer of 1972 [just one year prior to his death] Bruce decided to publish a book on wing chun kung fu with Ohara Publications. I was then the publisher of that company. Bruce didn't want to use his name because the art was so different from his jeet kune do. Instead he was planning to use an alias. . . . Even though Bruce decided not to use his name or photos in the wing chun book, he put his whole heart and energy into its production. . . . For two weeks Bruce . . . worked from morning until night, Monday through Friday. 'Bruce never quit,' recalled Ed Ikuta, the photographer. 'He just kept going and everything had to be precisely right.' . . . Before the book went to the printer, Bruce learned that recovery for his friend James [Jimmy Lee] would be slow and also learned that he was almost broke. His savings was rapidly being depleted and his medical costs were skyrocketing. . . . Although Bruce could really have used the money from the book since he hadn't completely recovered from his back injury and also an addition to the family (daughter Shannon), he nevertheless pitied his friend and handed over the title to James without a second thought. 'Can you do me a favor and give Jimmy the advance (royalty) right away?' he asked me. 'He needs the bread more than me.'" Uyehara, Mitoshi, *Bruce Lee: The Incomparable Fighter*, pp. 129–131.

7. "Wing Chun: The Kung Fu That Emphasizes Equally Strong Defense and Attack" by Peter Bennett, published in *Black Belt*, September 1972, pp. 22–27.

8. "When Bruce came back to Hong Kong, he came to see my family, and had a good chat with my father. Often, he came with gifts. . . . When 'Fist of Fury' was shown, Bruce invited my father out to tea at Golden Crown Restaurant. . . . Then he gave us several tickets to see the film. Many in the [Wing Chun] Institute had enjoyed this opportunity." Yip Chun, "The Bruce Lee Story," originally published in *The Star* (Hong Kong), March 17–20, 1973. Republished in *Bruce Lee: Superstar from Hong Kong*, Bruce Lee Jeet Kune Do Club, Hong Kong, 1980, p. 22.

9. *Bruce Lee: Superstar from Hong Kong*, Bruce Lee Jeet Kune Do Club, Hong Kong, 1980, p. 22.

10. "When my father passed away, I got out the phone book to try to call Bruce, but someone prevented me from doing so, and I never did." Yip Chun quoted in Li, Paul, *From Limited to Limitless: The Ways of Bruce Lee*, Oriental Resources Company, Hong Kong, 1998, p. 112.

11. "My father reminded [Bruce] that Chinese Kung Fu is one of the sophisticated arts of China, that we need Kung Fu techniques to defend ourselves and to keep good health, and that the techniques of Chinese Kung Fu should not be taught freely to foreigners (it was typically Chinese traditional thinking of the old Kung Fu masters). Bruce Lee promised to bear this in mind before he left for the USA. But soon after Bruce Lee had reached the USA, he set up a gymnasium, admitted foreign students, and taught them [Wing Chun] techniques, to the surprise and disappointment of his master." Yip Chun quoted from Yip Chun, *116 Wing Tsun Dummy Techniques as Demonstrated by Grandmaster Yip Man*, technical advisor Leung Ting, Leung Ting Publication & Distribution, Hong Kong, 1981, p. 109.

12. Luo Yao quoted in Li, Paul, *From Limited to Limitless: The Ways of Bruce Lee*, p. 111.

13. Liang Xiang quoted in Li, Paul, *From Limited to Limitless: The Ways of Bruce Lee*, p. 111.

14. Wong Shun Leung quoted in Li, Paul, *From Limited to Limitless: The Ways of Bruce Lee*, p. 112.

15. Yip Chun, "The Bruce Lee Story," originally published in *The Star* newspaper (Hong Kong), March 17–20, 1973. Republished in *Bruce Lee: Superstar from Hong Kong*, Bruce Lee Jeet Kune Do Club, Hong Kong, 1980, pp. 22–24.

16. "On the seventh day after a Chinese funeral, the equivalent of a wake is held at the person's home, because it is believed that the spirit of the dead comes back on that day. It was set for 8 p.m., but Bruce showed up at seven to make sure he was the first one there. He humbly apologized to Ip Chun and the rest of Ip Man's family for missing the funeral." Information provided by Yip Chun to Matthew Polly as cited in Polly, Matthew, *Bruce Lee: A Life*, p. 400.

17. Yip Chun, "The Bruce Lee Story," originally published in *The Star* newspaper (Hong Kong), March 17–20, 1973. Republished in *Bruce Lee: Superstar from Hong Kong*, Bruce Lee Jeet Kune Do Club, Hong Kong, 1980, pp. 22–24.

18. Unless otherwise indicated, the biographical material on Chan Wai Man is drawn from the online article "Famous Movie Star and Respected Gangster — Profile of 14K Triad Boss Michael Chan" at gangstersinc.org/profiles/blogs/famous-movie-star-and-respected-gangster-profile-of-14k-triad-bos.

19. Chan Wai Man quoted from the online article "Hong Kong Triad Legend: Michael Chan Wai-Man. Honor Among Thieves in Old Chinese Secret Societies" at facebook.com/watch/?v=647459335739053.

20. "Actually, back when I was eighteen years old, I was a policeman for two years. No-one knows this! Then they discovered my triad background and I got kicked out!" Chan Wai Man quoted in the online article at tapatalk.com/groups/bruceleelivetributeforum/90s-chan-wai-man-interview-t4554.html.

21. Chan Wai Man quoted from the online article "Hong Kong Triad Legend: Michael Chan Wai-Man."

22. Chan Wai Man quoted from the online article "Hong Kong Triad Legend: Michael Chan Wai-Man."

23. Chan Wai Man's fighting titles as per the video "Hong Kong Triad Boss Chan Wai Man Said Only Idiot Would Fight with Bruce Lee" at youtube.com/watch?v=E5guO9xMCyM.

24. "Bruce Lee was my good friend, long before he made films, when we were both still at school. We went to different schools, but we knew each other well." Chan Wai Man quoted from an interview in *Martial Arts Illustrated*, republished online at tapatalk.com/groups/bruceleelivetributeforum/90s-chan-wai-man-interview-t4554.html.

25. Chan Wai Man quoted from the video "Hong Kong triad boss Chan Wai Man said only idiot would fight with Bruce Lee."

26. "He easily beat me in arm wrestling. Even Bolo Yeung lost to him in wrist wrestling." Chan Wai Man quoted from the video "Hong Kong triad boss Chan Wai Man said only idiot would fight with Bruce Lee." See also: "One day he [Bruce Lee] came back and he told me, 'Ho, that guy Bolo is a powerful guy. He can bench press over 400 pounds.' But then he says, 'But he cannot handle me in the Indian Arm Wrestling; I beat him all the time.'" Mitoshi Uyehara interview with the author, 1994.

27. Chan Wai Man quoted from the video "Hong Kong triad boss Chan Wai Man said only idiot would fight with Bruce Lee":

> *Interviewer*: "There was a hearsay at the time, I hear that there's a Lau Dai Chuen who challenged Bruce . . ."
> *Chan Wai Man*: "I know. Bruce Lee beat him with one punch."
> *Interviewer*: "Do you believe it?"
> *Chan Wai Man*: "I believe, I believe that's true."

28. Chan Wai Man quoted from the video "Hong Kong triad boss Chan Wai Man said only idiot would fight with Bruce Lee."

29. "Look at his [Bruce Lee's] speed, power and skill — if you get caught by him, he can beat you with one punch. He can knock you down with one punch. It's easy for him." Chan Wai Man quoted from the video "Hong Kong triad boss Chan Wai Man said only idiot would fight with Bruce Lee."

30. Chan Wai Man quoted from the video "Hong Kong triad boss Chan Wai Man said only idiot would fight with Bruce Lee."

31. "The *Rush Hour* star [Jackie Chan] told the Guangzhou-based *Southern People Weekly* magazine that he had been 'bullied' by triads, or the Chinese organized crime societies, that were once powerful and thrived in the Asian financial hub. 'In the past, when they bullied me, I hid in the United States. They opened fire at me once I got off the aeroplane,' Hong Kong's *South China Morning Post* quoted him as saying in the magazine interview published last week. 'From that moment on, I needed to carry a gun every day when I went out,' said the Hong Kong born star, who has played a hero cop that took on crime lords in his hugely popular Cantonese crime action film series Police Story." From the article "Jackie Chan Investigated for Taking on Triad Gang with 'Guns and Grenades'" at businessinsider.com/jackie-chan-probed-for-guns-and-grenades-2012-12.

32. Chan Wai Man quoted from the video "Hong Kong Triad Boss Said Nobody Dares to Provoke Bruce Lee to Fight" at youtube.com/watch?v=O8egoMcgbJc.

33. Chan Wai Man quoted from the video "Hong Kong triad boss Chan Wai Man said only idiot would fight with Bruce Lee."

34. Golden Harvest Studios purchased the home for Bruce Lee and assigned title in the property to Lo Yuen Enterprises Limited, a company that was created presumably for tax purposes, on August 2, 1972. Li, Paul, *From Limited to Limitless: The Ways of Bruce Lee*, p. 101.

35. Herb Jackson quoted at rumsoakedfist.org/viewtopic.php?p=453261&sid=05c324 cf5c3e11b4dcc0fd8071c1feca.

36. Herb Jackson interview with the author, June 1993.

37. This is a viewpoint shared by Hayward Nishioka: "I've sparred [heavyweight Karate champion] Joe Lewis and I've sparred Bruce Lee. Now Joe Lewis knocked the wind out of me with a sidekick when we sparred, but nobody kicked harder than Bruce Lee did." Hayward Nishioka interview with the author, December 1993.

38. Herb Jackson interview with the author, June 1993.

39. "And as soon as I finish with all these films in Hong Kong, I would like to move back to the States and just stay there." Bruce Lee quoted from his interview with Alex Ben Block in Little, John (editor), *Bruce Lee: Words from a Master*, p. 62.

CHAPTER SEVENTEEN: ENTER THE EXTRAS

1. Jon Benn interview with the author, December 1994.

2. Bolo Yeung interview with the author, November 1993. Bruce Lee had evidently acquired the machine while living in Los Angeles, as Mike Stone remembered

Bruce using it: "It's minor electric shock treatment that you put on your muscles to increase their pulse and repetition . . . Bruce believed it would enhance his skill and ability. But he went over the top. One to ten, he would crank the dial up to seven or eight, enough to curl his hair." Mike Stone quoted in Polly, Matthew, *Bruce Lee: A Life*, p. 205.

3. John Saxon quoted from the article "The Amazing Feats of the Little Dragon," *Bruce Lee Forever Fanzine*, Nov./Dec. 2022, p. 23.

4. Bolo Yeung quoted in Clouse, Robert, *The Making of Enter the Dragon*, Unique Publications, Burbank, California, 1987, pp. 144–148.

5. In Bruce Lee's letter to Ted Ashley, then chairman of the board at Warner Bros., in April 1973, he writes: "You see, Ted, my obsession is to make, pardon the expression, the fuckingest action motion picture that has ever been made." Reprinted in Little, John (editor), *Bruce Lee: Letters of the Dragon*, 1998, p. 178.

6. According to Linda Lee, "there were hundreds of extras, most of them just young punks." Lee, Linda, *Bruce Lee: The Man Only I Knew*, p. 182. Robert Clouse, the director of *Enter the Dragon*, put the number at 400: "We had as many as 400 extras in the tournament scenes." Clouse, Robert, *The Making of Enter the Dragon*, p. 134.

7. "They are not movie professionals or actors; the extras that work on Chinese films are a bunch of young punks. They bring them in to play in the crowd scenes." Linda Lee quoted from the article "A Candid Interview with Mrs. Bruce Lee" by Mike Anderson, *Professional Karate*, Summer 1974. See also: "Many of them [the extras hired for the film] belonged to rival street gangs. Confrontations staged for the camera often broke down into real battles. Many of these young men were poor with little to look forward to in their lives. Bruce used to sit among these men when he wasn't needed in a scene. As he practiced his moves and kicks, the extras would sit on the grass, much of which we had to paint green, or be sitting on top of the walls. Sometimes one of the men would decide to challenge Bruce." Clouse, Robert, *The Making of Enter the Dragon*, p. 134. See also: "The problem usually occurred when Golden Harvest, unknowingly, would hire unvetted extras, due mainly out of desperation and lack of workforce. More often than not, [they] were young triad members, who it seemed in many cases weren't even bothered about getting paid or not, as their main objective was to get close to Bruce. Then, of course, as expected, [they] would often attempt to see whether he was good a fighter as portrayed on the screen." Stunt person Lam Ching-Ying quoted in Kerridge, Steve, and Chua, Darren, *Bruce Lee: The Intercepting Fist*, section "A Challenging Situation."

8. Andre Morgan interview with the author, September 1994.

9. The author believes that there is something of the "Rashomon Effect" at play in the accounts that follow. That is, an instance or instances "when the same event is described in significantly different (often contradictory) ways by different people who were involved." (This definition of the Rashomon Effect is taken from dictionary.com/e/pop-culture/the-rashomon-effect/.) That Bruce Lee

had at least two fights on the set of *Enter the Dragon* is beyond dispute, as there exists photographs from one and two newspaper accounts of the other. (The two newspaper articles were "Bruce Just Too Good," *China Mail*, March 16, 1973, and "Superstar is Challenged, so . . . Bruce Floors Actor," *The Star* (Hong Kong), March 16, 1973. The photographic sequence was taken by David Friedman, whom Warner Bros. had hired to take pictures throughout the shooting of the film and who happened to be on set the day one of these fights took place.) What occurred during these fights, however, is something for which there exists no uniform consensus, as each of the witnesses claims to have seen something different than the others. Consequently, the researcher into the matter is left with the perplexing task of attempting to find consistency in the various accounts, so that a clear picture of what actually occurred might be arrived at. Compounding matters is the fact that in all but a few instances the witnesses were recalling an event that they observed occur over a quarter of a century after it took place.

10. Ahna Capri's film is available to watch on YouTube.

11. "The guy said something to the effect that Bruce was 'a movie star, not a martial artist.'" Bob Wall interview with the author, July 1993. See also: "Some kid was sitting on a wall and he was saying something to Bruce, obviously in Cantonese, which I didn't understand, and apparently he was questioning whether or not he was just an actor, or could he really do any of the things that he had been doing." John Saxon interview with the author, March 22, 1996.

12. "This guy was saying, 'I don't believe that you can do it' and went on like this." Linda Lee quoted in the article "A Candid Interview with Mrs. Bruce Lee."

13. "I saw a young extra sitting on a wall, loudly address Bruce in Cantonese. I don't know exactly what he said, but I gathered it was something like: 'You're just an actor, for the movies!'" John Saxon quoted from the online article "Interview with John Saxon" at bruceleelives.co.uk/saxon.html.

14. The extra said he [Bruce] "wasn't much of a fighter" and "it's easy to see his martial arts wasn't any good." Bob Wall interview with the author, July 1993.

15. "And Bruce said, 'Oh, really? Well come on down.'" Bob Wall interview with the author, July 1993; "He [Bruce Lee] just said, 'Come down here and we'll settle it.'" Linda Lee quoted from the article "A Candid Interview with Mrs. Bruce Lee"; "Bruce beckoned to him to come down off the wall. The kid foolishly did." John Saxon quoted from the online article "Interview with John Saxon."

16. Bob Wall interview with the author, July 1993.

17. Bob Wall interview with the author, July 1993.

18. "[The extra] quickly received a lightning crack to his face." John Saxon quoted from the online article "Interview with John Saxon"; see also: "According to one witness, Shih Kien, it happened so fast that he was not able to see it clearly. When the fight began, he just saw Bruce dash towards the extra, then, it was too fast to see anything. The next moment, he saw the extra half-kneeled with his back stuck unto the wall. . . . Henry Wong, who was filming *Enter the Dragon*

behind-the-scenes footage, coincidentally witnessed and shot the entire fight. His recollections on the fight matched about 60%–70% to Shih Kien's description. However, unlike Shih Kien, he saw very clearly about the fight from the angle where he was standing. He said Bruce's first strike was two kicks to the extra and the extra fell way back to the wall." Paul Li Chi-Yuan quoted from an online interview at tapatalk.com/groups/bruceleelivestributeforum/paul-li-t3406-s10.html.

19. Bob Wall quoted in the article "Bruce Lee as Seen Through the Eyes of Fellow Martial Artists," *The Bruce Lee Memorial Issue*, pp. 54–55. See also: "Bruce blocked the extra from moving his body and used his forehand to press against the extra's neck." Bruce Lee historian Paul Li Chi-Yuan quoted from an online interview.

20. "But Shih thought Bruce was a bit hesitant to strike because he paused for a second." Bruce Lee historian Paul Li Chi-Yuan quoted from an online interview.

21. ". . . and his [Bruce Lee's] back hand kept up with the attack." Bruce Lee historian Paul Li Chi-Yuan quoted from an online interview. See also: "[Bruce] nailed him in the face repeatedly." Bob Wall interview with the author, July 1993. See also: "Bruce literally drove him into a wall and pummeled him." Ahna Capri quoted from the article "The Amazing Feats of the Little Dragon," *Bruce Lee Forever Fanzine*, Nov./Dec. 2022, p. 23.

22. "He bloodied his mouth," Bob Wall "quoted in the article "Bruce Lee as Seen Through the Eyes of Fellow Martial Artists," *The Bruce Lee Memorial Issue*, p. 55. "And the kid had a bloody nose." John Saxon interview with the author March 22, 1996. See also: "He [Bruce Lee] messed up his face real good. . . . he bloodied the guy up pretty good." Bob Wall interview with the author, July 1993.

23. Bob Wall "quoted in the article "Bruce Lee as Seen Through the Eyes of Fellow Martial Artists," *The Bruce Lee Memorial Issue*, p. 55.

24. "His reaction to the affair when he returned to shoot the fight scene immediately afterwards? He went to get a drink of water. No big deal." Bob Wall interview with the author, July 1993.

25. Bob Wall quoted from the online interview "Exclusive: Interview with Bob Wall" at cityonfire.com/feature-bob-wall-interview/.

26. John Saxon quoted from the online article "Interview with John Saxon."

27. Clouse, Robert, *The Making of Enter the Dragon*, p. 134. See also: "The kid with his foot tapped on the ground, which Bruce told me later is how they challenged each other." Ahna Capri quoted from the article "The Amazing Feats of the Little Dragon," *Bruce Lee Forever Fanzine*, Nov./Dec. 2022, p. 22.

28. All action and dialogue from this incident unless otherwise indicated is drawn from Henry Wong's recollection, as quoted in Clouse, Robert, *The Making of Enter the Dragon*, pp. 158–160.

29. "One day, in the studio, I met an extra. When I got close to him, he challenged the validity of my Kung Fu. I saw his pride." Wong Shun Leung quoting Bruce Lee's recounting of the fight, published in the online article "Wong Shun Leung — The Death of Bruce Lee" by Wong Shun Leung at vingtsunserbia.wordpress.com/about/articles/wong-shun-leung-the-death-of-bruce-lee/.

30. "I said, 'If I do not have real Kung Fu, I don't think you will have it. You are stupid!'" Wong Shun Leung quoting Bruce Lee's recounting of the fight, published in the online article "Wong Shun Leung — The Death of Bruce Lee."

31. "I asked him to come down to fight. He asked, 'How should we play?' I answered, 'Fight. This is the way we play.'" Wong Shun Leung quoting Bruce Lee's recounting of the fight, published in the online article "Wong Shun Leung — The Death of Bruce Lee."

32. "Then he challenged me to fight. I was very angry." Wong Shun Leung quoting Bruce Lee's recounting of the fight, published in the online article "Wong Shun Leung — The Death of Bruce Lee."

33. "With a shout, I kicked at his lower abdomen." Wong Shun Leung quoting Bruce Lee's recounting of the fight, published in the online article "Wong Shun Leung — The Death of Bruce Lee."

34. Wong Shun Leung quoting Bruce Lee's recounting of the fight, published in the online article "Wong Shun Leung — The Death of Bruce Lee."

35. "He then ran towards me. I kicked again, but this time, I kicked at his chest. He was hurt. He looked bad. He did not make any sound." Wong Shun Leung quoting Bruce Lee's recounting of the fight, published in the online article "Wong Shun Leung — The Death of Bruce Lee."

36. Wong Shun Leung quoting Bruce Lee's recounting of the fight, published in the online article "Wong Shun Leung — The Death of Bruce Lee."

37. "And then Robert Wall. You know Robert Wall? He goes, 'Hey, me, me come in.'" Bolo Yeung interview with the author, November 1993.

38. "And then Robert Wall with a sidekick — boom!" Bolo Yeung interview with the author, November 1993.

39. "Bruce Lee only used a little bit of power, but Robert Wall used a lot." Bolo Yeung interview with the author, November 1993.

40. "[Bob Wall said:] 'Come on!' Once again, sidekick — boom! Robert Wall kicked this guy." Bolo Yeung interview with the author, November 1993.

41. "Bruce Lee is sit down." Bolo Yeung interview with the author, November 1993.

42. "And some people tell him [Bruce] he [broke the guy's] ribs." Bolo Yeung interview with the author, November 1993. Henry Wong confirmed that the young man's ribs were broken, but he believed it was a result of one of Bruce's kicks (rather than Bob Wall's): "They fight. Not long. Bruce broke the extra's rib." Henry Wong quoted in Clouse, Robert, *The Making of Enter the Dragon*, p. 160.

43. "Bruce gave him money to go see doctor. Give mother $20,000 (HK) which was $4,000 (US). I know — I was there. Give money to mother. She take to hospital." Henry Wong quoted in Clouse, Robert, *The Making of Enter the Dragon*, p. 160. Bolo confirms that the extra was taken to the hospital: "So, he go to hospital." Bolo Yeung interview with the author, November 1993.

44. "Bruce want my film. Get rid of it. I say I have to get it to lab. Part of things I shot that day." Henry Wong quoted in Clouse, Robert, *The Making of Enter the Dragon*, p. 160.

45. "Later sent all film to Warner Bros. All gone. When Bruce die Golden Harvest call me, ask where all film was. 'How much dollars you want,' they say? 'You tell what you want.' I say 'I am sorry, but do not have the film. All gone.'" Henry Wong quoted in Clouse, Robert, *The Making of Enter the Dragon*, p. 160.

46. Madalena Chan and Henry Wong quoted from the video "Actor Challenged Bruce Lee on the SET of *Enter the Dragon* . . . NEW STORY!" at youtube.com /watch?v=ulRwj7dXuA8.

47. Madalena Chan quoted from the video "Actor Challenged Bruce Lee on the SET of *Enter the Dragon* . . . NEW STORY!"

48. "So, the kid did, right? Of course, he never pushed Bruce out of the ring. And then Bruce said, 'Okay. My turn.' So, he tells the kid, 'Okay, I'm going to hit you right here [gesturing to the left side of the kid's face].' And Bruce says, 'Are you ready?' And the kid says, 'What do you mean ready?' Before he said anything [completed his sentence] his teeth got fallen out of the mouth — so fast." Madalena Chan quoted from the video "Actor Challenged Bruce Lee on the SET of *Enter the Dragon* . . . NEW STORY!"

49. Robert Clouse quoted from Clouse, Robert, *The Making of Enter the Dragon*, p. 134.

50. Jim Kelly quoted from the article "No Business Like Show Business," *Fighting Stars*, Vol. 1, No. 1, October 1973, p. 31.

51. The extra actually had a point here — but for the wrong reason. In one or two instances, Gil Hubbs, the cinematographer for the film, did need to speed up the camera, but only so that Bruce's moves would register on film. According to director Robert Clouse: "I have been asked many times if Bruce was really as fast as people claimed. All I can say is he had the fastest reflexes I've ever seen. In one shot, Bruce was supposed to be in a stand-off with Bob Wall. In order to see his hand lash out and hit Bob, we had to speed the camera to 32 frames. At normal speed it didn't show on film." Clouse, Robert, *The Making of Enter the Dragon*, p. 136.

52. Andre Morgan, quoted in Dennis, Felix, and Atyeo, Don, *Bruce Lee: King of Kung Fu*, p. 27.

53. "The long-haired actor had challenged Lee to show him his boxing style. He had been watching the superstar making the movie *Enter the Dragon*. This film is Lee's first attempt at an international release. According to reliable sources, the youth leapt from the sidelines and challenged Lee to a fight." From the newspaper article "Superstar is Challenged, so . . . Bruce Floors Actor" by Christine Chow, *The Star* (Hong Kong), March 16, 1973. See also: "According to witnesses, the man aged about 20, appeared suddenly on the set. He told Lee he had seen Lee perform a lot of Jeet Kune Do, a form of martial art, on the screen and wanted to see it in real life." From the newspaper article "Bruce Just Too Good," published in the *China Mail*, March 16, 1973.

54. Linda Lee quoted from the article "A Candid Interview with Mrs. Bruce Lee."

55. "Bruce Lee was sitting down. And then [the extra] said, 'What is Jeet Kune Do?' Then Bruce Lee say, 'You want to see?' He [the stuntman] say, 'Yes. I want to see!'" Bolo Yeung interview with the author, November 1993.

56. "Putting aside his beloved chrysanthemum tea, Bruce would eventually call the loud one over. Bruce would never begin the encounter, but would ask the fellow if he knew anything about Jeet Kune Do. The fighter would grin back at the mob of his buddies and say that he knew as much as he needed to know." Clouse, Robert, *The Making of Enter the Dragon*, p. 134.

57. "And [Bruce said], 'Come here.'" Bolo Yeung interview with the author, November 1993.

58. "And some guy said 'You are fast but you have no power!' But he was fast and he had the power." Bolo Yeung interview with the author, November 1993.

59. "The witness said the man sneered when Lee set himself in a stance — and that was too much for the actor." From the newspaper article "Bruce Just Too Good," *China Mail*, March 16, 1973.

60. Andre Morgan quoted in Dennis, Felix, and Atyeo, Don, *Bruce Lee: King of Kung Fu*, p. 27.

61. "Bruce sort of played with him like a cat with a mouse." Andre Morgan, quoted in Dennis, Felix, and Atyeo, Don, *Bruce Lee: King of Kung Fu*, p. 27.

62. Clouse, Robert, *The Making of Enter the Dragon*, p. 134.

63. "Lee, angered at the youth's challenge, swung his fists at him and badly cut his mouth." From the newspaper article "Superstar Is Challenged, so . . . Bruce Floors Actor" by Christine Chow, *The Star* (Hong Kong), March 16, 1973.

64. "The kid wouldn't sit down and he tried to kick Bruce in the face." Andre Morgan, quoted in Dennis, Felix, and Atyeo, Don, *Bruce Lee: King of Kung Fu*, p. 27.

65. "Bruce wouldn't move as the kick would invariably fall short." Clouse, Robert, *The Making of Enter the Dragon*, p. 136.

66. "Bruce lost his temper, just for a second, and smashed the kid in the mouth one good one with his foot . . . not hard, just enough to cut his lip and let him know the game was over." Andre Morgan, quoted in Dennis, Felix, and Atyeo, Don, *Bruce Lee: King of Kung Fu*, p. 27; "He [Bruce Lee] floored a young man with a kick after the man had challenged his ability at the martial arts. . . . He lashed out with a kick and the man fell." From the newspaper article "Bruce Just Too Good," *China Mail*, March 16, 1973.

67. "Bruce did one swift kick and the guy's teeth went flying and the fight was over." David Friedman, the on-set photographer for Warner Bros., quoted from the online interview "Dave Friedman: Filming the Dragon" by Mark Edward Harris at bandwmag.com/articles/dave-friedman-filming-the-dragon.

68. "He followed up with a kick which sent the youth sprawling on the ground, almost unconscious." From the newspaper article "Superstar Is Challenged, so . . . Bruce Floors Actor" by Christine Chow, *The Star* (Hong Kong), March 16, 1973.

69. From the newspaper article "Superstar Is Challenged, so . . . Bruce Floors Actor" by Christine Chow, *The Star* (Hong Kong), March 16, 1973.

70. From the newspaper article "Bruce Just Too Good," *China Mail*, March 16, 1973.

71. Raymond Chow quoted from the newspaper article "Superstar Is Challenged, so . . . Bruce Floors Actor" by Christine Chow, *The Star* (Hong Kong), March 16, 1973.

72. Andre Morgan interview with the author, September 1994.

73. "The next day the guy was found floating in Victoria Harbor . . . that's what I'm told. That was just hearsay. One thing for sure. That extra didn't show up for work anymore." David Friedman quoted from the online interview "Dave Friedman: Filming the Dragon."

74. "Somebody stabbed him to death." Mitoshi Uyehara interview with the author, 1994.

75. "Bruce told me [that] the next day the guy got stabbed. I said, 'how come?' He said because Bruce was sort of like a hero, and when this guy challenged him it was like he put down [their] hero, right? And he said some gang jumped on him that night or the following day. And he heard that the kid got killed." Mitoshi Uyehara interview with the author, 1994.

CHAPTER EIGHTEEN: THE FINAL MATCH

1. "About two months before he died he gave me a phone call. He wanted to come to my institute and take some photographs. That was a Sunday. My family had stayed in the house for a week and they needed to go out for an excursion, so I refused his suggestion." Wong Shun Leung quoted from the online article "Bruce Lee and His Friendship with Wong Shun Leung."

2. Wong Shun Leung quoted from the online article "Bruce Lee and His Friendship with Wong Shun Leung."

3. "[Bruce Lee] called me up and wanted me to participate in the making of *The Game of Death*." Wong Shun Leung quoted from the online article "Bruce Lee and His Friendship with Wong Shun Leung."

4. "[Bruce Lee] had also invited me to the studio to attend a screen test." Wong Shun Leung quoted from the online article "Bruce Lee and His Friendship with Wong Shun Leung."

5. To wit: Bruce had used trapping and vertical fist striking against Robert Baker in their battle in *Fist of Fury*; he did likewise against Chuck Norris during their fight sequence in *The Way of the Dragon*; and had employed the techniques of slapping hand (*pak sao*) and pulling hand (*lop sau*) against Bob Wall (as well as against certain of the guards in his battle in the cavern sequence) in *Enter the Dragon*.

6. "I did not promise to act in the film, yet I still went to attend the screen test to please him." Wong Shun Leung quoted from the online article "Bruce Lee and His Friendship with Wong Shun Leung."

7. "I brought along a student named Wan on my trip to the studio." Wong Shun Leung quoted from the online article "Bruce Lee and His Friendship with Wong Shun Leung."

8. Wong Shun Leung quoted from the online article "Bruce Lee and His Friendship with Wong Shun Leung."

9. Wong Shun Leung quoted from the online article "Bruce Lee and His Friendship with Wong Shun Leung."

10. Wong Shun Leung quoted from the online article "Bruce Lee and His Friendship with Wong Shun Leung."

11. "I really hoped that the dull look in his eyes was the result of overwork, but I was only explaining it away. I could not wipe away the unlucky feeling. Owing to the fact that his situation might get worse if he knew it, I did not tell him about it." Wong Shun Leung quoted from the online article "Bruce Lee and His Friendship with Wong Shun Leung."

12. "As for the fact that he didn't show up for Sifu's [Yip Man's] funeral, this was definitely a breach in terms of the decorum of the martial arts world. I think people can't forget their 'roots.' After all, even if you break off on your own and start a great new martial art of your own, you'll never forget the foundations you built with your teachers." Wong Shun Leung's statement in the Hong Kong press as presented in Li, Paul, *From Limited to Limitless: The Ways of Bruce Lee*, p. 112.

13. "Here it is: if you can move with your tools from any angle, then you can adapt to whatever the object is in front of you. And the clumsier, the more limited the object, the easier for you to pot-shot it. That's what it amounts to." Bruce Lee quoted from a dialogue he had with his student Daniel Lee over the phone in 1971 that was recorded by Daniel Lee.

14. Wan Kam Leung quoted from an interview on the Hong Kong radio program *Dragon Seeks Its Path*. Transcript at tapatalk.com/groups/bruceleelivestributeforum/wan-kam-leung-interview-t3707.html. See also: "About two or three months before he died, I had paid Bruce a visit. We discussed and compared the results of our researches on Kung Fu in Bruce's study." Wong Shun Leung quoted from the online article "Bruce Lee and His Friendship with Wong Shun Leung."

15. Wong and Lee's dialogue quoted in the online article "Bruce Lee and His Friendship with Wong Shun Leung."

16. "Being good in gung fu does not mean adding more but to be able to get off with sophistication and ornamentation and be simply simple — like a sculptor building a statue, not by adding, but by hacking away the unessential so that the truth will be revealed unobstructed — artlessness." Bruce Lee quoted from *Jeet Kune Do: Bruce Lee's Commentaries on the Martial Way*, p. 255. See also: "It's not daily increase but daily decrease — hack away the unessential!" Bruce Lee quoted from his essay "What It All Amounts To," published in Lee, Bruce, and Little, John (editor), *The Tao of Gung Fu*, p. 173.

17. Wong Shun Leung and Bruce Lee's dialogue as reported by Wan Kam Leung, quoted from his interview on the Hong Kong radio program *Dragon Seeks Its Path*.

18. "There's also an air-pressure booster where you punch and the air cushion will bounce back instantly. It's really an eye-opener for me." Wan Kam Leung,

quoted from his interview on the Hong Kong radio program *Dragon Seeks Its Path.*

19. Wan Kam Leung, quoted from his interview on the Hong Kong radio program *Dragon Seeks Its Path.*

20. Wong Shun Leung quoting Bruce Lee in the article "The Death of Bruce Lee" by Wong Shun Leung, available online at vingtsunserbia.wordpress.com/about /articles/wong-shun-leung-the-death-of-bruce-lee/.

21. Wong Shun Leung quoting Bruce Lee in the article "The Death of Bruce Lee."

22. Wong Shun Leung quoting Bruce Lee in the article "The Death of Bruce Lee."

23. "In telling me these two events, Bruce's aim was to prove that he would fight with anybody at any time. He was like a wounded beast. He did not have to care about any other thing." Wong Shun Leung quoting Bruce Lee in the article "The Death of Bruce Lee."

24. "It all started when Bruce asked my Sifu about his opinion on his kick. Sifu commented that Bruce retreated his hands/legs quicker than his punches/kicks. Bruce denied and claimed that both his punches/kicks hit and retreated equally fast. So, the two martial arts fanatics started to 'Gong Sau' (talking hand)." Wan Kam Leung, quoted from his interview on the Hong Kong radio program *Dragon Seeks Its Path.*

25. Bruce Lee and Wong Shun Leung's dialogue as reported by Wong Shun Leung in the online article "Bruce Lee and His Friendship with Wong Shun Leung."

26. "To show respect, Bruce reserved his real ability to avoid hurting Sifu." Wan Kam Leung, quoted from his interview on the Hong Kong radio program *Dragon Seeks Its Path.*

27. ". . . it was an exciting sparring match and very realistic, but they stopped whenever someone might get seriously hurt and re-started again and again." Wan Kam Leung quoted from the documentary *Wong Shun Leung: The King of Talking Hands.*

28. "Sifu was wearing a yellow long sleeve Montagut shirt and Bruce was bare-chested and dressed in a track pant. This gave him more freedom to move and execute his punches and kicks flexibly." Wan Kam Leung, quoted from his interview on the Hong Kong radio program *Dragon Seeks Its Path.*

29. "[Bruce's muscles were] toned and shapely carved." Wan Kam Leung, quoted from his interview on the Hong Kong radio program *Dragon Seeks Its Path.*

30. Unless otherwise indicated, the account of the sparring match between Wong Shun Leung and Bruce Lee is drawn from Wong Shun Leung's account in the online article "Bruce Lee and His Friendship with Wong Shun Leung."

31. This is precisely the means of attack (Attack By Drawing) that Bruce had incorporated into his Jeet Kune Do arsenal for this very purpose: "The attack by drawing is an attack or counterattack initiated upon luring the opponent into a commitment by leaving him an apparent opening or executing movements that he may try to time and counter. . . . It's usually best, whenever possible, to draw your opponent into leading before hitting out on your own account. By forcing

your opponent to commit himself to a decided step, you can be moderately certain of what he is about to do. His commitment will deprive him of the ability to change his position and guard swiftly enough to deal successfully with any offensive you may yourself adopt." Lee, Bruce, *The Tao of Jeet Kune Do*, Ohara Publications, Santa Clarita, California, 1975, p. 199.

32. Wan Kam Leung, quoted from his interview on the Hong Kong radio program *Dragon Seeks Its Path*.

33. Wan Kam Leung, quoted from his interview on the Hong Kong radio program *Dragon Seeks Its Path*.

34. Wan Kam Leung, quoted from his interview on the Hong Kong radio program *Dragon Seeks Its Path*. See also: "Bruce Lee's kicks were lightning fast, heavy and aggressive . . . Sifu's footwork, hand techniques, timing and the way in which he would take angles was very sharp." Wan Kam Leung quoted from the documentary *Wong Shun Leung: The King of Talking Hands*.

35. Wong Shun Leung and Bruce Lee's actions as reported by Wan Kam Leung, quoted from his interview on the Hong Kong radio program *Dragon Seeks Its Path*.

36. Wong Shun Leung and Bruce Lee's actions as reported by Wan Kam Leung, quoted from his interview on the Hong Kong radio program *Dragon Seeks Its Path*.

37. "Then both continued to squabble in a jovial manner. In fact, Bruce still respected Sifu very much." Wong Shun Leung and Bruce Lee's actions as reported by Wan Kam Leung, quoted from his interview on the Hong Kong radio program *Dragon Seeks Its Path*.

38. "I witnessed my Sifu, Wong Shun Leung, beimo with Bruce Lee in his house." Wan Kam Leung quoted from the documentary *Wong Shun Leung: The King of Talking Hands*.

39. Wan Kam Leung, quoted from his interview on the Hong Kong radio program *Dragon Seeks Its Path*. See also: "If I really had to pick a winner, I would say Bruce won. To be honest, if Bruce used all his strength to hit my master, there is no way he would not collapse. His legs were really powerful. I don't think there is anyone that can endure one of his kicks." Wan Kam Leung quoted in Polly, Matthew, *Bruce Lee: A Life*, pp. 806–810.

40. "Bruce told Sifu: 'You cannot stand still. If you intend to move, the heels must leave the ground and then the steps will become nimble. Once the heels are not fixed to the ground, you'd have a greater mobility and your movement would be faster. However, once you are getting ready to fight, your heel should then avoid leaving the ground because your body will be *floating* if your heels leave the ground. And if so, even [if] your punch has landed on your opponent, the destructive power will be much reduced.' What Bruce said really made a lot of sense to me. I learnt from their sparring and was inspired by Bruce's words." Wan Kam Leung, quoted from his interview on the Hong Kong radio program *Dragon Seeks Its Path*.

41. "[Sifu] quite agreed with Bruce's point of view. Since Sifu's 'turning horse' was also not turning his heels, but instead was using the center line to turn his toes and feet, this restricted and slowed down his movement. Thus, he accepted Bruce's advice and from then onwards, he adapted to this new change." Wan Kam Leung, quoted from his interview on the Hong Kong radio program *Dragon Seeks Its Path*.

42. Wan Kam Leung, quoted from his interview on the Hong Kong radio program *Dragon Seeks Its Path*.

43. "Undeniably, my Sifu [Wong Shun Leung] said that Bruce Lee, after going overseas and returning to Hong Kong, his martial arts insight inspired my Sifu, too. So, they, mutually, how you say, taught, learned and both grew." Cliff Au Yeung quoted from the video "Cliff Au Yeung on Bruce Lee and Wong Shun Leung's Relationship (English Subtitled)" at youtube.com/watch?v=OfRJkMuQSWw.

44. Both Lee and Wong came to embrace the viewpoint that one's art should not limit or otherwise bind the individual practitioner: "A style should never be considered gospel truth, the laws and principles of which can never be violated. Man, the living, creating individual, is always more important than any established style." Bruce Lee quoted from his article "Liberate Yourself from Classical Karate," published in *Black Belt*, September 1971. "As long as the art remains logical, it doesn't matter what you call it, and it doesn't matter if what you're doing isn't 'Wing Chun' as such. If it's logical, if it works, then you can use it to make your art your slave, not your master." Wong Shun Leung quoted from the article "Bruce Lee's Teacher" by Bey Logan, *Combat*, Vol. 12, No. 9, August 1986.

45. "Bruce and my master shook hands after the coffee and Bruce told him he should come visit him again when he was free." Wan Kam Leung quoted in Polly, Matthew, *Bruce Lee: A Life*, p. 806.

46. Wan Kam Leung, quoted from his interview on the Hong Kong radio program *Dragon Seeks Its Path*. See also: "After we got back to the studio, my master took off his shirt and I had to massage him with some Chinese herbal ointment. His arms were black-and-blue. Good thing my master wore a long-sleeve shirt so Bruce couldn't see his bruises." Wan Kam Leung quoted in Polly, Matthew, *Bruce Lee: A Life*, pp. 806–810. See also: "After the beimo, we went back to Sifu's school where Sifu then showed me his upper arm . . . it was covered in bruises, caused by defending against Bruce Lee's kicks, so I helped Sifu by rubbing Dit Dar Jau [traditional bruise medicine] on his injuries, but I didn't tell anyone the story about how I helped Sifu apply the Dit Dar Jau." Wan Kam Leung quoted from the documentary *Wong Shun Leung: The King of Talking Hands*.

EPILOGUE

1. "Forensic pathologist Michael Hunter believes Lee suffered from an 'adrenal crisis' thanks to an overdose of cortisone, which Lee took for back pain." "How Did Bruce Lee Die? Inside the Icon's Death and Final Moments" at factinate.com/editorial /how-did-bruce-lee-die/. See also: "Autopsy: The Last Hours of Bruce Lee" at

podcasts.apple.com/gb/podcast/the-last-hours-of-bruce-lee/id1484888427 ?i=1000539633008.

2. "Bruce Lee Died of Heatstroke, Book Claims" at dailytelegraph.com.au/news /nsw/bruce-lee-died-of-heatstroke-book-claims/news-story/30c31527a46aafb 9fbfd6fb38398c599. See also: "Most recently, author Matthew Polly determined that, following the surgical removal of Lee's sweat glands in 1972 to prevent unsightly sweating on camera, the intensely physical actor likely suffered a deadly heat stroke." From the online article "How Did Bruce Lee Die? Inside the Icon's Death and Final Moments."

3. "Bruce Lee Likely 'Died from Drinking Too Much Water': Doctors" at national post.com/news/world/bruce-lee-died-from-drinking-too-much-water.

4. "Epilepsy Could Solve Mystery of Kung Fu Legend's Death" at theguardian .com/science/2006/feb/25/film.filmnews.

5. "Bruce Lee: The Mystery Surrounding the Martial Artist's Death" by Rachel Chang at biography.com/news/bruce-lee-death-mystery. See also: "Professor R.D. Teare, professor of forensic medicine at the University of London. . . . decided that the edema had been caused by hypersensitivity to either meprobamate or aspirin, or a combination of the two, two of the compounds in Equagesic [the headache drug that Bruce took on the day he died]. However unusual this might be — and cases were rare — this was the only feasible solution. The view was accepted by the jury and a verdict of misadventure returned." Lee, Linda, *Bruce Lee: The Man Only I Knew*, pp. 202–203.

6. "He told me he had just been offered a million dollars for a film to be produced by Dino De Laurentiis [on behalf of Italy's Titanus Studios]." Stirling Silliphant quoted from the article "Up Close & Personal with Stirling Silliphant," by John Corcoran, *Kick*, October 1980, p. 54.

7. "At that time, there were numerous people (i.e. agents) who pleaded with Bruce to make movies for the companies they represented so that they could earn great commissions. Like Andrew Vajna; Bruce would often go to his office for script discussions and producer, Carlo Ponti (husband of Sophia Loren then) would be in Andrew Vajna's office to persuade Bruce to make a movie for his Italian company." Robert Chan interview published in Chang, Chaplin, *Bruce Lee — The Man That They Knew*, Hong Kong, 2013. See also: "After the production of *Enter the Dragon* I asked Bruce why he did not return to Hong Kong as before to prepare his following films. He answered, 'That's enough for Hong Kong. My next aim will be Italy.' He said he would cooperate with Sophia Loren's husband, an outstanding Italian film producer. . . . Mr. Carlo Ponti invited Bruce to act in his film. The content of that film was a mixture of an Eastern Kung Fu expert and Western civilization. Bruce had studied carefully the scenario." Bruce Lee's mother Grace Lee quoted from "An Interview with Bruce Lee's Mother," published in *Bruce Lee: The Fighting Spirit* magazine, Bruce Lee Jeet Kune Do Club, Hong Kong, 1978, p. 62.

8. Dennis, Felix, and Atyeo, Don, *Bruce Lee: King of Kung Fu*, p. 71.

9. "One day he asked me, he said, 'Would you like to come to Run Run Shaw's studio? Run Run Shaw wants me to do a film for him.' He said, 'Why don't you take your wife, I'll take Linda, and we'll go.' And Run Run Shaw sent a Bentley or something over. And Run Run Shaw was courting him a great deal you know. But I remember his attitude was, Run Run was offering him half a mil, and he said, 'Why should I do a film for half a mil? If Marlon Brando can get two mil, I can.' [Rolls his eyes.] Okay. This was a lotta money in those days." John Saxon interview with the author, March 22, 1996.

10. Interview with Andy Vajna: "We were in negotiations about a multi-film project and signed a contract that he would get my house if he engaged in a few movies for me, but unfortunately he died soon after," mandiner.hu/cikk/20120806_andy _vajna_mindent_el_lehet_intezni.

11. Dennis, Felix, and Atyeo, Don, *Bruce Lee: King of Kung Fu*, p. 71.

12. Bruce Lee letter to his attorney, Adrian Marshall, July 20, 1973, published in *Muscle & Fitness*, March 1994.

13. "I talked to Bruce on the phone twice to try to convince him to do *The Silent Flute*. Jimmy Coburn even flew to Hong Kong to talk to him about it. But we couldn't persuade him to do the film. He felt it was behind him, something in his past." Stirling Silliphant quoted in the article "Up Close & Personal with Stirling Silliphant," by John Corcoran, *Kick*, October 1980, p. 55. See also: "Spoke to Stirling, and I told him that between you and him I'll thrust our silent flute in your hands." Bruce Lee's letter to James Coburn, June 13, 1973, published in Little, John (editor), *Bruce Lee: Letters of the Dragon*, p. 350.

14. "I had reached the point of feeling the film might never be done until the night I came from a screening of *Enter the Dragon* with Sy Weintraub. Sy also knew Bruce and had studied with him. Sy said to me, 'You've got to get Bruce and you back together again. You must do *The Silent Flute*.' Sy believed in the film. As you know, Jimmy Coburn and Bruce Lee and I had worked on the script well over a year together. It was actually Bruce's film. It was his very spirit. So Sy called Bruce on a Tuesday or Wednesday, and made a date for us to fly out Friday of that week to spend the weekend with Bruce in Hong Kong to discuss what we needed to do to put him and *The Silent Flute* back together again. Bruce had agreed to that meeting. The day before we would have flown out — he died." Stirling Silliphant quoted in the article "Up Close & Personal with Stirling Silliphant," by John Corcoran, *Kick*, October 1980, p. 55. See also: "By the way, Sy Weintraub had just called and will be flying here to H.K., supposedly to have devised a super plan for me." Bruce Lee letter to his attorney, Adrian Marshall, July 20, 1973, published in *Muscle & Fitness*, March 1994.

15. "I, Bruce Lee, will be the first highest paid Oriental super star in the United States. . . . Starting 1970, I will achieve world fame and from then onward till the end of 1980 I will have in my possession $10,000,000." Bruce Lee's handwritten goal entitled "My Definite Chief Aim," January 1969, qz.com/932799/bruce-lee -achieved-all-his-life-goals-by-32-by-committing-to-one-personality-trait.

16. Mitoshi Uyehara interview with the author, 1994.
17. Muhammad Ali interview with the author, April 25, 1994.
18. Roberto Duran interview with the author, April 19, 1994.
19. George Foreman quoted in the online article "George Foreman: Bruce Lee Could've Been a World Champion Boxer" at boxingdaily.com/boxing-news/george-foreman-bruce-lee-couldve-been-a-world-champion-boxer/.
20. Sugar Ray Leonard quoted from the online article "What Sugar Ray Took from Bruce Lee" at wingchunnews.ca/what-sugar-ray-took-from-bruce-lee-2/.
21. Leo Fong interview with the author, June 1994.
22. James DeMile quoted from the video "Bruce Lee VS Pro Fighters."
23. Ed Hart interview with the author, August 1993.
24. Don Wilson quoted from the article "The Fine Art of the Fight Scene," *Martial Arts Legends*, January 1993.
25. Benny Urquidez quoted in the article "Benny the Jet," *Fighting Stars*, April 1978.
26. Larry Hartsell interview with the author, July 12, 1994.
27. Chan Wai Man quoted from an interview in *Martial Arts Illustrated*, republished online at tapatalk.com/groups/bruceleelivestributeforum/90s-chan-wai-man-interview-t4554.html.
28. Chuck Norris quoted from *Deadly Hands of Kung Fu*, January 1976.
29. Mike Stone quoted from the article "Bruce Lee Touched the Lives of the Greats," published in *Black Belt Magazine's Best of Bruce Lee #2*, Rainbow Publications, Burbank, California, 1975, p. 52.
30. Joe Lewis interview with the author, June 1993.
31. Ernest Lieb quoted from the essay "An Objective Evaluation of the Combative Skill of Bruce Lee by Those Who Know What It Is," Little, John (editor), *Bruce Lee: Artist of Life*, pp. 478–479.
32. Louis Delgado quoted in the article "Kata: Karate's Better Half" by Pat Alston, *Black Belt*, November 1969, p. 27.
33. Fred Wren quoted from the essay "An Objective Evaluation of the Combative Skill of Bruce Lee by Those Who Know What It Is," Little, John (editor), *Bruce Lee: Artist of Life*, pp. 482–483.
34. Jim Kelly quoted from the article "Whatever Happened to Jim Kelly?" by David W. Clary, *Black Belt*, May 1992.
35. Bob Wall interview with the author, August 1993.
36. Conor McGregor quoted from the online article "Conor McGregor Claimed Bruce Lee Could Have Been a 'World Champion in MMA'" at sportbible.com/ufc/news-legends-conor-mcgregor-claimed-bruce-lee-could-have-been-an-mma-world-champion-20200110.
37. Georges St-Pierre quoted from the article "UFC's Georges St-Pierre Says Bruce Lee Changed His Life — 'I Won a Lot of Fights from What He Taught Me'" at scmp.com/sport/martial-arts/mixed-martial-arts/article/3087905/ufcs-georges-st-pierre-says-bruce-lee-changed.

38. Kenny Florian quoted from the online article "The MMA World Pays Tribute to Bruce Lee 40 Years after His Death" by Michael Stets at bleacherreport.com /articles/1710603-the-mma-world-pays-tribute-to-bruce-lee-40-years-after-his -death.

39. Anderson Silva quoted from the online article "Anderson Silva Talks God, Training, Bruce Lee and Life After Fighting" at google.ca/amp/s/lowkickmma.com/anderson -silva-talks-god-training-bruce-lee-and-life-after-fighting-17132/%3famp.

40. Eddie Bravo quoted in the online article "Eddie Bravo Became a Jiu Jitsu Legend with One Win. Can His Fighting Style Now Conquer MMA?" by Josh Chesler at ocweekly.com/eddie-bravo-became-a-jiu-jitsu-legend-with-one-win -can-his-fighting-style-now-conquer-mma-6483814/.

41. Rickson Grace quoted in the online article "Rickson Gracie on If Bruce Lee Was Legit" at bjjee.com/articles/rickson-gracie-on-if-bruce-lee-was-legit/, and Rickson Gracie quoted in the article "Rickson Gracie: The Ultimate Gracie Fighter — Undefeated and on a Roll," *Full Contact*, December 1994.

42. Roy Nelson quoted from the online article "The MMA World Pays Tribute to Bruce Lee 40 Years after His Death."

43. Michelle Waterson quoted from the online article "The MMA World Pays Tribute to Bruce Lee 40 Years after His Death."

44. Scott Coker quoted from the online article "The MMA World Pays Tribute to Bruce Lee 40 Years after His Death."

45. Dana White quoted from the online article "Dana White Calls Bruce Lee the Father of MMA but He Actually Rejected the Style" by Bob Garcia at sportscasting.com/dana-white-calls-bruce-lee-the-father-of-mma-but-he -actually-rejected-the-style/.

46. Hayward Nishioka interview with the author, July 1994.

47. Gene LeBell interview with the author, August 1993.

48. Wally Jay interview with the author, September 1993.

49. Jesse Glover interview with the author, September 1993.

BIBLIOGRAPHY

INTERVIEWS
Alex Richter (September 3, 2021)
Allen Joe (April 1994)
Andre Morgan (September 1994)
Dr. Anthony Drohomyrecky (June 22, 2021)
Blake Edwards (April 8, 1996)
Bob Wall (July 1993)
Bolo Yeung (November 1993)
David Peterson (September 15, 2012)
Doug Palmer (August 2, 1993)
Dr. Burt Seidler (June 11, 1998)
Ed Hart (August 1993)
Gene LeBell (August 1993)
George Lee (March 1994)
Hayward Nishioka (December 1993)
Herb Jackson (June 1993)
Jesse Glover (September 1993)
Jhoon Rhee (August 1993)
Joe Lewis (July 1993)
John Saxon (March 22, 1996)
Jon Benn (December 1994)
Kareem Abdul-Jabbar (August 1993)
Larry Hartsell (July 12, 1994)
Leo Fong (June 1994)
Linda Lee Cadwell (July 1993)
Mark Komuro (1996)
Mitoshi Uyehara (1994)
Muhammad Ali (April 25, 1994)
Raymond Chow (June 12, 1996)
Richard Bustillo (June 1994)
Robert Lee (June 5, 1996)

Roberto Duran (April 19, 1994)
Skip Ellsworth (August 1993)
Taky Kimura (1994)
Ted Wong (June 1, 1993)
Wally Jay (September 1993)
Yip Chun (August 12, 2009)

FACEBOOK MESSAGES

Alex Richter to the author, September 3, 2021.
Leo Fong to the author, August 12, 2021.
Steve Golden to the author, September 16, 2021.

MAGAZINES

Black Belt: November 1967; 1968 Yearbook; November 1969; 1969 Yearbook;
    September 1971; September 1972; August 1974; January 1979; July 1982.
Combat, May 1995.
Deadly Hands of Kung Fu, January 1976.
Fighting Stars: Vol. 1, No. 1, October 1973; October 1976; April 1978; August 1983.
Full Contact, December 1994.
Inside Kung Fu: September 1985; January 1991; March 1994.
Kick, October 1980.
Martial Arts Legends, January 1993.
Muscle & Fitness, March 1994.
Official Karate, July 1980.
Penthouse: February 1983; March 1983.
Professional Karate, Summer 1974.

SPECIAL PUBLICATIONS

The Best of Bruce Lee magazine, Rainbow Publications, Los Angeles, 1974.
The Bruce Lee Memorial Issue, Rainbow Publications, Los Angeles, 1974.
Black Belt Magazine's Best of Bruce Lee #2, Rainbow Publications, Burbank, California,
    1975.
Bruce Lee: Studies on Jeet Kune Do, Bruce Lee Jeet Kune Do Club, Hong Kong,
    1976.
Bruce Lee: His Unknowns in Martial Arts Learning, Bruce Lee Jeet Kune Do Club,
    Hong Kong, 1977.
Reminiscence of Bruce Lee, Wong Shun Leung, Bruce Lee Jeet Kune Do Club,
    Hong Kong, 1978.
Bruce Lee: The Fighting Spirit magazine, Bruce Lee Jeet Kune Do Club, Hong
    Kong, 1978.
Bruce Lee: Superstar from Hong Kong, Bruce Lee Jeet Kune Do Club, Hong Kong, 1980.

Mystery of Bruce Lee, Bruce Lee Jeet Kune Do Club, Hong Kong, 1980.
Knowing Is Not Enough: The Official Newsletter of Jun Fan Jeet Kune Do / Bruce Lee Educational Foundation, Spring 1999, Vol. 3, No. 1.

NEWSPAPERS
Hong Kong

Hong Kong newspaper article on inter-school boxing match (name of paper unknown), March 30, 1958.
China Mail, November 19, 1971.
Hong Kong Star, November 1971.
Hong Kong Standard, February 10, 1973.
The Star, March 16, 1973.
China Mail, March 16, 1973.
The Star, March 17, 1973.

Singapore

New Nation (Singapore), August 14, 1972.
New Nation (Singapore), August 15, 1972.

America

Chinese Pacific Weekly, November 26, 1964.
Chinese Pacific Weekly, December 17, 1964.
Chinese Pacific Weekly, January 7, 1965.
Chinese Pacific Weekly, January 14, 1965.
Chinese Pacific Weekly, January 28, 1965.
Seattle Post-Intelligencer (sports section), December 31, 1966.
Seattle Times, 1967.
St. Paul Dispatch, July 18, 1968.
Charlotte, North Carolina newspaper, October 24, 1969.
Miami Beach Sun, October 24, 1969.
Washington Star (Sportweek section), August 16, 1970.

BOOKS AND ARTICLES

Bax, Paul, *Disciples of the Dragon: Reflections from the Students of Bruce Lee*, first edition, Outskirts Press, Inc., Denver, 2008.
Bax, Paul, and Steve Smith, *Disciple of the Dragon: Reflections of Bruce Lee's Student, Jesse Glover (Disciples of the Dragon Book 2)*, self-published, Amazon Publishing, 2019, Kindle edition.
Block, Alex Ben, *The Legend of Bruce Lee*, Dell Publishing Co., Inc., New York, 1974.
Chan, Shun-hing, and Beatrice Leung, *Changing Church and State Relations in Hong Kong, 1950–2000*, HK University Press, Hong Kong, 2003.

Chang, Chaplin, *Bruce Lee — The Man That They Knew*, Hong Kong, 2013.

Chun, Yip, *116 Wing Tsun Dummy Techniques as Demonstrated by Grandmaster Yip Man*, technical advisor Leung Ting, Leung Ting Publication & Distribution, Hong Kong, 1981.

Chwoon, Tan Hoo, *Bruce Lee in His Greatest Movie: The Orphan*, Noel B Caros Productions, Singapore, 1998.

Clausnitzer, Rolf, *My Wing Chun Kung Fu Journey: From Bruce Lee to Wong Shun Leung*, self-published, Amazon Publishing, 2020, Kindle edition.

Clouse, Robert, *The Making of Enter the Dragon*, Unique Publications, Burbank, California, 1987.

Cowles, Joseph, *Wu Wei Gung Fu*, self-published, circa 1981.

Dennis, Felix, and Don Atyeo, *Bruce Lee: King of Kung Fu*, Straight Arrow Books, San Francisco, 1974.

Inosanto, Dan, and Alan Sutton, *Jeet Kune Do: The Art and Philosophy of Bruce Lee*, Know Now Publishing Company, Los Angeles, California, 1976.

Glover, Jesse, *Bruce Lee: Between Wing Chun and Jeet Kune Do*, Glover Publications, 1976.

Glover, Jesse R., *Bruce Lee's Non-Classical Gung Fu*, Glover Publications, Seattle, 1978.

Gunaratna, Henepola, *The Four Foundations of Mindfulness in Plain English*, Wisdom Publications, Somerville, Massachusetts, 2012.

Ing, Ken, *Wing Chun Warrior: The True Tales of Wing Chun Kung Fu Master Duncan Leung, Bruce Lee's Fighting Companion*, Blacksmith Books, Hong Kong, 2010, Kindle edition.

Inosanto, Daniel, *Absorb What Is Useful (A Jeet Kune Do Guidebook: Volume Two)*, Action Pursuit Group, Burbank, California, 1982.

Kennedy, Brian, and Elizabeth Guo, *Jingwu: The School That Transformed Kung Fu*, Blue Snake Books, Berkeley, California, 2010.

Kerridge, Steve, and Darren Chua, *Bruce Lee: The Intercepting Fist*, On the Fly Productions Ltd., England, 2020.

Lee, Bruce, and John Little (editor), *Bruce Lee — The Tao of Gung Fu: A Study in the Way of Chinese Martial Art*, Tuttle Publishing, Boston, 1997.

Lee, Bruce, *Chinese Gung Fu: The Philosophical Art Of Self-Defense*, Oriental Book Sales, Oakland, 1963.

Lee, Bruce, *The Tao of Jeet Kune Do*, Ohara Publications Inc., Santa Clarita, California, 1975.

Lee, Chow-Kan, and Tak Chiu Wong, *Forever Superstar Bruce Lee*, Hong Kong, 2000.

Lee, J. Yimm, and Bruce Lee (technical editor), *Wing Chun Kung Fu: Chinese Art of Self-Defense*, Ohara Publications Inc., Santa Clarita, California, 1972.

Lee, Linda, *Bruce Lee: The Man Only I Knew*, Warner Paperback Library, New York, 1975.

Lee, Linda, *The Life and Tragic Death of Bruce Lee*, A Star Book, W.H. Allen & Co., Ltd. London, 1975.

Leung, Shum, and Jeanne Chin, *The Secrets of Eagle Claw Kung Fu: Ying Jow Pai*, Charles Tuttle Publishing, Boston, 2001.

Li, Paul, *From Limited to Limitless: The Ways of Bruce Lee*, Oriental Resources Company, Hong Kong, 1998.

Little, John (editor), *Bruce Lee: Letters of the Dragon*, Tuttle Publishing, Boston, 1998.

Little, John, *Bruce Lee: The Art of Expressing the Human Body*, Tuttle Publishing, Boston, 1998.

Little, John (editor), *Bruce Lee: Artist of Life*, Tuttle Publishing, Boston, 1999.

Little, John (editor), *Jeet Kune Do: Bruce Lee's Commentaries on the Martial Way*, Tuttle Publishing, Boston, 1997.

Little, John (editor), *Bruce Lee: Words from a Master*, Contemporary Books, Chicago, 1999.

Magnan-Park, Aaron Han Joon, "Restoring the Transnational from the Abyss of Ethnonational Film Historiography: The Case of Chung Chang Wa," published in the *Journal of Korean Studies*, Vol. 16, No. 2 (Fall 2011).

Palmer, Doug, *Bruce Lee: Sifu, Friend and Big Brother*, Chin Music Press Inc., Seattle, 2020.

Polly, Matthew, *Bruce Lee: A Life*, Simon and Schuster, New York, 2018, Kindle edition.

Russo, Charles, *Striking Distance: Bruce Lee & the Dawn of Martial Arts in America*, University of Nebraska Press, Nebraska, 2016, Kindle edition.

Subramaniam, P., PhD, (general editors) Dr. Shu Hikosaka, Asst. Prof. Norinaga Shimizu ,& Dr. G. John Samuel, (translator) Dr. M. Radhika, *Varma Cuttiram: A Tamil Text on Martial Art from Palm-Leaf Manuscript*. Madras: Institute of Asian Studies, 1994.

Suzuki, Daisetz, Teitaro, *The Lankavatara Sutra*, published online at lirs.ru/do/lanka_eng/lanka-nondiacritical.htm.

Thomas, Bruce, *Bruce Lee: Fighting Spirit*, Frog Ltd., Berkeley, California, 1994.

Uyehara, Mitoshi, *Bruce Lee: The Incomparable Fighter*, Ohara Publications Inc., Santa Clarita, California, 1988.

Wing, Rick L., *Showdown in Oakland: The Story Behind the Wong Jack Man – Bruce Lee Fight*, self-published, Amazon Publishing, San Francisco, 2013, Kindle edition.

Yutang, Lin, *The Wisdom of Laotse*, Random House, New York, 1948.

Zhao TX, Liu B, Wei YX, Wei Y, Tang XL, Shen LJ, Long CL, Lin T, Wu SD, Wei GH, "Clinical and Socioeconomic Factors Associated with Delayed Orchidopexy in Cryptorchid Boys in China: A Retrospective Study of 2423 Cases," *Asian Journal of Andrology*, May–June 2019; 21(3): 304–308. Published December 18, 2018, online at doi: 10.4103/aja.aja_106_18.

VIDEOS

"According to Joe Lewis, Bruce Lee Was by Far the Greatest" at youtube.com/watch ?v=1X2byotY22o.

"Actor Challenged Bruce Lee on the SET of *Enter the Dragon* . . . NEW STORY!" at youtube.com/watch?v=ulRwj7DXuA8.

"Brother Gregory of SFXC Recalls Bruce Lee" (Part Two), Bruce Lee Club Channel at youtube.com/watch?v=77uvKCIIxLM.

"Bruce Lee" at youtube.com/watch?v=uOE3P7kDdgo.

Bruce Lee interviewed by Daniel Lee at youtube.com/watch?v=1UtUgOgRrXA.

"Bruce Lee SFXC The Return of the Dragon to Saint Francis Xavier's College 13th March 1973 Second Edition (26th March 2017)" at youtube.com/watch?v=ILG to6xvNcM.

"Bruce Lee VS Pro Fighters" at youtube.com/watch?v=_Yf-Cpvvucs&feature=emb _imp_woyt.

"Bruce Lee's Challenger talks of Bruce's death 1973" at youtu.be/IUPDCo4-rqY.

Bruce Lee's demonstration on Hong Kong's TVB at youtube.com/watch?v=hDM2 _uV-grU.

"Chinese Mafia — Hop Sing Tong/Raymond 'Shrimp Boy' Chow" at youtube.com /watch?v=5eGGvxPGeXI.

Chuck Norris interview with David Brenner on *Nightlife*, broadcast date: November 19, 1986, at youtube.com/watch?v=j331wiSUhVo&t=2s.

"Cliff Au Yeung on Bruce Lee and Wong Shun Leung's Relationship (English Subtitled)" at youtube.com/watch?v=OfRJkMuQSWw.

"George Dillman on Bruce Lee" at youtube.com/watch?v=J7cGj2RbfdE.

Grace and Robert Lee interview on "Good Night America" with Geraldo Rivera, 1976, at youtube.com/watch?v=atur4sJN96s.

"Grandmaster William Cheung on Meeting Bruce Lee" at youtube.com/watch?v =NzRU21NBYRA.

"Hong Kong Triad Boss Chan Wai Man Said Only Idiot Would Fight with Bruce Lee" at youtube.com/watch?v=E5guO9xMCyM.

"Hong Kong Triad Boss Said Nobody Dares to Provoke Bruce Lee to Fight" at youtube.com/watch?v=O8egoMcgbJc.

"Hong Kong Triad Legend: Michael Chan Wai-Man. Honor Among Thieves in Old Chinese Secret Societies" at facebook.com/watch/?v= 647459335739053.

"Interview Wong Shun Leung (Ving Tsun) about Bruce Lee" at youtube.com/watch?v =w8qg1R4d-Q4.

Joe Orbillo on Bruce Lee at the Jun Fan Jeet Kune Do Nucleus Seminar, San Francisco, January 11, 1997, at youtube.com/watch?v=iw6W1MMKm4o.

Leo Fong quoting Bruce Lee from an online video interview at dailymotion.com /video/x2qmb8c.

Longstreet: The Way of the Intercepting Fist at youtube.com/watch?v=1_C6wKGL _ug.

"Remembering Bruce Lee — Max Lee" at youtube.com/watch?v=Nu6g42YFoFM.

Ryan O'Neal versus Joe Frazier sparring match at youtube.com/watch?v=6ilMU8y RCyo&t=143s.

DOCUMENTARIES

Bruce Lee: A Warrior's Journey, produced and directed by John Little, Warner Bros. 2000.

The Grandmaster & The Dragon: William Cheung and Bruce Lee, directed by Michael Sealey and Nick Wolff, fsharetv.co/movie/the-grandmaster-&-the -dragon:-william-cheung-&-bruce-lee-episode-1-tt2063811#.

Wong Shun Leung: The King of Talking Hands, produced and directed by John Little, Northern River Productions, 2016 © David Peterson.

RADIO/AUDIO

"Autopsy: The Last Hours of Bruce Lee" at podcasts.apple.com/gb/podcast/the-last -hours-of-bruce-lee/id1484888427?i=1000539633008.

Chan Wai Man quoted from an audio series called Paths of Little Dragon on Commercial Radio in Hong Kong (courtesy of Paul Li).

Lam Ching Ying's interview with Joe Hung (audio courtesy of Paul Li).

Radio Television Hong Kong program, *Asian Threads*, podcast.rthk.hk/podcast/item .php?pid=363&eid=22299&lang=zh-CN.

ONLINE ARTICLES

"Anderson Silva Talks God, Training, Bruce Lee and Life After Fighting" at lowkickmma.com/anderson-silva-talks-god-training-bruce-lee-and-life-after -fighting-17132/?amp.

Andy Vajna interview at mandiner.hu/cikk/20120806_andy_vajna_mindent_el _lehet_intezni.

Bob Baker's journal entry for November 21, 1971, published online at entertainment .ha.com/itm/movie-tv-memorabilia/documents/robert-baker-journal -making-fist-of-fury-with-color-fight-scene-snapshots-from-the-set/a/7241 -89466.s?ic16=ViewItem-BrowseTabs-Inventory-BuyNowFromOwner -ThisAuction-120115.

"A Brief History of Chinese Kung-Fu: Part 2" by David A. Ross at fightingarts.com /reading/article.php?id=477.

"A Brief History of Lei Tai Fighting in Hong Kong" by Bernard Kwan at benotdefeatedbytherain.blogspot.com/2015/06/a-brief-history-of-ring-fighting -in.html.

"Bruce Lee & William Cheung: The Early Years," posted on William Cheung's website: wingchunacademy.wordpress.com/2011/03/14/bruce-lee-william-cheung -the-early-years/.

"Bruce Lee and His Friendship with Wong Shun Leung" at wongvingtsun.co.uk /wslbl.htm.

"Bruce Lee Died of Heatstroke, Book Claims" at dailytelegraph.com.au/news/nsw

/bruce-lee-died-of-heatstroke-book-claims/news-story/30c31527a46aafb9fbfd6
fb38398c599.

"Bruce Lee Real Fight with Western Boxing Champion Lau Dai Chuen" at
wingchunnews.ca/bruce-lee-real-fight-with-western-boxing-champion-lau
-dai-chuen/.

"Bruce Lee vs. Wong Jack Man: Fact, Fiction and the Birth of the Dragon" by
Charles Russo at vice.com/en/article/d7my3v/bruce-lee-vs-wong-jack-man
-fact-fiction-and-the-birth-of-the-dragon.

"Bruce Lee: The Mystery Surrounding the Martial Artist's Death" by Rachel
Chang at biography.com/news/bruce-lee-death-mystery.

"Bruce Lee's Contest Diary Exposed! 11 seconds KO Japanese Karate Black Belt
Challenger" at daydaynews.cc/en/constellation/314599.html.

"Bruce Lee's Forgotten Child Star Start: Before *Enter the Dragon* and Breaking Into
Hollywood, the Martial Arts Actor Was Hong Kong's 'Little Dragon Li' After
Landing His First Role as a Baby" by Douglas Parkes at scmp.com/magazines/style
/celebrity/article/3167557/bruce-lees-forgotten-child-star-start-enter-dragon-and.

Bruce Lee's business card with rates at pinterest.ca/pin/bruce-lees-rate-card-for
-private-tuition-as-well-as-his-group-classes-this-is-one-of-the-many-items-of
-removable-memorabilia-in-the-treas—243053711112825413/.

Bruce Lee's diary entry for November 1, 1960, is reproduced online at daydaynews
.cc/en/entertainment/314599.html.

Bruce Lee's handwritten goal entitled "My Definite Chief Aim," January, 1969, at
qz.com/932799/bruce-lee-achieved-all-his-life-goals-by-32-by-committing-to
-one-personality-trait/.

Bruce Lee's letter to Bob Baker, May 25, 1971, posted online at entertainment.ha
.com/itm/movie-tv-memorabilia/documents/bruce-lee-handwritten-letter-signed
-bruce-written-to-bob-baker-regarding-a-shoot-for-black-belt-magazine-promoting
-mentor-jame/a/7241-89442.s?ic16=ViewItem-BrowseTabs-Inventory-BuyNow
FromOwner-ThisAuction-120115.

Bruce Lee's letter to Bob Baker, June 17, 1970, posted online at entertainment.ha
.com/itm/movie-tv-memorabilia/documents/bruce-lee-handwritten-letter
-signed-bruce-written-to-bob-baker-informing-him-to-forget-about-sending-stuff
-as-excessive-in/a/7241-89425.s?ic16=ViewItem-BrowseTabs-Auction-Archive
-ThisAuction-120115.

Bruce Lee's letter to Bob Baker, September 10, 1970, posted online at entertainment.ha
.com/itm/movie-tv-memorabilia/documents/bruce-lee-handwritten-letter
-signed-bruce-written-to-bob-baker-regarding-baker-s-help-in-lee-s-back
-recovery/a/7241-89431.s?ic16=ViewItem-BrowseTabs-Auction-Archive
-ThisAuction-120115. "Bruce Lee's Real Fighting Account 15 Years Ago" by Lang
Ngan, published in the Hong Kong magazine *Superstar of the Generation —
Bruce Lee*, 1973, reproduced at tapatalk.com/groups/bruceleelivestributeforum/
bruce-lee-rooftop-fight-t3663.html.

Bruce Lee's letter to Wong Shun Leung, dated January 11, 1970, can be viewed online at jkd.com.hk/Chi/Photo_Gallery/images/wong_letter_big.jpg.

"Bruce Lee's Real Fight with Lau Dai-Chuen: Truth or Fake?!" at wingchunnews.ca /bruce-lees-real-fight-with-lau-dai-chuen-truth-or-fake/.

Cambridge dictionary at dictionary.cambridge.org/dictionary/english/research.

Chan Wai Man quoted in the online article at tapatalk.com/groups /bruceleelivestributeforum/90s-chan-wai-man-interview-t4554.html.

Chaplin Chang's interview at bruceleedivinewind.com/chaplinchang.html.

"Conor McGregor Claimed Bruce Lee Could Have Been a 'World Champion in MMA'" at sportbible.com/ufc/news-legends-conor-mcgregor-claimed-bruce-lee -could-have-been-an-mma-world-champion-20200110.

"Dana White Calls Bruce Lee the Father of MMA but He Actually Rejected the Style" by Bob Garcia at sportscasting.com/dana-white-calls-bruce-lee-the-father -of-mma-but-he-actually-rejected-the-style/.

"Dave Friedman: Filming the Dragon" by Mark Edward Harris at bandwmag.com /articles/dave-friedman-filming-the-dragon.

"Doing Research (6): Working the Beat — One Journalist's Efforts at Perfecting the Fine Art of Hanging Out" by Charles Russo at chinesemartialstudies. com/2016/05/05/doing-research-6-working-the-beat-one-journalists-efforts-at -perfecting-the-fine-art-of-hanging-out/.

"Eddie Bravo Became a Jiu Jitsu Legend with One Win. Can His Fighting Style Now Conquer MMA?" by Josh Chesler at ocweekly.com/eddie-bravo-became-a-jiu -jitsu-legend-with-one-win-can-his-fighting-style-now-conquer-mma-6483814/.

"Epilepsy Could Solve Mystery of Kung Fu Legend's Death" at theguardian.com /science/2006/feb/25/film.filmnews.

"Esther Eng" at web.archive.org/web/20161221000604/https://wfpp.cdrs.columbia .edu/pioneer/esther-eng-2/.

"Famous Movie Star and Respected Gangster — Profile of 14K Triad Boss Michael Chan" at gangstersinc.org/profiles/blogs/famous-movie-star-and-respected -gangster-profile-of-14k-triad-bos.

"George Foreman: Bruce Lee Could've Been a World Champion Boxer" at boxingdaily .com/boxing-news/george-foreman-bruce-lee-couldve-been-a-world-champion -boxer/.

"Golden Gate Girl" at lost-films.eu/films/show/id/4109.

"A Grandmaster Remembers Bruce Lee" at cheungsmartialarts.com/wp-content /uploads/2021/12/A-Grandmaster-Remembers-Bruce-Lee.pdf?v=3e8d115eb4b3.

Herb Jackson quoted at rumsoakedfist.org/viewtopic.php?p=453261&sid=05c324cf5c 3e11b4dccofd8071c1feca.

"The History of Karate in America" at usadojo.com/the-history-of-karate-in-america/.

"How Did Bruce Lee Die? Inside the Icon's Death and Final Moments" at factinate .com/editorial/how-did-bruce-lee-die/.

"Increases in Chinese Population" at countryeconomy.com/demography/population /china?year=1973.

Inflation calculator of DollarTimes at dollartimes.com/inflation/inflation.php
?amount=275&year=1967.

"An Interview with Bruce Lee's Brother, Robert Lee" by Andrew Heskins at
easternkicks.com/features/an-interview-with-bruce-lees-brother-robert-lee.

"Interview with John Saxon" at bruceleelives.co.uk/saxon.html.

"Interview with Wing Chun Grandmaster Yip Man," published in *New Martial
Hero* magazine #56, Hong Kong, 1972, naamkyun.com/2012/03/interview-with
-wing-chun-grandmaster-yip-man/.

"Interview with Wong Shun Leung and Barry Lee" at wingchunlexicon.com
/interview-with-wong-shun-leung-and-barry-lee/.

"Jackie Chan Investigated for Taking on Triad Gang with 'Guns and Grenades'" at
businessinsider.com/jackie-chan-probed-for-guns-and-grenades-2012-12.

James DeMile's statements on his Facebook page (which were republished online) at
tapatalk.com/groups/bruceleelivestributeforum/james-w-demille-and-bl-falling
-out-t3474.html.

James Lee's letter to Gene Snelling Jr., North Carolina, circa 1965, from oakauctions
.com/Important__Bruce_Lee__James_Yimm_Lee__Archive_rela-LOT6591.aspx.

"Joe Lewis: Legendary American Kickboxer" at usadojo.com/joe-lewis/.

Karate competition record of Chuck Norris at karate-in-english-lewis-wallace
.blogspot.com/2008/03/chuck-norris-accurate-record.html.

Karate competition record of Joe Lewis at karate-in-english-lewis-wallace.blogspot
.com/2008/03/joe-lewis-karate-and-full-contact.html.

"Keeping Kung Fu Secrets Grandmaster David Chin: Grandmaster David Chin's
Legacy of Hop Gar Rebels and Guang Ping Tai Chi Revolutionaries" at
usadojo.com/keeping-kung-fu-secrets-grandmaster-david-chin/.

"Kung Fu Master of Shaw Brothers' Golden Era Still Shines" by Alex Choi Ingamells
at bangkokpost.com/life/arts-and-entertainment/435642/kung-fu-master-of-shaw
-brothers-golden-era-still-shines.

"Legendary Joe Lewis: I Never Lost My World Full Contact Karate/Kickboxing
Titles to Anyone" by Tim Tal at bzfilm.com/talks-interviews/exclusive-interview
-with-the-great-joe-lewis/.

Leo Fong's interview at usadojo.com/wp-content/uploads/2017/02/fma-Digest
-Special-Edition-Leo-Fong.pdf.

Linda Lee's letter to Bob Baker, December 17, 1971, at entertainment.ha.com/itm
/movie-tv-memorabilia/documents/linda-lee-handwritten-letter-signed-bruce
-linda-written-to-bob-and-bev-baker-regarding-bruce-s-completion-of-jing
-mo-moon-/a/7241-89448.s?ic16=ViewItem-BrowseTabs-Inventory
-BuyNowFromOwner-ThisAuction-120115.

"Lives of Chinese Martial Artists (5): Lau Bun — A Kung Fu Pioneer in America"
at chinesemartialstudies.com/2013/02/20/lives-of-the-chinese-martial-artists-5
-lau-bun-a-kung-fu-pioneer-in-america/.

Michael Dorgan's biographical information per his website: taichisanjose.com
/articles-bruce-lee-toughest-fight.

"The MMA World Pays Tribute to Bruce Lee 40 Years After His Death" by Michael
    Stets at bleacherreport.com/articles/1710603-the-mma-world-pays-tribute-to
    -bruce-lee-40-years-after-his-death.
"Off the Wall with Bob Wall" by Terry Wilson at usadojo.com/off-the-wall-with
    -bob-wall/.
Paul Li Chi-Yuan quoted from an interview at tapatalk.com/groups
    /bruceleelivestributeforum/paul-li-t3406-s10.html.
"Profile: Jimmy Wang Yu" by Ben Johnson at kungfumovieguide.com/profile-jimmy
    -wang-yu/.
Rick Wing's biography at shaolinlomita.com/masters/master-rick-wing/.
"Rickson Gracie on If Bruce Lee Was Legit" at bjjee.com/articles/rickson-gracie-on
    -if-bruce-lee-was-legit/.
"'Rocky IV' at 35: Sylvester Stallone Was in the ICU After a Dolph Lundgren
    Punch Actually Connected" by Ryan Parker at hollywoodreporter.com/movies
    /movie-news/rocky-iv-at-35-sylvester-stallone-was-in-the-icu-after-a-dolph
    -lundgren-punch-actually-connected-4097952/.
Ryan O'Neal's biography online at biography.com/actor/ryan-oneal.
"Shinpu-Ren Lineage: Yon Pon Gun" at prescottkarate.com/shinpu-ren-lineage-yon
    -pon-gun.html.
"Sylvester Stallone on 'Rocky II' Sparring Partner Roberto Duran" by Jack
    Beresford at ultimateactionmovies.com/sylvester-stallone-interview-rocky-ii/.
"Soke Yoichi Nakachi" bio at spiritforcekarate.yolasite.com/expanded-history
    -nakachi.php.
Tang Sang's biography at en-academic.com/dic.nsf/enwiki/5668864.
"Thread: Lau Bun Stories" at kungfumagazine.com/forum/showthread.php?39874
    -Lau-Bun-Stories/page5.
"Through a Lens Darkly (62): Chan Bing's Choy Li Fut Students, 1967" by
    benjudkins at chinesemartialstudies.com/2019/10/20/through-a-lens-darkly-62
    -chan-bings-choy-li-fut-students-1967/.
"The Tongs of Chinatown: 'I Was There' — A Conversation with Bill Lee" by
    Michael Zelenko at foundsf.org/index.php?title=The_Tongs_of_Chinatown.
"Truth Is a Pathless Land," August 3, 1929, at jkrishnamurti.org/about-dissolution
    -speech.
"UFC's Georges St-Pierre Says Bruce Lee Changed His Life — 'I Won a Lot of Fights
    from What He Taught Me'" at scmp.com/sport/martial-arts/mixed-martial-arts
    /article/3087905/ufcs-georges-st-pierre-says-bruce-lee-changed.
"Uncovering Bruce Lee's Public School Years" by Devin Israel Cabanilla at iexaminer
    .org/uncovering-bruce-lees-public-school-years/.
Wan Kam Leung's interview transcript from Hong Kong Radio program *Dragon
    Seeks Its Path*. Transcript at tapatalk.com/groups/bruceleelivestributeforum/wan
    -kam-leung-interview-t3707.html.
"What Sugar Ray Took from Bruce Lee" at wingchunnews.ca/what-sugar-ray-took
    -from-bruce-lee-2/.

"William Cheung and Bruce Lee Story" at karateforums.com/william-cheung-and
-bruce-lee-story-vt2268.html.

"Wong Shun Leung — The Death of Bruce Lee" by Wong Shun Leung at
vingtsunserbia.wordpress.com/about/articles/wong-shun-leung-the-death-of
-bruce-lee/.

"Yip Man: Wing Chun Legend and Bruce Lee's Formal Teacher" by *Black Belt*
magazine, August 12, 2013, at blackbeltmag.com/yip-man-wing-chun-legend
-and-bruce-lees-formal-teacher.

"Young Bruce Lee, Part I: Street Brawling and Cha-Cha Dancing in Seattle" by
Billy Potts, November 19, 2020, at zolimacitymag.com/young-bruce-lee-part-i
-street-brawling-and-cha-cha-dancing-in-seattle-chinatown/.

Wong Jack Man's online interview at taichisanjose.com/wong-jack-man-interview.

Wong Shun Leung quoted in *Qi Magazine* at web.archive.org/web/20070928072440
/http://vingtsunupdate.com/index.php?option=com_content&task=view&id=8
2&Itemid=76.

ACKNOWLEDGMENTS

The author is indebted to the many people over the course of several decades spent researching Bruce Lee's life, art and philosophy. Particular thanks are extended to those who befriended and trained with Bruce and who were willing to speak to me on the record about the man and the real fights they saw him engage in. Their names can be found in the "interviews" section of the book's Bibliography. Special thanks are due to Kent and Teresa Chin, who took the time to translate all of the Chinese language newspaper and magazine articles I sent them. Gratitude is further extended to my friends and colleagues (some still with us, some passed on) from the Jun Fan Jeet Kune Do Nucleus, who gave considerably of themselves over many years to the effort of preserving and perpetuating Bruce Lee's art. Thank you also to Jeet Kune Do authority Chris Kent, who became my sounding board for the book's content from time to time, along with Alex Richter, the "Kung Fu Genius" podcaster (who also provided some fascinating details of his research into Bruce Lee's fight with Lau Dai Chuen), and to Ving Tsun sifu, David Peterson, who first opened my eyes to the contributions made to Bruce Lee's martial development by his teacher, the late, great Wong Shun Leung. I must also acknowledge Andy Kimura (the son of Bruce Lee's highest-ranked student, Taky Kimura), who continues the Kimura legacy of teaching Bruce Lee's art of Jun Fan Gung Fu/Jeet Kune Do in Seattle, Washington. I am beholden to Bruce's students Taky Kimura, Ted Wong, Herb Jackson, Jesse Glover, Ed Hart, Skip Ellsworth, Daniel Lee, Steve Golden, Larry Hartsell and Richard Bustillo (among others) who took me into their confidence and shared their friendship. A special acknowledgment is extended to

Bruce Lee historian and author Steve Kerridge (UK), and to people such as James Bishop (USA), Paul Bax (USA), Paul Li (Hong Kong), Charles Russo (USA) and Matthew Polly (USA) for their research and publications. Mr. Kerridge must further be acknowledged for graciously allowing me to use his copyrighted images of Bruce for the cover art of this book. Speaking of which, a huge thank you to Ben Little for his brilliant cover art concept and design, which perfectly captures the intensity and power of Bruce Lee. And, above all, to my awesome family: Terri, Riley, Taylor, Brandon and Ben for their feedback and support during the writing.

INDEX

ABOUT THE AUTHOR

JOHN LITTLE is the bestselling author of *The Donnellys (Volume One and Two)*, *Who Killed Tom Thomson?*, *The Warrior Within: The Philosophies of Bruce Lee To Better Understand the World Around You and Achieve a Rewarding Life*, *Bruce Lee: The Art of Expressing the Human Body*, among others. His articles have appeared in every martial arts publication in North America. Little is also an award-winning documentary filmmaker. He resides in Muskoka, Ontario, with his wife Terri and children Riley, Taylor, Brandon and Ben.